ATLAS

LONDON, NEW YORK
MUNICH, MELBOURNE, DELHI

LONDON, NEW YORK
MUNICH, MELBOURNE, DELHI

Cartographic Director Andrew Heritage
Senior Cartographic Manager David Roberts
Senior Cartographic Editor Simon Mumford
Digital Cartography and Packaging Encompass Graphics Limited
Database Editors Cambridge International Reference on Current Affairs (CIRCA)
Project Cartographer Rob Stokes, Iorwerth Watkins
Project Editor Sam Atkinson
Art Editor Karen Gregory
Systems Co-ordinator Philip Rowles
Production Michelle Thomas
3D Globes Planetary Visions Ltd., London

First published in Great Britain in 2001 by
Dorling Kindersley Limited, 80 Strand, London WC2R 0RL
A Penguin Company
Second Edition 2004

Previously published as the Ultimate Pocket Book of the World Atlas & Factfile
Copyright © 1996, 1998, 2001, 2003, 2004 Dorling Kindersley Limited, London

This edn produced for The Book People Ltd, Hall Wood Avenue, Haydock, St
Helens, WA11 9UL

See our complete catalogue at
www.dk.com

ISBN-13: 978-1-4053-0329-3
ISBN-10: 1-4053-0329-8

Printed and bound in Singapore by Star Standard

For the very latest information, visit:
www.dk.com and click on the Maps & Atlases icon

Key to map symbols

ELEVATION

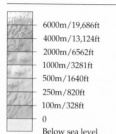

6000m/19,686ft
4000m/13,124ft
2000m/6562ft
1000m/3281ft
500m/1640ft
250m/820ft
100m/328ft
0
Below sea level

▲ Mountain

• Depression

BORDERS

▬▬▬ Full international

- - - - Disputed *de facto*

•••••• Territorial claim

×-×-×-× Cease-fire line

▮▮▮▮▮ Undefined

──── State/Province

DRAINAGE FEATURES

──── River

──── Seasonal river

▮▮▮▮▮ Canal

⬭ Lake

⬭ Seasonal lake

SETTLEMENTS

● Capital city

◎ Major town

○ Minor town

● Major port

COMMUNICATIONS

──── Major road

──── Rail

✈ International airport

◈ Insight; facts, figures and amazing information from around the world

NAVIGATOR

The navigator device can be used to quickly move around the atlas. Using this example, the next map to the north of page 128 can be found on page 120.

4
Atlas contents

North & Central America 16-17

South America 38-39

Africa 50-51

Europe 62-63

6
Factfile contents

Factfile contents

The Political World

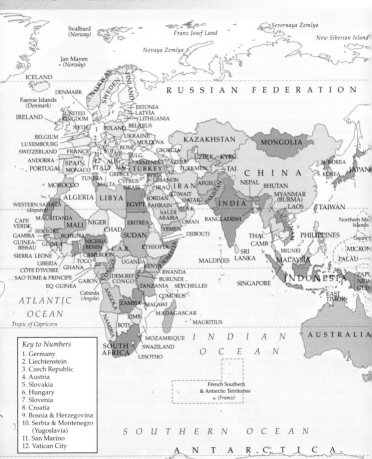

Svalbard *(Norway)*

Jan Mayen *(Norway)*

Franz Josef Land

Severnaya Zemlya

New Siberian Island

Novaya Zemlya

ICELAND

DENMARK

Faeroe Islands *(Denmark)*

IRELAND

UNITED KINGDOM

NORWAY

SWEDEN

FINLAND

RUSSIAN FEDERATION

ESTONIA

LATVIA

LITHUANIA

BELARUS

POLAND

NETH.

BELGIUM

LUXEMBOURG

SWITZERLAND

FRANCE

ANDORRA

PORTUGAL

SPAIN

MONACO

UKRAINE

MOLDOVA

GEORGIA

KAZAKHSTAN

MONGOLIA

C H I N A

N. KOREA

S. KOREA

JAPAN

UZBEK.

KYRG.

TURKMEN.

TAJ.

ROM.

BULG.

GREECE

ITALY

MAC.

ALB.

TURKEY

ARMENIA

AZERB.

AZ.

SYRIA

CYPRUS

ISRAEL

LEBANON

IRAQ

I R A N

AFGH.

NEPAL

BHUTAN

MOROCCO

MALTA

TUNISIA

ALGERIA

LIBYA

EGYPT

JORDAN

KUWAIT

BAHRAIN

SAUDI ARABIA

QATAR

U.A.E.

OMAN

PAKISTAN

INDIA

BANGLADESH

MYANMAR (BURMA)

LAOS

TAIWAN

WESTERN SAHARA *(disputed)*

CAPE VERDE

MAURITANIA

MALI

NIGER

CHAD

SUDAN

ERITREA

YEMEN

DJIBOUTI

Northern Mariana Islands

Guam

VIETNAM

THAI.

CAMB.

PHILIPPINES

MICRON.

PALAU

SENEGAL

GAMBIA

GUINEA-BISSAU

GUINEA

SIERRA LEONE

LIBERIA

CÔTE D'IVOIRE

BURKINA

GHANA

TOGO

BENIN

NIGERIA

CAMEROON

C.A.R.

ETHIOPIA

UGANDA

SOMALIA

SRI LANKA

MALDIVES

SINGAPORE

BRUNEI

MALAYSIA

INDONESIA

EAST TIMOR

PAPUA NEW GUINEA

SAO TOME & PRINCIPE

EQ. GUINEA

GABON

CONGO

DEM. REP. CONGO

RWANDA

BURUNDI

KENYA

TANZANIA

SEYCHELLES

Cabinda *(Angola)*

ANGOLA

ZAMBIA

MALAWI

COMOROS

ATLANTIC OCEAN

Tropic of Capricorn

NAMIBIA

ZIMB.

BOTS.

MOZAMBIQUE

MADAGASCAR

MAURITIUS

I N D I A N

O C E A N

AUSTRALIA

SOUTH AFRICA

SWAZILAND

LESOTHO

Key to Numbers
1. Germany
2. Liechtenstein
3. Czech Republic
4. Austria
5. Slovakia
6. Hungary
7. Slovenia
8. Croatia
9. Bosnia & Herzegovina
10. Serbia & Montenegro (Yugoslavia)
11. San Marino
12. Vatican City

French Southern & Antarctic Territories *(France)*

S O U T H E R N   O C E A N

A N T A R C T I C A

The Political World

ARCTIC OCEAN

Greenland (Denmark)

Arctic Circle

Alaska (US)

C A N A D A

ATLANTIC OCEAN

Aleutian Islands (US)

P A C I F I C O C E A N

UNITED STATES OF AMERICA

Midway Islands (US)

Hawaii (US)

MEXICO

Bermuda (UK)

BAHAMAS

BELIZE

CUBA

DOM. REP. Puerto Rico (US)
ST KITTS & NEVIS
ANTIGUA & BARBUDA
DOMINICA
ST LUCIA
BARBADOS
ST VINCENT &
THE GRENADINES
GRENADA
TRINIDAD & TOBAGO

Tropic of Cancer

GUATEMALA
EL SALVADOR
HONDURAS
NICARAGUA
PANAMA

JAMAICA
HAITI
COSTA RICA
VENEZUELA
COLOMBIA

French Guiana (France)

MARSHALL ISLANDS

WALLIS & FUTUNA (France)

Palmyra Atoll (US)

Galapagos Islands (Ecuador)

GUYANA
SURINAME

Equator

NAURU

K I R I B A T I

Tokelau (NZ)

Cook Islands (NZ)

ECUADOR

PERU

B R A Z I L

TUVALU

SOLOMON ISLANDS

VANUATU

FIJI

Niue (NZ)

French Polynesia (France)

Pitcairn Islands (UK)

BOLIVIA

PARAGUAY

Tropic of Capricorn

New Caledonia (France)

TONGA

American Samoa (US)

SAMOA

CHILE

P A C I F I C O C E A N

ARGENTINA

URUGUAY

NEW ZEALAND

CHILE

Falkland Islands (UK)

South Georgia & South Sandwich Islands (UK)

CONTINENTAL KEY

North & Central America

South America

Africa

Europe

NW/SE Asia

Australasia & Oceania

ANTARCTICA

Antarctic Circle

The Physical World

Spitsbergen

Franz Josef Land

Severnaya Zemlya

ARCTIC

New Siberian Islands

Laptev Sea

Greenland Sea

Novaya Zemlya

Kara Sea

Barents Sea

Norwegian Sea

Arctic Circle

Denmark Strait

Iceland

Scandinavia

North European Plain

Siberia

ASIA

Khrebet Cher

Lena

Ural Mountains

British Isles

North Sea

Baltic Sea

EUROPE

Volga

Ob'

Yenisey

Altai Mountains

Gobi

Manchurian Plain

Bay of Biscay

Alps

Danube

Caucasus

Black Sea

Lake Balkhash

Tien Shan

Yellow River

Sea of Japan (East Sea)

Hok

Azores

Iberian Peninsula

Mediterranean Sea

Anatolia

Caspian Sea

Aral Sea

Iranian Plateau

Hindu Kush

Plateau of Tibet

Kyushu

Madeira

Canary Islands

Atlas Mts

Zagros Mts

Syrian Desert

Indus

Himalayas

Mount Everest 29,035ft (8850m)

Yangtze

East China Sea

Taiwan

Tropic of Cancer

Sahara

Nile

Red Sea

Arabian Peninsula

Thar Desert

Ganges

Deccan

South China Sea

Philip

AFRICA

Sahel

Niger

Arabian Sea

Bay of Bengal

Mekong

Philippine Islands

Cape Verde Islands

Lake Chad

Ethiopian Highlands

Horn of Africa

Sri Lanka

Malay Peninsula

Equator

Gulf of Guinea

Congo

Congo Basin

Great Rift Valley

Lake Victoria

Kilimanjaro 19,340ft (5895m)

Somali Basin

Seychelles

Sumatra

Borneo

Celebes

East Indies

Ne Gui

ATLANTIC

Angola Basin

Zambezi

INDIAN

Java Sea

Java

Timor Sea

OCEAN

Mid-Atlantic Ridge

Namib Desert

Kalahari Desert

Madagascar

Mauritius

Réunion

Ninetyeast Ridge

Great Sandy Desert

AUSTRALI

Tropic of Capricorn

Cape Basin

Cape of Good Hope

Mozambique Channel

OCEAN

Nullarbor Plain

Southwest Indian Ridge

Kerguelen

Southeast Indian Ridge

Tasman

South Indian Basin

Antarctic Circle

SOUTHERN

ANTARCTICA

The Physical World

O C E A N

Siberian Sea

Chukchi Sea

Bering Strait

Bering Sea

Aleutian Islands

Northwest
Pacific
Basin

P o l y n e s i a

Hawaiian Islands

Pacific Mountains

ronesia

ia

olomon
slands

al

Fiji

ew Caledonia

sman
ea

North
Island

New
Zealand

O C E A N

Beaufort Sea

Brooks Range

Mount McKinley
(Denali)
20,322ft (6194m)

Mackenzie

Coast Mountains

Coast Ranges

Vancouver
Island

Gulf of
Alaska

Queen Elizabeth
Islands

Ellesmere Island

Baffin
Island

Baffin
Bay

Greenland

Arctic Circle

Great Bear
Lake

Great Slave
Lake

Hudson
Bay

NORTH
AMERICA

R O C K Y   M o u n t a i n s

Great Plains

Mississippi

Great Lakes

Appalachian Mts.

Labrador
Sea

Grand Banks
of Newfoundland

North American
Basin

Mid-Atlantic Ridge

Gulf of
Mexico

West Indies

Caribbean
Sea

Galapagos
Islands

ATLANTIC

O C E A N

Tropic of Cancer

P A C I F I C

O C E A N

Equator

Amazon

Amazon Basin

SOUTH
AMERICA

Peru
Basin

A n d e s

Brazil
Basin

East Pacific Rise

Easter Island

Cerro
Aconcagua
22,831ft
(6959m)

Gran
Chaco

Pantanal

Pampas

Tropic of Capricorn

Southwest

Pacific

Basin

Argentine
Basin

Patagonia

Falkland Islands

South Georgia

Tierra del Fuego

Cape Horn

Drake Passage

South Sandwich
Islands

Antarctic
Peninsula

Antarctic Circle

O C E A N

Time zones

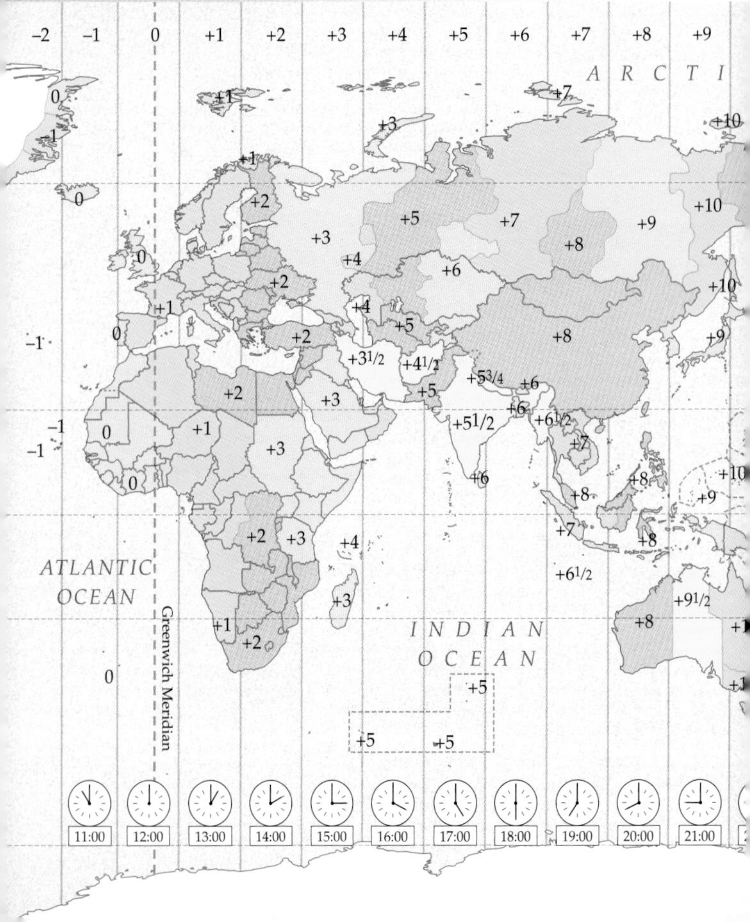

-2 | -1 | 0 | +1 | +2 | +3 | +4 | +5 | +6 | +7 | +8 | +9

A R C T I

+7

+10

0

+1

+3

+10

0

+1

+2

+5

+7

+9

+10

0

+3

+4

+6

+8

+10

0

+2

+4

+5

+8

+9

-1

0

+1

+2

+3½

+4½

+2

+3

+2

+5

+5¾

+6

+6

-1
-1

0

+1

+3

+5½

+6½

+6½

+2

ATLANTIC
OCEAN

0

+6

+2

+3

+4

+8

+8

+10

+9

+7

+8

+9

+2

+3

+6½

+8

+9½

+1

+2

+3

I N D I A N
O C E A N

+8

0

+5

+5

+5

Greenwich Meridian

| 11:00 | 12:00 | 13:00 | 14:00 | 15:00 | 16:00 | 17:00 | 18:00 | 19:00 | 20:00 | 21:00 |

Time zones

The
World's
Regions

North & Central America

ATLANTIC OCEAN

St Pierre & Miquelon (France)

Sargasso Sea

Bermuda (UK)

Virgin Islands (US)
British Virgin Islands (UK)
Anguilla (UK)
ST KITTS & NEVIS
ANTIGUA & BARBUDA
Guadeloupe (France)
ST LUCIA
BARBADOS
DOMINICA
GRENADA
TRINIDAD & TOBAGO

Turks & Caicos Islands (UK)
Puerto Rico (US)
DOMINICAN REPUBLIC
Montserrat (UK)
Martinique (France)
ST VINCENT & THE GRENADINES
Netherlands Antilles (Neth.)
Aruba (Neth.)

BAHAMAS
HAITI

CUBA

SOUTH AMERICA

Andes

Equator

Great Lakes
Lake Superior
Lake Huron
Lake Michigan
Lake Erie
Lake Ontario

Appalachian Mountains

Ohio

UNITED STATES OF AMERICA

Missouri
Mississippi
Arkansas

Great Plains

Cayman Islands (UK)
JAMAICA
BELIZE
GUATEMALA
HONDURAS
NICARAGUA
EL SALVADOR
COSTA RICA
PANAMA

Gulf of Mexico

Galápagos Islands (Ecuador)

Mount Whitney 14,495ft (4418m) ▲
Death Valley -282ft (-86m)

Rio Grande

Colorado

M E X I C O

Sierra Madre Occidental

PACIFIC OCEAN

Clipperton Island (French Polynesia)

Tropic of Cancer

Equator

0 km   1000
0 miles   1000

Western Canada & Alaska

RUSSIAN
FEDERATION

Wrangel I.

ARCT

OCEA

◆ *In 1867 William Henry Seward negotiated the purchase of Alaska from Russia for the price of $7,200,000, which amounted to around two cents per acre (0.4 hectares).*

Arctic Circle

Attu I.

*Bering
Sea*

Bering Strait

St. Lawrence I.

Brooks Range

Prudhoe
Bay

Rat Is.

Aleutian Islands

Nunivak I.

Yukon

ALASKA
(part of USA)

*Mt McKinley
20,322ft (6194m)*

Alaska Range

Fairbanks

Umnak I.
Dutch Harbor
Unalaska I.

Kodiak I. ○Kodiak

Anchorage

Valdez
Cordova

YUKON
TERRITOR

Rocky

◆ *The Aleutian Islands span some 1200 miles (1800 km) and by crossing the 180° line of longitude, form both the most easterly and westerly extents of the USA.*

*Gulf
of
Alaska*

WHITEHORSE

JUNEAU

B
CO

PACIFIC

OCEAN

Ketchikan

Prince Rupert

Queen Charlotte Is.

*Queen Charlotte
Sound*

◆ *On July 9, 1958 a massive landslide dropped 40 million cubic yards (30.6 million cu m) of rock into Lituya Bay creating a wave 1720 ft (524 m) high.*

Port Hardy
Vancouver I.

VICTORIA

| 0 km | 400 |
| 0 miles | 400 |

A   B   C   D

C

Queen Elizabeth Islands

Axel Heiberg Island

Ellesmere Island

Greenland
(Danish external territory)

◇ Despite an area of 769,900 sq miles (1,994,000 sq km) the northerly province of Nunavut has only 13 miles (21 km) of highway.

Bathurst I.

Devon Island

Baffin Bay

Melville Island

Resolute

Lancaster Sound

Davis Strait

Viscount Melville Sound

Somerset Island

Banks Island

Beaufort Sea

Prince of Wales I.

Baffin Island

Amundsen Gulf

Victoria Island

nuvik

King William I.

IQALUIT

N U N A V U T

Arctic Circle

Kugluktuk

Hudson Strait

Great Bear L.

Southampton I.

NORTHWEST

TERRITORIES

Mackenzie

YELLOWKNIFE

Great Slave L.

Dubawnt

Rankin Inlet

Hudson Bay

QUEBEC

Hay River

Fort Smith

Churchill

ISH
MBIA

Fort
St. John

ALBERTA

Fort McMurray

L. Athabasca

MANITOBA

C A N A D A

nce
eorge

Grande Prairie

SASKATCHEWAN

Flin Flon

Thompson

ONTARIO

EDMONTON

Saskatchewan

◇ Some 7% of Canada's 3.5 million sq miles (9.2 million sq km) land area is devoted to grain production yielding around 26 million tons (tonnes) of wheat every year.

amloops

Leduc

Red Deer

Prince Albert

L. Winnipeg

Saskatoon

Yorkton

ancouver

Calgary

REGINA

Kelowna

Lethbridge

Estevan

Brandon

WINNIPEG

U S A

Eastern Canada

NUNAVUT

Southampton I.

Coats I.

Salisbury I.
Nottingham I.

Ivujivik

Mansel I.

Hudson Bay

Péninsu d'Ungav

◆ The largest hydroelectric complex
in Canada at James Bay produces
over 16,000 megawatts of power.

MANITOBA

Inukjuak

L. Min

◆ The Trans-Canada Highway, running
from St John's in the east to
Victoria in the west, is
4860 miles (7820 km) long.

Belcher Is.
(Nunavut)

Kuujjuarapik

Winisk

James
Bay

Severn

Winisk

Attawapiskat

Akimiski I.
(Nunavut)

C A N A Eastma

Attawapiskat

Albany

L. Seul

 O N T A R I O

Moosonee

QU

L. Mistassin

Kenora

Armstrong

L. Nipigon

Cochrane

Rés. Gou

Lake
of the
Woods

Thunder Bay

Timmins

MINNESOTA

Lake Superior

Wawa

◆ Lake Superior is the largest freshwater
lake in the world covering an area
of 32,150 sq miles (83,268 sq km).

Sault
Sainte Marie

Sudbury

Ottawa

North Bay

OTTAWA

WISCONSIN

Lake
Michigan

Lake
Huron

Peterborough

Oshawa

TORONTO

Lake
Ontario

Kingst

UNITED STATES

MICHIGAN

Kitchener

Hamilton

NEW
YOR

IOWA

OF AMERICA

London

Windsor

Lake Erie

St. Catharines

ILLINOIS

INDIANA

OHIO

PENNSYLVANIA

A   B   C   D

Baffin I.

Hudson Strait

Akpatok I.
(Nunavut)

Ungava
Bay

*Labrador
Sea*

ATLANTIC

OCEAN

◇ Canada has the world's longest coastline
(including those of 52,455 islands) with a
total length of 151,394 miles (243,638 km).

Kuujjuaq

Nain

Hopedale
Makkovik

Cartwright

Schefferville

Labrador

NEWFOUNDLAND
& LABRADOR

Strait of Belle Isle

Smallwood
Reservoir

Réservoir
Caniapiscau

Newfoundland

D   A

E   B   C

Réservoir
Manicouagan

Havre-
Saint-Pierre

Ile d'Anticosti

Gander

Grand Falls

Corner Brook

ST JOHN'S

Sept-Îles

Channel-Port-
aux-Basques

C. Race

St. Lawrence

Gulf of St. Lawrence

St Pierre
& Miquelon
*(French territorial
collectivity)*

L. Saint-Jean
Jonquière

Gaspé

Cabot Strait

Chicoutimi

Bathurst

PRINCE
EDWARD
ISLAND

QUÉBEC

NEW

Sydney

FREDERICTON

BRUNSWICK Moncton CHARLOTTETOWN

Trois-Rivières MAINE

NOVA SCOTIA

Sherbrooke

Saint John

Dartmouth

Montreal

Yarmouth

HALIFAX

ATLANTIC

NEW
HAMPSHIRE

OCEAN

VERMONT

◆ The Bay of Fundy has the world's
highest tidal range with water's rising
20-50ft (5-15m) every high tide.

MASSACHUSETTS

RHODE ISLAND

0 km   300

CONNECTICUT

0 miles   300

USA: The Northeast

◆ The Chicago River originally flowed into Lake Michigan, but was reversed in 1900 by the completion of a canal.

MINNESOTA

Lake Superior

Superior
Ironwood
Marquette
Sault Ste Marie
Iron Mountain
Ladysmith
Cheboygan

WISCONSIN
MICHIGAN
Lake Huron

Eau Claire
Traverse City
Green Bay
Oshkosh
La Crosse
Lake Michigan
Bay City
Saginaw
Flint

IOWA
MADISON
Grand Rapids
LANSING
Milwaukee
Waukegan
Ann Arbor
Detroit
Rockford
Chicago
Lake Erie
Aurora
Gary
South Bend
Toledo
Cleveland
Erie
Joliet
Rock Island
Fort Wayne
Youngstown
Akron
Galesburg
Peoria
Mansfield
Canton
Wheeling

ILLINOIS
INDIANA
OHIO
Champaign
Muncie
COLUMBUS
SPRINGFIELD
INDIANAPOLIS
Decatur
Dayton
Effingham
Terre Haute
Cincinnati

Bloomington
MISSOURI
East St Louis
Huntington
Mt. Vernon
Louisville
CHARLESTON
Evansville
FRANKFORT
Lexington
WEST VIRGINIA
Carbondale
Owensboro
Richmond
Paducah
KENTUCKY
Hopkinsville
Bowling Green
London

ARKANSAS

CANADA
ONTARIO

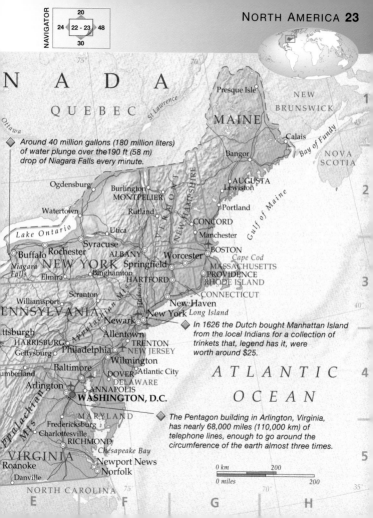

N A D A

QUEBEC

St Lawrence

Ottawa

NEW
BRUNSWICK

MAINE

Presque Isle

Bay of Fundy

NOVA
SCOTIA

Calais

Bangor

◊ Around 40 million gallons (180 million liters)
of water plunge over the 190 ft (58 m)
drop of Niagara Falls every minute.

Ogdensburg

Burlington
MONTPELIER

AUGUSTA
Lewiston

Watertown

Rutland

Portland

Lake Ontario

Utica

CONCORD

Manchester

Gulf of Maine

Buffalo Rochester

Syracuse

ALBANY

Worcester

BOSTON

*Niagara
Falls*

NEW YORK

Springfield

MASSACHUSETTS

PROVIDENCE

Elmira

Binghamton

HARTFORD

RHODE ISLAND

Scranton

CONNECTICUT

Williamsport

New Haven

ttsburgh

ENNSYLVANIA

Hudson

Long Island

Newark New York

◊ In 1626 the Dutch bought Manhattan Island
from the local Indians for a collection of
trinkets that, legend has it, were
worth around $25.

Allentown

HARRISBURG

TRENTON

NEW JERSEY

Gettysburg

Philadelphia

umberland

Wilmington

Baltimore

DOVER Atlantic City

ATLANTIC

Arlington

DELAWARE

ANNAPOLIS

WASHINGTON, D.C.

MARYLAND

OCEAN

◊ The Pentagon building in Arlington, Virginia,
has nearly 68,000 miles (110,000 km) of
telephone lines, enough to go around the
circumference of the earth almost three times.

Fredericksburg

Charlottesville

RICHMOND

Chesapeake Bay

VIRGINIA

Newport News

Roanoke

Norfolk

Danville

NORTH CAROLINA

0 km   200

0 miles   200

Appalachian Mts

USA: Central States

◆ At 20,016 ft (6104 m), or almost 4 miles (6 km) in length, the Fort Peck Dam is the largest earth-filled hydraulic dam in the US.

◆ The Great Salt Lake is a remnant of the prehistoric Lake Bonneville, which once covered almost 20,000 square miles (51,800 sq km) of western Utah.

◆ The world's largest organism is a 200 acre (81 hectares) grove of aspen trees in Utah. Derived from a single tree it has hundreds of suckers growing from its root system.

CANADA

MANITOBA

Lake of the Woods

ONTARIO

Lake Superior

MINNESOTA

Grand Forks

Virginia

Duluth

DAKOTA

Moorhead

Brainerd

BISMARCK

Fargo

◇ Access to the St Lawrence Seaway via the Great Lakes makes Duluth the most westerly Atlantic port in the US, some 1100 miles (1770 km) from the Atlantic ocean.

Aberdeen

St Cloud

WISCONSIN

DAKOTA

Minneapolis

Watertown

SAINT PAUL

MICHIGAN

PIERRE

Rochester

Mitchell

Sioux Falls

Lake Michigan

Mason City

Missouri

Dubuque

Sioux City

IOWA

Cedar Rapids

OHIO

ASKA

Columbus

DES MOINES

Davenport

North Platte

Omaha

Council Bluffs

ILLINOIS

INDIANA

Platte

LINCOLN

Burlington

Hastings

Kirksville

Mississippi

◇ Between 1950 and 1994 Kansas suffered over 2000 tornadoes, claiming around 200 lives and causing in excess of $1.2 billion damage.

St Joseph

kley

Hays

Kansas City

Independence

Missouri

Saint Louis

ANSAS

TOPEKA

Kansas City

JEFFERSON CITY

Ohio

Pratt

MISSOURI

KENTUCKY

Dodge

Wichita

Springfield

Arkansas

Ozark Plateau

OKLAHOMA

ARKANSAS

TENNESSEE

0 km   200
0 miles   200

Hells Canyon is the deepest in the US, with cliffs up to 7900 ft (2408 m) high.

At Black Rock Desert on October 15, 1997, ThrustSSC, driven by Andy Green, became the first land vehicle to break the sound barrier by achieving a speed of 763 mph (1228 km/h).

Death Valley is not only the lowest point in North America at 282 ft (86 m) below sea level, it is also the hottest, with a maximum air temperature of 134°F (57°C) recorded in 1913.

The Golden Gate Bridge, completed in 1937, has 80,000 miles (129,000 km) of wire in its two main cables, weighing a total of 22,200 tons (tonnes).

USA: The Southwest

◆ The Colorado River has cut down some 6242 ft (2000 m) into the Colorado Plateau to form the Grand Canyon, exposing rock strata over 2 billion years old.

◆ Meteor Crater was formed when a meteor about 150 ft (46 m) across struck the desert at about 40,000 mph (64,372 km/h) creating a bowl shaped depression 4,150ft (1,265m) wide and 570ft (174m) deep.

◆ The first atomic bomb was tested at Trinity Site near Alamogordo on July 16, 1945 yielding an explosive force equivalent to 20,000 tons (tonnes) of TNT from around 2.2 lbs (1 kg) of plutonium-239.

NEVADA

UTAH

COLORADO

L. Powell

Farmington

Grand Canyon

Painted Desert

Rio Grande

L. Mead

Colorado Plateau

Los Alamos

Gallup

SANTA FE

Flagstaff

Albuquerque

Pecos

Colorado

Prescott

A R I Z O N A

N E W

CALIFORNIA

Glendale

Scottsdale

M E X I C O

PHOENIX

Mesa

Sonoran

Roswell

Yuma

Desert

Casa Grande

Alamogordo

Artesia

Tucson

Las Cruces

Carlsbad

Douglas

El Paso

Rio Grande

Baja California

Golfo de California

M E X I

PACIFIC

OCEAN

0 km   200

0 miles   200

KANSAS

100°   95°

OKLAHOMA

Ponca City
Enid   Tulsa
Broken Arrow

35°

Borger   OKLAHOMA CITY   Shawnee
Pampa
Amarillo   Norman   Arkansas   ARKANSAS

                    Lawton   Red River
nadian
            Red River
ovis   Vernon   Paris

                    Wichita Falls
Brownfield   Lubbock   Denton   ◇ On January 10, 1901
                                        Longview   the Lucas Gusher blew
Hobbs   Fort Worth   Arlington   oil 100 ft (30 m) into the
            Sweetwater   Dallas   Tyler   air, flowing at 100,000
Big Spring   Abilene   barrels a day until it was
Odessa   Jacksonville   eventually capped nine
        Midland   Brazos   days later.
San Angelo   Waco   Toledo Bend Res.
Pecos   Colorado   Neches

T   E   X   A   S   LOUISIANA
                                        30°
                L. Travis   Bryan
        Edwards   AUSTIN   Beaumont
        Plateau   Houston   Port Arthur
        San Antonio   Pasadena
                                Texas City
    Del Rio   Victoria   Galveston
                San Antonio   Freeport
    Eagle Pass

                    Corpus Christi   Gulf
        Laredo   Kingsville
                            o f
                Padre Island
                            Mexico
                                        5
            Rio Grande

CO   Brownsville

E   100°   F   G   95°   H   25°

USA: The Southeast

MISSOURI

ILLINOIS

KENTUCKY

OKLAHOMA

Fayetteville

Walnut Ridge

Clarksville

NASHVILLE
Murfreesbor

Fort Smith

ARKANSAS

Memphis

TENNESSE

Chattanooga

North Little Rock
LITTLE ROCK
Hot Springs

Florence

Huntsville

Pine
Bluff

Gadsden

ATLANT

Texarkana

Ouachita

Columbus

Birmingham

Monroe

MISSISSIPPI

Demopolis

MONTGOMERY

Shreveport

LOUISIANA

JACKSON

Meridian

Colum

Red R.

Pearl

ALABAMA

Alexandria

Hattiesburg

Dothan

Lake Charles

BATON ROUGE

Gulfport

Mobile

TALLAHASS

Lafayette

Biloxi

Pensacola

Metairie

New Orleans

Panama City

*Mississippi
Delta*

◆ In August 1992 Hurricane Andrew
cut a swath through southern Florida
and Louisiana with winds of up to
175 mph (281 km/h), causing $25 billion
of damage.

◆ The Mississippi is the world's third
largest river and moves over a billion
tons (tonnes) of sediment a year.

G u l f   o f   M e x i c o

0 km   200

0 miles   200

A   B   C   D

VIRGINIA

Kingsport

Winston-Salem

Durham
RALEIGH

Roanoke

75°

Cape Hatteras

35° 1

Knoxville

NORTH CAROLINA

Greensboro

Asheville Gastonia Charlotte

Fayetteville Havelock

Greenville Spartanburg

COLUMBIA

SOUTH CAROLINA

Florence

Wilmington

Cape Fear

Athens

L. Marion

2

Augusta

Macon

Savannah

Charleston

◇ The carnivorous Venus's-flytrap plant, found
only on the wet coastal plains of North and
South Carolina, can count. They require two
separate stimuli on trigger hairs before the
trap is sprung to avoid "false alarms"
caused by raindrops, twigs, etc.

GEORGIA

Savannah

ATLANTIC

Valdosta

Brunswick

any

Jacksonville

OCEAN

30° 3

FLORIDA

Daytona Beach

Orlando

Cape Canaveral

Melbourne

◇ Lake Okeechobee is actually a shallow,
slow moving river, 150 miles (240 km) long
and 50 miles (80 km) wide, flowing
southward at the rate of 6 inches (15 cm)
a day.

Tampa

earwater

Petersburg

L. Okeechobee

West Palm Beach

4

Fort Myers

The Everglades

Pompano Beach

Fort Lauderdale

Miami Beach

Miami

Grand Bahama I.

BAHAMAS

25°

Key West

Florida Keys Straits of Florida

New Providence

Andros I.

75°

5

E F G H

Mexico

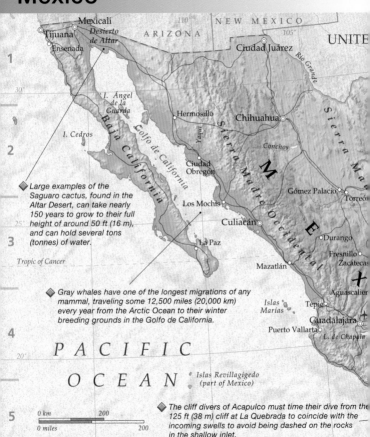

◆ Large examples of the Saguaro cactus, found in the Altar Desert, can take nearly 150 years to grow to their full height of around 50 ft (16 m), and can hold several tons (tonnes) of water.

◆ Gray whales have one of the longest migrations of any mammal, traveling some 12,500 miles (20,000 km) every year from the Arctic Ocean to their winter breeding grounds in the Golfo de California.

◆ The cliff divers of Acapulco must time their dive from the 125 ft (38 m) cliff at La Quebrada to coincide with the incoming swells to avoid being dashed on the rocks in the shallow inlet.

Map labels:

NEW MEXICO
ARIZONA
UNITE[D]
Tijuana
Mexicali
Ensenada
Desierto de Altar
Ciudad Juárez
Rio Grande
I. Ángel de la Guarda
Hermosillo
Chihuahua
Sierra Ma[dre]
I. Cedros
Baja California
Golfo de California
Yaqui
Conchos
M E
Ciudad Obregón
Gómez Palacio
Torreó[n]
Los Mochis
Culiacán
Sierra Madre Occidental
Durango
La Paz
Fresnillo
Zacatecas
Tropic of Cancer
Mazatlán
Aguascalie[ntes]
Islas Marías
Tepic
Guadalajara
Puerto Vallarta
L. de Chapala
PACIFIC OCEAN
Islas Revillagigedo (part of Mexico)

0 km   200
0 miles   200

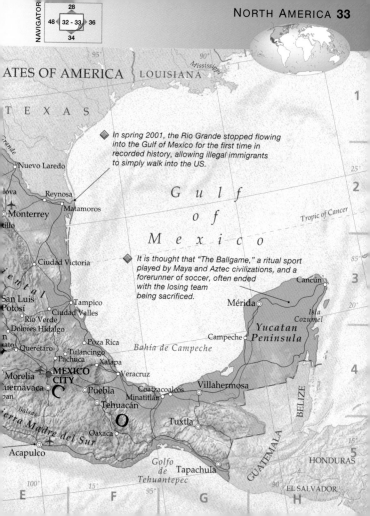

ATES OF AMERICA LOUISIANA

Mississippi

T E X A S

1

Nuevo Laredo

lova   Reynosa

Monterrey   Matamoros

tillo

25°   2

G u l f

o f

M e x i c o

Tropic of Cancer

Ciudad Victoria

85°   3

Cancún

San Luis
Potosí   Tampico   Mérida

Río Verde   Ciudad Valles   Isla
Cozumel

Dolores Hidalgo   Campeche   Yucatan

ato   Querétaro   Poza Rica   *Bahía de Campeche*   Peninsula

Tulancingo

Pachuca   Xalapa

Morelia   **MEXICO
CITY**   Veracruz   Villahermosa   20°   4

uernavaca   C   Puebla   Coatzacoalcos
Minatitlán

an   Tehuacán   BELIZE

O   Tuxtla   GUATEMALA

Balsas

erra Madre del Sur   Oaxaca

Acapulco   15°

*Golfo
de*   Tapachula   HONDURAS

100°   *Tehuantepec*

15°   95°   90°   EL SALVADOR

E   F   G   H

In spring 2001, the Rio Grande stopped flowing
into the Gulf of Mexico for the first time in
recorded history, allowing illegal immigrants
to simply walk into the US.

It is thought that "The Ballgame," a ritual sport
played by Maya and Aztec civilizations, and a
forerunner of soccer, often ended
with the losing team
being sacrificed.

Central America

95°   90°   85°

MEXICO
1

Usumacinta   Belize City

Flores   San Ignacio   ✈ BELMOPAN

BELIZE

GUATEMALA   Gulf of Honduras   Islas de la Bahía

Huehuetenango   Cobán   Lago   Puerto   Puerto Cortés   Trujillo
                         de Izabal   Barrios   San Pedro   La Ceiba
15°   Zacapa   Sula
Quezaltenango
2   HONDURAS   Pate
GUATEMALA CITY   Santa Rosa
                  de Copán   La Esperanza   Comayagua   Juticalpa
Escuintla   ✈ TEGUCIGALPA
                  Santa Ana   San Miguel

SAN SALVADOR   ✈ San Miguel   NIC
EL SALVADOR
                  Choluteca   Somoto   Jinotega
                         Estelí   Matagalpa
3   Gulf of Fonseca   Chinandega   León
                         Corinto
                                                  Juigalpa
PACIFIC   MANAGUA
                                  Granada   Lago de
                                  Rivas   Nicaragua

OCEAN

◆ Unique freshwater species of shark and swordfish have
10°   evolved in the long period since Lake Nicaragua was cut   Península de   Liberia
      off from the Pacific Ocean by a belt of volcanic cones.   Nicoya

4   Puntarenas   Ala

                                                                SAN JC

      ◆ The strongest living creature is the Rhinoceros Beetle
      found in the jungles of Costa Rica, which can support
      up to 850 times it's own body weight, equivalent to
      a human carrying about 70 tons (tonnes).

5
   0 km   200
   ├──┼──┼──┼──┤
   0 miles   200

        A   B   C   D

Greater Antilles

HAITI

80°

75°

1

The Blue Hole in Lighthouse Reef, a submerged cave some 1000 ft (300 m) in diameter and 400 ft (120 m) deep, was originally explored by Jacques Cousteau, co-inventor of the aqualung.

JAMAICA

as Santanilla
art of Honduras)

Bajo Nuevo
(part of Colombia)

2

15°

Cayos Miskitos

C a r i b b e a n

I. de Providencia
(part of Colombia)

S e a

3

I. de San Andrés
(part of Colombia)

Islas del Maíz
efields

Gatun Locks on the Panama Canal are 110 ft (33 m) wide and 1000 ft (303 m) long, took four years to build and required 2 million cubic yards (1.5 million cu m) of concrete.

4

10°

OSTA
ICA

Limón

Colón

Gulf
of
Darien

PANAMA

PANAMA CITY

Penonomé

Panama
Canal

Isla del
Rey

COLOMBIA

David

Golfo
de
Chiriquí

Santiago

Chitré
Las Tablas

Golfo
de
Panamá

5

80°

75°

E

F

G

H

The Caribbean

Gulf 85° UNITED STATES *Grand* Freeport

of OF AMERICA *Bahama I.* Great Abaco

1 25° *Mexico* New Providence

NASSAU Eleuthera I.

Tropic of Cancer *Andros I.* Cat I.

Santaren Channel Great

Matanzas Exuma I. Long I.

HAVANA Mayagua

Pinar del Río Santa Clara Acklins I.

2 Cienfuegos **CUBA** Great

Yucatan Channel Isla de la Juventud Camagüey Holguín Inagua

Greater Bayamo Guantánamo

Cayman Islands George Town Santiago Cap-Haïtie

(UK dependent de Cuba Gonaïves **HAI**

territory) **PORT-AU-PRINCE**

Montego Bay **KINGSTON** Jérémie Jac

3 ◆ The Bee Hummingbird, found in Cuba, *Antil*

is the smallest bird in the world. An adult **JAMAICA** Navassa Island

male measures around 2.2 inches (5.7 cm) (US unincorporated

from beak to tail and weighs about territory)

0.06 oz (1.6 gms).

Caribbean

15° HONDURAS

4 *Sea*

NICARAGUA

0 km 200

5 0 miles 200

10° COLOMBIA

A 85° B 80° C 75° D

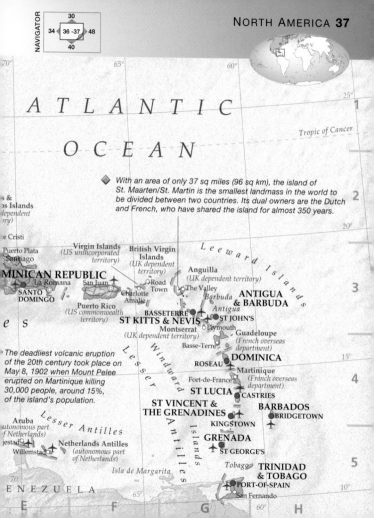

70°   65°   60°

ATLANTIC

25°   1

OCEAN

Tropic of Cancer

◆ With an area of only 37 sq miles (96 sq km), the island of St. Maarten/St. Martin is the smallest landmass in the world to be divided between two countries. Its dual owners are the Dutch and French, who have shared the island for almost 350 years.

2

20°

s &
os Islands
(dependent
ory)

e Cristi

Puerto Plata
Santiago

MINICAN REPUBLIC

La Romana   San Juan

SANTO
DOMINGO   Charlotte
Amalie
Puerto Rico
(US commonwealth
territory)

e   s

Virgin Islands
(US unincorporated territory)

British Virgin
Islands
(UK dependent
territory)

Road
Town

L e e w a r d   I s l a n d s

Anguilla
(UK dependent territory)
●The Valley

Barbuda

**ANTIGUA
& BARBUDA**

3

Antigua

BASSETERRE   ★**ST JOHN'S**

ST KITTS & NEVIS
Montserrat
(UK dependent territory)   Plymouth

Guadeloupe
(French overseas
department)

Basse-Terre

DOMINICA

15°

The deadliest volcanic eruption
of the 20th century took place on
May 8, 1902 when Mount Pelee
erupted on Martinique killing
30,000 people, around 15%,
of the island's population.

Lesser   Antilles

ROSEAU

Martinique
(French overseas
department)

Fort-de-France

ST LUCIA   CASTRIES

W i n d w a r d   I s l a n d s

**ST VINCENT &
THE GRENADINES**

BARBADOS
●**BRIDGETOWN**

KINGSTOWN

4

Aruba
(autonomous part
of Netherlands)
jestad   Netherlands Antilles
(autonomous part
of Netherlands)
Willemstad

Lesser   Antilles

GRENADA

ST GEORGE'S

Tobago

**TRINIDAD
& TOBAGO**

5

70°

Isla de Margarita

ENEZUELA   65°

PORT-OF-SPAIN

San Fernando   60°   10°

South America

A   B   C   D   E

ATLANTIC

OCEAN

Lesser Antilles

Greater Antilles

Hispaniola

Puerto
Rico

Caribbean Sea

Jamaica

Isthmus of
Panamá

Trinidad

French
Guiana
(France)

*(claimed by
Venezuela)*

SURINAME

GUYANA

*(claimed by
Suriname)*

Tumuc-Humac
Mountains

G u i a n a   H i g h l a n d s

Orinoco

VENEZUELA

Caroní

Meta

COLOMBIA

Magdalena

Cauca

Río Negro

Represa
Balbina

A m a z o n

B a s i n

Içá

Putumayo

Napo

Marañón

Amazon

Juruá

Purus

Madeira

Amazon

Xingu

Tocantins

Serra do Cachimbo

Serra Formosa

B R A Z I L

Brazilian
Highlands

Planalto
da
Borborema

São Francisco

Represa de
Sobradinho

Araguaia

Serra do Roncador

Planalto de

Chapada dos Parecis

Mato Grosso Highlands

Chapada dos Parecis

BOLIVIA

Beni

Madre de Dios

Altip

Lake
Titicaca

P E R U

A n d e s

Ucayali

ECUADOR

Chimborazo
20,702ft (6310m)

1   2   3   4

80° 70° 60° 50° 40° 10°

Tropic of Capricorn

ATLANTIC

OCEAN

South Georgia
(UK)

South Sandwich
Islands
(UK)

South Orkney Islands

Serra Geral

Lagoa dos Patos

URUGUAY

Mirim Lagoon

Río de la Plata

PARAGUAY

Paraná

Pilcomayo

Gran Chaco

Mesopotamia

Pampas

A R G E N T I N A

C H I L E

Atacama

Cerro Ojos
del Salado
(12,572ft)
6880m

Cerro Aconcagua
22,834ft
(6959m)

Colorado

Río Negro

Bahía Blanca

Golfo San Matías

Península
Valdés

Gulf of San Jorge

Bahía Grande

Chubut

Desado

Chico

P a t a g o n i a

Falkland Islands
(UK)
West Falkland
East Falkland

Scotia Sea

Tierra del Fuego

Cape Horn

Drake Passage

South Shetland Islands

ANTARCTICA

Strait of
Magellan

Isla de Chiloé

PACIFIC

OCEAN

Isla San Ambrosio
(Chile)

Isla San Félix
(Chile)

Islas Juan Fernández
(Chile)

Tropic of Capricorn

0 km   1000
0 miles   1000

Northern South America

Caribbean Sea

Gulf of Venezuela

PANAMA

PACIFIC OCEAN

Ríohacha
Santa Marta
Barranquilla
Cartagena
Valledupar
Maicao
Coro
Maracaibo
Cabimas
CARAC
Maracay
Ciudad Ojeda
Lago de Maracaibo
Barquisimeto
Valencia
Valera
Acarigua
San Jua
de los Morro
Sincelejo
Montería
Mérida
Guanare
Cúcuta
Barinas
San Cristóbal
San Fernando
Bello
Bucaramanga
Arauca
VEN
Medellín
Barrancabermeja
Arauca
Quibdó
Itagüí
Puerto Carreño
Manizales
Tunja
Yopal
Pereira
Meta
Armenia
Ibagué
BOGOTÁ
COLOMBIA
Buenaventura
Villavicencio
Cali
Guaviare
Orinoco
Popayán
Neiva
San José del Guaviare
Pasto
Florencia
Mitú
Esmeraldas
Mocoa
Tulcán
Ibarra
QUITO
Puaricor
Manta
Santo Domingo de los Colorados
Caquetá
Portoviejo
Ambato
Guayaquil
Riobamba
ECUADOR
Milagro
Putumayo
Cuenca
Golfo de Guayaquil
Machala
Loja
PERU

Magdalena
Cauca
Apure
Guárico

The first coffee seedlings were brought to Colombia in 1804 by Jesuit Missionaries, today Colombia produces over a million tons (tonnes) of coffee beans every year.

Nestling between snow capped peaks, at 9350 ft (2850 m) Quito is the second highest capital in the world.

0° Equator

GRENADA

ntilles

Isla de Margarita
Carúpano
TRINIDAD
& TOBAGO

Cumaná
Barcelona
Maturín
El Tigre
Tucupita

Ciudad Bolívar
Ciudad Guayana

UELA

Embalse
de Guri

Cuyuni

Salto
Ángel

G u i a n a
Highlands

Caura
Caroní
Paragua

noco

Orinoco

The Serpent's Mouth

**ATLANTIC
OCEAN**

◆ The Guyana shield is one of the
Earth's oldest surfaces, formed
around 4 billion years ago.

(claimed by Venezuela)

Bartica
Rockstone
Linden
GEORGETOWN
New Amsterdam
PARAMARIBO

Nieuw
Amsterdam
St-Laurent-
du-Maroni
Sinnamary
Kourou

GUYANA

*W.J. van
Blommesteinmeer*

SURINAME

Essequibo

Courantyne

French
Guiana
*(French overseas
department)*

CAYENNE

Maroni

◆ Angel Falls
(Salto Ángel)
plunge 3121 ft
(951 m) to form
the world's
highest waterfall.

Acarai Mts.

*(claimed by
Suriname)*

(claimed by Suriname)

◆ The European Space Agency launch
facility at Kourou takes advantage
of the Earth's spin near the
Equator to gain 10 percent
more payload than an equivalent
launch at Cape Canaveral in the US.

Equator

A m a z o n

B R A Z I L

B a s i n

Amazon

◆ 2.47 acres (one hectare) of Amazon rain forest
can contain more than 750 types of trees and
1500 plant species, amounting to around
900 tons (tonnes) of living plant material.

0 km   200

0 miles   200

Peru, Bolivia & North Brazil

VENEZUELA

COLOMBIA

Guia

Boa Vista

Guian

ECUADOR

Equator

Rio Negro

Repre Balbi

Putumayo

Napo

Iquitos

Amazon

Manaus

Amazon

Marañón

Moyobamba

Juruá

Amazon Basi

Piura

Tarapoto

B R A

Chiclayo

Saña

Trujillo

Pucallpa

Ucayali

Porto Velho

Purus

Chimbote

Huaraz

Huánuco

Rio Branco

Huacho

Huacho

La Oroya

Riberalta

Callao

Puerto
Maldonado

Madre de Dios

Beni

Guapore

LIMA

Huancayo

P

E

R

U

Ayacucho

Pisco

Ica

Cusco

Trinidad

PACIFIC
OCEAN

Nazca

Puno

B O L I V I A

Arequipa

*Lake
Titicaca*

LA PAZ

Cochabamba

Montero

Santa Cruz

Tacna

Oruro

Puerto Suá

Lago Roopó

SUCRE

Potosí

Uyuni

Tupiza

PARAGU

Tarija

C H I L E

ARGENTINA

◆ *Lake Titicaca is the largest lake in South
America at 3220 sq miles (8340 sq km)
and with an altitude of 12,500 ft (3810 m)
it is also the world's highest navigable lake.*

BOLIVIA'S TWO CAPITALS

La Paz - legislative and
administrative capital

Sucre - legal capital

French Guiana
(French overseas department)

◇ The Amazon River is 4195 miles (6751 km) long with
a peak flow of 7 million cubic feet (198,229 cu m) of
water entering the Atlantic Ocean every second.

'ighlands

Macapá

Ilha Caviana de Fora

ATLANTIC

Equator

Amazon

Belém

Ilha de Marajó

Santarém

OCEAN

São Luís

Paranaíba

San Fernando
de Noronha
(part of Brazil)

Fortaleza

Represa de
Tucuruí

Imperatriz

Teresina

Mossoró

Natal

Z

I

L

Carolina

Campina
Grande

João
Pessoa

Juàzeiro do Norte

São Francisco

Recife

Represa de
Sobradinho

Juàzeiro

Maceió

Aracaju

ato Grosso

Taguatinga

Feira de Santana

Salvador

Brazilian

Cuiabá

Anápolis

BRASÍLIA

Itabuna

Goiânia

Highlands

Vitória da Conquista

Montes Claros

Governador Valadares

Uberlândia

Uberaba

Belo Horizonte

Divinópolis

Vitória

ampo
rande

Ribeirão Preto

Campos

Marília
Campinas

Nova
Iguaçu

Juiz de Fora

Londrina

Sorocaba

Taubaté

Rio de Janeiro

Tropic of Capricorn

São Paulo

Xingu

Pires

Araguaia

Tocantins

Paraná

Paraná

1

2

3

4

5

Paraguay, Uruguay & South Brazil

◆ Formed by river deposits washed
down from the Andes and Brazilian
Shield, the Gran Chaco is virtually
free of stones. It is composed of
sand and silt sediments that are
up to 10,000 ft (3050 m) thick.

◆ The Itaipú hydroelectric scheme is
able to produce more power than
10 average nuclear reactors; it supplies
26% of the electrical power consumption
of Brazil and 78% for Paraguay.

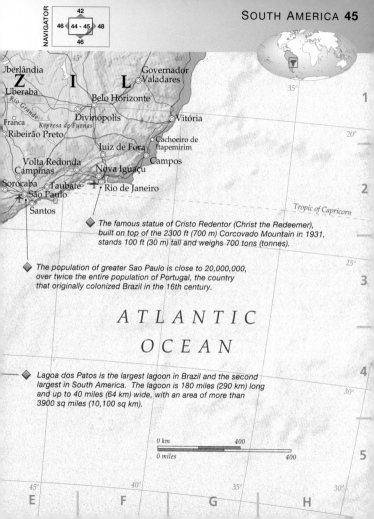

Jberlândia
Z   I   L
Uberaba
Rio Grande
Franca
Represa de Furnas
Ribeirão Preto
Volta Redonda
Campinas
Sorocaba
São Paulo
Santos
Taubaté

Governador
Valadares
Belo Horizonte
Divinópolis
Vitória
Cachoeiro de
Itapemirim
Juiz de Fora
Nova Iguaçu
Campos
Rio de Janeiro

Tropic of Capricorn

◆ The famous statue of Cristo Redentor (Christ the Redeemer),
built on top of the 2300 ft (700 m) Corcovado Mountain in 1931,
stands 100 ft (30 m) tall and weighs 700 tons (tonnes).

◆ The population of greater Sao Paulo is close to 20,000,000,
over twice the entire population of Portugal, the country
that originally colonized Brazil in the 16th century.

A T L A N T I C

O C E A N

◆ Lagoa dos Patos is the largest lagoon in Brazil and the second
largest in South America. The lagoon is 180 miles (290 km) long
and up to 40 miles (64 km) wide, with an area of more than
3900 sq miles (10,100 sq km).

0 km   400
0 miles   400

Southern South America

BRAZIL

BRAZIL

PARAGUAY

BOLIVIA

URUGUAY

PERU

CHILE

ARGENTINA

The world's tallest, active volcano is the Guallatiri volcano in northern Chile. It stands 19,918 ft (6071 m) tall, and last erupted in 1987.

The driest place on earth is the Atacama Desert in Chile with an average rainfall of 0.004 inches (0.1 mm) per year. Until recently some places had received no rain for over 400 years.

Tropic of Capricorn

Tropic of Capricorn

PACIFIC

OCEAN

Posadas

Formosa

Corrientes

Concordia

BUENOS AIRES

Gualeguaychú

La Plata

Río de la Plata

Uruguay

Paraná

Paraná

Resistencia

Vera

Rosario

Junín

Santa Fe

Paraná

Río Cuarto

Bermejo

Pilcomayo

Gran Chaco

San Salvador de Jujuy

Salta

San Miguel de Tucumán

Santiago del Estero

Laguna Mar Chiquita

Córdoba

Villa Mercedes

Salado

Pampas

Chuquicamata

Calama

San Juan

La Rioja

Mendoza

Godoy Cruz

Rancagua

SANTIAGO

Cerro Aconcagua 22,831ft (6959 m)

Desierto de Atacama

Arica

Iquique

Tocopilla

Antofagasta

Chañaral

Copiapó

Vallenar

La Serena

Coquimbo

Illapel

La Ligua

Viña del Mar

Valparaíso

San Antonio

Pichilemu

Talca

Linares

Curicó

Islas Juan Fernández (to Chile)

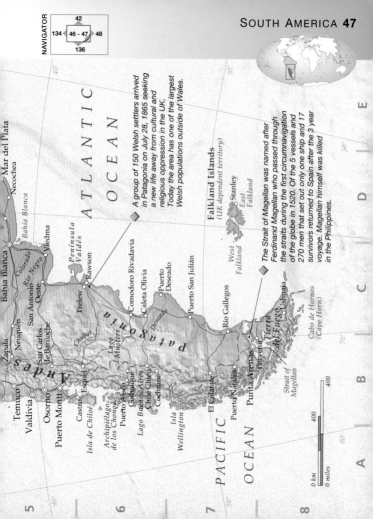

ATLANTIC

OCEAN

A group of 150 Welsh settlers arrived in Patagonia on July 28, 1865 seeking a new life away from cultural and religious oppression in the UK. Today the area has one of the largest Welsh populations outside of Wales.

Falkland Islands
(UK dependent territory)

Stanley
East
Falkland

West
Falkland

The Strait of Magellan was named after Ferdinand Magellan who passed through the straits during the first circumnavigation of the globe in 1520. Of the 5 vessels and 270 men that set out only one ship and 17 survivors returned to Spain after the 3 year voyage. Magellan himself was killed in the Philippines.

Mar del Plata

Necochea

Bahía Blanca

Colorado
Río Negro
Bahía Blanca

Viedma

Península
Valdés

San Antonio
Oeste

Rawson

Trelew

Comodoro Rivadavia

Caleta Olivia

Puerto
Deseado

Neuquén

Zapala

San Carlos
de Bariloche

Chubut

Esquel

Lago
Musters

Deseado

Puerto San Julián

Puerto Aisén
Coihaique

Lago Buenos Aires
Chile Chico
Cochrane

Río Gallegos

El Calafate

Puerto Natales

Punta Arenas

Porvenir

Tierra
del Fuego

Ushuaia

Cabo de Hornos
(Cape Horn)

Strait of
Magellan

Temuco

Valdivia

Osorno

Puerto Montt

Castro

Isla de Chiloé

Archipiélago
de los Chonos

Isla
Wellington

PACIFIC

OCEAN

Patagonia

Andes

0 km   400
0 miles   400

The Atlantic Ocean

◆ The North Atlantic Deep Water Current is an oceanic "river" that carries around twenty times more water than all the rivers of the world put together.

◆ The Gulf Stream travels across the Atlantic Ocean at up to 110 miles (170 km) a day.

Svalbard (Norway)

Barents Sea

Arctic Circle

Scandinavia

EUROPE

Baltic Sea

Black Sea

Danube

Red Sea

Port Said

Tropic of Cancer

Nile

ARCTIC OCEAN

Greenland Sea

Jan Mayen (Norway)

North Sea

Rotterdam

Alps

Mediterranean Sea

Sahara

AFRICA

Faeroe Is. (Denmark)

British Isles

Gibraltar

Atlas Mts.

Ellesmere I.

Greenland (Denmark)

Denmark Strait

Iceland

Azores (Portugal)

Madeira (Portugal)

Canary Is. (Spain)

Canary Basin

Niger

Baffin Bay

Labrador Sea

Grand Banks

Newfoundland Basin

CAPE VERDE

Cape Verde

Mid-Atlantic Ridge

Baffin I.

Davis Strait

St. Lawrence

New York

Bermuda (UK)

Sargasso Sea

West Indies

Caribbean Sea

Arctic Circle

Hudson Bay

NORTH AMERICA

Great Lakes

Gulf of Mexico

Tropic of Cancer

Mississippi

More large rivers drain into the Atlantic, than any other ocean, including the Amazon, Congo and Mississippi. These three alone deposit around 4560 tonnes of sediment per sq mile per year.

ATLANTIC OCEAN

PACIFIC OCEAN

SOUTH AMERICA

Andes

Amazon

Paraná

Rio de Janeiro

Buenos Aires

Cape Horn

Tropic of Capricorn

Equator

Gulf of Guinea

Congo

Lake Victoria

Lake Nyasa

Equator

Tropic of Capricorn

Cape Town

Cape of Good Hope

Mid-Atlantic Ridge

Walvis Ridge

Angola Basin

Cape Basin

Brazil Basin

Rio Grande Rise

Argentine Basin

Fernando de Noronha (Brazil)

Ascension I. (St Helena)

St Helena (UK)

Ilha da Trindade (Brazil)

Tristan da Cunha (St Helena)

Gough I. (Tristan da Cunha)

Atlantic-Indian Ridge

Bouvet I. (Norway)

Atlantic-Indian Basin

Falkland Is. (UK)

South Georgia (UK)

South Sandwich Is. (UK)

Scotia Sea

South Orkney Is.

South Shetland Is.

Weddell Sea

Bellingshausen Sea

ANTARCTICA

Antarctic Circle

0 km   2000
0 miles   2000

5
6
7
8

Africa

ATLANTIC OCEAN

Caspian Sea

The Gulf

Tropic of Cancer

Arabian Peninsula

Gulf of Aden

S O M A L I A

E U R O P E

Caucasus

Black Sea

A S I A

Syrian Desert

Cyprus

Mediterranean Sea

Sicily

Iberian Peninsula

Madeira (Portugal)

Islas Canarias (Spain)

Ceuta (Spain)

Melilla (Spain)

Atlas Mountains

TUNISIA

MOROCCO

WESTERN SAHARA (disputed)

Tropic of Cancer

MAURITANIA

SENEGAL

GAMBIA

GUINEA-BISSAU

GUINEA

SIERRA LEONE

LIBERIA

ALGERIA

S a h a r a

Ahaggar

MALI

Senegal

Niger

BURKINA

CÔTE D'IVOIRE (IVORY COAST)

GHANA

TOGO

BENIN

S a h e l

NIGER

Niger

NIGERIA

EQUATORIAL GUINEA

Gulf of Guinea

SÃO TOMÉ &

LIBYA

Libyan Desert

Tibesti

CHAD

EGYPT

Nile

Red Sea

Blue Nile

White Nile

S u d d

SUDAN

ERITREA

DJIBOUTI

ETHIOPIA

Ethiopian Highlands

UGANDA

Lake Turkana

Lake

CENTRAL AFRICAN REPUBLIC

CAMEROON

Uele

Congo

O

COMOROS

Mayotte
(France)

MADAGASCAR

Tropic of Capricorn

INDIAN

OCEAN

Mozambique Channel

Kilimanjaro
19,341ft (5895m)

BURUNDI

TANZANIA

Lake Natron

Lake Nyasa

Lake
Tanganyika

MALAWI

MOZAMBIQUE

SWAZILAND

DEM. REP.
CONGO

ANGOLA

ZAMBIA

ZIMBABWE

Zambezi

LESOTHO

GABON

Cabinda
(Angola)

Bié
Plateau

BOTSWANA

Kalahari
Desert

Orange River

SOUTH
AFRICA

NAMIBIA

Namib Desert

Cape of
Good Hope

Ascension I.
(St Helena)

St Helena
(UK)

ATLANTIC

OCEAN

Tropic of Capricorn

Tristan da Cunha
(St Helena)

Gough Island
(Tristan da Cunha)

0 km   1000

0 miles   1000

A   B   C   D   E

5

6

7

8

Northwest Africa

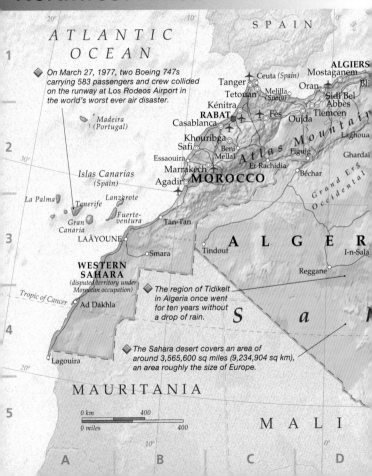

ATLANTIC
OCEAN

SPAIN

◆ On March 27, 1977, two Boeing 747s
carrying 583 passengers and crew collided
on the runway at Los Rodeos Airport in
the world's worst ever air disaster.

ALGIERS

Mostaganem

Tanger ⊕ Ceuta (Spain) Oran ◉ Bl

Tetouan ◉ Melilla Sidi Bel
(Spain) Abbès

Kénitra Fes Tlemcen

RABAT ⊕ Oujda

Casablanca

Madeira
(Portugal)

Khouribga Atlas Mountain Laghoua

Safi Beni
Mellal Figuig Ghardaï

Essaouira Er Rachidia Grand Erg

Marrakech Béchar Occidental

Islas Canarias
(Spain)

Agadir **MOROCCO**

La Palma Lanzarote

Tenerife

Gran Fuerte-
Canaria ventura Tan-Tan

A L G E R

LAÂYOUNE Tindouf I-n-Sala

Smara

Reggane

**WESTERN
SAHARA**
(disputed territory under
Moroccan occupation)

◆ The region of Tidikelt
in Algeria once went
for ten years without
a drop of rain.

Tropic of Cancer

Ad Dakhla **S** a

◆ The Sahara desert covers an area of
around 3,565,600 sq miles (9,234,904 sq km),
an area roughly the size of Europe.

Lagouira

MAURITANIA

0 km 400

0 miles 400

MALI

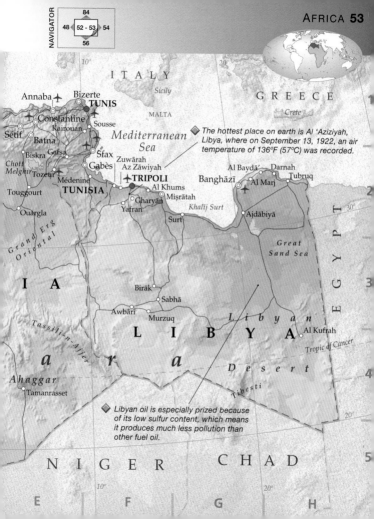

10°

I T A L Y

Sicily

G R E E C E

Crete

MALTA

Annaba ✈ Bizerte ✈
  ○ ● TUNIS
  ○ Constantine
  ○ Sousse
Sétif ○ Kairouan
Batna ✈
Biskra Gafsa ✈ Sfax
Chott ○ Tozeur ○ Gabès
Melghir Médenine Zuwārah
Touggourt ✈ TUNISIA Az Zāwiyah
  ○ Gharyān ✈ TRIPOLI
Ouargla ○ Yafran Al Khums
  Misrātah
  Surt

Mediterranean Sea

◆ The hottest place on earth is Al 'Azīzīyah, Libya, where on September 13, 1922, an air temperature of 136°F (57°C) was recorded.

Al Baydā' Darnah
Banghāzī ○ Tubruq
  Al Marj
  Ajdābiyā

Khalīj Surt

G R E E C E

E G Y P T

20°

Great Sand Sea

30°

I A

Birāk ○
  ○ Sabhā
Awbārī ○
  Murzuq

Libyan

L I B Y A ○ Al Kufrah

Tropic of Cancer

Tassili-n-Ajjer

a   r   a

Desert

Ahaggar
Tamanrasset ○

Tibesti

◆ Libyan oil is especially prized because of its low sulfur content, which means it produces much less pollution than other fuel oil.

20°

N I G E R   C H A D

10°   20°

E   F   G   H   5

When first opened in 1869, the Suez Canal consisted of a channel 26 ft (8 m) deep and 200 to 300 ft (60 to 90 m) wide at the surface. Construction involved the excavation and dredging of 97 million cubic yards (74 million cubic metres) of material.

For thousands of years the Nile has supported cultivation in the Aswan region, despite it being one of the driest places on Earth, with an average of only 0.02 inches (0.5 mm) of rain per year.

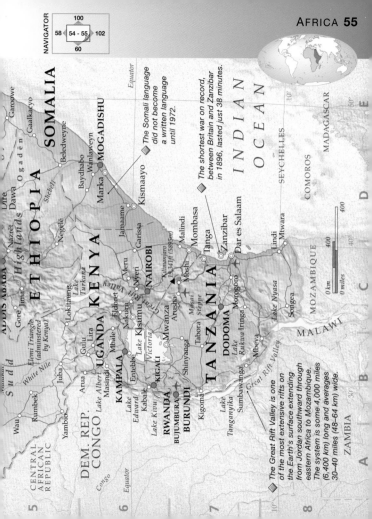

0 km 400
0 miles 400

Tropic of Cancer

20°

10°

WESTERN
SAHARA
*(disputed territory
under Moroccan occupation)*

Bîr
Mogreïn

'Erg Iguîdi

Kâghet

El Hank

E'

◆ *Despite a population of 2,500,000 there are
fewer than 6000 telephones in Mauritania,
roughly one for every 416 people.*

Fdérik Zouérat

Ouarâne

S

20°

Nouâdhibou

Akchâr

Choûm

Atâr

El Mreyyé

**CAPE
VERDE**

Ilhas de Barlavento
Santo
Antão
São
Vicente São
Nicolau Sal
Boa Vista
Santiago Maio
Fogo **PRAIA**
Ilhas de Sotavento

Akjoujt

Rkîz

NOUAKCHOTT

MAURITANIA

Aleg

Senegal

Kiffa

Aoukâr

A T L A N T I C

O C E A N

Saint Louis

Kaédi

Nioro

SENEGAL

DAKAR
Mbaké
Diourbel
Kaolack

Aleg

Kayes

S

Ségou

Ban

BAMAKO

◆ *Gambia is only around 20 miles (32 km)
wide and 300 miles (483 km) long;
its unusual shape and size are down
to territorial compromises arising from
19th-century Anglo-French rivalry
in western Africa.*

BANJUL **GAMBIA**
Bignona
BISSAU

**GUINEA-
BISSAU**
Boké

Gambia

Niger

Gaoual

Labé

Bafing

Bougouni

Siguiri

Odienné

Bo

Diou

GUINEA

Kindia

Kankan

**CÔTE
D'IVOIRE
(IVORY COAS**

◆ *Monrovia, named after the fifth US President
James Monroe, was founded in 1830 by the
American Colonization Society as a settlement
for freed American slaves.*

CONAKRY

FREETOWN

**SIERRA
LEONE**

Bo

Tubmanburg

LIBERIA

YAMOUSSOUKRO

Lac

Ko

MONROVIA
Buchanan

Zwedru

Gagno

◆ *A Ruppell's Griffen Vulture collided with a
commercial airliner at 37,000 ft (11,277 m) above
Côte d'Ivoire to earn the posthumous distinction
of the highest flying bird ever recorded.*

Harper

Abidj

20°

10°

A   B   C   D   E

A L G E R I A

L I B Y A

◆ In the late 1960s and early 1970s a series of catastrophic droughts caused the Sahara Desert to advance southward up to 60 miles (100 km) into the Sahel region. The loss of human life by starvation and disease was estimated in 1973 to be 100,000.

Tropic of Cancer

ech

aoudenni

Taoudenni

'Erg-In-Sâkâne

S   a   h   a   r   a

Tessalit

Tibesti

Azaouâd

Araouane

Adrar des Ifôghas

Assamakka

Ténéré du Tafassâsset

M A L I

Massif de l'Aïr

Ténéré

ac

Tombouctou

Gao

Ansongo

Agadez

Grand Erg de Bilma

C H A D

Lac
Niangay

Hombori

N I G E R

Tahoua

opti

a   h   e   l

Maradi

Zinder

Nguigmi
Gouré

Lake Chad

BURKINA

NIAMEY

Sokoto

OUAGADOUGOU

Sokoto

Katsina

Fáda-
Ngourma

Gusau

Kano

Maiduguri

oudougou

Kandi

Zaria

Wa

Kainji
Reservoir

Kaduna

Kumo

BENIN

ongola

Natitingou

Parakou

N I G E R I A

*Jos
Plateau*

Tamale

Sokodé

Ilorin

Niger

ABUJA

Benue

GHANA

Oyo

Ogbomosho

*Gulf
Mountains*

yani

Lake
Volta

Abomey

Ede

Enugu

C.A.R.

amasi

Ibadan

Benin
City

amankese

Nsawam

Lagos

Sapele

Onitsha

Aba

Calabar

ACCRA

LOMÉ

**PORTO-
NOVO**

Bight of Benin

Gulf of Guinea

Port Harcourt

*Mouths
of the Niger*

C A M E R O O N

Lake Volta is one of the largest man-made lakes in the world covering 3283 sq miles (8502 sq km), or 3.6% of Ghana's area

EQUATORIAL
GUINEA

The eye of an ostrich is bigger than it's brain. They are the largest bird on earth. An adult male can stand 8 ft (2.5 m) tall, weigh up to 300 lbs (135 kg), and run at around 30 mph (48 km/h).

Pygmies that inhabit the Congo Basin grow to be only 3 or 4 feet (0.9 to 1.2 m) tall at adulthood. The name, "Pygmy," is derived from the Greek word, pyme, which means "a cubit in height."

The vast sand flats surrounding Lake Chad were once covered by water. Changing climatic patterns caused the lake to shrink and desert now covers much of its previous area.

EGYPT

Tropic of Cancer

LIBYA

SUDAN

Sahara

Ennedi

CHAD

Tibesti

Faya

Biltine

Abéché

Mongo

Am Timan

Ati

NDJAMENA

Massif des Bongo

Ndélé

Obia

CENTRAL AFRICAN REPUBLIC

Mao

Bol

Chari

Sarh

Goré

Bongor

Laï

Kousséri

Lake Chad

NIGER

Maroua

Guider

Bossangoa

Sibut

ALGERIA

Tropic of Cancer

Garoua

Moundou

Ngaoundéré

NIGERIA

Banyo

Bamenda

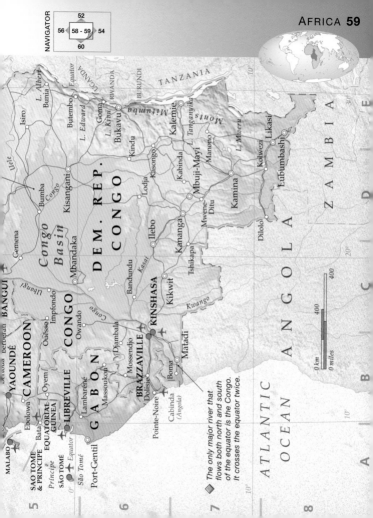

L. Albert
Isiro
Bunia
UGANDA
Butembo
Goma
RWANDA
TANZANIA
Uele
L. Eduard
L. Kivu
Bukavu
BURUNDI
Monts
Mitumba
Gemena
Bumba
Congo
Kisangani
Kindu
Kalemie
L. Tanganyika
Congo
Basin
DEM. REP.
CONGO
Kasongo
Kabinda
Manono
L. Mweru
Kolwezi
Likasi
Lubumbashi
Mbandaka
Lodia
Mbuji-Mayi
Kamina
ZAMBIA
Ubangi
CONGO
Bandundu
Kasai
Ilebo
Kananga
Mwene-
Ditu
Dilolo
Impfondo
Ouésso
Owando
Bandundu
Kwilu
Tshikapa
Mossendjo
Djambala
KINSHASA
Kikwit
A N G O L A
CAMEROON
Yaoundé
Ebolowa
Oyem
Bata
LIBREVILLE
GABON
Lambaréné
Massoukou
BRAZZAVILLE
Dolisie
Kwango
Matadi
Boma
Cabinda
(Angola)
Pointe-Noire
MALABO
EQUATORIAL
GUINEA
SÃO TOMÉ & PRÍNCIPE
Príncipe
SÃO TOMÉ
São Tomé
Equator
Port-Gentil

A T L A N T I C
O C E A N

The only major river that
flows both north and south
of the equator is the Congo.
It crosses the equator twice.

0 km 400
0 miles 400

Southern Africa

DEM. REP.
CONGO

Lak
Tanganyik

1

Cabinda
(Angola)
Cabinda

Congo

Uíge

Ambriz

N'Dalatando

Lucapa

Saurimo

Ndola
Mufulira

LUANDA

Malanje

Chingola

Cuanza

Kitwe
Luanshya

A N G O L A

**ATLANTIC
OCEAN**

Sumbe

Kuito

Huambo

Zambezi

ZAMBIA

Lobito
Benguela

Menongue

LUSAKA

2

Lubango

Cubango

Choma

Namibe

N'Giva

Zambezi

Livingstone

Lake
Kariba

Tombua

Rundu

Okavango

Victoria
Falls

Chitungwi

Cunene

ZIMB

◆ The Okavango River pours
some 14.4 billion cubic yards
(11 billion cu m) of water into
the Okavango Delta each year.
It drains away through a maze of
lagoons, channels, and islands
covering around 5800 sq miles
(15,000 sq km) before eventually
disappearing into the sands of the
Kalahari Desert to the south.

*Etosha
Pan*

Tsumeb

Okavango Delta

Grootfontein

Maun

Bulawayo
Francistown

NAMIBIA

Ghanzi

3

Namib Desert

WINDHOEK

Kalahari

BOTSWANA

Mahalapye

Limpopo

Swakopmund

Rehoboth

Desert

GABORONE

Walvis Bay

Lobatse

PRETOR

Tropic of Capricorn

Mmabatho

Soweto

Johannesburg

◆ The Kalahari Desert is the largest
continuous sand surface in the world.
Iron oxide gives the sand a distinctive red
color to the sand, which is over
200 ft (60 m) deep in places.

Keetmanshoop

Kroons

4

Lüderitz

Karasburg

Vaal

Kimberley

MASER

Orange

BLOEMFONTEIN

LESOTHO

SOUTH AFRICA'S THREE CAPITALS

Pretoria - administrative capital
Cape Town - legislative capital
Bloemfontein - financial capital

S O U T H

Middelburg

Drakensberg

A F R I C A

Beaufort West

East
Londo

5

Bellville

CAPE TOWN

Cape of Good Hope

George

Port
Elizabeth

0 km   400
0 miles   400

10°   20°

10°

20°

30°

0°   10°   20°

A   B   C   D

40°
50°

◇ Coco de Mer, or the double coconut palm, produces some of the largest seeds in the plant kingdom. Weighing up to 60 lbs (27 kg), they take around ten years to ripen.

Inner Islands

VICTORIA • *Mahé*

Amirante Islands

SEYCHELLES

1

TANZANIA

Mbala

Kasama

MALAWI

Mzuzu

Ipika

LONGWE

Salima

Lake
Nyasa

Rovuma

Aldabra Group

Farquhar Group

COMOROS

Grande Comore

MORONI

Mohéli *Anjouan*

Outer Islands

10°

2

Blantyre

Tete

Mocímboa da Praia

Mamoudzou

Mayotte
(French territorial collectivity)

Antsohihy

Antsirañana

Ambanja

Antalaha

Zomba

Nacala

M
O
Z
A
M
B
I
Q
U
E

Nsanje

Nampula

Moçambique

HARARE

Mocuba

Climolo

Quelimane

Beira

Mahajanga

MADAGASCAR

Fenoarivo

3

WE

Morondava

ANTANANARIVO

Toamasina

Fianarantsoa

Ambositra

MAURITIUS

PORT LOUIS

Inhambane

Xai-Xai

Mozambique Channel

Toliara

Ihosy

Mananjary

Saint-Denis

Réunion
(French overseas department)

Mascarene Islands

20°

MAPUTO

BABANE

VAZILAND

Farafangana

Vangaindrano

4

ermaritzburg

rban

Amboasary

◇ Thought to have been extinct for 70 million years, a living coelacanth was netted in the Indian Ocean in 1938. They are powerful predators averaging 5 feet (1.5 m) in length and weighing about 100lbs (45 kg).

Tropic of Capricorn

I   N   D   I   A   N

O   C   E   A   N

5

40°
50°
60°
30°

E   F   G   H

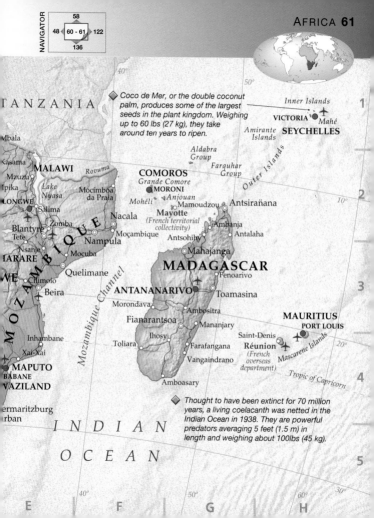

Europe

ICELAND

*Norwegian
Sea*

Faeroe Islands
(Denmark)

Shetland Islands

Outer
Hebrides

*British
Isles*

*North
Sea*

Orkney
Islands

Ireland   Isle of Man
(to UK)

IRELAND   *Britain*

DENMARK

*Celtic
Sea*

**UNITED
KINGDOM**

Nor

NETHERLANDS

English Channel   **BELGIUM**

Channel Is
(UK)   **LUX.**   **GERMANY**

**CZE
REPU**

Loire

Bay of Biscay   **FRANCE**

*Massif
Central*

SWITZ.

LIECH.

AUST

*Mont Blanc
15,771ft 4807m*

SLOVEN

PORTUGAL

Duero

Iberian

Pyrenees

MONACO

**SAN
MARINO**

CRO

**BOS
& H**

Tagus

SPAIN

*Peninsula
Guadalquivir*

ANDORRA

Corsica

**VATICAN
CITY**

ITAL

*Madeira
(to Portugal)*

Strait of Gibraltar

Balearic Islands

Sardinia

*Tyrrhenian
Sea*

Gibraltar
(UK)

Mediterra

Sicily

*Canary Islands
(to Spain)*

Atlas   Mountains

AFRICA

*ATLANTIC
OCEAN*

MALTA

0 km   800

0 miles   800

Arctic Circle

Limit of winter pack ice

Lof

A   B   C   D

NAVIGATOR

137
48 | 62 - 63 | 94
50

Barents Sea

North Cape   Ostrov Kolguyev

Arctic Circle

Ob

Irtysh

FINLAND

Kola
Peninsula

White
Sea

Ural Mountains

Northern Dvina

Lake Onega

R   U   S   S   I   A   N

Aland

Lake
Ladoga

F   E   D   E   R   A   T   I   O   N

ESTONIA

LATVIA

LITHUANIA
SS.

Caspian Plain

Central
Russian
Upland

Volga Uplands

Ural

Volga

Aral Sea

Syr Darya

BELARUS

Pripet
Marshes

Dnieper Lowlands

Don

Ural

Amu Dary

European Plain

Dnieper

UKRAINE

Bug

Dniester

Carpathian Mountains

Caspian
Sea

AKIA

MOLDOVA

NGARY

Sea of
Azov

Caucasus

ROMANIA

Crimea

El'brus
18,510ft
(5642m)

RB;
MON,
UGO)

Danube

Black Sea

BULGARIA

Balkan Mountains

MACED;

TURKEY

ANIA

Aegean
Sea

Anatolia

A   S   I   A

Zágros Mountains

GREECE

Peloponnese

e a

Crete

Cyprus

Tigris

Euphrates

The North Atlantic

◆ At 840,000 sq miles (2,175,600 sq km), Greenland is the largest island in the world. However, 650,000 sq miles (1,638, 400 sq km) of this is a massive ice sheet so heavy that the central land area has sunk to form to a basin more than 1000 ft (300 m) below sea level.

◆ The Jakobshavn Glacier, often moving 100 feet (30 m) a day, is among the world's fastest glaciers, and calves around 1350 icebergs every year.

NUNAVUT

Devon Island

Ellesmere Island

Nares Strait

Qaanaaq

Innaanganeq

Knud Rasmussen Land

Savissivik

Qimusseriarsuaq

Baffin Bay

Kullorsuaq

CANADA

Hudson Bay

Péninsule d'Ungava

QUEBEC

Ungava Bay

Baffin Island

Hudson Strait

Frobisher Bay

Cumberland Sound

Limit of summer pack ice

Davis Strait

Qeqertarsuaq

Qeqertarsuaq

Qasigiannguit

Sisimiut

Kong Frederik IX Land

Greenland
(Danish external territory)

Maniitsoq

NUUK

Kong Christian IX Land

Gunnbjørn Field 3700m

Paamiut

Ivittuut

Ammassalik

Qaqortoq

Kong Frederik VI Kyst

Denmark

Nanortalik

Limit of winter pack ice

Nunap Isua (Kap Farvel)

ATLANTIC OCEAN

Fa.

NEWFOUNDLAND & LABRADOR

Labrador Sea

Arctic Circle

0 km   800

0 miles   800

ARCTIC OCEAN

Kap Morris Jesup

ncoln ea

Wandel Sea

Nord

Kong Frederik VIII Land

rristian x Land

Greenland Sea

Daneborg

Kong Oscar Fjord

Ittoqqortoormiit

ittivaq

angikajik

rait

Limit of winter pack ice

ICELAND

Siglufjördhur

ayrï o Húsavík

o Seydhisfjördhur

ÝKJAVÍK

foss

tsey

Svalbard
(Norwegian dependency)

Spitsbergen

Longyearbyen

Barentsberg o

Storfjorden

Kvitøya

Nordaustlandet

Kong Karls Land

Barentsøya

Edgeøya

Bjørnøya
(Norway)

Zemlya Frantsa-Iosifa

Novaya Zemlya

Nordkapp
(North Cape)

Barents Sea

Arctic Circle

R U S S I A N   F E D E R A T I O N

FINLAND

Norwegian Sea

Jan Mayen
(Norway)

Faeroe Islands
(Denmark)

Tórshavn o

Shetland Islands

N O R W A Y

S W E D E N

Gulf of Bothnia

◆ With temperatures ranging from 59° F (15° C) in the summer to -40° F (-40° C) in the winter, vegetation on Svalbard consists mostly of lichens and mosses; the only trees are the tiny polar willow and the dwarf birch.

◆ Greenland's deeply indented coastline is 24,430 miles (39,330 km) long, a distance roughly equivalent to the Earth's circumference at the Equator.

◆ Even though only one twentieth of Iceland's potential geothermal power has been harnessed, around 89% of houses are heated geothermally.

E   F   G   H

1   2   3   4   5

Scandinavia & Finland

◆ The North Cape Current warms the northern coasts of Norway, Finland, and Russia's Kola Peninsula with water temperatures of 39–54° F (4–12° C), allowing this area of the Barents Sea to remain free of pack ice throughout the winter.

◆ The sun is continuously visible from late May to late July in Tromsø because of its position well north of the Arctic Circle.

◆ Scandinavia is still recovering from the last ice age, when the land was depressed 2000 ft (600 m) by the weight of the ice. Today the earth's crust is "rebounding" at the rate of 0.3 inches (9 mm) a year in the Gulf of Bothnia.

RUSSIAN FEDERATION

Barents Sea

ARCTIC OCEAN

Norwegian Sea

FINLAND

LAPLAND

Arctic Circle

FINLAND
Vaasa
Seinäjoki
Jyväskylä
Savonlinna
Imatra
Lappeenranta
Kouvola
Kotka
Vantaa
Tampere
Hämeenlinna
Riihimäki
Pori
Rauma
Turku
Espoo
HELSINKI
Åland
Mariehamn
Gulf of Finland

ESTONIA

LATVIA

LITHUANIA

BELARUS

KALININGRAD
(part of Russian
Federation)

POLAND

GERMANY

Sundsvall
Gulf
of
Bothnia
Gävle
Falun
Borlänge
Uppsala
Västerås
STOCKHOLM
Nyköping
Örebro
Norrköping
Linköping
Skövde
Vättern
Jönköping
Borås
Vänern
Karlstad
Visby
Gotland
Öland
Kalmar
Växjö
Karlskrona
Kristianstad
Bornholm
Rønne
Baltic Sea

S W E D E N

N O R W A Y

Hermansverk
Lillehammer
Hamar
Gjøvik
Mjøsa
OSLO
Moss
Fredrikstad
Halden
Porsgrunn
Skien
Arendal
Kristiansand
Stavanger
Haugesund
Bergen
Aurlandsvangen
Sørfjorden
Setesdal
Drammen
Hønefoss

Skagerrak

DENMARK
Jylland
Silkeborg
Herning
Esbjerg
Vejle
Randers
Århus
Odense
Aabenraa
COPENHAGEN
Sjælland
Nykøbing
Helsingborg
Malmö
Halmstad
Frederikshavn
Ålborg
Hjørring
Göteborg
Trollhättan

◆ The sauna is a Finnish institution with some 2 million sauna facilities to serve a population of just 5 million.

◆ The 10-mile (16-km) bridge and tunnel link across the Øresund sound is one of the largest infrastructure projects in European history. It connects the Danish capital Copenhagen to the Swedish port of Malmö.

The Low Countries

THE NETHERLANDS' TWO CAPITALS

Amsterdam - Capital
The Hague - Seat of Government

◆ The Netherlands is the lowest country in the world. It is estimated that 30 percent of the land is below sea level with the lowest point some 23 ft (6.7 m) below sea level.

◆ The inner city of Amsterdam is divided by its network of canals into some 90 "islands" linked together by approximately 1300 bridges and viaducts.

◆ The port of Rotterdam, combined with Europoort (which handles vessels too large to reach Rotterdam), is the largest in the world in terms of capacity, handling around 325 million tons (tonnes) of cargo every year.

GERMANY

NETHERLANDS

North Sea

Waddeneilanden

Schiermonnikoog
Ameland
Terschelling
Vlieland
Texel

Delfzijl
Emmen
Hengelo
Enschede
Almelo
Groningen
Assen
Heerenveen
Leeuwarden
Meppel
IJssel
Zwolle
Deventer
Apeldoorn
Arnhem
Nijmegen
Bergs
Waal
Amersfoort
Ede
Oss
's-Hertogenbosch
Utrecht
Hilversum
AMSTERDAM
Lelystad
Purmerend
Hoorn
Gouda
Lek
Zoetermeer
Leiden
Haarlem
Delft
THE HAGUE
Rotterdam
Dordrecht
Alkmaar
Den Helder
IJsselmeer

GERMANY

FRANCE

BELGIUM

LUXEMBOURG

Zeebrugge
Oostende
Brugge
Roeselare
Ieper
Kortrijk
Mouscron
Tournai
Terneuzen
Sint-Niklaas
Gent
Aalst
Mechelen
BRUSSELS
La Louvière
Mons
Turnhout
Antwerpen
Leuven
Tienen
Charleroi
Dinant
Namur
Hasselt
Genk
Seraing
Liège
Maastricht
Heerlen
Venlo
Verviers
Bastogne
LUXEMBOURG
Diekirch
Arlon
Esch-sur-Alzette

Flanders
Schelde
Ardennes
Meuse
Sambre
Ourthe
Sûre
Our
Moselle

♦ *Belgium and the Netherlands have an underground boundary that differs from the surface boundary shown on maps. In 1950, the two countries agreed to move the underground boundary so as not to divide coal mines between the two countries.*

♦ *On August 23, 1914 three weeks after Britain entered World War I, the 70,000 strong British Expeditionary Force encountered the advancing German army for the first time at the battle of Mons.*

♦ *Echternach is the home of the only religious dancing procession remaining in the Western world. Every year since the 15th century thousands of pilgrims have marched down the streets of the town performing a ritual dance involving specific movements, music, and prayers.*

0 km   50
0 miles   50

A | B | C | D | E
5 | 6 | 7 | 8

The British Isles

After the surrender of the German fleet in 1918 and its internment in Scapa Flow, over 50 ships were scuttled by the German crews on June 21, 1919, to prevent them falling into British hands.

With a depth of 788 ft (240 m) and a length of about 23 miles (36 km), Loch Ness contains the largest volume of fresh water in Great Britain.

Midges have the fastest wing-beat of any insect, and are able to flap their wings at around 63,000 beats per minute.

The Giant's Causeway comprises approximately 37,000 dark basalt polygonal columns packed together; they were formed by volcanic activity some 55 million years ago.

Lerwick

Shetland Islands

Faroe Islands

ATLANTIC

OCEAN

North Sea

Newcastle upon Tyne

Orkney Islands
Kirkwall

Thurso

Moray Firth

Elgin

Aberdeen

Ullapool

Inverness

Dundee

Loch Ness

SCOTLAND

Grampian Mts.

Perth

Stirling

Firth of Forth

EDINBURGH

Isle of Lewis
Stornoway

The Minch

Isle of Skye

Ben Nevis
▲4406 ft (1343m)

Fort William

Loch Lomond

Glasgow

Greenock

Southern Uplands

Outer Hebrides

The Little Minch

Isle of Mull

Oban

Jura

Ayr

North Uist

South Uist

Islay

Isle of Arran

Barra

UNITED KINGDOM

France, Andorra & Monaco

Work began on the 31-mile (50-km) Channel Tunnel in 1987. Earth was removed at the rate of 2400 tons (tonnes) a day until completion, seven years later. Around 10.5 million cu yards (8 million cu m) had been excavated.

Champagne bottles are placed neck down into a freezing brine bath (bac à glace), freezing only the bottle's neck to form a plug that keeps the wine – and the bubbles – in the bottle while sediments are removed.

On July 1, 1916, the British suffered 58,000 casualties on the opening day of the Somme Offensive. Five months later, after advancing only a few miles, there had been 420,000 British, 200,000 French, and 500,000 German casualties.

North Sea

English Channel

GERMANY

NETHERLANDS

UNITED KINGDOM

BELGIUM

LUXEMBOURG

F R A N C E

PARIS

Strasbourg
Colmar
Mulhouse
Belfort
Vosges
Thionville
Metz
Nancy
Épinal
Vesoul
Besançon
Saône
Dijon
Nevers
Auxerre
Troyes
Bar-le-Duc
Châlons-en-Champagne
Reims
Laon
Marne
Meuse
Moselle
Dunkerque
Lille
Douai
Arras
Amiens
Beauvais
Calais
Boulogne-sur-Mer
Channel Tunnel
Somme
Rouen
Dieppe
Seine
Versailles
Chartres
Mantes-la-Jolie
Orléans
Blois
Bourges
Le Mans
Tours
Poitiers
Angers
Laval
Loire
Rennes
St-Brieuc
St-Malo
St-Lô
Caen
Cherbourg
Le Havre
Alençon
Normandie
Bretagne
Quimper
Brest
Île d'Ouessant
Lorient
Belle Île
St-Nazaire
Nantes
la Roche-sur-Yon

Channel Islands
(UK crown dependency)
Guernsey
Jersey

Mont Blanc
15771ft (4807m) ▲

ITALY

*Ligurian
Sea*

Bastia

*Corse
(Corsica)*

Ajaccio

Sardinia

Villeurbanne
Annecy
Chambéry
Lyon
St-Etienne
Grenoble
Roanne
St-Chamond
Valence
Le Puy
Mende
Clermont
Ferrand
Aurillac
Rodez
Privas
Albi
Montauban
Toulouse
Auch
Agen
Cahors
Lot
Dordogne
Périgueux
Angoulême
Bordeaux
Mont-de-Marsan
Bayonne
Pau
Tarbes
Carcassonne
ANDORRA
ANDORRA
LA VELLA
Perpignan
Narbonne
Béziers
Montpellier
Nîmes
Arles
Marseille
Toulon
Avignon
Aix-en-
Provence
Provence
Cannes
Nice
MONACO
MONACO
Côte d'Azur
Îles
d'Hyères

Rhône

*Golfe
du Lion*

*Massif
Central*

Cévennes

Tarn

Garonne

P y r e n e e s

SPAIN

*Bay of
Biscay*

Mediterranean Sea

*Balearic
Islands*

◆ The word denim comes from "de Nîmes,"
this being the town where the fabric was
originally produced.

◆ One of history's great leaders,
Napoleon Bonaparte was born
on August 15, 1769, at Ajaccio
in Corsica.

◆ The lowest point in Andorra is Riu Runer
at 2756 ft (840m) above sea level.

◆ The Tour de France bicycle race is typically held over
some 20 day-long stages covering
around 2200 miles (3600 km) for
the coveted yellow jersey.

0 km   100
0 miles   100

5   6   7   8

A   B   C   D   E

Spain & Portugal

ATLANTIC

OCEAN

◆ Port has been produced in the Duoro Valley under strict regulation since the 1750s. Brandy is added to the grape juice to fortify and strengthen the wine.

◆ Portugal is one of the world's largest producers of cork and has regulations protecting cork trees dating back to 1320.

◆ Gibraltar was seized by a combined Anglo-Dutch fleet under Admiral Rooke in 1704. British sovereignty was then formalized in 1713 by the Treaty of Utrecht, and Gibraltar eventually became a British colony in 1830.

Ferrol · A Coruña (La Coruña) · Avilés · Gijon (X

Galicia · Lugo · Oviedo · *Cordillera Cantábrica*

Santiago de Compostela · León

Pontevedra · Ourense (Orense)

Vigo · *Emb. de Ricobayo* · Palenci

Minho · Chaves · Braganca · Valladolid

Viana do Castelo · Braga · *Duero*

Póvoa de Varzim · Guimarães · Vila Real · Zamora

Matosinhos · Porto · S P

Vila Nova de Gaia · *Douro* · Viseu · Salamanca

Aveiro · Áv

Coimbra · *Sistema Centr*

Covilhã · Plasencia

Figueira da Foz

PORTUGAL · *Tagus*

Castelo Branco · *Tagus*

Caldas da Rainha · Cáceres

Sintra · Santarém · Portalegre · Mérida · *Guadian*

Cascais

LISBON · Badajoz

Setúbal

Alcácer do Sal

Sines · Beja · *Sierra Morena* · Córdoba

Algarve · *Guadalquivir* · *Andaluci*

Lagos · Sevilla

Cabo de São Vicente · Faro · Olhão · Huelva · Anteque

El Puerto de Santa María · Málaga

Cádiz · Marbe

Algeciras · Gibralt (UK)

Ceuta (S

MOROCCO

Bay of Biscay

F R A N C E

Santander

Donostia-San Sebastián

Bilbao

z-Gasteiz

Miranda
de Ebro

Logroño

Pamplona
(Iruña)

Huesca

Soria

Zaragoza

Lleida

ANDORRA

Figueres

Girona (Gerona)

Costa Brava

Cataluña

Terrassa

Mataró

Sabadell

Barcelona

L'Hospitalet de Llobregat

Reus

Tarragona

Tortosa

◇ Work continues on the Sagrada Família, Gaudí's unfinished cathedral. Begun in 1882 the masterpiece is still without a roof.

P A I N

govia

MADRID

Getafe

Toledo

Teruel

Cuenca

Castelló
de la Plana

Palma

Mallorca

Menorca

Albacete

dad Real

Valencia

Gandía

Eivissa

Islas Baleares
(Balearic Islands)

Formentera

Elda

Benidorm

Linares

Cieza

Alicante

Elche

Costa Blanca

Murcia

◇ Seat of many great civilizations throughout history, the name Mediterranean translates as "sea between the lands."

én

Lorca

rra Nevada

Motril

Almería

sta del Sol

M e d i t e r r a n e a n   S e a

A L G E R I A

Golfe du
Lion

EUROPE

Pyrenees

Sistema
Ibérico

Ebro

Júcar

Segura

País Valenciano

Germany & The Alpine States

The Kiel Canal is one of the busiest in the world, with around 45,000 ships a year passing between the Baltic and the North Sea

Early in the morning of Sunday, August 13, 1961, work began on the Berlin Wall, which would eventually run for 66 miles (107 km) between east and west Berlin, cutting through 192 streets.

The German Bundestag, or Parliament, based in Berlin, has 672 members and is the world's largest elected legislative body.

North Sea

Baltic Sea

SWEDEN

DENMARK

POLAND

NETHERLANDS

GERMANY

Jylland

Fyn

Sjælland

Falster

Bornholm (Denmark)

Rügen

North Frisian Islands

BERLIN

Frankfurt an der Oder

Cottbus

Dresden

Leipzig

Potsdam

Dessau

Halle

Magdeburg

Wolfsburg

Braunschweig

Salzgitter

Göttingen

Kassel

Hannover

Hildesheim

Paderborn

Bielefeld

Osnabrück

Münster

Hamm

Dortmund

Bochum

Recklinghausen

Essen

Duisburg

Düsseldorf

Wuppertal

Leverkusen

Emden

Oldenburg

Bremen

Bremerhaven

Cuxhaven

Hamburg

Lüneburg

Lübeck

Neumünster

Kiel

Flensburg

Schwerin

Wismar

Rostock

Neubrandenburg

Stralsund

Greifswald

Müritz

Mecklenburger Bucht

Fehmarn

Fehmarn Belt

Femer Belt

Mecklenburg

Saale

Elbe

Spree

Ems

55°

15°

5°

10°

HUNGARY

CZECH REPUBLIC

At 528 ft (161 m) the spire of Ulm Cathedral is the tallest in the world.

Hollabrunn

Krems an der Donau

VIENNA

Sankt Pölten Baden

Eisenstadt

Wiener Neustadt

Sopron

Linz

Wels

Enns

Mur

AUSTRIA

Bruck an der Mur

Judenburg

Graz

Klagenfurt

Celje

Maribor

Kranj

Koper

LJUBLJANA

SLOVENIA

Salzburg

Bad Ischl

Villach

Lienz

Hallein

Tauern

Gulf of Venice

CROATIA

Regensburg

Ingolstadt

Landshut

Inn

Augsburg

Bavarian Alps

Innsbruck

Tirol

München

Born in Salzburg on January 27, 1756, Wolfgang Amadeus Mozart was already writing music by the age of five, and at eleven he produced his first opera.

The glass roof over the Olympic stadium in München (Munich) measures 914,940 sq ft (85,000 sq m) making it the biggest structure of its kind in the world.

Frankfurt am Main

Offenbach

Darmstadt Würzburg

Erlangen

Nürnberg

Heidelberg

Mannheim

Heilbronn

Ulm

Stuttgart

Reutlingen

Schwäbische Alb

Bregenz

LIECHTENSTEIN

VADUZ

Lake Constance

Feldkirch

Bohemian Forest

Schwarzwald

ITALY

FRANCE

Kaiserslautern

Saarbrücken

Karlsruhe

Pforzheim

Freiburg im Breisgau

Mosel

Rhine

Neckar

Wiesbaden

Mainz

Schaffhausen

Zürich

Zürichsee

Zug

Luzern

Chur

Locarno

Lugano

Lake Maggiore

Lake Lugano

SWITZERLAND

BERN

Basel

Delémont

Biel

Thunersee

Brig

Sion

Monthey

Matterhorn 14,691ft (4478m)

St Gothard tunnel is 10.14 miles (16.32 km) long, making it the second longest road tunnel in the world.

Lac de Neuchâtel

Yverdon

Lausanne

Genève

Lake Geneva

0 km 100

0 miles 100

In April 1998 a violin made by Italian master Stradivari at Cremona in around 1680 sold at Christie's in London for £947,500.

San Marino formed in AD 301 is the oldest, and, at 24 sq-mi (61 sq km), one of the smallest, republics in the world.

CZECH REPUBLIC

SLOVAKIA

HUNGARY

SLOVENIA

CROATIA

BOSNIA & HERZEGOVINA

AUSTRIA

FRANCE

GERMANY

SWITZERLAND

LIECHTENSTEIN

Adriatic Sea

Udine

Trieste

Gulf of Venice

Piave

Bolzano

Dolomitche

Trento

Bergamo

Vicenza

Verona

Treviso

Mestre

Venezia

Po Delta

Ancona

Pescara

Ascoli Piceno

L'Aquila

Brescia

Lago di Como

Lago Maggiore

Lake Maggiore

Monza

Milano

Novara

Torino

Aosta

Alessandria

Piacenza

Cremona

Parma

Reggio nell Emilia

Mantova

Adige

Po

Modena

Ferrara

Bologna

Ravenna

Forlì

Rimini

SAN MARINO

Prato

Firenze

Arezzo

Perugia

Foligno

Terni

Viterbo

ROME

Tevere

Lago Trasimeno

Toscana

Siena

Grosseto

Arno

ITALY

Genova

Golfo di Genova

Savona

San Remo

La Spezia

Viareggio

Pisa

Livorno

Ligurian Sea

Isola d'Elba

Arcipelago Toscano

Corsica (part of France)

The medical school at Salerno is the oldest in Europe, established during the 11th and 12th centuries.

Mt Etna began some 300,000 years ago as a submarine volcano and has since grown to a cone with a base 30 miles (48 km) wide and 10,958 ft (3340 m) high.

The George cross that appears on the Maltese flag was awarded to the islanders by King George VI of Britain for their heroism during World War II.

Strait of Otranto

Bari
Altamura
Brindisi
Potenza
Lecce
Taranto
Gallipoli
Benevento
Golfo di Taranto
Ionian Sea
Napoli
Salerno
Crotone
Torre del Greco
Catanzaro
Isola di Capri
Golfo di Salerno
Cosenza
Tyrrhenian Sea
Isola Stromboli
Reggio di Calabria
Isola Eolie
Isola Lipari
Isola Vulcano
Stretto di Messina
Isola d'Ustica
Messina
Cefalù
Sicilia (Sicily)
Palermo
Catania
Siracusa
Ragusa
VALLETTA
Trapani
Caltanissetta
Isole Egadi
Enna
Agrigento
MALTA
Marsala
Gozo
Malta Channel
Isola di Pantelleria
Isole Pelagie
Strait of Sicily

Sardegna (Sardinia)
Alghero
Nuoro
Oristano
Mediterranean Sea
Iglesias
Cagliari

TUNISIA

Mediterranean Sea

0 km   100
0 miles   100

BELARUS

LATVIA

LITHUANIA

◆ Warsaw was home to the world's first public library, opened in 1747.

KALININGRAD
(part of Russian Federation)

E

D

C

B

A

SWEDEN

Baltic Sea

Bornholm
(part of Denmark)

DENMARK

Gulf of Danzig

Courland Lagoon

◆ Hitler's demand in 1939 that Gdansk be returned to German control precipitated the invasion of Poland which ultimately led to World War II.

Elblag

Olsztyn

Ostrołeka

Białystok

Lublin

Ostrowiec
Świętokrzyski

WARSAW

Narew

Wisła

Bug

M a z u r y

Gdynia
Gdańsk

Grudziądz

Bydgoszcz

Toruń

Płock

Radom

Kielce

Słupsk

Włocławek

Wisła

Warta

Człuchów

Noteć

Piła

Koszalin

Łódź

P O L A N D

Poznań

Kalisz

Wrocław

Szczecin

Gorzów
Wielkopolski

Oder

Zielona
Góra

Legnica

Warta

Pomeranian
Bay

*Zalew
Szczeciński*

GERMANY

◆ In November 1989 the so-called "Velvet Revolution" saw Czechoslovakia split into the Czech Republic and Slovakia.

0 km   100
0 miles   100

UKRAINE

Dniester

San

Rzeszów

Kraków Tarnów

Wodzisław

Bielsko-Biała

Śląski

Rybnik

Gliwice

Carpathian Mts.

Laborec

Prešov

Košice

Rožňava

Lučenec Ózd

Miskolc

Nyíregyháza

Debrecen

Békéscsaba

R O M A N I A

Mureş

Szeged

Kecskemét

Szolnok

BUDAPEST

Danube

G r e a t H u n g a r i a n P l a i n

Tisza

Poprad

Zvolen

Banská Bystrica

Martin

Žilina

S L O V A K I A

Nitra

Trenčín

Váh

BRATISLAVA

Morava

Piešťany

Trnava

Győr

Tatabánya

Székesfehérvár

Veszprém
Balaton

Sopron

Szombathely

Zalaegerszeg

Nagykanizsa

H U N G A R Y

Danube

Sió

Szekszárd

Baja

Kaposvár

Drava

Pécs

Raab

A U S T R I A

S L O V E N I A

ITALY

C R O A T I A

*Adriatic
Sea*

B O S N I A -
H E R Z E G O V I N A

SERBIA & MONTENEGRO
(YUGOSLAVIA)

Sudeten

Vltava

PRAGUE

Kladno

Vary

Plzeň

C Z E C H   R E P U B L I C

Pardubice

Stratonice

Tábor

Jihlava

České
Budějovice

Prostějov

Brno

Ostrava

Olomouc

◆ Built in 1357, Charles Bridge was the
only crossing point of the Vltava in
Prague until the 19th century.

◆ With a surface area of around
231 sq mi (598 sq km) Lake Balaton
has an average depth of only 11 ft (3.25 m).

◆ The Great Hungarian Plain (Alföld) stretches
south from Budapest to the borders of Croatia and Serbia and east to Ukraine and
Romania. It covers an area of 20,000 sq miles (51,800 sq km)
and is almost completely flat.

50°

45°

Southeast Europe

At 11:15 am, on June 28, 1914, Archduke Francis Ferdinand and his wife were shot dead by Gavrilo Princip in Sarajevo. This single act precipitated World War I, which eventually lead to the death of almost 9 million troops.

Born in Zagreb in 1892, Marshall Tito was the president of the former Yugoslavia from 1953 until his death in 1980.

The Danube forms all or part of the border between nine different European nations, Germany, Austria, Slovakia, Hungary, Croatia, Serbia & Montenegro (Yugoslavia), Romania, Bulgaria, and the Ukraine.

SLOVAKIA

AUSTRIA · HUNGARY

ROMANIA

BULG

Danube

Danube

SLOVENIA

CROATIA

ZAGREB

Varaždin
Koprivnica
Čakovec
Samobor
Karlovac
Ogulin
Gospić
Bihać
Sisak
Prijedor
Una
Sava
Banja Luka
Ključ
Rep. Srpska
Knin
Šibenik
Split
Zadar
Dugi Otok
Pag
Cres
Krk
Rijeka
Pula
Virovitica
Bjelovar
Nova Gradiška
Slavonski Brod
Osijek
Đakovo
Doboj
Modriča
Bosanski Šamac
Tuzla
Zvornik
Drina
Loznica
Šabac
Sava
BOSNIA & HERZEGOVINA
Zenica
SARAJEVO
Srebrenica
Fed. Bosna i Hercegovina
Jajce
Livno
Konjic
Foča
Mostar
Makarska
Korčula
Brač
Hvar
Dinaric Alps
D i n a r i c A l p s
Vareš
Sombor
Subotica
Bačka Topola
Kanjiža
Vojvodina
Novi Sad
Zrenjanin
Vršac
Pančevo
BELGRADE
Smederevo
Serbia
SERBIA & MONTENEGRO
(YUGOSLAVIA)
MONTENEGRO
Kragujevac
Čačak
Kraljevo
Kopaonik
Kosovska
Niš
Aleksinac
Kruševac
Morava
Zaječar
Bijelo Polje
45°

20°

15°

45°

1

2

3

4

Macedonia's capital, Skopje, was hit by a devastating earthquake in 1963. Around 80% of the city's buildings were damaged or destroyed and over 1000 people killed.

European eels migrate thousands of miles from their birthplace in the Sargasso Sea to live most of their 10-year lives in Lake Ohrid, before returning to the Atlantic to spawn and die.

Under an extreme communist regime between 1944 and 1991, Albania was for many years the only officially atheist state in the world.

The Mediterranean

POLAND

UKRAINE

CZECH REP.

R O P E

30°

Dnieper

Don

50°

1

AUSTRIA

SLOVAKIA

HUNGARY

Hungarian

Plain

Carpathians

MOLDOVA

RUSSIAN

FEDERATION

SLOVENIA

CROATIA

BOS. &

HERZ.

SERB.

& MON.

(YUGO.)

ROMANIA

Danube

Delta

Sea

of Azov

Crimea

BULGARIA

Balkan Mts.

Danube

Black Sea

Caucasus Mts.

2

Adriatic Sea

Dinaric Alps

ALBANIA

MACEDONIA

Rhodope Mts.

Pindus Mts.

Bosporus

GEORGIA

I T A L Y

Naples

Aegean

Sea

Lesbos

GREECE

Piraeus

Izmir

T U R K E Y

Anatolia

3

Ionian

Sea

Peloponnese

Kos

Taurus Mts.

Lake

Van

Sicily

MALTA

Rhodes

Cyprus

SYRIA

Euphrates

Tigris

r a n e a n   S e a

Crete

LEBANON

Anti-Lebanon

IRAQ

4

Gulf of Sirte

Haifa

ISRAEL

Nile

Delta

Port Said

JORDAN

Syrian Desert

A S I A

30°

Suez Canal

L I B Y A

Nile

EGYPT

SAUDI

ARABIA

5

C A

Libyan

Desert

Red Sea

Arabian

Peninsula

20°

30°

40°

E   F   G   H

Bulgaria & Greece

ROMANIA

SERBIA & MONTENEGRO (YUGOSLAVIA)

BULGARIA

TURKEY

Black Sea

Danube

Dobrich
Varna
Razgrad
Ruse
Shumen
Burgas
Pleven
Vratsa
Gabrovo
Sliven
Stara Zagora
Yambol
Orestiada
Loveth
Kazanlŭk
Plovdiv
Khaskovo
Komotini
Alexandroúpoli
Samothráki
SOFIA
Pazardzhik
Velingrad
Xánthi
Kavála
Pernik
Petrich
Drama
Serres
Thásos
Blagoevgrad
Kilkís
Stymónas
Thessaloníki
Kalamariá
Katerini
Véroia
Vólos
Kozáni
Lárisa
Flórina
Tríkala
Kárpenísi
Kardítsa
Lake Ohrid
Lake Prespa
Ioánnina
Préveza
Kérkyra
Kérkyra

MACEDONIA

GREECE

ALBANIA

Thracian Sea

Vóreioi Sporádes

Límnos

Mitilíni

Akrotírio Pínnes
Akrotírio Drépano
Akrotírio Palioúri

Thermaïkós Kólpos

Marmara Denizi

Danube
Olt

Sofia's skyline is dominated by the gold domes of the Alexander Nevski Memorial Church, which took craftsmen and artists some thirty years to build between 1882 and 1912.

Built between 447 and 438 BCE, the Parthenon survived almost unscathed for over 2000 years until, in 1687, a gunpowder magazine beneath the building exploded causing considerable damage.

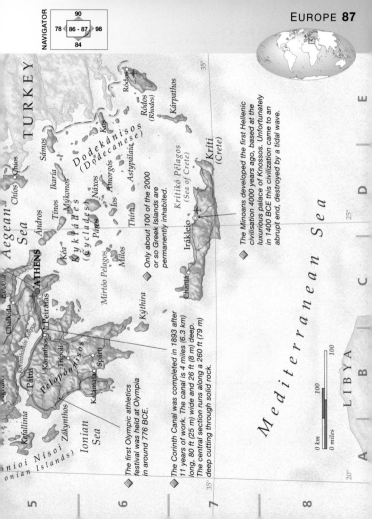

TURKEY

Aegean
Sea

Chíos ○Chíos

Samos

Ikaría

Dodekánisos
(Dodecanese)

Ródos
Ródos
(Rhodes)

Kárpathos

Tínos
Mýkonos
Kykládes
(Cyclades)

Náxos

Íos

Amorgós

Astypálaia○

Ándros

Kéa

Páros

Thíra

Kos

Mílos

Mirtóo Pélagos

Kritikó Pélagos
(Sea of Crete)

ATHENS

Chalkída

Évvoia

Peiraiás

Irákleio

Kríti
(Crete)

Chaniá

◇ The Minoans developed the first Hellenic
civilisation 4000 years ago, based at the
luxurious palace of Knossos. Unfortunately
in 1400 BCE this civilization came to an
abrupt end, destroyed by a tidal wave.

Kórinthos Kórinthos Díþ
Korinthiakós Kólpos

Pátra

Trípoli

Pelopónnisos

Spárti

Kalamáta○

Kýthira

◇ Only about 100 of the 2000
or so Greek Islands are
permanently inhabited.

Mediterranean Sea

LIBYA

100

100

0 km
0 miles

Kefalloniá

Zákynthos

Ionian
Sea

nioi Nísoi
onian Islands)

◇ The first Olympic athletics
festival was held at Olympia
in around 776 BCE.

◇ The Corinth Canal was completed in 1893 after
11 years of work. The canal is 4 miles (6.3 km)
long, 80 ft (25 m) wide and 26 ft (8 m) deep.
The central section runs along a 260 ft (79 m)
deep cutting through solid rock.

35°

35°

25°

20°

A   B   C   D   E

5   6   7   8

The Baltic States & Belarus

◆ Rich oil shale deposits in northern Estonia are quarried, crushed, and heated to produce almost 32,000 barrels of oil a day.

◆ Low salinity and the shallow coastal waters cause pack ice to accumulate at the head of the Gulf of Bothnia and off Finland during most winters; occasionally the ice becomes banked up in pressure ridges that are almost 50 ft (15 m) high.

E D E R A T I O N

Western Dvina

Vitsyebsk
Orsha
Horki
Mahilyow
Krychaw

Lyepyel'
Barysaw
Zhodzina
Byarezino
Zhlobin
Svyetlahorsk
Homyel'

B E L A R U S

Maladzyechna
Rechytsa
Kalinkavichy

MINSK
Babruysk

Kyyivs'ke
Vdskh.

Dnieper

Ptsich

Slutsk
Salihorsk
Mazyr

Druskininkai
Baranavichy
Luninyets

Pripet Marshes

Hrodna
Neman
Vawkavysk
Slonim
Pinsk

Pripet

Kobryn

Brest

U K R A I N E

P O L A N D

♦ Formed in 1945 from the northern half of German East Prussia, and ceded to Russia under the Potsdam agreement, Kaliningrad oblast became a true enclave, completely separated from the rest of Russia, when Lithuania and Belarus achieved their independence in 1991.

♦ Covering an area of approximately 104,000 sq miles (270,000 sq km) Pripet Marshes are the largest area of marshland in Europe.

♦ Following the break up of the Soviet Union the Commonwealth of Independent States was established on December 8, 1991 by a treaty signed at Minsk, with the intent of coordinating the foreign policies of the newly independent former Soviet republics.

0 km 100
0 miles 100

Ukraine, Moldova & Romania

POLAND

BELARUS

Pripet

Pripet Marshes

◇ On April 25, 1986, engineers accidentally initiated an uncontrolled chain reaction in the number 4 reactor of the Chornobyl' nuclear power plant. The resulting explosion released 8 tons (tonnes) of radioactive material in the world's worst ever nuclear accident.

Kovel'

Luts'k

Korosten

Rivne

L'viv

Zhytomyr

SLOVAKIA

Ternopil'

U K

◇ Vlad Dracula or Vlad the Impaler was the real life prince upon whom Bram Stoker based his famous Count Dracula. Dracula was born in Transylvania in 1431 in the town of Sighisoara.

Uzhhorod

Ivano-Frankivs'k

Khmel'nyts'kyy

Vinny

Kam''yanets'-Podil's'kyy

Chernivtsi

Dniester

Satu Mare

HUNGARY

Baia Mare

Oradea

Dej

Suceava

Botoșani

Râbnița

Bălți

MOLDOVA

Dubăsari

Transylvania

Cluj-Napoca

Iași

CHIȘ

Arad

Alba Iulia

Târgu Mureș

Piatra-Neamț

Tiraspo

Sighisoara

Bacău

Tighina

Deva

ROMANIA

Siret

Basarabeasca

Timișoara

Sibiu

Focșani

Galați

Reni

Carpații Meridionali

Brașov

Reșița

Râmnicu Vâlcea

Buzău

Brăila

Tulcea

Târgoviște

Ploiești

Drobeta-Turnu Severin

Pitești

Craiova

BUCHAREST

Consta

Eforie Su

SERBIA & MONTENEGRO (YUGOSLAVIA)

Corabia

Oltu

Danube

Giurgiu

Mangalia

BULGARIA

30°　　　　　35°　　　　　40°

RUSSIAN

FEDERATION

Shostka

Chernihiv

Chornobyl'

Kyyivs'ke Vdskh.

Sumy

KIEV

Kaniys'ke Vdskh.

ila Tserkva　　Lubny　　　Kharkiv

A I N E

Cherkasy　　　　Poltava

Kremenchuts'ke Vdskh.　　Kremenchuk

Oleksandriya　　　　　Slov''yans'k

Kirovohrad　　　　　　Pavlohrad

Dnipropetrovs'k　　　Horlivka

Kryvyy Rih　　Nikopol'　　Zaporizhzhya

Mykolayiv　*Kakhovs'ka Vdskh.*

Kherson　*Dnieper*　Kakhovka　Melitopol'　Berdyans'k

Odesa

Karkinits'ka Zatoka

Kryms'kyy Pivostriv

Yevpatoriya

Simferopol'

Sevastopol'　　Yalta

Pivdennyy Buh

Donets

Syeverodonets'k

Luhans'k

Kostyantynivka

Makiyivka　Yenakiyeve

Donets'k　Krasnyy Luch

Mariupol'

Sea of Azov

Kerch

Black Sea

RUSSIAN

FEDERATION

◆ A monument in central Kiev stands as testament to the 7-12 million Ukrainian peasants who died during the Great Famine of 1932–33.

◆ In 1872 an ironworks was founded at Donets'k by British industrialist John Hughes (from whom the town's pre-Revolutionary name Yuzovka was derived) to produce rails for the growing Russian transportation network.

Odesa was one of the major flashpoints in the Russian Revolution of 1905, and was the scene of the mutiny on the warship Potemkin, when sailors protesting against the serving of rotten meat eventually threw the officers overboard.

0 km　　　100
0 miles　　　100

50°

1

2

3

4

45°

5

40°

E　　　F　　　G　　　H

35°

European Russia

The port of Murmansk remains ice free throughout the winter thanks to the Gulf Stream, whereas St. Petersburg 600 miles (965 km) to the south on the Baltic Sea is ice-bound between December and May.

ARCTIC OCEAN

Karskoye More

Novaya Zemlya

Ostrov Vaygach

Barents Sea

Ostrov Kolguyev

Vorkuta

Usa

(Ural Mountains)

Arctic Circle

Pechora

Ukhta

Mezen'

Syktyvkar

Murmansk

Kol'skiy Poluostrov

Arkhangel'sk

Pinega

Beloye More

Severnaya Dvina

Kotlas

RUSSIAN FEDERATION

Petrozavodsk

Onega

Vologda

Onezhskoye Ozero

Cherepovets

Tver'

FINLAND

Ladozhskoye Ozero

Rybinskoye Vdkhr.

NORWAY

SWEDEN

Arctic Circle

Novgorod

Velikiye Luki

Smolensk

Sankt Petersburg

Gulf of Finland

Pskov

ESTONIA

Norwegian Sea

Gulf of Bothnia

Baltic Sea

LATVIA

LITHUANIA

BELARUS

0 km 400

0 miles 400

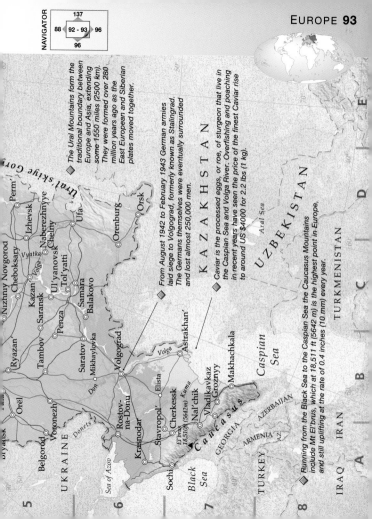

The Ural Mountains form the traditional boundary between Europe and Asia, extending some 1550 miles (2500 km). They were formed over 280 million years ago as the East European and Siberian plates moved together.

From August 1942 to February 1943 German armies laid siege to Volgograd, formerly known as Stalingrad. The Germans themselves were eventually surrounded and lost almost 250,000 men.

Caviar is the processed eggs, or roe, of sturgeon that live in the Caspian Sea and Volga River. Overfishing and poaching in recent years have seen the price of the finest Caviar rise to around US $4000 for 2.2 lbs (1 kg).

Running from the Black Sea to the Caspian Sea the Caucasus Mountains include Mt El'brus, which at 18,511 ft (5642 m) is the highest point in Europe, and still uplifting at the rate of 0.4 inches (10 mm) every year.

North & West Asia

ARCTIC

1 80°

Franz Josef Land

Severnaya
Zemlya

Svalbard
(Norway)

Norwegian
Sea

North Cape

Barents
Sea

Novaya Zemlya

Kara Sea

Nor

2 Arctic Circle

60°

Gulf of Bothnia

Lake
Onega

Northern
Dvina

RUSSIAN

Centr

West Siberian

Ob'

Yenisey

Chulym

Lake Ladoga

Plain

Ob'

Irtysh

Irtysh

Ishim

North
Sea

Baltic Sea

Volga

Central Russian
Upland

Volga

KALININGRAD
(Russ. Fed.)

A

S

3 EUROPE

Don

Ural

KAZAKHSTAN

Ozero
Zaysan

Aral Sea

Lake
Balkhash

Ili

Tien Shan

40°

Danube

Black Sea

Caucasus

Caspian Sea

UZBEKISTAN

KYRGYZSTAN

GEORGIA

ARMENIA AZERB.

TURKMEN.

Amu Darya

TURKEY

Lake
Van

TAJIKISTAN

4 SYRIA

LEBANON

IRAQ

Tigris

IRAN

AFGHANISTAN

Tibetan
Plateau

Himalaya

Mediterranean
Sea

ISRAEL

JORDAN

Euphrates

KUWAIT

Ganges

BAHRAIN

QATAR

U.A.E.

Tropic of Cancer

20°

Nile

Red Sea

SAUDI
ARABIA

The Gulf

OMAN

Arabian
Sea

Bay of
Bengal

5 AFRICA

YEMEN

Gulf of Aden

Socotra (Yemen)

20° A 40° B 60° C 80° D

NAVIGATOR
137
62 94-95 134
106
120°   140°

NORTH & WEST ASIA **95**

O C E A N

OCEAN

140°

160°

180°

80°

1

Ozero
Taymyr

Laptev Sea

New Siberian Islands

East Siberian
Sea

Wrangel Island

erian Lowland

Anabar

Olenёk

Lena

Yara

Indigirka

Kolyma

Long Strait

Chukchi
Sea

Bering Strait

erian Plateau

F E D E R A T I O N

Arctic Circle

Velikaya

2

60°

b   e   r   i   a

Lena

Amga

Bering
Sea

Chona

Vitim

Lake
Baikal

Argun

Amur

Zeya

Sea of
Okhotsk

Kamchatka

Aleutian Islands

3

I   A

Sakhalin

Kurile Islands

(administered by
Russian Federation,
claimed by Japan.)

40°

obi

Sea of
Japan
(East Sea)

Yellow River

Yangtze

East
China
Sea

P A C I F I C

O C E A N

4

Tropic of Cancer

20°

South
China
Sea

0 km   800

0 miles   800

5

120°   140°   160°   180°

E   F   G   H

Russia & Kazakhstan

NORWAY
DENMARK
SWEDEN
FINLAND
ARCTIC
Arctic Circle
Barents Sea
GERMANY
KALININGRAD
(part of Russian
Federation)
POLAND
EST.
Pskov
LAT.
LITH.
BELARUS
Murmansk
Zemly
Fran
Ios
Novaya Zemlya
Karskoye More
Sankt-Peterburg
Novgorod
Arkhangel'sk
UKRAINE
MOLDOVA
Bryansk
Cherepovets
MOSCOW
Vologda
Yaroslavl'
Tula
Ryazan'
Voronezh
Nizhniy
Novgorod
Kazan'
Izhevsk
Kirov
Syktyvkar
Perm'
Vorkuta
Salekhard
Nori'
Zapadno-
Sibirskaya
Ravnina
Ob'
R U
Rostov-
na-Donu
Volgograd
Samara
Ural'sk
Ufa
Serov
Yekaterinburg
Nizhnevartovsk
F E D
Sochi
Stavropol'
Nal'chik
GEORGIA
Groznyy
ARM.
Makhachkala
AZ.
Astrakhan'
Orenburg
Orsk
Chelyabinsk
Kostanay
Rudnyy
Petropavlovsk
Omsk
Krasnoya
Tomsk
Novosibirsk
Aktau
Kokshetau
ASTANA
Pavlodar
Barnaul
Kemerov
Caspian Sea
K A Z A K H S T A N
Karaganda
Novokuzne
Semipalatinsk
Ust'-
Kamenogors
Aral
Sea
Zhezkazgan
Kyzylorda
Balkhash
Ozero
Balkhash
TURKMENISTAN
UZBEKISTAN
Shymkent
Taraz
Taldykorgan
Almaty
IRAN
KYRGYZSTAN
CHINA
Ural'skiye Gory
Don
Volga
Ural
Volga

A   B   C   D
1   2   3   4   5

OCEAN

Ostrov
Vrangelya

80°   180°   70°

Arctic Circle

160°

60°

Vostochno-
Sibirskoye
More

Pevek

Anadyr'

Severnaya
Zemlya

120°

140°

Ambarchik

Bering
Sea

1

Novosibirskiye
Ostrova

100°

180°

Ostrov
Taymyr

More
Laptevykh

170°

Ossora

2

Ozero Taymyr

Tiksi

Verkhoyanskiy Khrebet

Ust'-Kamchatsks

Poluostov
Kamchatka

Olenek

Lena

Magadan

Petropavlovsk
-Kamchatskiy

160°

dnesibirskoye
Ploskogor'ye

Okhotsk

I A N

Suntar

Yakutsk

Sea of
Okhotsk

3

i b i r
(Siberia)

A T I O N

Lena

Sakhalin

150°

Komsomol'sk-
na-Amure

Kuril'skiye Ostrova

ansk   Bratsk

Skovorodno

Yuzhno-
Sakhalinsk

4

Ozero
Baykal

Blagoveshchensk

Khabarovsk

JAPAN

40°

Irkutsk   Chita

Amur

Ulan-Ude

C H I N A

Vladivostok

◆ The Trans-Siberian Railroad, completed in 1916, runs
5866 miles (9440 km) between Moscow and Vladivostok.
Crossing eight time zones, the journey takes eight days.

0 km   500
0 miles   500

5

130°

NGOLIA

100°   110°   120°

Turkey & the Caucasus

An average of 50,000 commercial ships pass through the Bosporus a year, along with thousands of ferries and smaller passenger boats. The strait is three times busier than the Suez Canal and four times as busy as the Panama Canal.

ROMANIA

Black Sea

BULGARIA

25°

30°

35°

Edirne
Kırklareli
GREECE
Tekirdağ
Bosporus
İstanbul
40°
Marmara
Denizi
İzmit
Bursa
Çanakkale
Balıkesir
Eskişehir
Manisa
Uşak
Afyon
Kütahya
İzmir
Denizli
İsparta
Aydın
Muğla
Antalya
Bodrum
Dalaman

Zonguldak
Karabük
Adapazarı
Çankırı
ANKARA
Kırıkkale

Sinop
Kastamonu
Samsu
Öt

Küre Dağları

Kızıl Irmak

Çorum
Toka
Siv

T U R

Anatolia

Nevşehir
Kayseri
Tuz Gölü
Niğde
Konya
Kahram
maraş
Ereğli
Adana
Osmaniye
Tarsus
Toros Dağları
Mersin
Gazian
İskenderun
Antakya

Çanakkale Boğazı (Dardanelles)

Lésvos
Chíos
25°
Sámos

Kriti

Ródos
Kárpathos
Megísti

35°

Antalya Körfezi

TURKISH REPUBLIC OF NORTHERN CYPRUS
(recognized only by Turkey)
Girne (Kyrenia)
Gazimağusa (Famagusta)
NICOSIA
Paphos
Larnaca
Limassol

CYPRUS

LEBANON

M e d i t e r r a n e a n   S e a

30°

35°

A   B   C   D

1

2

3

4

5

RUSSIAN FEDERATION

◆ An earthquake struck Armenia in 1988, killing 55,000 people and devastating the country's infastructure.

Caspian Sea

Gagra
Sokhumi
Och'amch'ire
K'ut'aisi
Caucasus
Enguri
P'ot'i
GEORGIA
Bat'umi
T'BILISI
Rust'avi
Hopa
Kura
Quba
abzon
Rize
Vanadzor
Gänca
Mingäçevir
Sumqayıt
gı Karadeniz Dağları
Gyumri
Kars
ARMENIA
AZERBAIJAN
BAKU
Erzincan
Erzurum
Sevana Lich
YEREVAN
Nagornyy Karabakh
Xankändi
Büyükağrı Dağı (Mount Ararat)
Aras
Naxçıvan
Aras
Länkäran
16,853ft (5137m)
AZERBAIJAN

◆ Azerbaijan has substantial oil reserves located in and around the Caspian Sea. They were some of the earliest oilfields in the world to be exploited.

E Y
Muş
Van Gölü
Güney Doğu Toroslar
Van
älazig
Siirt
Kurdistan
alatya
iyarbakır
Batman
I R A N
iyaman
Mardin

◆ The salty water of Lake Van inhibits all animal life except the Darekh, a small fish that has adapted to the harsh conditions.

Şanliurfa

◆ Atatürk Dam, one of the largest dams in the world, was completed in 1990. The reservoir behind the dam covers an area of 315 sq miles (816 sq km) and often requires interruptions in the flow of the Euphrates River to maintain water levels.

S Y R I A
I R A Q

0 km   200
0 miles   200

The Near East

TURKEY

IRAQ

Al Qāmishlī

Al Ḩasakah

Al Jazīrah

Tigris

Euphrates

Dayr az Zawr

Ar Raqqah

S Y R I A

Buḩayrat
al-Asad

Ḩalab

Idlib

Aʿzāz

Orontes

Ḩamāh

Ḩimş

Tudmur

Al Lādhiqīyah

Ṭarṭūs

Tripoli

LEBANON

Baalbek

Zaḩle

Anti-Lebanon

DAMASCUS

BEIRUT

Litani

Saïda

CYPRUS

Mediterranean
Sea

◆ The Euphrates is 1700 miles (2470 km) long and drains an
area of 171,000 sq mi (443,000 sq km). Although less than
30 percent of the river's drainage basin is in Turkey, about
95 percent of the river's water originates in the
Turkish highlands.

◆ Manufactured by a secret process,
Damascus steel was much prized
in the preindustrial era as an
extremely hard metal used for high

◆ Lebanon only has one permanent river, the Nahr el Litani,
which runs for 110 miles (175 km).

0 km   100
0 miles   100

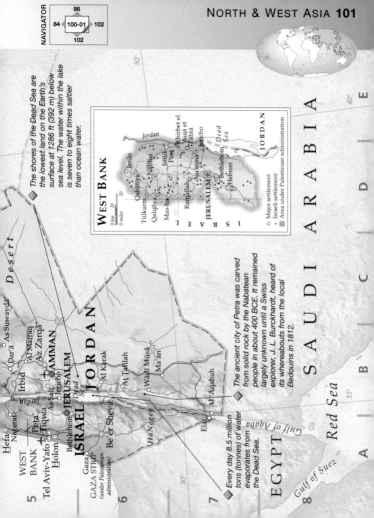

The shores of the Dead Sea are the lowest land on the Earth's surface at 1286 ft (392 m) below sea level. The water within the lake is seven to eight times saltier than ocean water.

WEST BANK

Jordan

Jenin
Ţūlkarm
Qalqīlyah
Nāblus
Jiftlik Post
Khirbet el Auja et Tahta
Jericho
Mas-ha
Ramallah
Su'eima
Bethlehem
Hebron
JERUSALEM

I S R A E L

J O R D A N

Dead Sea

0 km   20
0 miles   20

○ Major settlement
• Israeli settlement
▨ Area under Palestinian administration

S A U D I   A R A B I A

Desert

As Suwaydā'
Darʿā   Al Mafraq
Az Zarqā'
Irbid   AMMAN
Nazareth   As Salţ
Haifa   Jericho   Dead Sea
Peta   JERUSALEM
Tiqwa   Bethlehem
Tel Aviv-Yafo   Hebron
Holon
WEST BANK
GAZA STRIP
(under Palestinian administration)
GAZA   Be'er Sheva

ISRAEL
JORDAN
Al Karak
At Ţafīlah
Wādī Mūsā
Maʿān

The ancient city of Petra was carved from solid rock by the Nabatean people in about 400 BCE. It remained largely unknown until a Swiss explorer, J.L. Burckhardt, heard of its whereabouts from the local Bedouins in 1812.

Ha Negev
Elat
Al ʿAqabah

EGYPT

Gulf of Aqaba

Gulf of Suez

Red Sea

Every day 8.5 million tons (tonnes) of water evaporates from the Dead Sea.

The Middle East

In the 10th century, the Grand Vizier of Persia took his entire library with him wherever he went. The 117,000 volume library was carried by camels trained to walk in alphabetical order.

Four thousand years ago Babylonian law laid down a minimum wage for every class of workers in the kingdom.

RUSSIAN FEDERATION

KAZAKHSTAN

UZBEKISTAN

TURKMENISTAN

Syr Darya

Kyzyl Kum

Aral Sea

Ustyurt Plateau

UKRAINE

Sea of Azov

Black Sea

GEORGIA

Caucasus

ARMENIA

AZERBAIJAN

Caspian Sea

TURKEY

Anatolia

Euphrates

Van Gölü

Tigris

Khvoy

Maragheh

Arbil

Tabriz

Ardabil

Zanjan

Qazvin

Amol

Rasht

Sari

Gorgan

Sabzevar

Neyshabur

Mashhad

TEHRAN

Qom

Kashan

Arak

Hamadan

Sanandaj

Kermanshah

Esfahan

Yazd

Iranshahr

Plateau

Kerman

Zahedan

Bam

I R A N

Kuh-ha-ye Zagros

(Zagros Mountains)

Khash

PAKISTAN

AFGHANISTAN

Kirkuk

Al Mawsil (Mosul)

SYRIA

Syrian Desert

Behrat an Tharthar

I R A Q

BAGHDAD

Dezful

Bakhtaran

Ahvaz

Abadan

Al Basrah (Basra)

Euphrates

An Najaf

KUWAIT

KUWAIT CITY

Ka'b

Sakakah

An Nafud

Al Jawf

Tabuk

Tabal Sh

Bushehr

Bandar-e Bushehr

Shiraz

Bandar-e 'Abbas

LEBANON

CYPRUS

ISRAEL

JORDAN

Sinai

Dead Sea

0 km   400

0 miles   400

Saudi Arabia contains the world's largest oil reserves. The region can produce over 8 million barrels of oil every day.

Ar Rub' al Khali, also known as the Empty Quarter, is the largest uninterrupted sand desert in the world, with sand dune ridges up to 25 miles (40 km) long.

The name "Red Sea" is derived from the extensive blooms of algae that occasionally occur. These change color when they die, turning the sea's normally intense blue-green waters a deep red.

Every Muslim must make at least one pilgrimage to Mecca during their lifetime. Muslims regard the small shrine called the Ka'bah, located near the center of the Great Mosque in Mecca, as the most sacred place on Earth.

Central Asia

KAZAKHSTAN

Aral Sea

◆ Since 1960, the Aral Sea has shrunk by 40 percent, becoming extremely saline and consequently losing all but one of it's once-abundant fish species.

Ustyurt Plateau

Turan Lowland

Syr Darya

UZBEKISTAN

Nukus

Köneürgenç

Urganch

Uchquduq

Daşoguz

To'rtko'l

Zarafshon

Caspian

TURKMENISTAN

Türkmenbaşy

Hazar

Balkanabat

Aydar

Bereket

Turan

Garagum

Buxoro

Navoiy

Sea

Serdar

Seýdi

Samarqand

Bäherden

Amu Darya

Qarshi

Gökdepe

Türkmenabat

Büzmeýin

AŞGABAT

Mary

Saýat

Bayramaly

Garagumy Kanaly

Atamyrat

Kaka

Tedzhen

Murgap

Aqchah

Sheberghän

Mazar-e Sha

◆ The desert of Kara Kum (Garagum) occupies over 70 percent of Turkmenistan, severely limiting human settlement across much of the country.

Bälä Morghäb

Meymaneh

Gushgy

Darya-ye Morghäb

Herät

Harīrūd

I R A N

AFGHANISTAN

◆ The Kara Kum (Garagum) Canal, the world's longest irrigation canal, stretches some 683 miles (1100 km) and is known as the "River of Life" as it irrigates large areas of arid land.

Farāh

Gereshk

Kalā

Kandahār

Zaranj

Dasht-e Mārgow

Daryā-ye Helmand

0 km   200

0 miles   200

A   B   C   D

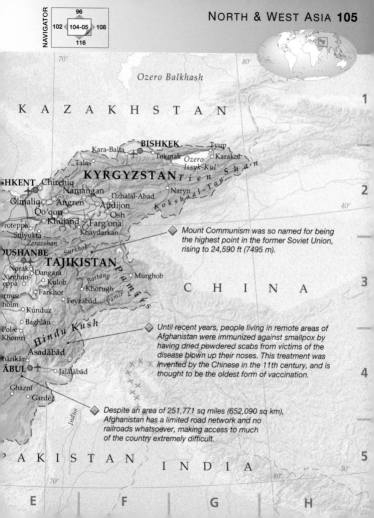

Ozero Balkhash

1

K A Z A K H S T A N

70°   80°

BISHKEK
Kara-Balta   Tyup
Talas   Tokmak   *Ozero*   Karakol
Issyk-Kul'
HKENT Chirchiq   KYRGYZSTAN *Tien Shan*   2
Namangan   Naryn
Olmaliq Angren   Dzhalal-Abad
Qo'qon   Osh
roteppa Khujand Farg'ona
Sulyukta   Khaydarkan

40°

Mount Communism was so named for being
the highest point in the former Soviet Union,
rising to 24,590 ft (7495 m).

Zeravshan
USHANBE   TAJIKISTAN
Norak Dangara   *Surkhob*   C H I N A
Jürghon- Kulob *Bartang*   Murghob
eppa Farkhor *Pamirs*   3
rmez- Khorugh
holm Kunduz Feyzabad *Pamir*
Baghlan

Pol-e *Hindu Kush*   Until recent years, people living in remote areas of
Khomri   Afghanistan were immunized against smallpox by
Asadabad   having dried powdered scabs from victims of the
harikar ABUL   disease blown up their noses. This treatment was
Jalalabad   invented by the Chinese in the 11th century, and is
Ghazni   thought to be the oldest form of vaccination.   4
Gardez

Indus   Despite an area of 251,771 sq miles (652,090 sq km),
Afghanistan has a limited road network and no
railroads whatsoever, making access to much
of the country extremely difficult.

P A K I S T A N   I N D I A   5
70°   80°   30°

E   F   G   H

South & East Asia

Black Sea

Caspian Sea

Aral Sea

Lake Balkhash

Syr Darya

Irtysh

Yenisey

Lake Baikal

Uvs Nuur

Hoosgol Nuur

MONGOLIA

Altai Mountains

Gobi

Yellow River

Tien Shan

A   S   I   A

Iranian Plateau

Hindu Kush

Takla Makan Desert

Kunlun Mountains

Altun Shan

C H I N A

The Gulf

Gulf of Oman

PAKISTAN

Indus

Sutlej

Thar Desert

Himalayas

Yamuna

Ganges

NEPAL

Plateau of Tibet

Brahmaputra

Saleween

Mekong

Yang

Mount Everest 29, 035ft (8850m)

BHUTAN

Rann of Kuchchh

Gulf of Khambhat

I N D I A

Deccan

Western Ghats

Eastern Ghats

BANGLADESH

MYANMAR (BURMA)

Irrawaddy

Red River

VIETNAM

LAOS

Hai

Arabian Sea

Laccadive Islands (to India)

Bay of Bengal

Andaman Islands (to India)

Andaman Sea

THAILAND

Mekong

CAMBODI

Tonle Sap

Gulf of Thailand

SRI LANKA

Gulf of Mannar

MALDIVES

Nicobar Islands (to India)

MALA

Singapo

Sumatra

Ja

Equator

INDIAN

OCEAN

0 km   1000

0 miles   1000

20° · 140° · 160° · 40°

Amur
Argun
at Khingan Range
Manchuria
Plain
Lake Khanka
Sakhalin
Hokkaido

JAPAN

Liao He
Yalu
**NORTH
KOREA**
**SOUTH
KOREA**
Sea of
Japan
(East Sea)

Great Plain of China

Yellow
Sea
Korea Strait
Shikoku
Kyushu

East China
Sea
Ryukyu Islands

TAIWAN
Taiwan Strait

*Philippine
Sea*

Luzon Strait

aracel Islands
disputed)
Luzon

South China
Sea

PHILIPPINES

Spratly
Islands
disputed)

RUNEI
Palawan
Sulu
Sea
Mindanao

IA
Celebes
Sea
Halmahera

orneo
NDONESIA
Moluccas
Seram
Celebes

Flores
Sea
Banda Sea
Lesser Sunda Islands
Arafura
Sea
Timor
EAST TIMOR

PACIFIC

OCEAN

Northern
Marianas Is.
(to US)

Guam
(to US)

M i c r o n e s i a

Equator

M e l a n e s i a

Bismarck Archipelago

Solomon
Islands

Pegunungan Maoke
New Guinea
Solomon
Sea

Coral
Sea

20°

Equator

140° · 160°

1
2
3
4
5

E · F · G · H

Western China & Mongolia

◇ The Altai Mountains provide one of the last refuges for the endangered snow leopard. There are thought to be only 600 animals left in the wild.

◇ The Turpan Depression is the lowest and hottest place in China. Temperatures can exceed 117°F (47°C) around the lake of Aydingkol Hu, which lies 505 ft (154 m) below sea level.

◇ Although forming around 20 percent of China's landmass, Tibet is sparsely populated, supporting only 1 percent of China's 1.3 billion population.

RUSSIAN FEL

KAZAKHSTAN

MONG

Zapadnyy Sayan

Yenisey

Hövsgöl Nuur

Ulaangom

Uvs Nuur

Ölgiy

Hyargas Nuur

Mörön

Altay

Charis Nuur

Tsetserle

Hankayn Nuruu

Altai Mountains

Hovd

Altay

Bayanhongor

Ulungur Hu

Gurbantünggüt Shamo

Karamay

Kuytun

Yining

Shihezi

ÜRÜMQI

Qitai

Turpan

Hami

Xingxingxia

Ejin

G

Go

Ozero Issyk-Kul'

KYRGYZSTAN

Tien Shan

Bosten Hu

Korla

Lop Nur

GANSU

Kashi

Tarim He

Tarim Basin

Yengisar

Shache

XINJIANG UYGUR

Ruoqiang

Qilian Shan

TAJIKISTAN

Yecheng

ZIZHIQU

Altun Shan

AFGH.

Moyu

(claimed by India)

Taklimakan Shamo

Qira

Kunlún Shan

Qaidam Pendi

Qinghai H

Golmud

Dulan

Karakoram Range

AKSAI CHIN (administered by China, claimed by India)

CHI

PAKISTAN

Kashmir

Indus

Qingzang Gaoyuan (Plateau of Tibet)

QINGHA

JAMMU AND KASHMIR

Rutog

Tongtian He

Bayan Har Sh

Yushu

DEMCHOK/DÊMOQOG (administered by China, claimed by India)

Gar

XIZANG ZIZHIQU (Tibet)

Tanggula Shan

Mekong

Amdo

Qamdo

Zanda

Brahmaputra

Nyima

Siling Co

Nagqu

INDIA

Tangra Yumco

Nam Co

Damxung

Nyainqêntanglha Shan

Jinsha

Himalayas

Lhazê

LHASA

NEPAL

Gyangzê

ARUNACHAL PRADESH (claimed by China)

▲ Mount Everest 29,035ft (8850m)

BHUTAN

INDIA

0 km   400
0 miles   400

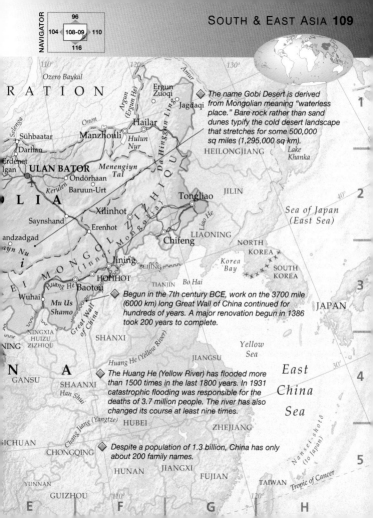

110°   120°   130°

Ozero Baykal

R A T I O N

Ergun
Zuoqi   Jagdaqi

Argun (Ergun He)

Onon

Selenga   Hailar

Sühbaatar   Manzhouli   Hulun
Darhan   Nur
Erdenet
Igan   ULAN BATOR   Menengiyn   HEILONGJIANG   Lake
                        Tal   Khanka

Ondörhaan

L I A   Kerulen   Baruun-Urt

Saynshand   Xilinhot   Tongliao   40°
           Erenhot   Chifeng   JILIN
andzagdad   Sea of Japan
ayn Nu   Jining   (East Sea)

i   LIAONING
EI MONGOL ZIZHIQU   Inner Mongolia   Liao He
Wuhai   Huang He   HOHHOT   BEIJING   NORTH
         Baotou   TIANJIN   KOREA   Korea   SOUTH
Mu Us   Bo Hai   Bay   KOREA
Shamo   JAPAN
NINGXIA HUIZU   Great Wall   SHANXI   30°
ZIZHIQU   of China

N   GANSU   SHAANXI   JIANGSU   Yellow   East
                 Han Shui   Sea   China
ICHUAN   Chang Jiang (Yangtze)   HUBEI   ZHEJIANG   Sea
CHONGQING   Nansei-shotō (to Japan)
                 HUNAN   JIANGXI   FUJIAN
YUNNAN   110°   TAIWAN   Tropic of Cancer
   GUIZHOU   120°

♦ The name Gobi Desert is derived from Mongolian meaning "waterless place." Bare rock rather than sand dunes typify the cold desert landscape that stretches for some 500,000 sq miles (1,295,000 sq km).

♦ Begun in the 7th century BCE, work on the 3700 mile (6000 km) long Great Wall of China continued for hundreds of years. A major renovation begun in 1386 took 200 years to complete.

♦ The Huang He (Yellow River) has flooded more than 1500 times in the last 1800 years. In 1931 catastrophic flooding was responsible for the deaths of 3.7 million people. The river has also changed its course at least nine times.

♦ Despite a population of 1.3 billion, China has only about 200 family names.

Eastern China & Korea

RUSSIAN FEDERATION

Whereas European languages such as English or French use an alphabet of 26 letters, the Chinese language uses a system of over 50,000 characters or symbols.

The "Yongle dadian," an encyclopedia of the Chinese Ming dynasty, had 22,937 chapters in 10,000 volumes. More than 2000 Chinese scholars worked on the book for 5 years before it was finished.

Tangshan, China, suffered the deadliest earthquake of the 20th century on July 28, 1976. One quarter of the population was killed or seriously injured, with an estimated death toll of 242,000 people.

Tiananmen Square in Beijing is the largest public square in the world covering an area of 100 acres (40.5 hectares).

MONGOLIA

NEI MONGOL (Inner Mongolia)

Ozero Baykal

Selenga

Onon

Shilka

Argun (Ergun He)

Amur (Heilong Jiang)

Xiao Hinggan Ling

HEILONGJIANG

Qiqihar

HARBIN

Jilin Mudanjiang

JILIN Chongjin

Huinjiang

Fushun

SHENYANG

Fuxin

LIAONING

Jinzhou Dandong

Haicheng

Anshan

Dalian

Yingkou

Bo Hai

Korea Bay

NORTH KOREA

PYONGYANG

Namp'o

Hamhung

Sea of Japan (East Sea)

SOUTH KOREA

SEOUL

Taejon

Taegu

Pusan

Lake Khanka

CHANGCHUN

Datong

BEIJING

TIANJIN

HEBEI

Tangshan

Shijiazhuang

TAIYUAN

SHANDONG

JINAN

Handan

Qingdao

NINGXIA

YINCHUAN

Qilian Shan

Great Wall of China

Qinghai Hu

Qaidam Pendi

XINJIANG UYGUR ZIZHIQU

Li is the family name for over 87 million people in China.

By far the biggest tidal bore in the World is the Ch'ien't'ang'kian (Hang-chou-fe) in China. At spring tides the wave attains a height of up to 25 ft (7.5 m) and a speed of 13-15 knots (24-27 km/h).

The Giant Bamboo is the fastest growing plant in the world, able to grow at the rate of 3 ft (90 cm) a day.

Paracel Islands (disputed by China, Taiwan and Vietnam)

Spratly Islands (disputed by China, Malaysia, Philippines, Taiwan and Vietnam)

(China and Taiwan claim all of each other's territory)

Japan

Ostrov Iturup

Ostrov Shikotan

Kurile Islands

Ostrov Kunashir

Nemuro

Kushiro

Kurile Islands
(administered by the
Russian Federation,
claimed by Japan)

Sea of
Okhotsk

Kitami

Abashiri

Hokkaidō

Asahikawa

Obihiro

Tomakomai

Ostrov
Sakhalin

La Pérouse Strait

Wakkanai

Rebun-tō

Rishiri-tō

Sapporo

Otaru

Hakodate

Okushiri-tō

Aomori

Hachinohe

Morioka

Akita

Honshū

Sendai

Fukushima

Kōriyama

Iwaki

Hitachi

Niigata

Sado

Shinano-gawa

Toyama

J A P A N

Sea of Japan

(East Sea)

RUSSIAN FEDERATION

CHINA

NORTH KOREA

Liancourt Rocks

At 33.4 miles (53.8 km), 14.3 miles (23.3 km) of
which lie under the Tsugaru Strait, the
Seikan Tunnel is the longest tunnel in the
world. Construction began in 1964 and
took 24 years to complete.

The Toyota Motor Co. Ltd was first established in 1937
as a spin-off from Toyoda Automatic Loom Works.
The company now produces 4.5 million cars a
year equivalent to one every six seconds.

The same family has occupied the Imperial Throne of Japan for the last 1300 years. The present-day emperor, Akihito, is the 125th in succession.

On August 12, 1990, Typhoon Winona, combined with the summer holiday rush, created the longest traffic jam in Japan's history, an 84-mile long tailback involving about 15,000 vehicles.

The longest bridge in the world is the Akashi Kaikyo Bridge linking Honshu and Shikoku, with a central span of 6352 ft (1991 m), the total length shore to shore is 12,831 ft (3,911 m) or 2.4 miles (3.9 km).

30°

140°

135°

130°

25°

PACIFIC OCEAN

Philippine Sea

Izu-shotō

Hachijō-jima

Aoga-shima

East China Sea

Ryūkyū-rettō

Okinawa

Naha

Tokuno-shima

Amami-O-shima

Ōsumi-shotō

Yaku-shima

Tanega-shima

Kagoshima

Miyazaki

Kumamoto

Kyūshū

Amakusa-nada

Nagasaki

Gotō-rettō

Sasebo

Fukuoka

Iki

Kitakyūshū

Shimonoseki

Tsushima

Korea Strait

Ōita

Matsuyama

Kōchi

Tokushima

Shikoku

Nakamura

Yamaguchi

Hiroshima

Okayama

Kurashiki

Matsue

Tottori

Oki-shotō

Hamada

Fukui

Biwa-ko

Wakayama

Ōsaka

Kōbe

Kyōto

Shingū

Nagoya

Okazaki

Hamamatsu

Kawasaki

Chiba

Yokohama

SOUTH KOREA

5

6

7

8

A

B

C

D

E

F

0 km 200

0 miles 200

Southern India & Sri Lanka

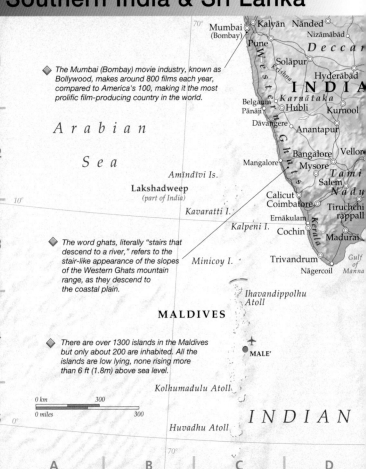

◆ The Mumbai (Bombay) movie industry, known as Bollywood, makes around 800 films each year, compared to America's 100, making it the most prolific film-producing country in the world.

◆ The word ghats, literally "stairs that descend to a river," refers to the stair-like appearance of the slopes of the Western Ghats mountain range, as they descend to the coastal plain.

◆ There are over 1300 islands in the Maldives but only about 200 are inhabited. All the islands are low lying, none rising more than 6 ft (1.8m) above sea level.

70°

Mumbai (Bombay)
Kalyān   Nānded
Nizāmābād
Pune
Deccar
Solāpur
Krishna
Hyderābād
INDIA
Karnātaka
Belgaum   Hubli   Kurnool
Pānāji
Dāvangere   Anantapur
Bangalore   Vellor
Mangalore   Mysore   *Tami*
Nādu
Salem
Calicut
Coimbatore   Tiruchchi
rāppall
Ernākulam   *Kerala*
Cochin   Madurai
Trivandrum   *Gulf*
Nāgercoil   *of Manna*

Arabian

Sea

Amīndīvi Is.

Lakshadweep
(part of India)

Kavaratti I.

Kalpeni I.

Minicoy I.

Ihavandippolhu Atoll

MALDIVES

● **MALE'**

Kolhumadulu Atoll

Huvadhu Atoll

I N D I A N

70°

10°

0°

0 km   300
0 miles   300

A   B   C   D

1

2

3

4

5

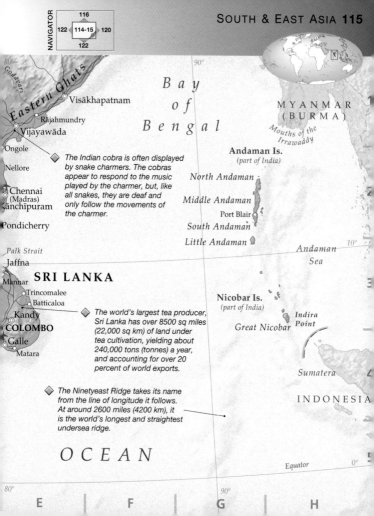

8068

Godāvari

Eastern Ghats

Visākhapatnam

Rājahmundry

Vijayawāda

Ongole

Nellore

Chennai
(Madras)
Kānchīpuram

Pondicherry

B a y
o f
B e n g a l

90°

M Y A N M A R
(B U R M A)

*Mouths of the
Irrawaddy*

Andaman Is.
(part of India)

North Andaman

Middle Andaman

Port Blair

South Andaman

Little Andaman

The Indian cobra is often displayed
by snake charmers. The cobras
appear to respond to the music
played by the charmer, but, like
all snakes, they are deaf and
only follow the movements of
the charmer.

Palk Strait

Jaffna

Mannar

SRI LANKA

Trincomalee

Batticaloa

Kandy

COLOMBO

Galle

Matara

*Andaman
Sea*

10°

Nicobar Is.
(part of India)

Great Nicobar

*Indira
Point*

The world's largest tea producer,
Sri Lanka has over 8500 sq miles
(22,000 sq km) of land under
tea cultivation, yielding about
240,000 tons (tonnes) a year,
and accounting for over 20
percent of world exports.

Sumatera

I N D O N E S I A

The Ninetyeast Ridge takes its name
from the line of longitude it follows.
At around 2600 miles (4200 km), it
is the world's longest and straightest
undersea ridge.

O C E A N

Equator   0°

80°   90°   G

E   F   G   H

North India, Pakistan & Bangladesh

◆ The Karakoram Highway was finally completed in 1978 after 24,000 workers had toiled for almost 20 years. The road climbs to 16,000 ft (4890 m) at the Khunjerab Pass.

(claimed by India)

Hindu Kush

K2 28,251ft (8

A "line of control" was agreed between India and Pakistan in 1972

Peshāwar
Mardān

Karakoram Range

AFGHANISTAN
ISLAMABAD
Rāwalpindi
Jhelum

Jamu & Kashmir

Gujrāt
Gujrānwāla
Amritsar
Jalandhar

Punjab
Sargodha
Lahore
Ludhiāna
Chandīgarh

Toba Kākar Range
Faisalābād
Okāra

Quetta
Dera Ghāzi Khān
Multān

IRAN

Chāgai Hills

PAKISTAN
Bahāwalpur

Meerut
Delhi
NEW DELHI

Shikārpur
Rahīmyār Khān
Bīkāner

Central Makrān Range
Lārkāna
Sukkur
Thar Desert
Rajasthān
Jaipur
Āgra

Nawābshāh
Jodhpur
Ajmer
Gwalior

Karāchi
Hyderābād
Kota

Tropic of Cancer

Rann of Kachchh
I N D

Mouths of the Indus
Gulf of Kachchh
Gāndhīdhām
Ahmadābād
Bhopā

0 km   200
0 miles   200

Arabian
Sea
Jāmnagar
Gujarāt
Rājkot
Indore
Vadodara
Madhy

Porbandar
Bhāvnagar
Narmada
Nāgpur

Sūrat
Mahārashtra

◆ On January 26, 2001 a massive earthquake devastated the Gujarat region of India, costing some 25,000 lives.

Gulf of Khambhāt
Damān

Nāshik
Nānded

Mumbai (Bombay)
Kalyān
Dec

✕✕✕ Ceasefire Line

Pune
Nizāmābād

Solāpur

80° | 90°

XINJIANGUYGUR
ZIZHIQU

◆ The northern ranges of the Himalayas contain the highest
mountains in the world, with average heights of more than
23,000 ft (7000 m) and many peaks higher
than 26,000 ft (8000m).

KSAI CHIN
dministered by China,
aimed by India

C H I N A QINGHAI

EMCHOK/DÉMQOG
dministered by China,
aimed by India

◆ Cerrapunji, 4232 ft (1290 m) above sea level, has an average annual
rainfall of 503 inches (1279 cm), although this is monsoon rain and
the winter is a virtual drought. The highest ever seasonal rainfall
was 901 inches (2290 cm).

XIZANG ZIZHIQU
(Tibet)

◆ In the kingdom of Bhutan, all
citizens officially become a
year older on New Year's Day.

ARUNACHAL PRADESH
(claimed by China)

H i m a l a y a s

N E P A L

Mount Everest
29,035ft (8850m)

●KATHMANDU   ★THIMPHU
○Gangtok   ★BHUTAN

○Guwāhati

○Dispur   ○Kohima

Bareilly

*Uttar
Pradesh*

○Lucknow   ○Birātnagar
○Saidpur
Kānpur ○Vārānasi ○Patna Jamālpur
○Allahābād   Gaya *Bihār* Rājshāhi ●BANGLADESH   ○Sylhet ○Imphāl

Brahmaputra

Ganges

Tropic of Cancer

I A   ○Dhanbād   *West* ●DHAKA
○Ranchi   *Bengal* ○Comilla   M Y A N M A R
○Kolkata   ○Khulna   (B U R M A)
(Calcutta)

Jabalpur

Jamuna

Chittagong

Pradesh

○Raipur   *Mouths of the Ganges*

an   *Mahānadi*   *Bay*
Orissa   ○Cuttack   *of*

◆ The heaviest hailstones
on record, weighing about
2.25 lbs (1 kg), are
reported to have killed 92
people in the Gopalganj
area of Bangladesh on
April 14, 1986.

Eastern Ghats   *Bengal*

āveri

Warangal   ○Visākhapatnam

30°

20°

Mainland Southeast Asia

Around 70 percent of the world's teak grows in the hills of northern Myanmar. However overexploitation means that supplies may soon be exhausted.

The *Anopheles* mosquito, which carries the malaria parsite *Plasmodium*, is estimated to have been responsible for half of all human deaths not caused by war.

VIET NAM

Qui Nhon

Nha Trang

Kông

Trà Vinh

Sŏc Trăng

Stœng Trêng

Đà Lat

Mekong

CAMBODIA

Kâmpóng Cham

Svay Riêng

Hô Chi Minh

Muang Khong

Phum Sngkê

Phûm Sâmraông

Bătdâmbâng

Samraong

Tônlé Sap

Kâmpóng Chhnăng

PHNOM PENH

Mekong

Mouths of the Mekong

Cân Tho

Ratchasima

BANGKOK

Ayutthaya

Chon Buri

Pattaya

CAMBODIA

Kâmpóng Saôm

Kâmpôt

Rach Gia

Kâmpot

Following years of conflict it is estimated that around 3 million landmines remain buried in the soils of Cambodia.

South   China   Sea

Ko Chang

Gulf of Thailand

Ko Phangan

Ko Samui

Nakhon Si Thammarat

Songkhla

Pattani

Yala

Malay   Peninsula

MALAYSIA

Ratchaburi

Res.

Ratchaburi

Chumphon

Hat Yai

Strait of Malacca

Tavoy

Mergui

Surat Thani

Trang

INDONESIA

Sumatra

Mergui Archipelago

Isthmus of Kra

Ko Phuket

Phuket

The world's smallest mammal is the bumblebee bat of Thailand, weighing less than 0.09 oz (2.5g).

Andaman   Sea

Nicobar Islands (part of India)

INDIAN   OCEAN

Bangkok has some of the worst traffic jams in the world. In July 1992, after a monsoon storm, it took 11 hours for one jam to clear.

South   China   Sea

0 km   200

0 miles   200

Maritime Southeast Asia

MYANMAR (BURMA)

THAILAND

LAOS

VIETNAM

CAMBODIA

Hainan Dao (to China)

Paracel Islands
(disputed by China, Taiwan and Vietnam)

South China Sea

0 km 400
0 miles 400

90°
100°
110°

1

2

3

4

5

Andaman Sea

Nicobar Islands (to India)

Isthmus of Kra

Gulf of Thailand

Spratly Islands
(disputed by China, Malaysia, Philippines, Taiwan and Vietnam)

◆ The Rafflesia plant has the largest flower in the world. The bloom, 3 ft (90 cm) in diamet attracts insects by imitating the foul smell of rotting flesh.

George Town
Bandaaceh
Kota Bharu
Kuala Terengganu
Kuantan
Kota Kinabalu
BANDAR SERI BEGAWAN
BRUNEI

Taiping Ipoh
Medan
Pematangsiantar
Pulau Simeulue
Danau Toba
Klang
Seremban
KUALA LUMPUR
MALAYSIA
Sibu
Sarawak
Pegunungan Muller
Bali

Sibolga
Pulau Nias
Johor Bahru
SINGAPORE
Kuching
Borneo

Equator

Sumatera (Sumatra)
Pekanbaru
Pontianak
Kapuas
Kalimantan
Samari
Balikpap

Padang
Pulau Siberut
Kepulauan Mentawai
Batang Hari
Jambi
Bangka
Selat Karimata

Palembang
Banjarmasin

Bengkulu
IND
D

Pulau Belitung
Tegal
Java Sea
Maka

Pegunungan Barisan

Bandarlampung
Cirebon
Pekalongan
Semarang
Surabay
Kudus
Matara

Selat Sunda
JAKARTA
Bogor
Sukabumi
Bandung
Cilacap
Magelang
Yogyakarta
Surakarta
Denpasar
Jembe
Malang
Kediri
Madiun
Bali
Lo

Jawa (Java)

INDIAN

OCEAN

◆ In August 1883 a devastating volcanic eruption destroyed most of the island of Krakatau and triggered a tsunami that claimed around 33,000 lives.

10°
10°

Equator

Strait of Malacca

90°
100°

A   B   C   D

Luzon Strait
Babuyan Channel
Philippine

Sea

Tuguergarao
Ilagan
guio
Luzon
geles Dagupan
Cabanatuan
NILA Lucena
tangas Naga
Mindoro Legaspi
doro *Sibuyan Sea*

PHILIPPINES

◆ The Philippines take their name from Philip II of Spain, who was king when the islands were colonized during the 16th century.

Roxas City
Straits
Iloilo Cadiz
Bacolod Cebu
City *Bohol Sea*
Iligan Butuan
Cagayan de Oro
amboanga *Mindanao*
Davao

P A C I F I C

Yap

MICRONESIA

Sulu Archipelago
General
Santos
Sulu Sea
Celebes Sea
Davao Gulf

Vau

Kepulauan Talaud

PALAU

Manado
Gorontalo
Gulf of Tomini
Sulawesi (Celebes)
Kepulauan Banggai
Kepulauan Sula

alu

O C E A N

Babeldaob

◆ Indonesia is the world's largest archipelago with almost 14,000 islands stretching 3100 miles (5000 km) between the Indian and Pacific oceans.

Pulau Morotai
Pulau Halmahera
Molucca Sea
Maluku (Moluccas)
Halmahera Sea
Sorong
Jazirah Doberai
Pulau Biak

Equator

Jayapura

Sungai Mamberamo

N
Kendari
Parepare
Ujungpandang
Pulau Buton
Banda Sea

E
Wahai
Ambon
Pulau Buru
Ceram Sea
Pulau Seram

S
Pulau Kai
Kepulauan Kai

I
Pegunungan Maoke
Papua (Irian Jaya)

A
New
PAPUA

NEW
GUINEA

Guinea

es Sea
Flores
Tenggara
Pulau Alor
Pulau Wetar
Kepulauan Tanimbar
Pulau Yamdena

Sumba
Savu Sea
Kepulauan Leti
DILI
EAST TIMOR
Timor

Digul

Torres Strait

umba
Kupang
Timor Sea

A r a f u r a   S e a

AUSTRALIA

20° 130°

120° 130° 140° 10°

Northern Mariana Islands (to US)

Guam (to US)

10°

1

2

3

4

5

The Indian Ocean

With no part of the Maldives over 8ft (2.4m) above sea level, they are under great threat by global warming. There are over 2000 islands yet the total land area is only 115 sq miles.

Australian Basin

Exmouth Plateau

Tropic of Capricorn

AUSTRALASIA

Perth Basin

Fremantle

Naturaliste Plateau

Diamantina Fracture Zone

Wharton Basin

Broken Ridge

East Indiaman Ridge

Southern Indian Ridge

Southeast Indian Ridge

SOUTHERN OCEAN

South Indian Basin

◆ Every cubic mile (4.3 cu km) of seawater holds over 150 million tons (tonnes) of minerals.

Osborn Plateau

Ninetyeast Ridge

INDIAN OCEAN

Amsterdam Island

Île St-Paul

Central Indian Ridge

Crozet Basin

Kerguelen Plateau

Kerguelen

Banzare Seamounts

South West Indian Ridge

French Southern & Antarctic Territories (to France)

Crozet Islands

Heard & Mcdonald Islands (to Australian)

◆ The largest animal ever seen alive was a 113.5 ft (35 m), 170-ton (tonne) female blue whale.

MAURITIUS

Réunion (to France)

Farafangana

Madagascar Basin

Madagascar Plateau

Prince Edward Islands (to South Africa)

Mascarene Plain

Natal Basin

Davie Ridge

Mozambique Channel

Madagascar

(to France)

Durban

Enderby Plain

Atlantic-Indian Basin

Antarctic Circle

ANTARCTICA

Limit of winter pack ice

Limit of summer pack ice

Antarctic Circle

0 km 1500

0 miles 1500

40° 60° 80° 100° 120° 140° E

A B C D E

5 6 7 8

Australasia & Oceania

Philippine Sea

20°

Mid-Pacific Mountains

Wake Island (to US)

Northern Mariana Islands (to US)

MARSHALL ISLANDS

Saipan

Mariana Trench

Micronesia

Ratak Chain

Guam (to US)

Ratik Chain

Philippine Trench

Yap Trench

MICRONESIA

Caroline Islands

Chuuk Islands

Pohnpei

Kosrae

Nauru

NAURU

Banaba

KIRIBATI

Philippines

Babeldaob

Yap Trench

PALAU

Melanesia

Tungaru (Gilbert Islands)

Sulu Sea

Bismarck Archipelago

PAPUA NEW GUINEA

TUV

Celebes Sea

Bismarck Sea

SOLOMON ISLANDS

Borneo
Equator

Mount Wilhelm 14,793ft (4509m) ▲

New Guinea

Bougainville Island

Solomon Islands

Santa Cruz Islands

Celebes

Solomon Sea

Guadalcanal

Banda Sea

Arafura Sea

Torres Strait

VANUATU

North Fiji Basin

Vanua

Timor
Flores

Espíritu Santo

Malekula

Efate

Viti Levu

Timor Sea

Gulf of Carpentaria

Cape York Peninsula

Great Barrier Reef

Coral Sea

Coral Sea Islands (to Australia)

New Caledonia (to France)

Ashmore & Cartier Islands (to Australia)

Arnhem Land

Great Dividing Range

New Caledonia Ridge

Norfolk Ridge

Sou

Fiji Ba

INDIAN OCEAN

AUSTRALIA

Great Sandy Desert

Macdonnell Ranges

Simpson Desert

New Caledonia

Lord Howe Rise

Norfolk Island (to Australia)

Uluru (Ayers Rock) ▲

Gibson Desert

L. Eyre North

Grey Range

Lord Howe Island (to Australia)

North

20° Tropic of Capricorn

Great Victoria Desert

L. Torrens

Darling

Mount Kosciuszko 7310ft (2228m) ▲

Fiji Basin

North Island

NEW ZEALAND

Murray

Nullarbor Plain

Great Australian Bight

Kangaroo Island

Bass Strait

Tasman Sea

South Island

Aoraki (Mt Cook) 12,283ft (3744m) ▲

Cape Leeuwin

South Australian Basin

Tasmania

Antip

Tasman Plateau

Auckland Islands (to New Zealand)

Tasman Basin

100°

40°

120°

140°

A

B

C

D

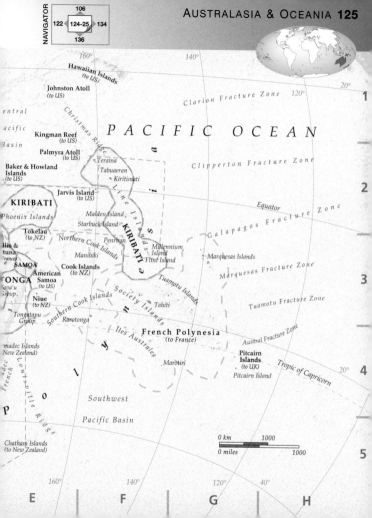

160°   140°   120°   20°   1

Hawaiian Islands
(to US)

Johnston Atoll
(to US)

Clarion Fracture Zone

entral
acific
Basin

PACIFIC OCEAN

Christmas Ridge

Kingman Reef
(to US)

Palmyra Atoll
(to US)

Clipperton Fracture Zone

Baker & Howland
Islands
(to US)

Teraina
Tabuaeran
Kiritimati

JARVIS Island
(to US)

KIRIBATI

Equator   2

Galapagos Fracture Zone

Phoenix Islands

Malden Island
Starbuck Island

KIRIBATI

Tokelau
(to NZ)

Northern Cook Islands

Penrhyn

Millennium
Island
Flint Island

Line Islands

Marquesas Islands

His &
tuna
France

SAMOA

Manihiki

Marquesas Fracture Zone

American
Samoa
(to US)

Cook Islands
(to NZ)

TONGA

Society Islands

Tuamotu Islands   3

ava'u
roup.

Niue
(to NZ)

Southern Cook Islands

Tahiti

Tuamotu Fracture Zone

Tongatapu
Group

Rarotonga

Îles Australes

Austral Fracture Zone

madec Islands
New Zealand)

French Polynesia
(to France)

Marotiri

Pitcairn
Islands
(to UK)

Tropic of Capricorn   20°

adec
rench

Louisville Ridge

P

P   o   l   y   n   e   s   i   a

Pitcairn Island   4

40°

Southwest
Pacific Basin

Chatham Islands
(to New Zealand)

0 km   1000

0 miles   1000   5

160°   140°   120°   40°

E   F   G   H

The Southwest Pacific

30°

140° 150° 160° 170°

Guam
(US unincorporated
territory) HAGÁTÑA

**MARSHALL
ISLANDS** Ratak Chain

1

10° Yap Marianas Trench

Caroline Islands *M i c r o n e s i a*

Chuuk Is. Majuro

KOROR Pohnpei
PALIKIR

MICRONESIA Ralik Chain

PALAU Kosrae

BAIRIKI
Tarawa

◇ The Pitohui bird has a poison on its feathers and skin
similar to the poison arrow tree frog, making it the
only known example of a poisonous bird.

0° Equator **NAURU**
Banab

PAPUA NEW GUINEA

Bismarck Archipelago New Ireland

I N D O N E S I A
Mt Wilhelm
14,793ft (4509m) ▲ Madang Bougainville I. *M e l a n e s i a*
New Britain New
New Guinea Lae Georgia
Islands

3

PORT MORESBY *Solomon
Sea* **HONIARA** Santa Cruz Is.

10° *A r a f u r a* **SOLOMON
ISLANDS**

Torres Strait

S e a

**Arnhem
Land** Gulf of
Carpentaria *C o r a l   S e a* Banks Is.

4

VANUATU

◇ Found only in the rain forest of New Guinea,
Queen Alexandra's Birdwing, with a wingspan
of 11 inches (280 mm), is the
largest butterfly in the world. **PORT VILA**

Coral Sea Islands
(Australian external
territory) **New Caledonia**
(French overseas
territory)

20°

Great Barrier Reef

5

AUSTRALIA

NOUMÉA Îles
Loyauté

30°

140° 150° 160°

A B C D

180° *International Date Line*

170° *160°* *150°*

P A C I F I C   O C E A N

10°

1

◇ In 1994 the International Date Line was repositioned around Kiribati territory bringing Millennium Island 14 hours ahead of GMT, making it the first landfall for sunrise at the dawn of the new millennium.

Kingman Reef *(administered by US)* **Palmyra Atoll** *(administered by US)*

·Teraina
Tabuaeran

2

Baker & Howland Is. *(administered by US)*

Jarvis I. *(administered by US)*

·Kiritimati

L i n e   I s l a n d s

Tungaru (Gilbert Islands)

I R I B A T I *Phoenix Islands*

KIRIBATI

Equator *0°*

◇ Samoa is home to the world's smallest spider, the Patu marplesi, which spans a mere 0.0017 inches (0.04mm).

3

VALU

● **FONGAFALE**

Tokelau *(NZ dependent territory)*

Vostok I.

Millennium I.

10°

P o l y n e s i a

American Samoa *(US unincorporated territory)*

Flint I.

Northern Cook Is.

4

Wallis & Futuna *(French overseas territory)* **SAMOA** **ÁPIA**

○ **PAGO PAGO**

French Polynesia *(French overseas territory)*

FIJI *Vanua Levu*

Vava'u Group

Cook Islands *(in free assoc. with NZ)*

Îles de la Société

ith vu ● **SUVA**

Ha'apai Group

Niue *(in free assoc. with NZ)* ○ **ALOFI** *Southern Cook Is.*

● **PAPEETE** ○

Tahiti

TONGA

20°

● **NUKU'ALOFA**

AVARUA ●

Rarotonga

| 0 km | | 500 |
| 0 miles | | 500 |

5.

180° *170°* *International Date Line* *Tropic of Capricorn*

E F G H

Western Australia

On Christmas Day, 1974, Cyclone Tracy devastated Darwin with winds of up to 175 mph (280km/h) resulting in 66 deaths, thousands of injuries and 95 percent of the city destroyed.

One of the largest states in the world, with an area of more than 975,000 sq miles (2.5 million sq km), Western Australia covers a third of the Australian continent.

INDONESIA

Bali

Pulau Lombok

Jawa

Arafura Sea

Croker Island

Arnhem Land

Melville Island

Van Diemen Gulf

Bathurst Island

DARWIN

Pine Creek

Katherine

Daly Waters

Top Springs

Victoria River

Kununurra

Tanami Desert

Tennant Creek

NORTHERN TERRITORY

Macdonnell Ranges

Timor Sea

Cape Londonderry

Joseph Bonaparte Gulf

Wyndham

Kimberley Plateau

Halls Creek

Fitzroy Crossing

Lake Mackay

Bonaparte Archipelago

Heywood Islands

King Sound

Fitzroy River

Great Sandy Desert

Percival Lakes

INDIAN OCEAN

Broome

Eighty Mile Beach

Marble Bar

WESTERN

Port Hedland

Dampier

Onslow

Fortescue River

Hamersley Range

Ashburton

Exmouth Gulf

Exmouth

Eastern Australia

◇ The venom of the Sea Wasp, Marine Stinger, or Box Jellyfish can kill a person in between 30 seconds and four minutes.

◇ Australia's Great Barrier Reef is the world's largest area of coral islands and reefs, running for about 1,240 miles (2,000 km) along the coast of Queensland.

◇ Koalas feed only on nutrient-poor eucalypt leaves and consequently have evolved a low energy lifestyle based around sleeping for 20 hours each day.

Coral Sea Islands (to Australia)

Coral Sea

Great Barrier Reef

Whitsunday Group

Rockhampton

Mackay

Bowen

Townsville

Hinchinbrook Island

Charters Towers

Clermont

Emerald

Barcaldine

PAPUA NEW GUINEA

Great Dividing Range

Tully

Cairns

Port Douglas

Cooktown

Hughenden

Cloncurry

Winton

Longreach

Barcaldine

Princess Charlotte Bay

Torres Strait

Cape York

Cape York Peninsula

Mitchell River

Gilbert River

Gregory Range

Flinders River

Normanton

Burketown

Mount Isa

Selwyn Range

QUEENSLAND

INDONESIA

Wessel Islands

Groote Eylandt

Gulf of Carpentaria

Wellesley Islands

Arafura Sea

Arnhem Land

Barkly Tableland

NORTHERN

Daly Waters

Top Springs Roadhouse

Tennant Creek

Tanami Desert

TERRITORY

DARWIN

Pine Creek

Katherine

Alice Springs

Macdonnell Ranges

Tropic of Capricorn

AUSTRALIA

BRISBANE
Gold Coast
Surfers Paradise
Murwillumbah
Dalby
Toowoomba
Miles
Grafton
Coffs Harbour
Port Macquarie
St. George
Goondiwindi
Moree
Walgett
Armidale
Tamworth
Newcastle
Gosford
Cunnamulla
Nyngan
Dubbo
Parramatta
SYDNEY
Wollongong
Great Dividing Range
Grey Range
Bourke
Ivanhoe
Cootamundra
CANBERRA
AUSTRALIAN
CAPITAL TERRITORY
Cooma
Wilcannia
Wagga Wagga
Mount
Kosciuszko
7310 ft (2228 m) ▲
Albury
NEW SOUTH WALES
Lachlan River
Barrier Range
Broken Hill
Lake
Callabonna
Mildura
Ouyen
Bendigo
VICTORIA
MELBOURNE
Geelong
Traralgon
South East Point
Flinders Island
Lake
Blanche
Marree
Lake
Frome
Lake
Eyre North
Peterborough
Ballarat
Horsham
Warrnambool
King Island
Bass Strait
Banks Strait
Launceston
Cooper
Pedy
Lake
Eyre South
Crystal Brook
Gawler
ADELAIDE
Murray River
Portland
Mount Gambier
Marrawah
Burnie
Devonport
HOBART
Lake
Torrens
Whyalla
Port
Augusta
Eyre
Peninsula
TASMANIA
SOUTH AUSTRALIA
Lake
Gairdner
Port
Lincoln
Spencer Gulf
Kangaroo Island
Great
Victoria
Desert
Tarcoola
Penong
Ceduna
Murray River
Darling River
Barwon River

*The Platypus lives in an aquatic
environment, suckles its young
like a mammal, lays eggs, and
has webbed feet and a bill
resembling that of a duck.*

*Huge truck rigs known as
Road Trains, which can reach
up to 175 ft (53.5 m) in length,
carry freight across the vast
distances of the Australian interior.
They often have as many as three
trailers, weighing more than
100 tons (tonnes) in total.*

T a s m a n   S e a

0 km   400
0 miles   400

New Zealand

The lizardlike tuatara is found on some of the islands and rocky stacks off New Zealand. It is the sole remaining representative of the reptilian order Rhynchocephalia, which first evolved before the dinosaurs. It has a third 'eye' on the top of its head which is sensitive to light.

Ninety Mile Beach is in fact only about 60 miles long. Nevertheless, this still makes it one of the longest sandy beaches in the world.

Around AD 130 something in the order of 33 billion tons (tonnes) of pumice was ejected in a massive volcanic eruption that left a 20,000 sq mile (51,800 sq km) debris field and created an enormous caldera that subsequently became Lake Taupo.

More than 55 million sheep thrive in New Zealand's mild climate, outnumbering the human population by 15 to 1.

T a s m a n   S e a

N O R T H   I S L A N D

N E W   Z E A L A N D

Three Kings Islands

North Cape

Great Exhibition Bay

Te Kao
Kaitaia

Te Kuiti

Paihia
Whangarei

Ruawai
Warkworth
Kaikohe

Great Barrier Island

Hauraki Gulf

Whitianga
Manurewa

Takapuna
Auckland
Waiuku

Hamilton
Cambridge

Paeroa

Tauranga
Whakatane

Bay of Plenty

East Cape
Ruatoria

Rotorua
Lake Rotorua

Taupo
Lake Taupo

Gisborne

Wairoa

Hawke Bay

Napier
Hastings
Waipawa
Woodville

Taumarunui
Taihape

North Taranaki Bight

New Plymouth
Stratford

Hawera
South Taranaki Bight

Wanganui
Palmerston North

Cape Farewell

Cape Palliser

South Island

New Zealand has always been a leader in progressive social legislation. In 1893 it was the first country to grant women the right to vote.

The royal albatross colony on Otago Peninsula is the only mainland nesting site for these birds in the world. Soaring on wings up to 9'6" (3 m) across, breeding pairs mate for life and have been known to live for over 60 years.

The Kakapo is a nocturnal flightless parrot that lives in burrows. When in danger, its main form of defense is to remain perfectly still, which made it an easy target for predators such as the dogs, cats, rats, and ferrets that were introduced in the 19th century. Consequently it is in danger of extinction; in 1998 there were only 57 birds left in the wild.

PACIFIC OCEAN

Blenheim
Kaikoura
Wairau
Clarence
Richmond Ra.
Pegasus Bay
Rangiora
Christchurch
Banks Peninsula
Canterbury Bight
Oxford Plains
Hurunui
Otira
Ashburton
Mayfield
Rakaia
Fairlie
Timaru
Studholme
Oamaru
Waitaki
Mosgiel
Dunedin
Otago Peninsula
Balclutha
Clutha
Gore
Lumsden
Mataura
Invercargill
Foveaux Strait
Stewart Island
South West Cape
Halfmoon Bay
Riverton
Waiau
Te Anau
Lake Te Anau
Lake Manapouri
Milford Sound
Fiordland
Lake Wakatipu
Queenstown
Alexandra
Lake Wanaka
Wanaka
Haast
Fox Glacier
Mt Cook (Aoraki)
12,283 (3744m)
Southern Alps
Greymouth
Hokitika
Reefton
Westport

Though still the highest peak in New Zealand, at 12,394 ft (3744 m), a massive rock fall in 1991 reduced the height of the mountain by 66 ft (20 m).

0 km   100
0 miles   100

The Pacific Ocean

◆ Challenger Deep in the Mariana Trench is 35,838 ft (10,923 m), or almost 7 miles (11 km), below the surface of the Pacific. At this depth water pressures is around 16,000 lbs/sq inch (1,127 kg/cm sq).

Arctic Circle

Ob'
Yenisey
Lena

Bering Sea
Aleutian Basin
Aleutian Islands
Chinook Trough

Sea of Okhotsk

Kurile Islands
Kurile Trench
Northwest Pacific Basin

G o b i
Vladivostok
Sea of Japan (East Sea)
Mendocino

A S I A
Yellow River
Osaka
Tokyo
Yellow Sea
Nagoya

Yangtze
Shanghai
East China Sea
Japan

Midway Island (to US)
Hawaiian

Hong Kong (Xianggang)
Taiwan
Ryukyu Trench
Shikoku Basin

Tropic of Cancer

Wake Island (to US)
Mid Pacific Mountains
Johnston Atoll

Manila
Philippine Trench
Philippine Basin
Guam (to US)
Northern Mariana Islands (to US)

M i c r o n e s i a
MARSHALL ISLANDS
Central Pacific Basin
P A

Mekong
Philippines

36.201ft (11,034m)
Challenger Deep

Kingman

South China Sea
Borneo
Celebes Sea
Celebes

PALAU
MICRONESIA
Caroline Islands
Ontong Java Rise

Melanesian Basin

Baker & Howland (to US)

Singapore
Sumatra

Equator
Jakarta
Java
Banda Sea
East Indies
Java Sea

M e l a n e s i a
NAURU
KIRIBATI
Tokelau

New Guinea
Arafura Sea
Timor
Timor Sea

SOLOMON ISLANDS
Coral Sea
Wallis & Futuna (to France)
TUVALU

INDIAN

Coral Sea Islands (to Australia)
VANUATU
New Caledonia (to France)
FIJI
TONGA

SAM
Am
Sar

Great Barrier Reef
Great Dividing Range
Lord Howe Rise

Tropic of Capricorn

OCEAN
A U S T R A L I A

Kermadec Islands (to NZ)
Norfolk Island (to Australia)

Niu
(to

Great Australian Bight
Murray
Sydney
Tasman Sea

North Island

South Australian Basin
Tasmania
Hobart

New Zealand
Chatham Islands (to NZ)

0 km   2000
0 miles   2000

South Island
Campbell Plateau

International Dateline

◆ Manua Loa on the Big Island of Hawaii rises 33,132 ft (10,098 m) from the ocean floor to it's peak 13,677 ft (4169 m) above the surface of the Pacific Ocean, and contains around 9,700 cubic miles (39,731 cu km) of rock.

Pacific   Anta

Antarctic Circle
A N T A R C T I C A

A   B   C   D

Anchorage

Arctic Circle

Rocky Mountains

Hudson Bay

Labrador Sea

Gulf of Alaska

NORTH AMERICA

Vancouver

Cascadia Basin

◇ Pacific giant kelp can grow up to 18 inches (45 cm) a day, and may eventually reach up to 197 ft (60 m) or 34 times the height of the average man.

ATLANTIC OCEAN

Zone

San Francisco

Long Beach

Tropic of Cancer

array Fracture Zone

Molokai Fracture Zone

Gulf of California

Gulf of Mexico

Greater Antilles

Lesser Antilles

waiian Islands (US)

Clarion Fracture Zone

Middle America Trench

Caribbean Sea

C OCEAN

Clipperton Island (to France)

Panama City

◇ The Pacific Equatorial Counter Current flows eastward toward South America, carrying up to 40 million tons (tonnes) of warm water with it every second.

(to US)

Clipperton Fracture Zone

Guatemala Basin

mati smas Island

Galapagos Fracture Zone

BATI

Gallego Rise

Galapagos Islands (to Ecuador)

Bauer Basin

Galapagos Rise

Callao

SOUTH

Marquesas Islands

Marquesas Fracture Zone

French Basin

Mendaña Fracture Zone

Peru-Chile Trench

AMERICA

Tiki

ti

East Pacific Rise

Sala y Gomez (to Chile)

Isla San Ambrosio (to Chile)

Tropic of Capricorn

French Polynesia (to France)

Austral Fracture Zone

Easter Fracture Zone

Isla San Félix (to Chile)

iles

Îles Gambier

Pitcairn Islands (to UK)

Easter Island (to Chile)

Islas Juan Fernández (to Chile)

Andes

Panama

Valparaiso

Australes

Galapagos Chile Basin

hwest cific sin

Agassiz Fracture Zone

Chile Rise

Chile Trench

Eltanin Fracture Zone

Mornington Abyssal Plain

Cape Horn

Limit of winter pack ice

Southeast Pacific Basin

Bellingshausen Plain

Drake Passage

Peter I Island (to Norway)

Antarctic Circle

Amundsen Plain

Limit of summer pack ice

1

2

3

4

5

E   F   G   H

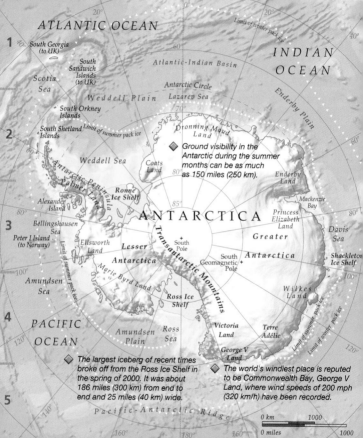

ATLANTIC OCEAN

1

South Georgia (to UK)

INDIAN OCEAN

Atlantic-Indian Basin

Scotia Sea

South Sandwich Islands (to UK)

Antarctic Circle

Lazarev Sea

Weddell Plain

Enderby Plain

South Orkney Islands

Limit of summer pack ice

Dronning Maud Land

2

South Shetland Islands

Weddell Sea

◆ Ground visibility in the Antarctic during the summer months can be as much as 150 miles (250 km).

Coats Land

Enderby Land

Antarctic Peninsula

Palmer Land

Ronne Ice Shelf

Mackenzie Bay

Alexander Island

A N T A R C T I C A

Princess Elizabeth Land

Bellingshausen Sea

+ *South Pole*

Greater

Davis Sea

3

Peter I Island (to Norway)

Ellsworth Land

Lesser Antarctica

South Geomagnetic Pole +

Antarctica

Shackleton Ice Shelf

Amundsen Sea

Marie Byrd Land

Transantarctic Mountains

Wilkes Land

Ross Ice Shelf

4

PACIFIC OCEAN

Amundsen Plain

Ross Sea

Victoria Land

Terre Adélie

◆ The largest iceberg of recent times broke off from the Ross Ice Shelf in the spring of 2000. It was about 186 miles (300 km) from end to end and 25 miles (40 km) wide.

George V Land

◆ The world's windiest place is reputed to be Commonwealth Bay, George V Land, where wind speeds of 200 mph (320 km/h) have been recorded.

5

Pacific-Antarctic Ridge

0 km   1000
0 miles   1000

A   B   C   D

160°
180°
Bering
Sea
Bering Strait
● Providleniya
Arctic Circle

A S I A

Chukchi
Sea

R U S S I A N

ALASKA
(to US)

NORTH AMERICA

Ostrov
Vrangelya

East
Siberian
Sea

F E D E R A T I O N

Limit of summer pack ice
● Tuktoyaktuk

Limit of permanent pack ice

Chukchi
Plain

Beaufort
Sea

Amundsen Gulf

120°

Canada
Basin

Chukchi
Plateau

Novosibirskiye
Ostrova

◇ The Arctic Ocean is the world's
smallest ocean with a total area of
5,440,000 sq miles (15,1000,000 sq km)
and is almost permanently covered
by pack ice.

Victoria
Island

Mendeleyev Ridge

120°

CANADA

Queen

100°

Makarov
Basin

A R C T I C

Severnaya
Zemlya

100°

Elizabeth

Islands

Ellesmere Island

+
North
Pole

O C E A N

Kara
Sea

● Dikson

Baffin
Island

Lincoln
Sea

85°

Nansen Basin

Sryalaya Anna
Trough

Ostrov
Belyy

Knud Rasmuss
Land

Franz
Josef Land

60°

Baffin
Bay

Wandel
Sea

Limit of permanent pack ice

Novaya
Zemlya

Greenland
(to Denmark)

Kong Frederik VIII

80°

Limit of summer

Svalbard
(to Norway)

The Arctic Lion's Main is the ◇
world's largest jellyfish, 7 ft
(2.1 m) in diameter. Its main
body trails tentacles up to
180 ft (55 m) in length.

Kong Land

Spitsbergen

● Longyearbyen

Bjørnøya
(to Norway)

Barents
Sea

Greenland
Sea

North Cape

0 km   500

0 miles   500

Jan Mayen
(to Norway)

Denmark Strait

20°

Iceland
Plateau

Norwegian
Sea

70°

● Murmansk

Kola
Peninsula

● Archangel

SWEDEN

NORWAY

FINLAND

E U R O P E

40°

The

Country

Factfiles

North & Central America

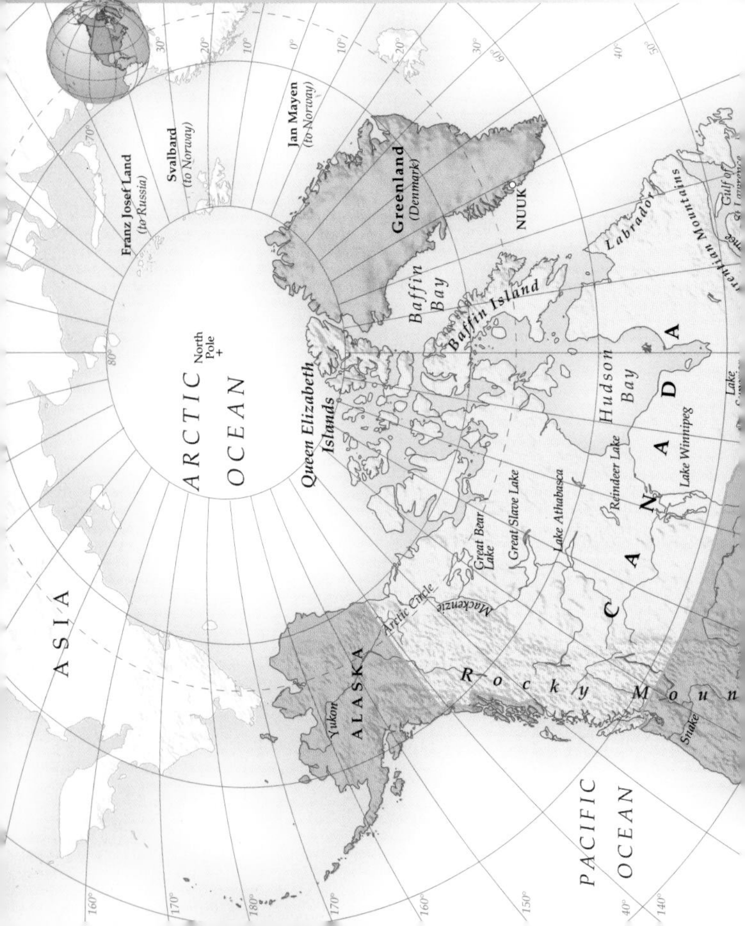

ASIA

ARCTIC OCEAN

North Pole

Franz Josef Land (to Russia)

Svalbard (to Norway)

Jan Mayen (to Norway)

Greenland (Denmark)

NUUK

Baffin Bay

Baffin Island

Labrador

Queen Elizabeth Islands

Hudson Bay

CANADA

Great Bear Lake

Great Slave Lake

Reindeer Lake

Lake Athabasca

Lake Winnipeg

Lake

Gulf of St Lawrence

Mackenzie

Arctic Circle

ALASKA

Yukon

Aleutian Mountains

Rocky Moun

Snake

PACIFIC OCEAN

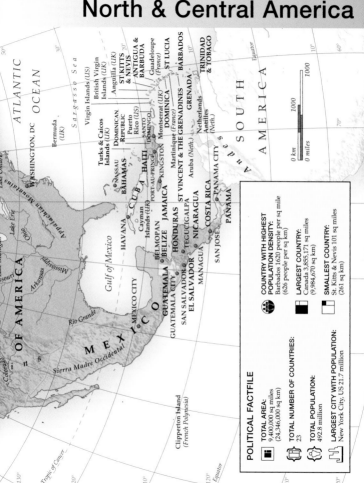

ATLANTIC OCEAN

Sargasso Sea

Bermuda *(UK)*

WASHINGTON, DC

Lake Ontario

Appalachian Mountains

Lake Erie

Ohio

Mississippi

Arkansas

Virgin Islands *(US)*

British Virgin
Islands *(UK)*

Anguilla *(UK)*

ST KITTS
& NEVIS

ANTIGUA &
BARBUDA

Guadeloupe
(France)

DOMINICA

ST LUCIA

BARBADOS

ST VINCENT & THE GRENADINES

GRENADA

TRINIDAD
& TOBAGO

Turks & Caicos
Islands *(UK)*

DOMINICAN
REPUBLIC

Puerto
Rico *(US)*

SANTO
DOMINGO

Martinique *(France)*

Netherlands
Antilles *(Neth.)*

Aruba *(Neth.)*

Montserrat *(UK)*

NASSAU

BAHAMAS

HAITI

PORT-AU-PRINCE

KINGSTON

JAMAICA

HAVANA

C U B A

Cayman
Islands *(UK)*

Gulf of Mexico

BELMOPAN

BELIZE

GUATEMALA CITY

GUATEMALA

SAN SALVADOR

EL SALVADOR

TEGUCIGALPA

HONDURAS

MANAGUA

NICARAGUA

SAN JOSÉ

COSTA RICA

PANAMA CITY

PANAMA

Andes

S O U T H   A M E R I C A

MEXICO CITY

Rio Grande

M E X I C O

Sierra Madre Occidental

Colorado

Clipperton Island
(French Polynesia)

O F   A M E R I C A

Tropic of Cancer

Equator

0 km   1000

0 miles   1000

COUNTRY WITH HIGHEST
POPULATION DENSITY:
Barbados 1620 people per sq mile
(626 people per sq km)

LARGEST COUNTRY:
Canada 3,855,171 sq miles
(9,984,670 sq km)

SMALLEST COUNTRY:
St Kitts & Nevis 101 sq miles
(261 sq km)

POLITICAL FACTFILE

TOTAL AREA:
9,400,000 sq miles
(24,346,000 sq km)

TOTAL NUMBER OF COUNTRIES:
23

TOTAL POPULATION:
492.8 million

LARGEST CITY WITH POPULATION:
New York City, US 21.7 million

South America

ATLANTIC

OCEAN

São Francisco

Represa de
Sobradinho

BRASÍLIA

B R A Z I L

Tocantins

PARAMARIBO

CAYENNE

Xingu

Araguaia

GEORGETOWN

French
Guiana
(France)

Amazon

SURINAME

GUYANA

Madeira

BOLIVIA

Guiana Highlands

CARACAS

Orinoco

Río Negro

B a s i n

SUCRE

Beni

LA PAZ

VENEZUELA

Meta

Guaviare

A m a z o n

Juruá

Purus

Madre de Dios

BOGOTÁ

Putumayo

Caquetá

Lake
Titicaca

Caribbean Sea

Magdalena

Cauca

Napo

P E R U

S. Titicaca

COLOMBIA

Marañón

A
n
d
e
s

LIMA

Isthmus of
Panama

Equator QUITO

ECUADOR

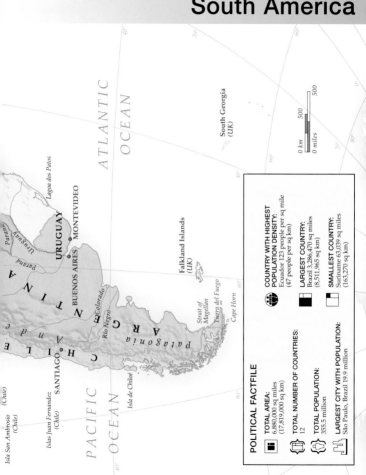

ATLANTIC

OCEAN

PACIFIC

OCEAN

Isla San Ambrosio *(Chile)*

Islas Juan Fernandez *(Chile)*

Isla de Chiloé

SANTIAGO

C H I L E

A n d e s

A R G E N T I N A

Patagonia

Rio Negro

Colorado

Tierra del Fuego

Strait of Magellan

Cape Horn

Falkland Islands *(UK)*

South Georgia *(UK)*

Paraná

Paraguay

Uruguay

Lagoa dos Patos

URUGUAY

MONTEVIDEO

BUENOS AIRES

0 km   500
0 miles   500

POLITICAL FACTFILE

TOTAL AREA:
6,880,000 sq miles
(17,819,000 sq km)

TOTAL NUMBER OF COUNTRIES:
12

TOTAL POPULATION:
355.5 million

LARGEST CITY WITH POPULATION:
São Paulo, Brazil 19.9 million

**COUNTRY WITH HIGHEST
POPULATION DENSITY:**
Ecuador 123 people per sq mile
(47 people per sq km)

LARGEST COUNTRY:
Brazil 3,286,470 sq miles
(8,511,965 sq km)

SMALLEST COUNTRY:
Suriname 63,039 sq miles
(163,270 sq km)

ATLANTIC
OCEAN

Black Sea

E U R O P E

Mediterranean Sea

The Gulf

A S I A

Syrian
Desert

Tropic of Cancer

Arabian Peninsula

Red Sea

ERITREA

ASMARA

DJIBOUTI

DJIBOUTI

ADDIS ABABA

ETHIOPIA

SOMALIA

Shebeli

Lake

CAIRO

Nile

EGYPT

KHARTOUM

Blue Nile

White Nile

S U D A N

CENTRAL AFRICAN
REPUBLIC

BANGUI

Libyan
Desert

L I B Y A

TRIPOLI

TUNIS

TUNISIA

ALGIERS

Atlas Mountains

Tibesti

NDJAMENA

CHAD

N I G E R

CAMEROON

NIGERIA

ABUJA

PORTO-NOVO

BENIN
TOGO

LOME

NIAMEY

OUAGADOUGOU

Niger

M A L I

BURKINA

GHANA

ALGERIA

MOROCCO

RABAT

Ceuta
(Spain)

Melilla
(Spain)

Madeira
(Portugal)

Islas Canarias
(Spain)

LAÂYOUNE

WESTERN
SAHARA
(disputed)

Tropic of Cancer

NOUAKCHOTT

MAURITANIA

Senegal

DAKAR

SENEGAL

BANJUL
GAMBIA

BISSAU

GUINEA-BISSAU

CONAKRY

GUINEA

FREETOWN

SIERRA LEONE

MONROVIA

LIBERIA

BAMAKO

Niger

YAMOUSSOUKRO

CÔTE
D'IVOIRE
(IVORY COAST)

ABIDJAN

S   a   h   a   r   a

Equator

COMOROS
MORONI
Mayotte
(France)

ANTANANARIVO

MADAGASCAR

Tropic of Capricorn

KENYA
NAIROBI

RWANDA
KIGALI
Lake Victoria
BUJUMBURA
BURUNDI
DODOMA

TANZANIA

Lake Tanganyika

DEM. REP.
CONGO

MALAWI
Lake Nyasa

LILONGWE

ZAMBIA

HARARE

LUSAKA

ZIMBABWE

Zambezi

MOZAMBIQUE

I N D I A N

O C E A N

BRAZZAVILLE

GABON

KINSHASA

Cabinda
(part of Angola)

ANGOLA

LUANDA

NAMIBIA

WINDHOEK

BOTSWANA

Kalahari
Desert

GABORONE

PRETORIA

MAPUTO

SWAZILAND
MBABANE

LESOTHO
MASERU

SOUTH
AFRICA

BLOEMFONTEIN

Orange River

CAPE TOWN
Cape of Good Hope

SÃO TOMÉ &
PRINCIPE

St Helena
(UK)

Ascension I.
(St Helena)

A T L A N T I C

O C E A N

Tropic of Capricorn

Equator

| 0 km | 1000 |
| 0 miles | 1000 |

POLITICAL FACTFILE

TOTAL AREA:
11,677,250 sq miles
(30,244,050 sq km)

TOTAL NUMBER OF COUNTRIES:
53

TOTAL POPULATION:
831.6 million

LARGEST CITY WITH POPULATION:
Cairo, Egypt 15.3 million

**COUNTRY WITH HIGHEST
POPULATION DENSITY:**
Mauritius 1671 people per sq mile
(645 people per sq km)

LARGEST COUNTRY:
Sudan 967,493 sq miles
(2,505,810 sq km)

SMALLEST COUNTRY:
Seychelles 176 sq miles
(455 sq km)

POLITICAL FACTFILE

 TOTAL AREA:
4,809,200 sq miles
(12,456,000 sq km)

 TOTAL NUMBER OF COUNTRIES:
43

 TOTAL POPULATION:
768.6 million

 LARGEST CITY WITH POPULATION:
Moscow, European Russia 13.2 million

**COUNTRY WITH HIGHEST
POPULATION DENSITY:**
Monaco 42,649 people per sq mile
(16,404 people per sq km)

LARGEST COUNTRY:
European Russia 1,527,341 sq miles
(3,955,818 sq km)

SMALLEST COUNTRY:
Vatican City, Italy 0.17 sq miles
(0.44 sq km)

REYKJAVÍK
ICELAND

Arctic Circle

*Norwegian
Sea*

Faeroe Islands
(Denmark)

Shetland Islands

*Outer
Hebrides*   *Orkney Islands*   OSLO

**British
Isles**   *North
Sea*

IRELAND   **DENMARK**

DUBLIN **UNITED
KINGDOM**   COPENHAGEN

LONDON   AMSTERDAM
NETH.   BERLIN
THE
Channel Is. BELGIUM HAGUE
(UK)   BRUSSELS   **GERMANY**
LUXEMBOURG   PRAGU
PARIS LUXEMBOURG
Loire   CZECH REPUBL
FRANCE *Rhine* LIECH. BRATISLA
Bay of Biscay   VIENNA
SWITZERLAND   **AUSTRIA**
Garonne   SLOVENI
LJUBLJANA
BERN   ZAGREB

ATLANTIC   MONACO   SAN MARINO
OCEAN   **PORTUGAL** *Duero*   **CROATIA**
ANDORRA   SARAJE
LISBON   MADRID   Corsica **BOSN.
Tagus   VATICAN CITY & HER**
SPAIN   ROME
Guadalquivir
Madeira
(Portugal)   **Gibraltar**
(UK)   *Balearic Islands*   Sardinia
Ceuta   *Me d i t e r r a*
(Spain) Melilla
Canary Islands   *(Spain)*
(Spain)   *A t l a s   M o u n t a i n s*   Sicily
A F R I C A   VALLETTA
MALTA

NORWAY

SW

Elbe

Ebro

NORWAY

DEN

FINLAND

Ural Mountains

Ob'

Irtysh

Northern Dvina

Lake Onega

Lake Ladoga

HELSINKI

STOCKHOLM

ESTONIA

TALLINN

R U S S I A N

F E D E R A T I O N

LATVIA

RĪGA

MOSCOW

Baltic Sea

LITHUANIA

VILNIUS

KALININGRAD

(Russ.Fed.)

MINSK

Volga

Ural

BELARUS

WARSAW

POLAND

Don

Aral Sea

KIEV

UKRAINE

SLOVAKIA

BUDAPEST

HUNGARY

MOLDOVA

Dnieper

CHIŞINĂU

ROMANIA

C a u c a s u s

Caspian Sea

BELGRADE

BUCHAREST

SERB.
& MON.
(YUGO)

Danube

Black Sea

A S I A

SOFIA

BULGARIA

SKOPJE

TURKEY

MACED.

TIRANA

ALBANIA

GREECE

ATHENS

Sea

Crete

Cyprus

0 km   1000

0 miles   1000

Asia

ARCTIC OCEAN

Franz Josef Land

Severnaya Zemlya

Kara Sea

Laptev Sea

EUROPE

RUSSIAN FEDERATIO

Ob

Irtysh

Yenisey

ASTANA

Lake Baikal

ANKARA
TURKEY
GEORGIA
TBILISI
KAZAKHSTAN
Aral Sea
Lake Balkhash
ULAN BATOR
MONGOLIA

Black Sea

Tropic of Cancer

NICOSIA
CYPRUS
ARMENIA
YEREVAN
AZERBAIJAN
BAKU
UZBEKISTAN
BISHKEK
KYRGYZSTAN

LEBANON
BEIRUT
SYRIA
DAMASCUS
TURKMENISTAN
ASHGABAT
TASHKENT

JERUSALEM
AMMAN
Tehrān
DUSHANBE
TAJIKISTAN

ISRAEL
JORDAN
BAGHDAD
IRAQ
IRAN
KABUL
ISLAMABAD
C H I N

KUWAIT
KŪWAIT
AFGHANISTAN

BAHRAIN
MANAMA
QATAR
PAKISTAN
NEW
DELHI
NEPAL
THIMPHU

RIYADH
DOHA
ABU DHABI
KATHMANDU
BHUTAN

SAUDI
ARABIA
U.A.E.
MUSCAT
Indus
Ganges
BANGLADESH
DHAKA

SANA
OMAN
I N D I A
MYANMAR
(BURMA)
VIETN.
HANOI
LAOS

YEMEN
Arabian
Sea
RANGOON
VIENTIANE
THAILAND

Socotra
(Yemen)
Bay of
Bengal
BANGKOK
CAMBODI

Laccadive
Islands
(India)
Andaman &
Nicobar Islands
(India)
PHN
PEN

Red Sea

Equator

MALE
COLOMBO
MAL

MALDIVES
SRI
LANKA
KUALA LUMPUR

SINGAPORE
I N

AFRICA

I N D I A N   O C E A N

JAKAR

Yang

East Siberian Sea

Aleutian Islands

Sea Of Okhotsk

Kurile Islands

NORTH KOREA
PYONGYANG
SEOUL
JAPAN
TOKYO
BEIJING
SOUTH KOREA

Ryukyu Islands

TAIPEI

TAIWAN

PACIFIC OCEAN

MANILA

PHILIPPINES

RUNEI
BANDAR SERI BEGAWAN

YSIA

D O N E S I A

DILI **EAST TIMOR**
Pante Maksar
(E.Timor)

A U S T R A L A S I A
& O C E A N I A

Tropic of Cancer

Equator

POLITICAL FACTFILE

TOTAL AREA:
16,838,365 sq miles
(43,608,000 sq km)

TOTAL NUMBER OF COUNTRIES:
49

TOTAL POPULATION:
3803.4 million

LARGEST CITY WITH POPULATION:
Tokyo, Japan 35.1 million

COUNTRY WITH HIGHEST POPULATION DENSITY:
Singapore 17,797 people per sq mile
(6885 people per sq km)

LARGEST COUNTRY:
Asiatic Russia 5,065,394 sq miles
(13,119,382 sq km)

SMALLEST COUNTRY:
Maldives 116 sq miles
(300 sq km)

0 km   1000
0 miles   1000

Australasia & Oceania

Philippine Sea

Wake Island
(to US)

Northern
Mariana
Islands
(US)

HAGÅTÑA
Guam
(US)

PALIKIR

MARSHALL
ISLANDS

MAJURO

Caroline Islands

KOROR
Babeldaob

MICRONESIA

BAIRIKI

PALAU

NAURU
NAURU

KIRIBATI

PAPUA NEW
GUINEA

TUVALU
FONGAFALE

A S I A

PORT MORESBY

SOLOMON
ISLANDS

HONIARA

VANUATU

Equator

PORT VILA

SUVA

Coral Sea
Islands
(Australia)

New Caledonia
(France)

FIJI

Ashmore &
Cartier Islands
(Australia)

NOUMÉA

INDIAN
OCEAN

AUSTRALIA

Norfolk Island
(Australia)

Tropic of Capricorn

Lake Eyre North

Lake Torrens
Lake Gairdner

Great Dividing Range

Darling

Lord Howe
Island
(Australia)

NEW
ZEALAND

Murray

CANBERRA

WELLINGTON

Tasman
Sea

Tasmania

Auckland Islands
(New Zealand)

Micronesia

Melanesia

Polynesia

POLITICAL FACTFILE

TOTAL AREA:
3,376,700 sq miles (8,745,750 sq km)

TOTAL NUMBER OF COUNTRIES:
14

TOTAL POPULATION:
30.6 million

LARGEST CITY WITH POPULATION:
Sydney, Australia 4.2 million

COUNTRY WITH HIGHEST POPULATION DENSITY:
Nauru 1522 people per sq mile
(587 people per sq km)

LARGEST COUNTRY:
Australia 2,967,893 sq miles
(7,686,860 sq km)

SMALLEST COUNTRY:
Nauru 8.1 sq miles (21 sq km)

Johnston Atoll
(US)

International Dateline

Baker & Howland
Islands
(US)

Jarvis Island
(US)

KIRIBATI

Phoenix Islands

KIRIBATI

Tokelau
(NZ)

Wallis &
Futuna
(Fr.) **SAMOA**
MATA'UTU o o APIA
American
Samoa
(US)

Cook Islands
(NZ)

o PAGO PAGO

TONGA

Niue
(NZ)

Marquesas Islands

PACIFIC

OCEAN

Equator

PAPEETE

Society Islands

NUKU'ALOFA

AVARUA o

French Polynesia
(France)

Iles Australes

Kermadec Islands
(New Zealand)

Pitcairn
Islands
(UK)

Tropic of Capricorn

International Dateline

Chatham Islands
(New Zealand)

| 0 km | 1000 |
| 0 miles | 1000 |

Key to factfile maps

FOREWORD

THIS FACTFILE is intended as a guide to a world that is continually changing as political fashions and personalities come and go. Nevertheless, all the material in these factfiles has been researched from the most up-to-date and authoritative sources to give an incisive portrait of the geographical, social, and economic characteristics that make each country unique.

KEY TO MAP SYMBOLS

ELEVATION

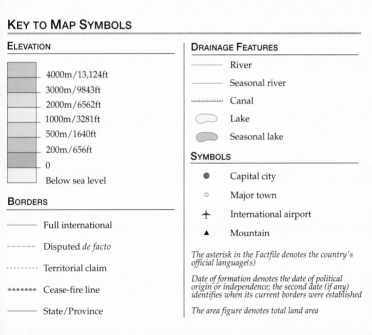

4000m/13,124ft
3000m/9843ft
2000m/6562ft
1000m/3281ft
500m/1640ft
200m/656ft
0
Below sea level

BORDERS

——— Full international

– – – – – Disputed *de facto*

·········· Territorial claim

✳✳✳✳✳✳✳ Cease-fire line

——— State/Province

DRAINAGE FEATURES

——— River

——— Seasonal river

⸽⸽⸽⸽⸽⸽⸽⸽ Canal

Lake

Seasonal lake

SYMBOLS

● Capital city

○ Major town

✈ International airport

▲ Mountain

The asterisk in the Factfile denotes the country's official language(s)

Date of formation denotes the date of political origin or independence; the second date (if any) identifies when its current borders were established

The area figure denotes total land area

Afghanistan

Landlocked in southwestern Asia, about 75% of Afghanistan is inaccessible. The strict Islamist regime imposed by the *taliban* was swept aside with the help of the US in 2001.

GEOGRAPHY

Predominantly mountainous. Highest range is the Hindu Kush. Mountains are bordered by fertile plains. Desert plateau in the south.

CLIMATE

Harsh continental. Hot, dry summers. Cold winters with heavy snow, especially in the Hindu Kush.

PEOPLE & SOCIETY

Mujahideen factions fought first against Soviet invaders (from 1979), and then against each other (after 1989), before the *taliban* won control in 1996. Under their strict Islamist regime women were denied all rights and ethnic tensions were exacerbated. The US assisted anti-*taliban* forces in 2001 as part of its "war on terrorism." A new democratic government struggles to maintain control over the war-ravaged country.

THE ECONOMY

Economy has collapsed: infrastructure destroyed. Illicit opium trade is the main earner. Hopes from oil pipelines crossing Afghan territory.

◆ **INSIGHT:** *The UN estimates that it could take 100 years to remove the ten million landmines laid in the country*

FACTFILE

OFFICIAL NAME: Islamic State of Afghanistan
DATE OF FORMATION: 1919
CAPITAL: Kabul
POPULATION: 23.3 million
TOTAL AREA: 250,000 sq. miles (647,500 sq. km)

DENSITY: 93 people per sq. mile
LANGUAGES: Pashtu*, Dari*, Tajik, other
RELIGIONS: Sunni Muslim 84%, Shi'a Muslim 15%, other 1%
ETHNIC MIX: Pashtun 38%, Tajik 25%, Hazara 19%, Uzbek, Turkmen, other 18%
GOVERNMENT: Transitional regime
CURRENCY: New afghani = 100 puls

Albania

Lying at the southeastern end of the Adriatic Sea, Albania was the last east European country to liberalize its economy. The regional wars of the 1990s have left a difficult legacy.

GEOGRAPHY

Narrow coastal plain. Interior is mostly hills and mountains. Forest and scrub cover over 40% of the land.

CLIMATE

Mediterranean coastal climate, with warm summers and cool winters. Mountains receive heavy rains or snows in winter.

PEOPLE & SOCIETY

The pace of economic reform remains a major issue, particularly since the chaos of the "pyramid" scheme collapse in 1997. Mosques and churches have reopened in what was once the world's only officially atheist state. Greek minority in the south suffers much discrimination.

◆ **INSIGHT:** *The Albanians' name for their country, Shqipërisë, means "Land of the Eagles"*

THE ECONOMY

Oil and gas reserves plus high growth rate have potential to offset rudimentary infrastructure and lack of foreign investment.

SERBIA & MONTENEGRO (YUGOSLAVIA)

Lake Scutari

Shkodër

Kukës

42°

Adriatic Sea

MACEDONIA

Durrës

✦ TIRANA

Elbasan

Lake Ohrid

41°

Lushnjë

Fier ○ Berat

Lake Prespa

Vlorë ○

Korçë ○

40°

Delvinë

Ionian Sea

GREECE

20°

▮	2000m/6562ft
▮	1000m/3281ft
▮	500m/1640ft
▮	200m/656ft
	Sea Level

0   50 km

0   50 miles

FACTFILE

OFFICIAL NAME: Republic of Albania
DATE OF FORMATION: 1912
CAPITAL: Tirana
POPULATION: 3.2 million
TOTAL AREA: 11,100 sq. miles (28,748 sq. km)
DENSITY: 302 people per sq. mile

LANGUAGES: Albanian*, Greek
RELIGIONS: Sunni Muslim 70%, Orthodox Christian 20%, Roman Catholic 10%
ETHNIC MIX: Albanian 93%, Greek 5%, other 2%
GOVERNMENT: Parliamentary system
CURRENCY: Lek = 100 qindarka (qintars)

Algeria

Africa's second-largest country, Algeria achieved independence from France in 1962. Today, its military-dominated government faces a severe challenge from Islamic extremists.

GEOGRAPHY

85% of the country lies within the Sahara Desert. Fertile coastal region with plains and hills rises from the southeast to the Atlas Mountains.

CLIMATE

Coastal areas are warm and temperate, with most rainfall during the mild winters. The south is very hot, with negligible rainfall.

PEOPLE & SOCIETY

Algerians are predominantly Arab, under 30 years of age, and urban. Most indigenous Berbers consider the mountainous Kabylia region in the northeast to be their homeland. The Sahara sustains just 500,000 people, mainly oil workers and Tuareg nomads with goat and camel herds, who move between the irrigated oases. In recent years, political violence has claimed the lives of 1500 people annually.

THE ECONOMY

Oil and gas exports. Political turmoil has led to exodus of skilled foreign labor. Limited agriculture.

◆ **INSIGHT**: The world's highest dunes are located in the deserts of east central Algeria

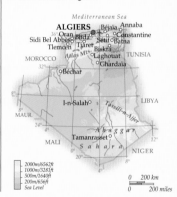

FACTFILE

OFFICIAL NAME: People's Democratic Republic of Algeria
DATE OF FORMATION: 1962
CAPITAL: Algiers
POPULATION: 31.4 million
TOTAL AREA: 919,590 sq. miles (2,381,740 sq. km)

DENSITY: 34 people per sq. mile
LANGUAGES: Arabic*, Tamazight, French
RELIGIONS: Sunni Muslim 99%, Christian and Jewish 1%
ETHNIC MIX: Arab 75%, Berber 24%, European and Jewish 1%
GOVERNMENT: Presidential system
CURRENCY: Algerian dinar = 100 centimes

Andorra

A tiny landlocked principality, Andorra lies high in the eastern Pyrenees between France and Spain. It held its first full elections in 1993. Tourism is the main source of income.

GEOGRAPHY

High mountains, with six deep, glaciated valleys that drain into the Valira River as it flows into Spain.

CLIMATE

Cool, wet springs followed by dry, warm summers. Mountain snows linger until March.

PEOPLE & SOCIETY

Immigration is strictly monitored and restricted by quota to French and Spanish nationals seeking employment in Andorra. A referendum in 1993 ended 715 years of semifeudal status, but Andorran society remains conservative. Divorce is illegal.

INSIGHT: *Andorra's coprincipality status dates from the 13th century. The "princes" are the president of France and the bishop of Urgel in Spain.*

THE ECONOMY

Tourism and duty-free sales dominate the economy. Strict banking secrecy laws and low consumer taxes promote investment and commerce. France and Spain effectively decide economic policy. Dependence on imported food and raw materials.

FACTFILE

OFFICIAL NAME: Principality of Andorra
DATE OF FORMATION: 1278
CAPITAL: Andorra la Vella
POPULATION: 68,243
TOTAL AREA: 181 sq. miles (468 sq. km)
DENSITY: 379 people per sq. mile

LANGUAGES: Spanish, Catalan*, French, Portuguese
RELIGIONS: Roman Catholic 94%, other 6%
ETHNIC MIX: Spanish 46%, Andorran 28%, other 18%, French 8%
GOVERNMENT: Parliamentary system
CURRENCY: Euro = 100 cents

Angola

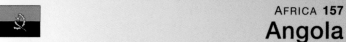

Located in southwest Africa, Angola suffered almost constant civil war following independence from Portugal in 1975. Hopes of a lasting end to war followed the latest peace deal in 2002.

GEOGRAPHY
Most of the land is hilly and grass-covered. Desert in the south. Mountains in the center and north.

CLIMATE
Varies from temperate to tropical. Rainfall decreases north to south. Coast is cooler and dry.

PEOPLE & SOCIETY
Civil war was fought between UNITA, representing the Ovimbundu, and the ruling Kimbundu-dominated MPLA. Free and fair elections in 1991–1992, after the MPLA had abandoned Marxism, failed to stall the war for long. Hundreds of thousands of people died. A peace deal in 2002 saw UNITA join the government.

◆ **INSIGHT:** *Angola has the greatest number of amputees (caused by landmines) in the world*

THE ECONOMY
Potentially one of Africa's richest countries, but civil war has hampered economic development. Oil and diamonds are exported.

2000m/6562ft
1000m/3281ft
500m/1640ft
200m/656ft
Sea Level

0   200 km
0   200 miles

FACTFILE

OFFICIAL NAME: Republic of Angola
DATE OF FORMATION: 1975
CAPITAL: Luanda
POPULATION: 13.9 million
TOTAL AREA: 481,351 sq. miles
(1,246,700 sq. km)
DENSITY: 29 people per sq. mile

LANGUAGES: Portuguese*, Umbundu, Kimbundu, Kikongo
RELIGIONS: Roman Catholic 50%, other 30%, Protestant 20%
ETHNIC MIX: Ovimbundu 37%, other 25%, Kimbundu 25%, Bakongo 13%
GOVERNMENT: Presidential system
CURRENCY: Readjusted kwanza = 100 lwei

Antarctica

The circumpolar continent of Antarctica is almost entirely covered by ice, some up to 1.2 miles (2 km) thick. It also contains 90% of the Earth's freshwater reserves.

GEOGRAPHY

The bulk of Antarctica's ice is contained in the Greater Antarctic Ice Sheet – a huge dome that rises steeply from the coast and flattens to a plateau in the interior.

CLIMATE

Powerful winds create a storm belt around the continent, which brings cloud, fog, and blizzards. Winter temperatures can fall to –112°F (–80°C).

PEOPLE & SOCIETY

No indigenous population. Scientists and logistical staff work at the 40 permanent, and as many as 100 temporary, research stations. A few Chilean settler families live on King George Island. Tourism is mostly by cruise ship to the Antarctic Peninsula. Annual tourist numbers had reached 17,000 by 2002.

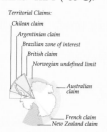

Territorial Claims:
Chilean claim
Argentinian claim
Brazilian zone of interest
British claim
Norwegian undefined limit
Australian claim
French claim
New Zealand claim

The Antarctic Treaty of 1959 holds all territorial claims in abeyance in the interest of international cooperation

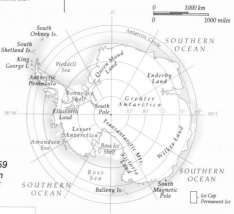

FACTFILE

DATE OF FORMATION: 1961
TOTAL AREA: 5,405,000 sq. miles (14,000,000 sq. km)

◆ **INSIGHT:** *If the ice sheets of Antarctica were to melt, the world's oceans would rise by as much as 200–210 ft (60–65 m)*

Antigua & Barbuda

A former colony of Spain, France, and the UK, Antigua and Barbuda lies at the outer edge of the Leeward Islands group in the Caribbean, and includes the uninhabited islet of Redonda.

GEOGRAPHY

Mainly low-lying limestone and coral islands with some higher volcanic areas. Antigua's coast is indented with bays and harbors.

CLIMATE

Tropical, moderated by trade winds and sea breezes. Humidity and rainfall are low for the region.

PEOPLE & SOCIETY

Population almost entirely of African origin, with small communities of Europeans and South Asians. Women's status has risen as a result of greater access to education. Wealth disparities are small and unemployment is low. Politics has been dominated for the past 40 years by the Bird family.

◆ **INSIGHT:** *In 1865, Redonda was "claimed" by an eccentric Englishman as a kingdom for his son*

THE ECONOMY

Tourism is the main source of revenue and the biggest provider of jobs. Fishing and sea-island cotton industries are expanding. High debt.

FACTFILE

OFFICIAL NAME: Antigua and Barbuda
DATE OF FORMATION: 1981
CAPITAL: St. John's
POPULATION: 67,448
TOTAL AREA: 170 sq. miles (442 sq. km)
DENSITY: 397 people per sq. mile

LANGUAGES: English*, English patois
RELIGIONS: Anglican 45%, other Protestant 42%, Roman Catholic 10%, other 2%, Rastafarian 1%
ETHNIC MIX: Black African 95%, other 5%
GOVERNMENT: Parliamentary system
CURRENCY: E. Caribbean $ = 100 cents

Argentina

Argentina occupies most of the southern portion of South America. After 30 years of intermittent military rule, multiparty democracy returned in 1983. The economy collapsed in 2001.

GEOGRAPHY

The Andes form a natural border with Chile in the west. East are the heavily wooded plains (Gran Chaco) and treeless but fertile Pampas plains. Bleak and arid Patagonia in the south.

CLIMATE

The Andes are semiarid in the north and snowy in the south. Pampas have a mild climate with summer rains.

PEOPLE & SOCIETY

People are largely of European descent; over one-third are of Italian origin. Indigenous peoples are now in a minority, living mainly in Andean regions or in the Gran Chaco. The middle classes were worst hit by the economic collapse of 2001–2002.

◆ **INSIGHT:** *The Tango originated in the poorer quarters of Buenos Aires at the end of the 19th century*

THE ECONOMY

Dependence on regional markets, principally Brazil, and poor investor confidence led to collapse in 2001–2002.

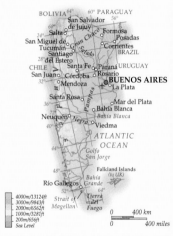

FACTFILE

OFFICIAL NAME: Republic of Argentina
DATE OF FORMATION: 1816
CAPITAL: Buenos Aires
POPULATION: 37.9 million
TOTAL AREA: 1,068,296 sq. miles
(2,766,890 sq. km)
DENSITY: 36 people per sq. mile

LANGUAGES: Spanish*, Italian, Amerindian languages
RELIGIONS: Roman Catholic 90%, other 6%, Protestant 2%, Jewish 2%
ETHNIC MIX: Indo-European 83%, Mestizo 14%, Jewish 2%, Amerindian 1%
GOVERNMENT: Presidential system
CURRENCY: Argentine peso = 100 centavos

Armenia

The smallest of the former USSR's republics, Armenia lies landlocked in the Lesser Caucasus Mountains. Since 1988, the confrontation with Azerbaijan has dominated national life.

GEOGRAPHY
Rugged and mountainous, with expanses of semidesert and a large lake in the east: Sevana Lich.

CLIMATE
Continental climate, with little rainfall in the lowlands. The winters are often bitterly cold.

PEOPLE & SOCIETY
Christianity is the dominant religion, but minority groups are well integrated. War with Azerbaijan over the enclave of Nagorno Karabakh forced 350,000 Armenians living in Azerbaijan to return home, many to live in poverty. There are close and important ties to the seven-million-strong Armenian diaspora.

◆ **INSIGHT:** *In the 4th century, Armenia became the first country to adopt Christianity as its state religion*

THE ECONOMY
Few natural resources. Agriculture accounts for over 20% of GDP. Main products are wine, tobacco, olives, and rice. Well-developed machine-building and manufacturing – includes textiles and bottling of mineral water.

FACTFILE
OFFICIAL NAME: Republic of Armenia
DATE OF FORMATION: 1991
CAPITAL: Yerevan
POPULATION: 3.8 million
TOTAL AREA: 11,506 sq. miles (29,800 sq. km)
DENSITY: 330 people per sq. mile

LANGUAGES: Armenian*, Azeri, Russian
RELIGIONS: Armenian Apostolic Church (Orthodox) 94%, other 6%
ETHNIC MIX: Armenian 93%, Azeri 3%, other 2%, Russian 2%
GOVERNMENT: Presidential system
CURRENCY: Dram = 100 luma

Australia

An island continent in its own right, Australia is the world's sixth-largest country. European settlement began over 200 years ago. Most Australians now live in cities along the coast.

GEOGRAPHY

Located between the Indian and Pacific Oceans, Australia has a variety of landscapes including tropical rainforests, the arid plateaus, ridges, and vast deserts of the "red center," the lowlands and river systems draining into Lake Eyre, rolling tracts of pastoral land, and magnificent beaches around much of the coastline. In the far east are the mountains of the Great Dividing Range. Famous natural features include Uluru (Ayers Rock) and the Great Barrier Reef.

CLIMATE

The west and south are semi-arid with hot summers. The arid interior can reach 120°F (50°C) in the central desert areas . The north is hot throughout the year, and humid during the summer monsoon. East, southeast, and southwest coastal areas are temperate.

PEOPLE & SOCIETY

The first settlers arrived in Australia at least 100,000 years ago. Today, the Aborigines make up less than 3% of the population. European colonization began in 1788, and was dominated by British and Irish immigrants, some of whom were convicts. White-only immigration drives brought many Europeans to Australia, but since the 1960s multi-culturalism has been encouraged and most new settlers are Asian; Cantonese is now the third most widely spoken language after English and Italian. Wealth disparities are small, but Aborigines, the exception in an otherwise integrated society, are marginalized: their average life expectancy is fully 20 years less than other Australians. Politics is increasingly right-wing and illegal immigration is a major concern. Obesity is a growing problem among adults.

FACTFILE

OFFICIAL NAME: Commonwealth of Australia
DATE OF FORMATION: 1901
CAPITAL: Canberra
POPULATION: 20 million
TOTAL AREA: 2,967,893 sq. miles (7,686,850 sq. km)

DENSITY: 7 people per sq. mile
LANGUAGES: English*, Italian, other
RELIGIONS: Various Protestant 38%, other 36%, Roman Catholic 26%
ETHNIC MIX: European 92%, Asian 5%, Aboriginal and other 3%
GOVERNMENT: Parliamentary system
CURRENCY: Australian dollar = 100 cents

THE ECONOMY

Efficient mining and agricultural industries: particular success in viticulture. Large resource base. Tourism growing. Concentration on Asian markets; hit hard by the 1997 financial crisis which tipped the region into recession. Japan remains the most important trading partner. Competition from Asian economies is intense. Protectionism abandoned to open up Australian markets. Shows strong economic growth but unemployment has been an issue.

◆ **INSIGHT:** *Sydney has the world's largest suburban area, a conurbation so vast that the city is twice as large as Beijing and six times the size of Rome*

Austria

Bordering eight countries in the heart of Europe, Austria was created in 1918 after the collapse of the Habsburg Empire. It joined the EU in 1995 and adopted the euro fully in 2002.

GEOGRAPHY

Mainly mountainous. Alps and foothills cover the west and south. Lowlands in the east are part of the Danube River basin.

CLIMATE

Temperate continental climate. The western Alpine regions have colder winters and more rainfall.

PEOPLE & SOCIETY

Austrian society is homogeneous. Though Austrians speak German, they like to stress their distinctive identity in relation to Germany. Minorities are few; there are some ethnic Croats, Slovenes, and Hungarians, plus refugees from conflict in former Yugoslavia. Though strongly Roman Catholic, Austrian society is less conservative than some southern German *Länder*. Class divisions remain strong.

THE ECONOMY

Large manufacturing base, despite lack of energy resources. The skilled labor force is key to the production of high-tech exports. Euro has boosted investment.

INSIGHT: *Many of the world's great composers were Austrian, including Mozart, Haydn, Schubert, and Strauss*

FACTFILE

OFFICIAL NAME: Republic of Austria
DATE OF FORMATION: 1918
CAPITAL: Vienna
POPULATION: 8.1 million
TOTAL AREA: 32,378 sq. miles (83,858 sq. km)
DENSITY: 254 people per sq. mile

LANGUAGES: German*, Croatian, Slovenian, Hungarian
RELIGIONS: Roman Catholic 78%, nonreligious 9%, other 8%, Protestant 5%
ETHNIC MIX: German 93%, Croat, Slovene, and Hungarian 6%, other 1%
GOVERNMENT: Parliamentary system
CURRENCY: Euro = 100 cents

Azerbaijan

Situated on the western coast of the Caspian Sea, Azerbaijan was the first Soviet republic to declare independence in 1991. Territorial disputes with Armenia have dominated politics since.

GEOGRAPHY
Caucasus Mountains in west, including Naxçivan exclave south of Armenia. Flat, low-lying terrain on the coast of the Caspian Sea.

CLIMATE
Low rainfall. Continental, with bitter winters, inland. Subtropical in coastal regions.

PEOPLE & SOCIETY
Azeris, a Muslim people with ethnic links to Turks, form a large majority. Thousands of Armenians, Russians, and Jews have left since independence. Influx of half a million Azeri refugees fleeing war with Armenia over the disputed enclave of Nagorno Karabakh. Armenians there operate de facto independence. The status of women deteriorated after the fall of communism but they are slowly regaining their position.

THE ECONOMY
Extensive oil and gas reserves have come on stream. Legacy of war still drains state resources. Industry antiquated; infrastructure poor.

INSIGHT: *The fire-worshipping Zoroastrian faith originated in Azerbaijan in the 6th century BCE*

FACTFILE

OFFICIAL NAME: Republic of Azerbaijan
DATE OF FORMATION: 1991
CAPITAL: Baku
POPULATION: 8.1 million
TOTAL AREA: 33,436 sq. miles (86,600 sq. km)
DENSITY: 242 people per sq. mile

LANGUAGES: Azeri*, Russian
RELIGIONS: Shi'a Muslim 68%, Sunni Muslim 26%, Russian Orthodox 3%, Armenian Orthodox 2%, other 1%
ETHNIC MIX: Azeri 90%, Dagestani 3%, Russian 3%, other 2%, Armenian 2%
GOVERNMENT: Presidential system
CURRENCY: Manat = 100 gopik

Bahamas

Located off the Florida coast in the western Atlantic, the Bahamas comprises an archipelago of some 700 islands and 2400 cays, only 30 of which are inhabited.

GEOGRAPHY
Long, mainly flat coral formations with a few low hills. Some islands have pine forests, lagoons, and mangrove swamps.

CLIMATE
Subtropical. Hot summers and mild winters. Heavy rainfall, especially in summer. Hurricanes can strike in July–December.

PEOPLE & SOCIETY
About 60% of the population live on New Providence. Tourism employs over 40% of the labor force. The remainder are engaged in traditional fishing and agriculture, or in administration. Haitian and Cuban immigrants form the poorest group in society. More women are now entering the professions. Government priorities are tackling narcotics trafficking and money laundering.

THE ECONOMY
Major tourist destination, especially for US visitors. Financial services: banking and insurance.

◆ **INSIGHT:** *Only a tiny fraction of the country's extensive merchant fleet is owned by Bahamians*

FACTFILE
OFFICIAL NAME: Commonwealth of the Bahamas
DATE OF FORMATION: 1973
CAPITAL: Nassau
POPULATION: 312,000
TOTAL AREA: 5382 sq. miles (13,940 sq. km)

DENSITY: 81 people per sq. mile
LANGUAGES: English*, English Creole, French Creole
RELIGIONS: Baptist 32%, other 29%, Anglican 20%, Roman Catholic 19%
ETHNIC MIX: Black African 85%, other 15%
GOVERNMENT: Parliamentary system
CURRENCY: Bahamian dollar = 100 cents

Bahrain

Bahrain is an archipelago of 49 islands between the Qatar peninsula and the Saudi Arabian mainland. Only three of the islands are inhabited. It was the first Gulf emirate to export oil.

GEOGRAPHY

All islands are low-lying. The largest, Bahrain Island, is mainly sandy plains and salt marshes.

CLIMATE

Summers are hot and humid. Winters are mild. Low rainfall.

PEOPLE & SOCIETY

The key social division is between the Shi'a majority and Sunni minority. Sunnis hold the best jobs in bureaucracy and business while Shi'as tend to do menial work. The al-Khalifa family has ruled since 1783, and only transformed Bahrain into a constitutional monarchy, with limited democracy, in 2002. Bahrain is socially liberal.

◆ **INSIGHT:** *The 16 Hawar Islands were awarded to Bahrain in 2001 after a lengthy dispute with Qatar*

THE ECONOMY

Main exports are refined petroleum and aluminum products. As oil reserves run out, gas is of increasing importance. Regional offshore banking center. Government debts are high.

FACTFILE

OFFICIAL NAME: Kingdom of Bahrain
DATE OF FORMATION: 1971
CAPITAL: Manama
POPULATION: 663,000
TOTAL AREA: 239 sq. miles (620 sq. km)
DENSITY: 2429 people per sq. mile

LANGUAGES: Arabic
RELIGIONS: Muslim (mainly Shi'a) 99%, other 1%
ETHNIC MIX: Bahraini 70%, Iranian, Indian, and Pakistani 24%, other Arab 4%, European 2%
GOVERNMENT: Monarchy
CURRENCY: Bahraini dinar = 1000 fils

Bangladesh

Bangladesh lies at the north end of the Bay of Bengal. It seceded from Pakistan in 1971 and, after much political instability, returned to democracy in 1991.

GEOGRAPHY
Mostly flat alluvial plains and deltas of the Brahmaputra and Ganges Rivers. Southeast coasts are fringed with mangrove forests.

CLIMATE
Hot and humid. During the monsoon, water levels can rise 20 ft (6 m) above sea level.

PEOPLE & SOCIETY
Bangladesh often suffers devastating floods, cyclones, and famine. Democracy was restored in 1991 after a period of military rule. Over half of the population lives in poverty, but living standards are improving. Women are prominent in politics, but their rights are neglected.

◆ INSIGHT: *Torrential monsoon rains flood two-thirds of the country every year*

THE ECONOMY
Agriculture is vulnerable to unpredictable climate. Bangladesh accounts for 80% of world jute fiber exports. Poor infrastructure deters investment. Growing textile industry.

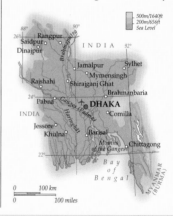

FACTFILE
OFFICIAL NAME: People's Republic of Bangladesh
DATE OF FORMATION: 1971
CAPITAL: Dhaka
POPULATION: 143 million
TOTAL AREA: 55,598 sq. miles (144,000 sq. km)

DENSITY: 2774 people per sq. mile
LANGUAGES: Bengali*, Urdu, Chakma, Marma, Garo, Khasi, Santhali, Tripuri, Mro
RELIGIONS: Muslim (mainly Sunni) 87%, Hindu 12%, other 1%
ETHNIC MIX: Bengali 98%, other 2%
GOVERNMENT: Parliamentary system
CURRENCY: Taka = 100 poisha

Barbados

Barbados is the most easterly of the Caribbean islands. Once solely inhabited by the native Arawak, Barbados was first colonized by British settlers in the 1620s.

GEOGRAPHY

Encircled by coral reefs. Fertile and predominantly flat, with a few gentle hills to the north.

CLIMATE

Moderate tropical climate. Sunnier and drier than its more mountainous neighbors.

PEOPLE & SOCIETY

Some latent tension between white community, which controls politics and much of the economy, and majority black population, but violence is rare. Increasing social mobility has enabled black Barbadians to enter the professions. Despite political stability, and good welfare and education services, pockets of abject poverty remain.

◆ **INSIGHT:** *Barbados retains a strong British influence and is referred to by its neighbors as "Little England"*

THE ECONOMY

Well-developed tourist industry based on climate and accessibility. Financial services and information processing are important new growth sectors. Sugar industry, once the main cash crop, now ailing.

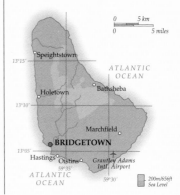

FACTFILE

OFFICIAL NAME: Barbados
DATE OF FORMATION: 1966
CAPITAL: Bridgetown
POPULATION: 269,000
TOTAL AREA: 166 sq. miles (430 sq. km)
DENSITY: 1620 people per sq. mile

LANGUAGES: Bajan (Barbadian English), English*
RELIGIONS: Anglican 40%, other 24%, nonreligious 17%, Pentecostal 8%, Methodist 7%, Roman Catholic 4%
ETHNIC MIX: Black African 90%, other 10%
GOVERNMENT: Parliamentary system
CURRENCY: Barbados dollar = 100 cents

Belarus

Literally "White Russia," Belarus lies landlocked in eastern Europe. It reluctantly became independent of the USSR in 1991. There are few resources other than agriculture.

GEOGRAPHY
Mainly plains and low hills. The Dnieper and Dvina Rivers drain the eastern lowlands. Vast Pripet Marshes in the southwest.

CLIMATE
Extreme continental climate. Winters are long, sub-freezing, but mainly dry; summers are hot.

PEOPLE & SOCIETY
Only 2% of people are non-Slav, so ethnic tension is minimal. Russian culture dominates; only 11% of the population is fluent in Belarussian. The government is keen to merge the country with Russia. Belarus was the slowest of the ex-Soviet states to implement political reform. Wealth is held by a small ex-communist elite. Fallout from 1986 Chernobyl nuclear disaster in Ukraine still seriously affects health and the environment.

THE ECONOMY
Low unemployment but high inflation. Outmoded industry; dependence on Russia for energy and raw materials. Privatization stalled.

◆ **INSIGHT:** *The number of cancer and leukemia cases has soared since the 1986 Chernobyl disaster*

FACTFILE

OFFICIAL NAME: Republic of Belarus
DATE OF FORMATION: 1991
CAPITAL: Minsk
POPULATION: 10.1 million
TOTAL AREA: 80,154 sq. miles (207,600 sq. km)
DENSITY: 126 people per sq. mile

LANGUAGES: Belarussian*, Russian*
RELIGIONS: Russian Orthodox 60%, other (including Muslim, Jewish, and Protestant) 32%, Roman Catholic 8%
ETHNIC MIX: Belarussian 78%, Russian 13%, Polish 4%, Ukrainian 3%, other 2%
GOVERNMENT: Presidential system
CURRENCY: Belarussian rouble = 100 kopeks

Belgium

Belgium lies in northwestern Europe. Its history has been marked by tensions between the majority Flemish and minority French-speaking communities.

GEOGRAPHY
Low-lying coastal plain covers two-thirds of the country. Land becomes hilly and forested in the southeast (Ardennes) region.

CLIMATE
Maritime climate with Gulf Stream influences. Temperatures are mild, with heavy cloud cover and rain. More rainfall and weather fluctuations at the coast.

PEOPLE & SOCIETY
Since 1970, Flemish-speaking regions have become more prosperous than those of the minority French-speakers (Walloons), overturning traditional roles and increasing friction. In order to contain tensions, Belgium began to move toward federalism in 1980. Both groups now have their own governments and control most of their own affairs.

THE ECONOMY
Variety of industrial exports, including steel, glassware, cut diamonds, and textiles. Very high levels of public debt. Bureaucracy larger than European average.

◆ INSIGHT: *The Ardennes region, in the southeast of the country, is famous for its forests, cuisine, and lakes*

FACTFILE

OFFICIAL NAME: Kingdom of Belgium
DATE OF FORMATION: 1830
CAPITAL: Brussels
POPULATION: 10.3 million
TOTAL AREA: 11,780 sq. miles (30,510 sq. km)
DENSITY: 813 people per sq. mile

LANGUAGES: Dutch*, French*, German*
RELIGIONS: Roman Catholic 88%, other 10%, Muslim 2%
ETHNIC MIX: Fleming 58%, Walloon 33%, other 6%, Italian 2%, Moroccan 1%
GOVERNMENT: Parliamentary system
CURRENCY: Euro = 100 cents

Belize

Belize lies on the eastern shore of the Yucatan Peninsula. Formerly called British Honduras, Belize was the last Central American country to gain its independence, in 1981.

GEOGRAPHY
Almost half the land area is forested. Low mountains in southeast. Flat swampy coastal plains.

CLIMATE
Tropical. Very hot and humid, with May–December rainy season.

PEOPLE & SOCIETY
English-speaking black Creoles are outnumbered by Spanish speakers, including native *mestizos* and immigrants from neighboring states. The Creoles have traditionally dominated society, but high levels of emigration to the US have weakened their influence. Newcomers provide manpower for agriculture. The Afro-Carib *garifuna* have their own language.

 INSIGHT: *Belize's barrier reef is the second-largest in the world*

THE ECONOMY
Agriculture and offshore banking are economic mainstays. Sugar, lobsters, shrimp, and textiles are exported. Hurricane damage is a recurring, and very serious, problem.

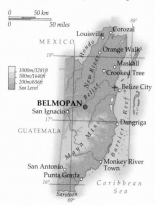

FACTFILE

OFFICIAL NAME: Belize
DATE OF FORMATION: 1981
CAPITAL: Belmopan
POPULATION: 236,000
TOTAL AREA: 8867 sq. miles (22,966 sq. km)
DENSITY: 27 people per sq. mile

LANGUAGES: English Creole, Spanish, English*, Mayan, Garifuna (Carib)
RELIGIONS: Roman Catholic 62%, other 20%, Anglican 12%, Methodist 6%
ETHNIC MIX: Mestizo 44%, Creole 30%, Maya 11%, Garifuna 7%, other 8%
GOVERNMENT: Parliamentary system
CURRENCY: Belizean dollar = 100 cents

Benin

Benin stretches north from the west African coast. In 1990, it became one of the pioneers of African democratization, ending 17 years of one-party Marxist-Leninist rule.

GEOGRAPHY
Sandy coastal region. Numerous lagoons lie just behind the shoreline. Forested plateaus inland. Mountains in the northwest.

CLIMATE
Hot and humid in the south. Two rainy seasons. Hot, dusty *harmattan* winds blow during the December–February dry season.

PEOPLE & SOCIETY
There are 42 different ethnic groups. The southern Fon have tended to dominate politics. Other major groups are the Adja and Yoruba. The northern Fulani follow a nomadic lifestyle. North–south tension is mainly due to the south being more developed. Voodoo is thought to have originated in Benin. Substantial differences in wealth reflect a strongly hierarchical society.

THE ECONOMY
Strong agricultural sector: cash crops include cotton, cocoa beans, and coffee. Large-scale smuggling is a serious problem. France is the main aid donor.

◆ INSIGHT:
Benin trains many doctors, but more of them work in France than in Benin

500m/1640ft
200m/656ft
Sea Level

0   100 km
0   100 miles

ATLANTIC OCEAN

📖 FACTFILE

OFFICIAL NAME: Republic of Benin
DATE OF FORMATION: 1960
CAPITAL: Porto-Novo
POPULATION: 6.6 million
TOTAL AREA: 43,483 sq. miles (112,620 sq. km)
DENSITY: 155 people per sq. mile

LANGUAGES: Fon, Bariba, Yoruba, Adja, Houeda, Somba, French*
RELIGIONS: Voodoo 50%, Muslim 30%, Christian 20%
ETHNIC MIX: Fon 47%, other 31%, Adja 12%, Bariba 10%
GOVERNMENT: Presidential system
CURRENCY: CFA franc = 100 centimes

Bhutan

Perched in the eastern Himalayas between India and China lies the landlocked Kingdom of Bhutan. It is largely closed to the outside world, to protect its culture and environment.

GEOGRAPHY
Low, tropical southern strip rising through fertile central valleys to high Himalayas in the north. Around 70% of the land is forested.

CLIMATE
South is tropical, north is alpine, cold, and harsh. Central valleys warmer in east than west.

PEOPLE & SOCIETY
The king was absolute monarch, until he devolved many powers in 1998. Most people originate from Tibet, and are devoutly Buddhist. A quarter are Hindu Nepalese, who settled in the south. Bhutan has 20 languages. In 1988, Dzongkha (a Tibetan dialect native to just 16% of the people) was made the official language. The Nepalese community regard this as "cultural imperialism" and there are considerable ethnic tensions.

THE ECONOMY
Reliant on trade with India. 80% of people farm their own plots of land and herd cattle and yaks. Steep land unsuited for cultivation. Development of cash crops for Asian markets.

INSIGHT: *To protect traditional Bhutanese values, television was banned in the country until 1999*

FACTFILE
OFFICIAL NAME: Kingdom of Bhutan
DATE OF FORMATION: 1656
CAPITAL: Thimphu
POPULATION: 2.2 million
TOTAL AREA: 18,147 sq. miles (47,000 sq. km)
DENSITY: 121 people per sq. mile

LANGUAGES: Dzongkha*, Nepali, Assamese
RELIGIONS: Mahayana Buddhist 70%, Hindu 24%, other 6%
ETHNIC MIX: Bhute 50%, other 25%, Nepalese 25%
GOVERNMENT: Monarchy
CURRENCY: Ngultrum = 100 chetrum

Bolivia

Landlocked high in central South America, Bolivia is one of the region's poorest countries. La Paz is the world's highest capital city: 13,385 feet (3631 m) above sea level.

GEOGRAPHY

A high windswept plateau, the *altiplano*, lies between two Andean mountain ranges. Semiarid grasslands to the east; dense tropical forests to the north.

CLIMATE

Altiplano has extreme tropical climate, with night-frost in winter. North and east are hot and humid.

PEOPLE & SOCIETY

The indigenous majority faces widespread discrimination. The economy remains under the control of a few wealthy Spanish-descended families, though Amerindian influence in politics is growing. Economic reform has widened the poverty gap.

◆ **INSIGHT:** *Bolivia has the highest golf course, ski run, and soccer stadium in the world*

THE ECONOMY

Gold, silver, zinc, and tin are mined. Oil and natural gas deposits being developed. Overseas investors are deterred by social problems. Lack of manufacturing: primary products vulnerable to world price fluctuations.

3000m/9843ft
2000m/6562ft
1000m/3281ft
500m/1640ft
200m/656ft
Sea Level

Guayaramerín
Riberalta
PERU
Lake Titicaca
LA PAZ
Cochabamba
Oruro
SUCRE
Potosí
CHILE
Tupiza
Tarija
ARGENTINA
Beni
Trinidad
BRAZIL
Montero
Santa Cruz
Puerto Suárez
Guaporé
Altiplano
Gran Chaco
PARAGUAY

0   200 km
0   200 miles

FACTFILE

OFFICIAL NAME: Republic of Bolivia
DATE OF FORMATION: 1825
CAPITALS: La Paz (administrative); Sucre (judicial)
POPULATION: 8.7 million
TOTAL AREA: 424,162 sq. miles (1,098,580 sq. km)

DENSITY: 21 people per sq. mile
LANGUAGES: Aymara*, Quechua*, Spanish*
RELIGIONS: Roman Catholic 93%, other 7%
ETHNIC MIX: Quechua 37%, Aymara 32%, mixed 13%, European 10%, other 8%
GOVERNMENT: Presidential system
CURRENCY: Boliviano = 100 centavos

Bosnia & Herzegovina

Perched in the highlands of southeast Europe, Bosnia and Herzegovina was the focus of the bitter ethnic conflict which accompanied the dissolution of the former Yugoslav state.

GEOGRAPHY
Hills and mountains, with narrow river valleys. Lowlands in the north. Mainly deciduous forest covers about half of the total area.

CLIMATE
Continental. Hot summers and cold, often snowy winters.

PEOPLE & SOCIETY
Despite sharing the same origin and spoken language, Bosnians have been divided by history between Orthodox Serbs, Roman Catholic Croats, and Muslim Bosniaks. Ethnic cleansing was practiced by all sides in the civil war displacing around 60% of the population. Refugees are still returning.

INSIGHT: *The country is split into two separate entities, the Muslim–Croat Federation and the Serb Republic*

THE ECONOMY
Bosnia has the potential to recover its status as a thriving market economy with a strong manufacturing base, but still struggles with the legacy of war. Little investment.

FACTFILE

OFFICIAL NAME: Bosnia and Herzegovina
DATE OF FORMATION: 1992
CAPITAL: Sarajevo
POPULATION: 4.1 million
TOTAL AREA: 19,741 sq. miles (51,129 sq. km)

DENSITY: 208 people per sq. mile
LANGUAGES: Serbo-Croat
RELIGIONS: Muslim 40%, Orthodox Christian 31%, Catholic 15%, other 14%
ETHNIC MIX: Bosniak 48%, Serb 38%, Croat 14%
GOVERNMENT: Parliamentary system
CURRENCY: Marka = 100 pfeninga

Botswana

Landlocked in the heart of southern Africa, Botswana boasts the world's largest inland river delta. Diamonds provide potential wealth, but the country is crippled by HIV/AIDS.

GEOGRAPHY

Lies on vast plateau, high above sea level. Hills in the east. Kalahari Desert in center and southwest. Swamps and salt pans elsewhere and in Okavango Basin.

CLIMATE

Dry and prone to drought. Summer wet season, April–October. Winters are warm, with cold nights.

PEOPLE & SOCIETY

Tswana make up 98% of the population. The San bushmen, the first inhabitants, are marginalized. They were ordered in 2002 to abandon their nomadic lifestyle. Botswana has the highest rate of HIV-positive adults in the world (38.8%).

◆ **INSIGHT:** *Water, Botswana's most precious resource, is honored in the name of the currency – pula*

THE ECONOMY

Diamonds are the leading export. Deposits of other minerals. Beef is exported to Europe. Tourism aimed at wealthy wildlife enthusiasts. AIDS is devastating the population.

FACTFILE

OFFICIAL NAME: Republic of Botswana
DATE OF FORMATION: 1966
CAPITAL: Gaborone
POPULATION: 1.6 million
TOTAL AREA: 231,803 sq. miles (600,370 sq. km)
DENSITY: 7 people per sq. mile

LANGUAGES: Setswana, English*, Shona, San, Khoikhoi, isiNdebele
RELIGIONS: Traditional beliefs 50%, Christian (mainly Protestant) 30%, other (including Muslim) 20%
ETHNIC MIX: Tswana 98%, other 2%
GOVERNMENT: Presidential system
CURRENCY: Pula = 100 thebe

Brazil

Covering almost half of South America, Brazil is the site of the world's largest and ecologically most important rainforest. The country has immense natural and economic resources.

GEOGRAPHY

Covering over one-third of Brazil's total land area, the rainforest grows around the massive Amazon River and its delta. Apart from the basin of the River Plate to the south, the rest of the country consists of highlands. The mountainous east is part-forested and part-desert. The coastal plain in the southeast has swampy areas. The Atlantic coastline is 1240 miles (2000 km) long.

CLIMATE

Brazil's share of the Amazon Basin, occupying half the country, has a model tropical equatorial climate. Temperatures are high with almost no seasonal variation. The Brazilian plateau has far greater ranges of temperature and rainfall. The east is very dry and suffers from frequent droughts. The south has hot summers and cool winters.

PEOPLE & SOCIETY

Diverse population includes Amerindians, blacks, European immigrants, and people of mixed race. Amerindians suffer prejudice from most other peoples in Brazil. Shanty towns in the cities attract poor migrants from the northeast. Urban crime, violent land disputes, and unchecked development in Amazonia tarnish Brazil's image as a modern nation. Catholicism and the family unit remain strong.

THE ECONOMY

Dominant regional economy. Huge potential for growth based on abundant natural resources. Brazil is a leading exporter of coffee, sugar, and orange juice. Social tension threatens stability. Debts are high.

Equator

COLOMBIA

PERU

FACTFILE

OFFICIAL NAME: Federative Rep. of Brazil
DATE OF FORMATION: 1822
CAPITAL: Brasília
POPULATION: 175 million
TOTAL AREA: 3,286,470 sq. miles (8,511,965 sq. km)
DENSITY: 54 people per sq. mile

LANGUAGES: Portuguese*, German, Italian, Spanish, Polish, Japanese, other
RELIGIONS: Roman Catholic 74%, Protestant 15%, atheist 7%, other 4%,
ETHNIC MIX: Black 53 %, mixed race 40%, White 6%, other 1%
GOVERNMENT: Presidential system
CURRENCY: Real = 100 centavos

Brazil

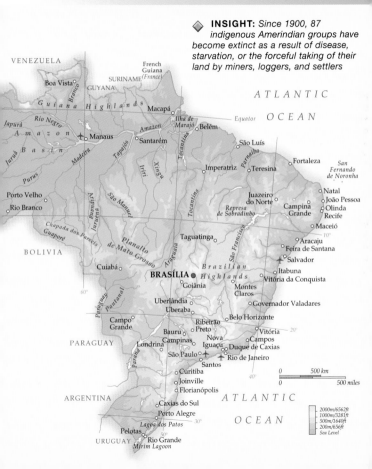

◆ **INSIGHT:** *Since 1900, 87 indigenous Amerindian groups have become extinct as a result of disease, starvation, or the forceful taking of their land by miners, loggers, and settlers*

VENEZUELA

French Guiana *(France)*

SURINAME

GUYANA

Boa Vista

Guiana Highlands

Rio Branco

Macapá

Ilha de Marajó

Belém

ATLANTIC

OCEAN

Equator

Japurá

Rio Negro

Amazon

Manaus

Santarém

São Luís

Amazon Basin

Madeira

Tapajós

Iriri

Xingu

Tocantins

Parnaíba

Teresina

Fortaleza

San Fernando de Noronha

Jurúá

Purus

Imperatriz

Porto Velho

Rio Branco

São Manuel

Tocantins

Juazeiro do Norte

Natal

João Pessoa

Olinda

Recife

Campina Grande

Maceió

Represa de Sobradinho

Chapada dos Parecis

Guaporé

Branco

Juruena

Planalto de Mato Grosso

Aracaju

São Francisco

Feira de Santana

Salvador

BOLIVIA

Cuiabá

Brazilian Highlands

Itabuna

Vitória da Conquista

BRASÍLIA

Taguatinga

Goiânia

Montes Claros

Governador Valadares

Uberlândia

Uberaba

Belo Horizonte

Campo Grande

Pantanal

Ribeirão Preto

Vitória

Bauru

Campinas

Nova Iguaçu

Campos

PARAGUAY

Londrina

Duque de Caxias

São Paulo

Rio de Janeiro

Santos

Paraná

Curitiba

Joinville

Florianópolis

ARGENTINA

Caxias do Sul

Porto Alegre

ATLANTIC

Lagoa dos Patos

OCEAN

Pelotas

Rio Grande

URUGUAY

Mirim Lagoon

0   500 km
0   500 miles

2000m/6562ft
1000m/3281ft
500m/1640ft
200m/656ft
Sea Level

Brunei

Lying on the northern coast of the island of Borneo, Brunei is surrounded and divided in two by the Malaysian state of Sarawak. It has been independent since 1984.

GEOGRAPHY

Mostly dense lowland rainforest and mangrove swamps, with some mountains in the southeast.

CLIMATE

Tropical. Six-month rainy season with very high humidity.

PEOPLE & SOCIETY

Malays benefit from positive discrimination. Many in the Chinese community are stateless. Since a failed rebellion in 1962, Brunei has been ruled by decree of the sultan. In 1990, "Malay Muslim Monarchy" was introduced, promoting Islamic values as state ideology. Women, less restricted than in some Muslim states, are obliged to wear headscarves but not the veil.

◆ **INSIGHT:** *The sultan spent US$450 million building the world's largest palace at Bandar Seri Begawan*

THE ECONOMY

Oil and natural gas reserves have brought one of the world's highest standards of living. Massive overseas investments. Major consumer of high-tech hi-fi, video equipment, and Western designer clothes.

FACTFILE

OFFICIAL NAME: Sultanate of Brunei
DATE OF FORMATION: 1984
CAPITAL: Bandar Seri Begawan
POPULATION: 341,000
TOTAL AREA: 2228 sq. miles (5770 sq. km)
DENSITY: 168 people per sq. mile

LANGUAGES: Malay*, English, Chinese
RELIGIONS: Muslim (mainly Sunni) 66%, Buddhist 14%, other 10%, Christian 10%
ETHNIC MIX: Malay 67%, Chinese 16%, other 11%, indigenous 6%
GOVERNMENT: Monarchy
CURRENCY: Brunei dollar = 100 cents

Bulgaria

Located in southeastern Europe, Bulgaria was under communist rule from 1947 to 1989. Since then, the country has made slow progress toward political and economic stability.

 GEOGRAPHY
Mountains run east–west across center and along southern border. Danube plain in north, Thracian plain in southeast. Black Sea to the east.

CLIMATE
Warm summers and snowy winters, especially in mountains. East winds bring seasonal extremes.

 PEOPLE & SOCIETY
The communists tried forcibly to suppress cultural identities, leading to a large exodus of Bulgarian Turks in 1989. Recent privatization programs have left many Turks landless and prompted further emigration. Roma suffer discrimination at all levels of society. Women have equal rights in theory, but society remains patriarchal. The former king Simeon II returned to become prime minister, taking the name Saxecoburggotski, in 2001.

THE ECONOMY
Good agricultural production, including grapes, for well-developed wine industry, and tobacco. Expertise in software development. Industry and infrastructure are outdated.

◆ **INSIGHT:** *Archaeologists have found evidence of wine-making in Bulgaria dating back over 5000 years*

 FACTFILE
OFFICIAL NAME: Republic of Bulgaria
DATE OF FORMATION: 1908
CAPITAL: Sofia
POPULATION: 7.8 million
TOTAL AREA: 42,822 sq. miles (110,910 sq. km)
DENSITY: 183 people per sq. mile

LANGUAGES: Bulgarian*, Turkish, Romani
RELIGIONS: Orthodox Christian 83%, Muslim 12%, other 4%, Catholic 1%
ETHNIC MIX: Bulgarian 84%, Turkish 9%, Roma 5%, other 2%
GOVERNMENT: Parliamentary system
CURRENCY: Lev = 100 stotinki

Burkina

Known as Upper Volta until 1984, the west African state of Burkina has been ruled by military dictators for most of its postindependence history. It is now a multiparty state.

GEOGRAPHY

The Sahara covers the north of the country. The south is largely savanna. The three main rivers are the Black, White, and Red Voltas.

CLIMATE

Tropical. Dry, cool weather November–February. Erratic rain March–April, mostly in southeast.

PEOPLE & SOCIETY

No single ethnic group is dominant, but the Mossi, from around Ouagadougou, have always played an important part in government. The people from the west are much more ethnically mixed. Extreme poverty has led to a strong sense of egalitarianism. Most women are still denied access to education, though their absence from public life belies their real power and social influence.

THE ECONOMY

Cotton is the major cash crop, but the soil quality is poor and worsening as the Sahara Desert encroaches.

◆ **INSIGHT:** *Droughts and poor soils mean that many Burkinabes seek work southward in Ghana and Côte d'Ivoire*

FACTFILE

OFFICIAL NAME: Burkina Faso
DATE OF FORMATION: 1960
CAPITAL: Ouagadougou
POPULATION: 12.2 million
TOTAL AREA: 105,869 sq. miles (274,200 sq. km)
DENSITY: 115 people per sq. mile

LANGUAGES: Mossi, Fulani, French*, Tuareg, Dyula, Songhai
RELIGIONS: Traditional beliefs 55%, Muslim 35%, Roman Catholic 9%, other Christian 1%
ETHNIC MIX: Other 50%, Mossi 50%
GOVERNMENT: Presidential system
CURRENCY: CFA franc = 100 centimes

Burundi

Small, densely populated and landlocked, Burundi lies just south of the equator, on the Nile–Congo watershed in central Africa. Ethnic tensions are the main factor in politics.

GEOGRAPHY

Hilly with high plateaus in center and savanna in the east. Great Rift Valley on western side.

CLIMATE

Temperate, with high humidity. Heavy and frequent rainfall, mostly October–May. Highlands have frost.

PEOPLE & SOCIETY

Burundi's postindependence history has been dominated by ethnic conflict – with repeated large-scale massacres – between majority Hutu and the Tutsi, who control the army. hundreds of thousands of people, have been killed since 1992. Twa pygmies are not involved in the conflict. Most people are subsistence farmers.

◆ **INSIGHT:** *Burundi's birth rate is one of the highest in Africa. On average women have seven children*

THE ECONOMY
Overwhelmingly agricultural economy. Small quantities of gold and tungsten. Potential of oil in Lake Tanganyika. Little prospect of lasting stability.

FACTFILE

OFFICIAL NAME: Republic of Burundi
DATE OF FORMATION: 1962
CAPITAL: Bujumbura
POPULATION: 6.7 million
TOTAL AREA: 10,745 sq. miles (27,830 sq. km)
DENSITY: 677 people per sq. mile

LANGUAGES: Kirundi*, French*, Kiswahili
RELIGIONS: Christian (mainly Roman Catholic) 60%, traditional beliefs 39%, Muslim 1%
ETHNIC MIX: Hutu 85%, Tutsi 14%, Twa 1%
GOVERNMENT: Transitional regime
CURRENCY: Burundi franc = 100 centimes

Cambodia

Located on the Indochinese peninsula in southeast Asia, Cambodia has emerged from two decades of civil war and invasion from Vietnam. Rice is the principal crop.

GEOGRAPHY
Mostly low-lying basin. Tônlé Sap (Great Lake) drains into the Mekong River. Forested mountains and plateau east of the Mekong.

CLIMATE
Tropical. High temperatures throughout the year. Heavy rainfall during May–October monsoon.

PEOPLE & SOCIETY
Under Pol Pot's Marxist Khmer Rouge regime, between 1975 and 1979, over one million Cambodians died. Effects of revolution and civil war are still felt and are reflected in the world's highest rate of orphans and widows. A fragile stability has lasted since elections in 1993. The Khmer Rouge discontinued its armed struggle after the death of Pol Pot in 1998. King Norodom Sihanouk remains a key figure in politics.

THE ECONOMY
Economy is still recovering from civil war. Modest trade in rubber and timber, and self-sufficiency in rice. Reliant on imports and aid. Small tax base limits the scope of reforms.

INSIGHT: *Cambodia has many impressive temples, dating from when the country was the center of the Khmer empire*

FACTFILE
OFFICIAL NAME: Kingdom of Cambodia
DATE OF FORMATION: 1953
CAPITAL: Phnom Penh
POPULATION: 13.8 million
TOTAL AREA: 69,900 sq. miles (181,040 sq. km)
DENSITY: 202 people per sq. mile

LANGUAGES: Khmer*, French, Chinese, Vietnamese, Cham
RELIGIONS: Buddhist 93%, Muslim 6%, Christian 1%
ETHNIC MIX: Khmer 90%, other 5%, Vietnamese 4%, Chinese 1%
GOVERNMENT: Parliamentary system
CURRENCY: Riel = 100 sen

Cameroon

Situated in the corner of the Gulf of Guinea, Cameroon was effectively a one-party state for 30 years. Multiparty elections were held in 1992, returning the former ruling party to power.

GEOGRAPHY

Over half the land is forested: equatorial rainforest in north, evergreen forest and wooded savanna in south. Mountains in the west.

CLIMATE

South is equatorial, with plentiful rainfall, declining inland. Far north is beset by drought.

PEOPLE & SOCIETY

Around 230 ethnic groups; no single group is dominant. The Bamileke is the largest, though it has never held political power. North–south tensions are diminished by the ethnic diversity. There is more rivalry between majority French- and minority English-speakers.

◆ **INSIGHT:** *Cameroon's name derives from the Portuguese word* camarões – *after the shrimp fished by the early European explorers*

THE ECONOMY

Moderate oil reserves. Very diversified agricultural economy – timber, cocoa, bananas, coffee. Self-sufficient in food. Fuel smuggling from Nigeria undermines refinery profits. Corruption.

2000m/6562ft
1000m/3281ft
500m/1640ft
200m/656ft
Sea Level

CHAD
Lake 0 16°
Chad 12°
NIGERIA Maroua
Garoua
12° 8°
Ngaoundéré
Bamenda Kumbo Meiganga
8° Bafoussam CENTRAL
Kumba Nkongsamba AFRICAN
Douala REPUBLIC
Edéa YAOUNDÉ
Mbalmayo 4°
ATLANTIC Ebolowa
OCEAN EQ.
GUINEA GABON CONGO

0 100 km
0 100 miles

FACTFILE

OFFICIAL NAME: Republic of Cameroon
DATE OF FORMATION: 1960
CAPITAL: Yaoundé
POPULATION: 15.5 million
TOTAL AREA: 183,567 sq. miles (475,400 sq. km)
DENSITY: 86 people per sq. mile

LANGUAGES: Bamileke, Fang, Fulani, French*, English*
RELIGIONS: Catholic 35%, traditional beliefs 25%, Muslim 22%, Protestant 18%
ETHNIC MIX: Highlanders 31%, other 39%, equatorial Bantu 19%, Kirdi 11%
GOVERNMENT: Presidential system
CURRENCY: CFA franc = 100 centimes

Canada

Canada extends from its long border with the US to the Arctic Ocean. The relationship of French-speaking Québec with the rest of the country has become a less contentious issue.

GEOGRAPHY

The world's second-largest country, stretching north to Cape Colombia on Ellesmere Island, south to Lake Erie, and across five time zones from the Pacific seaboard to Newfoundland. Arctic tundra and islands in the far north give way southward to forests, interspersed with lakes and rivers, and then the vast Canadian Shield, which covers over half the area of Canada. Rocky Mountains in west, beyond which are the Coast Mountains, islands, and fjords. Fertile lowlands in the east.

CLIMATE

Ranges from polar and subpolar in the north, to continental in the south. Winters in the interior are colder and longer than on the coast, with temperatures well below freezing and deep snow; summers are hotter. Pacific coast has the mildest winters.

PEOPLE & SOCIETY

Two-thirds of the population live in the Great Lakes–St. Lawrence lowlands, fostering some shared cultural values with the neighboring US. Important differences, however, include wider welfare provision and Common-wealth membership. The Québécois wish to preserve their culture and language from further Anglicization, and demand to be recognized as a "distinct society." The government welcomes ethnic diversity among immigrants, promoting a policy which encourages each group to maintain its own culture. Land claims made by the indigenous peoples are being redressed. Nunavut, an Inuit-governed territory which covers nearly a quarter of Canada's land area, was created from a portion of the Northwest Territories in 1999. Women are well represented at most levels of business and government.

FACTFILE

OFFICIAL NAME: Canada
DATE OF FORMATION: 1867
CAPITAL: Ottawa
POPULATION: 31.3 million
TOTAL AREA: 3,851,788 sq. miles (9,976,140 sq. km)
DENSITY: 9 people per sq. mile

LANGUAGES: English*, French*, other
RELIGIONS: Roman Catholic 44%, Protestant 29%, other 27%
ETHNIC ORIGIN: British, French and other European 27m, Asian 3m, Amerindian, Métis, and Inuit 1.3m
GOVERNMENT: Parliamentary system
CURRENCY: Canadian dollar = 100 cents

THE ECONOMY

Wide-ranging resources, providing exports, cheap energy, and raw materials for manufacturing, underpin a high standard of living. Manufactured exports have faced increasing competition since the mid-1980s, while prices for primary exports have fluctuated. Attempts to bring down the budget deficit saw welfare programs and defense spending cut. A record budget surplus was recorded in 1997-8. Unemployment has fallen steadily from a high of around 10% in the mid-1990s. Canada's close ties to the US inevitably mean't it was affected by the 2001 slowdown.

◆ **INSIGHT:** The magnetic north pole, where the dipping needle of a compass stands still, migrates across northern Canada

3000m/9843ft
2000m/6562ft
1000m/3281ft
500m/1640ft
200m/656ft
Sea Level

0   400 km

0   400 miles

Cape Verde

Off the west coast of Africa, in the Atlantic Ocean, lies the group of islands that make up Cape Verde, a Portuguese colony until it gained independence in 1975.

GEOGRAPHY
Ten main islands and eight smaller islets, all of volcanic origin. Mostly mountainous, with steep cliffs and rocky headlands.

CLIMATE
Warm, and very dry. Subject to droughts that can sometimes last for years at a time.

PEOPLE & SOCIETY
Most people are of mixed Portuguese–African origin; the rest are largely African, descended from slaves or more recent immigrants. Creolization of the culture negates ethnic tensions. 50% of the population live on Santiago. Over 600,000 Cape Verdeans now live abroad.

◆ **INSIGHT:** *Poor soils and lack of surface water mean that Cape Verde is dependent on food aid*

THE ECONOMY
Most people are subsistence farmers. Fish is the main export. Only minerals produced are salt, and volcanic rock for cement.

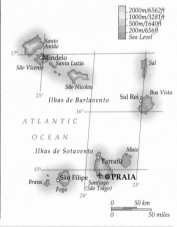

2000m/6562ft
1000m/3281ft
500m/1640ft
200m/656ft
Sea Level

Santo Antão
Mindelo
São Vicente
Santa Luzia
Sal
São Nicolau
Sal Rei
Boa Vista
Ilhas de Barlavento
ATLANTIC
OCEAN
Ilhas de Sotavento
Maio
Tarrafil
Brava
São Filipe
Santiago (São Tiago)
PRAIA
Fogo

0   50 km
0   50 miles

FACTFILE
OFFICIAL NAME: Republic of Cape Verde
DATE OF FORMATION: 1975
CAPITAL: Praia
POPULATION: 446,000
TOTAL AREA: 1557 sq. miles (4033 sq. km)
DENSITY: 287 people per sq. mile

LANGUAGES: Creole, Portuguese*
RELIGIONS: Roman Catholic 97%, other 2%, Protestant 1%
ETHNIC MIX: Mestiço 60%, African 30%, other 10%
GOVERNMENT: Mixed presidential–parliamentary system
CURRENCY: C.V. escudo = 100 centavos

Central African Republic

The Central African Republic (CAR) is a landlocked country lying between the basins of the Chad and Congo Rivers. The country is prone to coups; the last was in 2003.

GEOGRAPHY

Comprises a low plateau, covered by scrub or savanna. Equatorial rainforests in the south. The Ubangi River forms the border with the Democratic Republic of the Congo.

CLIMATE

The south is equatorial; the north is hot and dry. Rain occurs all year round, with heaviest falls between July and October.

PEOPLE & SOCIETY

The Baya and Banda are the largest ethnic groups, but the lingua franca is Sango, a trading creole spoken by the minorities in the south who have traditionally provided most political leaders. Women have considerable power. Ethnic diversity helps limit disputes. Less than 2% of the population live in the arid north.

THE ECONOMY

Dominated by subsistence farming. Exports include gold, diamonds, cotton, and timber. Self-sufficient in food. Instability and poor infrastructure hinder progress.

◆ **INSIGHT:** *"Emperor" Bokassa's eccentric rule from 1965 to 1979 was followed by military dictatorship until democracy was restored in 1993*

1000m/3281ft
500m/1640ft
200m/656ft
Sea Level

FACTFILE

OFFICIAL NAME: Central African Republic
DATE OF FORMATION: 1960
CAPITAL: Bangui
POPULATION: 3.8 million
TOTAL AREA: 240,534 sq. miles (622,984 sq. km)
DENSITY: 16 people per sq. mile

LANGUAGES: Sango, Banda, Gbaya, French*
RELIGIONS: Traditional beliefs 60%, Christian 35%, Muslim 5%
ETHNIC MIX: Baya 34%, Banda 27%, Mandjia 21%, Sara 10%, other 8%
GOVERNMENT: Transitional regime
CURRENCY: CFA franc = 100 centimes

Chad

Landlocked in north central Africa, Chad has had a turbulent history since independence from France in 1960. Intermittent periods of civil war followed a military coup in 1975.

GEOGRAPHY

Mostly plateaus sloping westward to Lake Chad. Northern third is Sahara. Tibesti Mountains in north rise to 10,826 ft (3300 m).

CLIMATE

Three distinct zones: desert in north, semiarid region in center, and tropics in south.

PEOPLE & SOCIETY

Half the population live in the southern fifth of the country. Northern third has only 100,000 people, mainly Muslim Toubou nomads. Democracy was restored in 1996 by ex-coup leader Idriss Déby. There is political strife between Muslims in the north and Christians in the south. The most recent conflict broke out in 1999.

◆ **INSIGHT:** *Lake Chad is slowly drying up – it is now estimated to be just 10% of the size it was in 1970*

THE ECONOMY

The discovery of substantial oil desposits, and the opening of a pipeline to the coast via Cameroon, promise to transform Chad's economy for the better.

| 3000m/9843ft |
| 2000m/6562ft |
| 1000m/3281ft |
| 500m/1640ft |
| 200m/656ft |
| Sea Level |

LIBYA

Tibesti

S a h a r a

NIGER

Lake Chad
Bol · Abéché

NIGERIA · Mongo · SUDAN

NDJAMENA

Bongor
Fianga · Benoy · Sarh · CENTRAL AFRICAN REPUBLIC

CAMEROON · Doba
Moundou

0   200 km
0   200 miles

📖 FACTFILE

OFFICIAL NAME: Republic of Chad
DATE OF FORMATION: 1960
CAPITAL: N'Djamena
POPULATION: 8.4 million
TOTAL AREA: 495,752 sq. miles
(1,284,000 sq. km)
DENSITY: 17 people per sq. mile

LANGUAGES: French*, Sara, Arabic*, Maba
RELIGIONS: Muslim 50%, traditional beliefs 43%, Christian 7%
ETHNIC MIX: Nomads (Tuareg and Toubou) 38%, Sara 30%, other 17%, Arab 15%
GOVERNMENT: Presidential system
CURRENCY: CFA franc = 100 centimes

Chile

Chile extends in a ribbon down the west coast of South America. It returned to elected civilian rule in 1989 after a referendum had rejected military dictator General Pinochet.

GEOGRAPHY
Fertile valleys in the center between the coast and the Andes. Atacama Desert in north. Deep sea channels, lakes, and fjords in south.

CLIMATE
Arid in the north. Hot, dry summers and mild winters in the center. Higher Andean peaks have glaciers and year-round snow. Very wet and stormy in the south.

PEOPLE & SOCIETY
Most people are of mixed Spanish–Amerindian descent, and are highly urbanized; a third of the population live in Santiago, many in large slums. There are three main indigenous groups, including the Rapa Nui of Easter Island. General Pinochet's dictatorship was brutally repressive, but the business and middle classes prospered.

THE ECONOMY
World's biggest copper producer. Growth in foreign investment due to political stability. Exports include wine, fishmeal, fruits, and salmon.

PERU
BOLIVIA
Arica
Iquique
Atacama Desert
Antofagasta
PACIFIC OCEAN
Viña del Mar
Valparaíso
Rancagua
SANTIAGO
Talcahuano
Talca
Concepción
Chillán
Temuco
Valdivia
Puerto Montt
Isla de Chiloé
Andes
ARGENTINA
Punta Arenas
Strait of Magellan
Cape Horn

4000m/13124ft
3000m/9843ft
2000m/6562ft
1000m/3281ft
Sea Level

0   300 km
0   300 miles

 INSIGHT: *Chile's Atacama Desert is the driest place on Earth*

FACTFILE
OFFICIAL NAME: Republic of Chile
DATE OF FORMATION: 1818
CAPITAL: Santiago
POPULATION: 15.6 million
TOTAL AREA: 292,258 sq. miles (756,950 sq. km)
DENSITY: 54 people per sq. mile

LANGUAGES: Spanish*, Amerindian languages
RELIGIONS: Roman Catholic 80%, other and nonreligious 20%
ETHNIC MIX: Mixed and European 90%, Amerindian 10%
GOVERNMENT: Presidential system
CURRENCY: Chilean peso = 100 centavos

China

Covering a vast area of eastern Asia, China is bordered by 14 countries. From the founding of Communist China in 1949, until his death in 1976, Mao Zedong dominated the country.

GEOGRAPHY

A land of huge physical diversity, China has a long Pacific coastline to the east. Two-thirds of the country is uplands. The southwestern mountains include Tibet, the world's highest plateau; in the northwest, the Tien Shan Mountains separate the arid Tarim and Dzungarian basins. The rolling hills and plains of the low-lying east are home to two-thirds of the population.

CLIMATE

China is divided into two main climatic regions. The north and west are semiarid or arid, with extreme temperature variations. The south and east are warmer and more humid, with year-round rainfall. Winter temperatures vary with latitude, but are warmest on the subtropical southeast coast. Summer temperatures are more uniform, rising above 70°F (21°C).

PEOPLE & SOCIETY

Most people are Han Chinese. The rest of the population belong to one of 55 minority nationalities, or recognized ethnic groups. Many of these groups have a disproportionate political significance as they live in strategic border areas. A policy of resettling Han Chinese in remote regions is deeply resented and has led to uprisings in Xinjiang and Tibet. The government has relaxed the one-child family policy for minorities after some small groups were brought close to extinction; Han Chinese still face controls. Chinese society is patriarchal in practice, and generations tend to live together. However, economic change is breaking down the social controls of the Mao era. Divorce and unemployment are rising; materialism has replaced the puritanism of the past. A resurgence of religious belief has occurred in recent years.

FACTFILE

OFFICIAL NAME: People's Rep. of China
DATE OF FORMATION: 960
CAPITAL: Beijing
POPULATION: 1.29 billion
TOTAL AREA: 3,705,386 sq. miles (9,596,960 sq. km)
DENSITY: 359 people per sq. mile

LANGUAGES: Mandarin*, other
RELIGIONS: Nonreligious 59%, traditional beliefs 20%, other 13%, Buddhist 6%, Muslim 2%
ETHNIC MIX: Han 92%, other 6%, Hui 1%, Zhuang 1%
GOVERNMENT: One-party state
CURRENCY: Yuan = 10 jiao = 100 fen

THE ECONOMY

China has shifted from a centrally planned to a market-oriented economy; liberalization has gone furthest in the south where the emerging business class is based. The Tenth Five-Year Plan (2001–2005) emphasizes rapid development, reforms, and improving competitiveness. The government now runs a record deficit of almost $40 billion. Trade entered a new era in 2000–2001. A substantial growth in imports followed a deal with the EU and the normalization of US trade relations, while a boost in exports aided a 7% growth in GDP in 2002.

INSIGHT: *China has the world's oldest continuous civilization. Its recorded history began 4000 years ago, with the Shang dynasty*

	4000m/13124ft
	3000m/9843ft
	2000m/6562ft
	1000m/3281ft
	500m/1640ft
	200m/656ft
	Sea Level

0   400 km
0   400 miles

Colombia

Lying in northwest South America, Colombia has coastlines on both the Caribbean and the Pacific. It is primarily noted for its coffee, emeralds, gold, and narcotics trafficking.

GEOGRAPHY
The densely forested and almost uninhabited east is separated from the western coastal plains by the Andes, which divide into three ranges (*cordilleras*) with intervening valleys.

CLIMATE
Coastal plains are hot and wet. The highlands are much cooler. The equatorial east has two wet seasons.

PEOPLE & SOCIETY
Most Colombians are of mixed blood. Blacks and Amerindians have the least political representation. The 40-year-long civil conflict has displaced millions of people, and left over 50,000 dead. The war is now entwined with the narcotics trade. Violent crime is common.

◆ **INSIGHT:** *Over 50% of the world's cocaine is produced in Colombia*

THE ECONOMY
Healthy and diversified export sector – includes coffee and coal. Considerable growth potential, but drugs-related violence and corruption deter foreign investors.

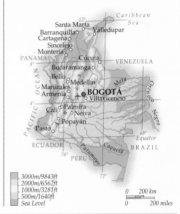

3000m/9843ft
2000m/6562ft
1000m/3281ft
500m/1640ft
Sea Level

0   200 km
0   200 miles

FACTFILE

OFFICIAL NAME: Republic of Colombia
DATE OF FORMATION: 1819
CAPITAL: Bogotá
POPULATION: 43.5 million
TOTAL AREA: 439,733 sq. miles (1,138,910 sq. km)
DENSITY: 108 people per sq. mile

LANGUAGES: Spanish*, Amerindian languages, English Creole
RELIGIONS: Catholic 95%, other 5%
ETHNIC MIX: Mestizo 58%, White 20%, European–African 14%, Black African 4%, Black Amerindian 3%, other 1%
GOVERNMENT: Presidential system
CURRENCY: Peso = 100 centavos

Comoros

Off the east African coast, between Mozambique and Madagascar, lies the archipelago republic of the Comoros, comprising three main islands and a number of smaller islets.

GEOGRAPHY
Main islands are of volcanic origin and are heavily forested. The remainder are coral atolls.

CLIMATE
Hot and humid all year round, especially on the coasts. November to May is hottest and wettest period.

PEOPLE & SOCIETY
The Comoros has absorbed a diversity of people over the years, including Africans, Arabs, Polynesians, and Persians. There have also been Portuguese, Dutch, French, and Indian immigrants. Ethnic discord is rare, but regional tensions between islands are marked. The country is politically unstable and there have been frequent coups over the last decade. A fragile new federal system has been in place since 2002. Wealth is concentrated among a political and business elite.

THE ECONOMY
One of the world's poorest countries. Subsistence-level farming. Vanilla and cloves are main cash crops. Lack of basic infrastructure.

◆ **INSIGHT:** *The Comoros is the world's largest producer of ylang-ylang – an extract from tree blossom used in manufacturing perfumes*

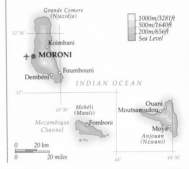

FACTFILE

OFFICIAL NAME: Union of the Comoros
DATE OF FORMATION: 1975
CAPITAL: Moroni
POPULATION: 749,000
TOTAL AREA: 838 sq. miles (2170 sq. km)
DENSITY: 870 people per sq. mile

LANGUAGES: Arabic*, Comoran*, French*
RELIGIONS: Muslim (mainly Sunni) 98%, other 1%, Roman Catholic 1%
ETHNIC MIX: Comoran 97%, other 3%
GOVERNMENT: Presidential system
CURRENCY: Comoros franc = 100 centimes

Congo

Astride the equator in west central Africa, this former French colony emerged from 20 years of Marxist-Leninist rule in 1990. Democracy was soon overshadowed by years of violence.

GEOGRAPHY

Mostly forest- or savanna-covered plateaus, drained by the Ubangi and Congo River systems. Narrow coastal plain is lined with sand dunes and lagoons.

CLIMATE

Hot, tropical. Temperatures rarely fall below 86°F (30°C). Two wet and two dry seasons. Rainfall is heaviest south of the equator.

PEOPLE & SOCIETY

One of the most tribally conscious and heavily urbanized countries in Africa. There are four main ethnic groups: Bakongo, Sangha, Teke, and Mbochi. Main tensions are between the Bakongo in the north and the Mbochi in the south. There has been a period of relative peace since 1999, though the Pool region, around Brazzaville, remains tense.

THE ECONOMY

Oil provides 95% of export revenue. Timber supplies. Substantial industrial base around Brazzaville and Pointe-Noire. Large foreign debt.

INSIGHT: *In 1970, Congo became the first African country to declare itself a communist state*

FACTFILE

OFFICIAL NAME: Republic of the Congo
DATE OF FORMATION: 1960
CAPITAL: Brazzaville
POPULATION: 3.2 million
TOTAL AREA: 132,046 sq. miles (342,000 sq. km)
DENSITY: 24 people per sq. mile

LANGUAGES: Kongo, Teke, Lingala, French*
RELIGIONS: Traditional 50%, Catholic 25%, Protestant 23%, Muslim 2%
ETHNIC MIX: Bakongo 48%, Sangha 20%, Teke 17%, Mbochi 12%, other 3%
GOVERNMENT: Presidential system
CURRENCY: CFA franc = 100 centimes

Congo, (DRC)

Lying in eastcentral Africa, the Democratic Republic of the Congo (DRC) is one of Africa's largest countries, and the scene of one of its worst regional wars.

GEOGRAPHY

Rainforested basin of Congo River occupies 60% of the land area. High mountain ranges and lakes stretch down the eastern border.

CLIMATE

Tropical and humid. Distinct wet and dry seasons south of the equator. The north is mainly wet.

PEOPLE & SOCIETY

There are over 12 main ethnic groups and around 190 smaller ones. The indigenous forest pygmies are now a marginalized group, victimized during the war. Civil war from 1996 drew neighboring countries into a long and bloody conflict. Peace was acheived in 2003 but tensions remain.

◆ **INSIGHT:** *The DRC's rainforests comprise 6% of the world's, and 50% of Africa's, remaining woodlands*

THE ECONOMY

Rich resource base: diamonds provide 85% of export earnings. Debt cancelled in 2003. War, corruption, and mismanagement have seen economy collapse.

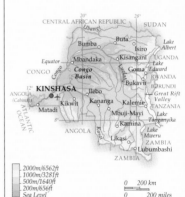

FACTFILE

OFFICIAL NAME: Democratic Republic of the Congo
DATE OF FORMATION: 1960
CAPITAL: Kinshasa
POPULATION: 54.3 million
TOTAL AREA: 905,563 sq. miles (2,345,410 sq. km)

DENSITY: 62 people per sq. mile
LANGUAGES: Kiswahili, Tshiluba, Kikongo, Lingala, French*
RELIGIONS: Traditional 50%, Christian 50%
ETHNIC MIX: Other 55%, Bantu and Hamitic 45%
GOVERNMENT: Transitional regime
CURRENCY: Congolese franc = 100 centimes

Costa Rica

Costa Rica is the most stable country in Central America. Its neutrality in foreign affairs is long-standing, but it has strong ties with the US. The national army was abolished in 1949.

GEOGRAPHY

Coastal plains of swamp and savanna rise to a fertile central plateau, which leads to a mountain range with active volcanic peaks.

CLIMATE

Hot and humid in coastal regions. Temperate central uplands. High annual rainfall.

PEOPLE & SOCIETY

Most people are *mestizo*, of partly Spanish origin. There is a black, English-speaking minority and around 5000 indigenous Amerindians. Plantation-owners are the wealthiest group, while over 25% of people live in poverty. Nonetheless, living standards are high for the region.

◆ **INSIGHT:** *Costa Rica's constitution is the only one in the world to forbid a national army*

THE ECONOMY

Bananas, beef, and coffee are the leading exports but are all vulnerable to fluctuating world prices. Tourism also fuels construction industry. State monopolies deter foreign investment. History of high inflation.

FACTFILE

OFFICIAL NAME: Republic of Costa Rica

DATE OF FORMATION: 1838

CAPITAL: San José

POPULATION: 4.2 million

TOTAL AREA: 19,730 sq. miles (51,100 sq. km)

DENSITY: 213 people per sq. mile

LANGUAGES: Spanish*, English Creole, Bribri, Cabecar

RELIGIONS: Roman Catholic 76%, other (including Protestant) 24%

ETHNIC MIX: Mestizo and European 96%, Black 2%, Chinese 1%, Amerindian 1%

GOVERNMENT: Presidential system

CURRENCY: Colón = 100 centimos

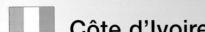

Côte d'Ivoire (Ivory Coast)

One of the larger nations along the coast of west Africa, Côte d'Ivoire is the world's biggest cocoa producer. An image of stability was rocked by civil war in 2002–2003.

GEOGRAPHY

Sandy coastal strip backed by a largely rainforested interior, and a savanna plateau in the north.

CLIMATE

High temperatures all year round. South has two wet seasons; north has one, with lower rainfall.

PEOPLE & SOCIETY

There are more than 60 tribes, the key ones being the Baoulé in the center, the Agni in the east, the Senufo in the north, and the Dan-Yacouba in the west. Regional migrants account for 40% of the population, fueling ethnic tensions. Christians in the south harbor resentment against non-Ivorian Muslims in the north.

◆ **INSIGHT:** *The Basilica of Our Lady of the Peace in Yamoussoukro is the second-largest church in the world*

THE ECONOMY

Main crops are cocoa and coffee. Expanding oil and gas industries. Instability threatens investment. Lack of professional training.

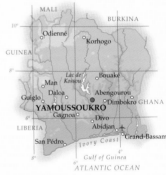

1000m/3281ft	
500m/1640ft	0 100 km
200m/656ft	0 100 miles
Sea Level	

📖 FACTFILE

OFFICIAL NAME: Republic of Côte d'Ivoire

DATE OF FORMATION: 1960

CAPITAL: Yamoussoukro

POPULATION: 16.7 million

TOTAL AREA: 124,502 sq. miles (322,460 sq. km)

DENSITY: 136 people per sq. mile

LANGUAGES: Akan, French*, Kru, Voltaic

RELIGIONS: Christian 29%, Muslim 25%, traditional beliefs 23%, other 23%

ETHNIC MIX: Other 30%, Baoulé 23%, Bété 18%, Senufo 15%, Agni-Ashanti 14%

GOVERNMENT: Presidential system

CURRENCY: CFA franc = 100 centimes

Croatia

Though it was controlled by Hungary from medieval times and was a part of the Yugoslav state for much of the 20th century, Croatia has a very strong national identity.

GEOGRAPHY
Rocky, mountainous Adriatic coastline is dotted with islands. Interior is a mixture of wooded mountains and broad valleys.

CLIMATE
The interior has a temperate continental climate. Mediterranean climate along the Adriatic coast.

PEOPLE & SOCIETY
Croats are ethnically similar to Bosniaks and Serbs. They are distinguished by their Roman Catholic faith and their use of the Latin alphabet. War greatly altered Croatia's ethnic makeup. Serbs now constitute just 4% of the population – not enough to warrant "minority rights" under the constitution.

◆ **INSIGHT:** *Croatia only regained control of Serb-occupied Eastern Slavonia, around Vukovar, in 1998*

THE ECONOMY
The war cost the economy an estimated $50 billion and there is persistently high unemployment. There has been steady growth since, and tourism has recovered.

FACTFILE
OFFICIAL NAME: Republic of Croatia
DATE OF FORMATION: 1991
CAPITAL: Zagreb
POPULATION: 4.7 million
TOTAL AREA: 21,831 sq. miles (56,542 sq. km)
DENSITY: 215 people per sq. mile

LANGUAGES: Croatian
RELIGIONS: Roman Catholic 88%, other 7%, Orthodox Christian 4%, Muslim 1%
ETHNIC MIX: Croat 90%, other 5%, Serb 4%, Bosniak 1%
GOVERNMENT: Parliamentary system
CURRENCY: Kuna = 100 lipas

Cuba

A former Spanish colony, Cuba is the largest island in the Caribbean and the only communist country in the Americas. It has been led by Fidel Castro since 1959.

GEOGRAPHY

Mostly fertile plains and basins. Three mountainous areas. Forests of pine and mahogany cover one-quarter of the country.

CLIMATE

Subtropical. Hot all year round, and very hot in summer. Heaviest rainfall in the mountains. Hurricanes can strike in the fall.

PEOPLE & SOCIETY

Castro's regime has reduced formerly extreme wealth disparities, given education a high priority, and established an efficient health service. Political dissent, however, is not tolerated. A dramatic fall in living standards since the late 1980s has led thousands of Cubans to flee to the US, to seek asylum. About 70% of Cubans are of Spanish descent, and ethnic tension is minimal.

THE ECONOMY

The 30-year-old US trade embargo continues. The sugar industry has collapsed and has been replaced as Cuba's main industry by tourism. The US dollar has been freely used since the 1990s, boosting investment but creating a "dollarized" elite.

◆ INSIGHT: *Most modern cars in Cuba are imported, along with computers, in exchange for sugar in a special trading deal with Japan*

FACTFILE

OFFICIAL NAME: Republic of Cuba
DATE OF FORMATION: 1902
CAPITAL: Havana
POPULATION: 11.3 million
TOTAL AREA: 42,803 sq. miles (110,860 sq. km)
DENSITY: 264 people per sq. mile

LANGUAGES: Spanish
RELIGIONS: Nonreligious 49%, Roman Catholic 40%, atheist 6%, other 4%, Protestant 1%
ETHNIC MIX: White 66%, European–African 22%, Black 12%
GOVERNMENT: One-party state
CURRENCY: Cuban peso = 100 centavos

Cyprus

Cyprus lies south of Turkey in the eastern Mediterranean.
Since 1974, it has been partitioned between the Turkish-
occupied north and the Greek-Cypriot south.

GEOGRAPHY
Mountains in the center-west
give way to a fertile plain in the east,
flanked by hills to the northeast.

CLIMATE
Mediterranean. Summers
are hot and dry. Winters are mild,
with snow in the mountains.

PEOPLE & SOCIETY
The Greek majority practice
Orthodox Christianity. Since the
16th century, a minority community of
Turkish Muslims has lived in the north
of the island. In 1974 Turkish troops
occupied the north, which was
proclaimed the Turkish Republic of
Northern Cyprus, but is recognized
only by Turkey. Over 100,000 mainland
Turks have settled there since. Wage
levels are on average three times
higher in the south, where the
tourist industry is booming.

THE ECONOMY
In the south, tourism is the
key industry. Shipping and light
manufacturing are also important. The
international isolation of the north has
starved it of vital foreign investment.

◆ **INSIGHT:** *The Green Line, which
separates north from south, was
opened for the first time in 2003*

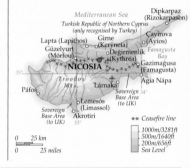

FACTFILE

OFFICIAL NAME: Republic of Cyprus
DATE OF FORMATION: 1960
CAPITAL: Nicosia
POPULATION: 797,000
TOTAL AREA: 3571 sq. miles
(9250 sq. km)
DENSITY: 223 people per sq. mile

LANGUAGES: Greek*, Turkish*
RELIGIONS: Orthodox Christian 73%,
Muslim 23%, other 4%
ETHNIC MIX: Greek 77%, Turkish 18%,
other 5%
GOVERNMENT: Presidential systems
CURRENCY: Cyprus pound = 100 cents
(Turkish lira in TRNC = 100 kurus)

Czech Republic

Once part of Czechoslovakia in central Europe, the Czech Republic became independent in 1993, after peacefully dissolving its federal union with Slovakia.

 GEOGRAPHY
Landlocked in central Europe. Bohemia, the western territory, is a plateau surrounded by mountains. Moravia, in the east, is characterized by hills and lowlands.

 CLIMATE
Cool, sometimes cold winters and warm summer months, which bring most of the annual rainfall.

 PEOPLE & SOCIETY
Secular and urban society, with high divorce rates. Czechs make up the vast majority of the population, while the next largest group are Moravians. The 300,000 Slovaks left after partition are now permitted dual citizenship. Ethnic tensions are few, but there is widespread hostility toward the Roma minority. A new commercial elite is emerging alongside postcommunist entrepreneurs.

 THE ECONOMY
Traditional heavy industries (machinery, iron, car-making) have been successfully privatized. Large tourism revenues. Skilled labor force. Rising unemployment.

◆ **INSIGHT:** *Charles University in Prague was founded in the 13th century.*

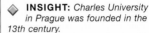

| 1000m/3281ft |
| 500m/1640ft |
| 200m/656ft |
| Sea Level |

0   50 km

0   50 miles

📖 FACTFILE

OFFICIAL NAME: Czech Republic

DATE OF FORMATION: 1993

CAPITAL: Prague

POPULATION: 10.3 million

TOTAL AREA: 30,450 sq. miles (78,866 sq. km)

DENSITY: 338 people per sq. mile

LANGUAGES: Czech*, Slovak, Hungarian

RELIGIONS: Roman Catholic 39%, atheist 38%, other 18%, Protestant 3%, Hussite 2%

ETHNIC MIX: Czech 81%, Moravian 13%, Slovak 6%

GOVERNMENT: Parliamentary system

CURRENCY: Czech koruna = 100 haleru

Denmark

Denmark occupies the Jutland peninsula and over 400 islands in southern Scandinavia. Greenland and the Faeroe Islands are self-governing associated territories.

GEOGRAPHY

Fertile farmland covers two-thirds of the terrain, which is among the flattest in the world. About 100 islands are inhabited.

CLIMATE

Damp, temperate climate with mild summers and cold, wet winters. Rainfall is moderate.

PEOPLE & SOCIETY

Society is homogeneous. Rising unemployment has fostered some ethnic tensions with the small immigrant population. Almost all women now work and 90% of children attend nurseries. Divorce rates are high and marriage is becoming less common. Income distribution is the most even in the West.

◆ **INSIGHT:** *Denmark is Europe's oldest kingdom – the monarchy dates back to the 10th century*

THE ECONOMY

Gas and oil reserves. The skilled workforce is key to high-tech industrial success. Strong currency affects competitiveness. Pigmeat and dairy products are exported.

FACTFILE

OFFICIAL NAME: Kingdom of Denmark
DATE OF FORMATION: 950
CAPITAL: Copenhagen
POPULATION: 5.3 million
TOTAL AREA: 16,639 sq. miles
(43,094 sq. km)
DENSITY: 324 people per sq. mile

LANGUAGES: Danish
RELIGIONS: Evangelical Lutheran 89%, other 10%, Roman Catholic 1%
ETHNIC MIX: Danish 96%, other (including Scandinavian and Turkish) 3%, Faeroese and Inuit 1%
GOVERNMENT: Parliamentary system
CURRENCY: Danish krone = 100 øre

Djibouti

A city-state with a desert hinterland, Djibouti lies in northeast Africa at the entrance to the Red Sea. Once known as the French Territory of the Afars and Issas, independence came in 1977.

GEOGRAPHY
Mainly low-lying desert and semidesert, with a volcanic mountain range in the north.

CLIMATE
Almost no rain, though the monsoon is very humid. The 109°F (45°C) heat of summer is unbearable.

PEOPLE & SOCIETY
The main ethnic groups are the Issas in the south, and the nomadic Afars in the north. Tensions between them developed into a guerrilla war in 1991–1994. Smaller tribal groups make up the rest of the population, and the rural peoples are mostly nomadic. Wealth is concentrated in Djibouti city. France exerts considerable influence in Djibouti, supporting it financially and maintaining a naval base and a military garrison.

THE ECONOMY
Djibouti's major assets are its ports in a key Red Sea location.

◆ **INSIGHT:** *Chewing the leaves of the mildly narcotic qat shrub is an age-old social ritual in Djibouti*

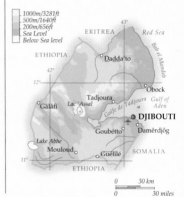

1000m/3281ft
500m/1640ft
200m/656ft
Sea Level
Below Sea level

ERITREA · Red Sea
ETHIOPIA
Bab el Mandeb
43°
Dadda'to
42°
12°
Obock
Tadjoura · Gulf of Aden
Gâlâfi · Lac 'Assal · Golfe de Tadjoura
● DJIBOUTI
Goubétto · Damêrdjôg
Lake Abhe
Mouloud · Guélilé
11° · SOMALIA
ETHIOPIA

0 ___ 30 km
0 ___ 30 miles

FACTFILE
OFFICIAL NAME: Republic of Djibouti
DATE OF FORMATION: 1977
CAPITAL: Djibouti
POPULATION: 652,000
TOTAL AREA: 8494 sq. miles (22,000 sq. km)
DENSITY: 73 people per sq. mile

LANGUAGES: Somali, Afar, French*, Arabic*
RELIGIONS: Muslim (mainly Sunni) 94%, Christian 6%
ETHNIC MIX: Issa 60%, Afar 35%, other 5%
GOVERNMENT: Presidential system
CURRENCY: Djibouti franc = 100 centimes

Dominica

Dominica is renowned as the Caribbean island that resisted European colonization until the 18th century. It achieved independence from the UK in 1978.

GEOGRAPHY

Mountainous and densely forested. Volcanic activity has given the land very fertile soils, hot springs, geysers, and black sand beaches.

CLIMATE

Tropical, cooled by constant trade winds. Heavy annual rainfall. Tropical depressions and hurricanes are likely June–November.

PEOPLE & SOCIETY

The majority of Dominicans are descendants of African slaves brought over to work on banana plantations. The Carib Territory on the northeast of the island is home to the only surviving indigenous community in the Caribbean. Wealth disparities are not as marked as elsewhere in the region, but the alleviation of poverty has become a major plank of government policy.

THE ECONOMY

Bananas and tourism are the economic mainstays, though preferential access for Dominican bananas to the EU has now gone.

INSIGHT: *Dominica is known as "Nature Island" due to its spectacular flora and fauna*

FACTFILE

OFFICIAL NAME: Commonwealth of Dominica
DATE OF FORMATION: 1978
CAPITAL: Roseau
POPULATION: 70,158
TOTAL AREA: 291 sq. miles (754 sq. km)

DENSITY: 242 people per sq. mile
LANGUAGES: French Creole, English*
RELIGIONS: Roman Catholic 77%, Protestant 15%, other 8%
ETHNIC MIX: Black 91%, mixed 6%, Carib 2%, other 1%
GOVERNMENT: Parliamentary system
CURRENCY: East Caribbean $ = 100 cents

Dominican Republic

The Dominican Republic occupies the eastern two-thirds of the island of Hispaniola in the Caribbean. Spanish-speaking, it seeks closer ties to the anglophone West Indies.

GEOGRAPHY

Highlands and rainforested mountains – including highest peak in Caribbean, Pico Duarte – interspersed with fertile valleys. Extensive coastal plain in the east.

CLIMATE

Hot and humid close to sea level, cooler at altitude. Heavy rainfall, especially in the northeast.

PEOPLE & SOCIETY

White landowners – especially those descended from the original Spanish settlers – and the military hold political power. Mixed-race majority control commerce and form bulk of the professional middle classes. White and mixed-race women are entering the professions. Great disparities of wealth exist; the black and Haitian-immigrant population occupy the bottom of the social ladder.

THE ECONOMY

Mining – mainly of nickel and gold – and sugar are major sectors. Hidden economy based on trans-shipment of narcotics to the US. Recent dramatic growth in tourism.

INSIGHT: *Santo Domingo is the oldest city in the Americas. It was founded in 1496 by the brother of Christopher Columbus*

	2000m/6562ft
	1000m/3281ft
	500m/1640ft
	200m/656ft
	Sea Level

0   50 km
0   50 miles

FACTFILE

OFFICIAL NAME: Dominican Republic
DATE OF FORMATION: 1865
CAPITAL: Santo Domingo
POPULATION: 8.6 million
TOTAL AREA: 18,679 sq. miles (48,380 sq. km)
DENSITY: 460 people per sq. mile

LANGUAGES: Spanish*, French Creole
RELIGIONS: Roman Catholic 92%, other and nonreligious 8%
ETHNIC MIX: Mixed 75%, White 15%, Black 10%
GOVERNMENT: Presidential system
CURRENCY: Dominican Republic peso = 100 centavos

East Timor

The world's youngest country, East Timor occupies the once Portuguese-owned eastern half of the island of Timor. Invaded by Indonesia in 1975, it became independent in 2002.

GEOGRAPHY

A narrow coastal plain gives way to forested highlands. Timor's mountain backbone rises to 9715 ft (2963 m).

CLIMATE

Tropical. Heavy rain in wet season (December–March), then dry and hot, particularly in the north.

PEOPLE & SOCIETY

The population is almost entirely Roman Catholic. The Timorese are a mix of Malay and Papuan peoples, and many indigenous Papuan tribes survive. There is an urban Chinese minority, and ethnic Indonesian settlers became numerous after annexation in 1975. Preindependence violence in 1999 was politically rather than ethnically motivated. Women do not have access to the professions and levels of domestic violence are notably high. Living standards are low.

THE ECONOMY

An agreement with Australia on sharing oil reserves under the Timor Sea was sealed in 2003. Violence in 1999 held back investment and damaged infrastructure. Coffee is the key export.

◆ **INSIGHT:** *Once dependent on sandalwood, the economy could be transformed by oil under the Timor Sea*

FACTFILE

OFFICIAL NAME: Democratic Republic of Timor Leste

DATE OF FORMATION: 2002

CAPITAL: Dili

POPULATION: 779,000

TOTAL AREA: 5756 sq. miles (14,874 sq. km)

DENSITY: 138 people per sq. mile

LANGUAGES: Tetum*, Bahasa Indonesia, Portuguese*

RELIGIONS: Catholic 95%, other 5%

ETHNIC MIX: Malay/Papuan groups c.85%, Indonesian c.13%, Chinese 2%

GOVERNMENT: Parliamentary system

CURRENCY: US dollar = 100 cents

Ecuador

Once part of the Inca heartland, Ecuador sits high on South America's western coast. Its territory includes the beautiful Galápagos Islands, 610 miles (970 km) to the west.

GEOGRAPHY

Broad coastal plain, inter-Andean central highlands, dense jungle in upper Amazon basin.

CLIMATE

The climate is hot and moist on the coast, cool in the Andes, and hot equatorial in the Amazon basin.

PEOPLE & SOCIETY

Over half of the population is of Amerindian–Spanish extraction (*mestizo*). Black communities exist on the coast. The strong and largely unified Amerindian movement is at the forefront of social protests. The US state aid agency estimates that as much as 70% of the population lives in poverty, predominantly in cities.

◆ **INSIGHT:** *Darwin's study on the Galápagos Islands in 1856 played a major part in his theory of evolution*

THE ECONOMY

The world's second-biggest banana producer, and a net oil exporter. Fishing industry. US dollar offers stability, but less control. Poor infrastructure and land productivity.

FACTFILE

OFFICIAL NAME: Republic of Ecuador
DATE OF FORMATION: 1830
CAPITAL: Quito
POPULATION: 13.1 million
TOTAL AREA: 109,483 sq. miles (283,560 sq. km)
DENSITY: 123 people per sq. mile

LANGUAGES: Spanish*, Quechua, other Amerindian languages
RELIGIONS: Roman Catholic 93%, Protestant, Jewish, and other 7%
ETHNIC MIX: Mestizo 55%, Amerindian 25%, White 10%, Black 10%
GOVERNMENT: Presidential system
CURRENCY: US dollar = 100 cents

Egypt

Occupying the northeast corner of Africa, Egypt is divided by the highly fertile Nile Valley. Its essentially pro-Western, military-backed regime is being challenged by Islamic fundamentalists.

GEOGRAPHY
Fertile Nile Valley separates arid Libyan Desert from smaller semiarid eastern desert. Sinai peninsula has mountains in south.

CLIMATE
Summers are very hot, but winters are cooler. Rainfall is negligible, except on the coast.

PEOPLE & SOCIETY
There is a long tradition of ethnic and religious tolerance, though the rise of Islamism has sparked clashes between Muslims and Copts (Coptic Christianity is one of the Church's earliest branches). Women play a full part in education and the economy, though this is threatened by Islamism. The rapidly growing population is a serious problem. Poverty is rife around Cairo, Africa's second-largest city.

THE ECONOMY
Oil and gas are main sources of revenue. Tolls from the Suez Canal. Successful tourist industry. High birthrate and rural poverty main problems.

◆ **INSIGHT:** *Egypt has been a major tourist destination since the 1880s*

Mediterranean Sea · Nile Delta
El Manşûra
Alexandria · Port Sa'îd · ISRAEL
Tantâ · Ismâ'îliya
Shubrâ el Kheima · Suez Canal · JORDAN
Monkhafad · El Gîza · Sinai
el Qattâra · El Faiyûm · CAIRO
LIBYA · 28°
Asyûṭ · Hurghada
Sohâg · Qena
Libyan · Luxor
Desert · Aswân
24° · Administrative border
Buheiret · Nâşir
SUDAN · Political border
28° · 32° · 36°

- 2000m/6562ft
- 1000m/3281ft
- 500m/1640ft
- 200m/656ft
- Sea Level
- Below Sea Level

0 ——— 200 km
0 ——— 200 miles

FACTFILE

OFFICIAL NAME: Arab Republic of Egypt
DATE OF FORMATION: 1936
CAPITAL: Cairo
POPULATION: 70.3 million
TOTAL AREA: 386,660 sq. miles (1,001,450 sq. km)
DENSITY: 183 people per sq. mile

LANGUAGES: Arabic*, French, English, Berber
RELIGIONS: Muslim (mainly Sunni) 94%, Coptic Christian and other 6%
ETHNIC MIX: Eastern Hamitic 90%, other (Nubian, Armenian, Greek) 10%
GOVERNMENT: Presidential system
CURRENCY: Egyptian pound = 100 piastres

El Salvador

El Salvador is Central America's smallest and most densely populated country. Already struggling to recover from a civil war in the 1980s, it was badly struck by earthquakes in 2001.

GEOGRAPHY

El Salvador is a narrow coastal belt backed by two mountain ranges. There is a central plateau. Located within a seismic zone, there are more than 20 volcanic peaks.

CLIMATE

Tropical coastal belt is very hot, with seasonal rains. Cooler, temperate climate in highlands.

PEOPLE & SOCIETY

Population is largely *mestizo*; ethnic tensions are few. The 1981–1991 civil war was fought between the US-backed right-wing government and left-wing FMLN guerrillas, over gross economic disparities, which still exist despite some reform. During the war 75,000 people died, many of whom were unarmed civilians. The FMLN gave up its arms in 1992 and is now the largest party in Congress.

THE ECONOMY

Overdependence on coffee, which accounts for majority of exports. Series of powerful earthquakes in early 2001 devastated infrastructure and deepened the country's reliance on aid. There are no significant resources.

◆ **INSIGHT:** *Independent since 1841, El Salvador is named after Jesus Christ, "the savior" of Christians*

FACTFILE

OFFICIAL NAME: Republic of El Salvador
DATE OF FORMATION: 1841
CAPITAL: San Salvador
POPULATION: 6.5 million
TOTAL AREA: 8124 sq. miles (21,040 sq. km)
DENSITY: 812 people per sq. mile

LANGUAGES: Spanish
RELIGIONS: Roman Catholic 80%, Evangelical 18%, other 2%
ETHNIC MIX: Mestizo 94%, Amerindian 5%, White 1%
GOVERNMENT: Presidential system
CURRENCIES: Salvadorean colón = 100 centavos; US dollar = 100 cents

Equatorial Guinea

Comprising the mainland territory of Río Muni and five islands on the west coast of central Africa, Equatorial Guinea lies, as its name suggests, just north of the equator.

GEOGRAPHY

The islands are mountainous and volcanic. The mainland is lower, with mangrove swamps along the coast.

CLIMATE

Bioko is extremely wet and humid. The mainland is only marginally drier and cooler.

PEOPLE & SOCIETY

Equatorial Guinea is the only Spanish-speaking country in Africa. Río Muni is sparsely populated and most people there are Fang, an ethnic group also found in Cameroon and northern Gabon. Bioko is populated mostly by Bubi and a minority of Creoles known as Fernandinos. Tensions between the two territories have been reignited by the discovery of oil off Bioko. What little wealth exists is concentrated in the ruling clan.

THE ECONOMY

Oil and gas reserves have come on stream; the government has promised to reinvest the new funds in development. Timber and coffee.

INSIGHT: *There is only one properly paved road, serving the president's hometown*

2000m/6562ft	
1000m/3281ft	
500m/1640ft	
200m/656ft	
Sea Level	

MALABO
3°30'N
Isla de Bioco
Bight of Biafra

ATLANTIC OCEAN
Gulf of Guinea
CAMEROON
Micomeseng
Bata   Niefang
Mbini   Mongomo
Río   Uolo
Muni
Cabo San Juan
Etembue   Cogo   Nsoc
Isla de Corisco
GABON

0   40 km
0   40 miles

FACTFILE

OFFICIAL NAME: Republic of Equatorial Guinea
DATE OF FORMATION: 1968
CAPITAL: Malabo
POPULATION: 483,000
TOTAL AREA: 10,830 sq. miles (28,051 sq. km)

DENSITY: 45 people per sq. mile
LANGUAGES: Spanish*, Fang, Bubi, French*
RELIGIONS: Roman Catholic 90%, other 10%
ETHNIC MIX: Fang 85%, other 11%, Bubi 4%
GOVERNMENT: Presidential system
CURRENCY: CFA franc = 100 centimes

Eritrea

Lying along the southwest shore of the Red Sea, Eritrea won a long war for independence from Ethiopia in 1993. The two neighbors fought a bitter border war in 1998–2000.

GEOGRAPHY
Mostly consists of rugged mountains, bush, and the Danakil Desert, which falls below sea level.

CLIMATE
Warm in the mountains; desert areas are hot. Droughts from July onward are common.

PEOPLE & SOCIETY
Tigrinya-speakers, mainly Orthodox Christians, are the most numerous of nine main ethnic groups. A strong sense of nationhood has been forged by war. Women played a vital role in combat. Over 80% of people are subsistence farmers. Multiparty elections, expected in 1997, have been persistently postponed.

◆ **INSIGHT:** *Eritrea is the only country to secede successfully in postcolonial Africa*

THE ECONOMY
Legacy of disruption and destruction from wars. Susceptible to drought and famine. Most of the population live at subsistence level. Potential for mining of gold, copper, silver, and zinc. Possible foreign earnings from oil exports.

	2000m/6562ft
	1000m/3281ft
	500m/1640ft
	200m/656ft
	Sea Level
	Below Sea Level

FACTFILE
OFFICIAL NAME: State of Eritrea
DATE OF FORMATION: 1993
CAPITAL: Asmara
POPULATION: 4 million
TOTAL AREA: 46,842 sq. miles (121,320 sq. km)
DENSITY: 88 people per sq. mile

LANGUAGES: Tigrinya*, English*, Tigre, Afar, Arabic*, Bilen, Kunama, other
RELIGIONS: Christian 45%, Muslim 45%, other 10%
ETHNIC MIX: Tigray 50%, Tigray and Kunama 40%, Afar 4%, other 6%
GOVERNMENT: Transitional regime
CURRENCY: Nakfa = 100 cents

Estonia

Traditionally the most Western-oriented of the Baltic states, Estonia is the smallest and most developed of the three and has the highest standard of living of any former Soviet republic.

GEOGRAPHY

Estonia's terrain is flat, boggy, and partly forested, with over 1500 islands. Lake Peipus forms much of the eastern border with Russia.

CLIMATE

Maritime, with some continental extremes. Harsh winters, with cool summers and damp springs.

PEOPLE & SOCIETY

Estonians are related ethnically and linguistically to the Finns. Friction between ethnic Estonians and the large Russian minority led to a reassertion of Estonian culture and language. Outright discrimination against the Russian language was only ended in 2000. Estonians are predominantly Lutheran. Families are small and divorce rates are high. Market reforms have increased prosperity; a few people have become very rich.

THE ECONOMY

Stable currency pegged to the euro. Good productivity. Timber and oil shale are the most important of few natural resources. Estonia is dependent on imported energy.

INSIGHT: *Estonia is a popular tourist destination for Finns, who come for the water and winter sports, architectural heritage, and nature tours*

FACTFILE

OFFICIAL NAME: Republic of Estonia
DATE OF FORMATION: 1991
CAPITAL: Tallinn
POPULATION: 1.4 million
TOTAL AREA: 17,462 sq. miles (45,226 sq. km)
DENSITY: 80 people per sq. mile

LANGUAGES: Estonian*, Russian
RELIGIONS: Evangelical Lutheran 56%, Russian Orthodox 25%, other 19%
ETHNIC MIX: Estonian 62%, Russian 30%, other 8%
GOVERNMENT: Parliamentary system
CURRENCY: Kroon = 100 senti

Ethiopia

Located in northeast Africa, the former empire of Ethiopia was a Marxist regime in 1974–1991. Now a free-market democracy, it has suffered a series of economic, civil, and natural crises.

GEOGRAPHY
Great Rift Valley divides mountainous northwest region from desert lowlands in northeast and southeast. Ethiopian Plateau is drained mainly by the Blue Nile.

CLIMATE
Moderate with summer rains. Highlands are warm, with night frost and snowfalls on the mountains.

PEOPLE & SOCIETY
76 Ethiopian nationalities speak 286 languages. Oromo (or Gallas) are the largest group. Ethnic representation is a major political issue. Orthodox Christianity has a very ancient history in Ethiopia. Former emperor Haile Selassie inspired Rastafarianism.

◆ **INSIGHT:** *King Solomon and the Queen of Sheba are said to have founded the Kingdom of Abyssinia (Ethiopia) c.1000 BCE*

THE ECONOMY
There is an overwhelming dependence on agriculture. War-damaged infrastructure and periodic serious droughts and famines undermine growth. Ethiopia is moving toward becoming a full market economy.

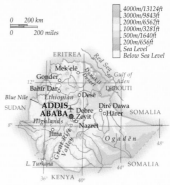

4000m/13124ft
3000m/9843ft
2000m/6562ft
1000m/3281ft
500m/1640ft
200m/656ft
Sea Level
Below Sea Level

0   200 km
0   200 miles

FACTFILE
OFFICIAL NAME: Federal Democratic Republic of Ethiopia
DATE OF FORMATION: 1896
CAPITAL: Addis Ababa
POPULATION: 66 million
TOTAL AREA: 435,184 sq. miles (1,127,127 sq. km)

DENSITY: 154 people per sq. mile
LANGUAGES: Amharic*, Tigrinya, other
RELIGIONS: Orthodox Christian 40%, Muslim 40%, traditional 15%, other 5%
ETHNIC MIX: Oromo 40%, Amhara 25%, other 20%, Sidamo 9%, Somali 6%
GOVERNMENT: Parliamentary system
CURRENCY: Ethiopian birr = 100 cents

Fiji

A volcanic archipelago in the southern Pacific Ocean, comprising two large islands and 880 islets. Severe tensions exist between native Fijians and the substantial Indian minority.

GEOGRAPHY
Main islands are mountainous, fringed by coral reefs. Remainder are limestone and coral formations.

CLIMATE
Tropical. High temperatures all year round. Cyclones are a hazard.

PEOPLE & SOCIETY
The British introduced workers from India in the late 19th century, and by 1946 their descendants outnumbered the indigenous Fijian population. Ethnic-Fijian nationalism is strong and the first ethnic Indian-dominated government was overthrown in 2000; serious tensions persist. Many Indo-Fijians have left the country. Women are lobbying for more rights.

◆ **INSIGHT:** *Both Fijians and Indians practice fire-walking; Indians walk on hot embers, Fijians on heated stones*

THE ECONOMY
Well-diversified economy based on sugar production, gold mining, timber, and commercial fishing. Tourists are returning after a drop in numbers prompted by instability.

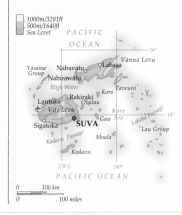

FACTFILE
OFFICIAL NAME: Republic of the Fiji Islands
DATE OF FORMATION: 1970
CAPITAL: Suva
POPULATION: 832,000
TOTAL AREA: 7054 sq. miles (18,270 sq. km)
DENSITY: 118 people per sq. mile

LANGUAGES: Fijian, English*, Hindi, Urdu, Tamil, Telugu
RELIGIONS: Hindu 38%, Methodist 37%, Catholic 9%, Muslim 8%, other 8%
ETHNIC MIX: Melanesian (Fijian) 48%, Indian 46%, other 6%
GOVERNMENT: Parliamentary system
CURRENCY: Fiji dollar = 100 cents

Finland

Finland's language and national identity have been influenced by both its Scandinavian and Russian neighbors. Once closely associated with the USSR, Finland is now a member of the EU.

GEOGRAPHY

South and center are flat, with low hills and many lakes. Uplands and low mountains in the north. 60% of the land area is forested.

CLIMATE

Long, harsh winters with frequent snowfalls. Short, warmer summers. Rainfall is low, and decreases northward.

PEOPLE & SOCIETY

More than half the population live in the five districts around Helsinki. The Swedish minority live mainly in the Åland Islands in the southwest. The Sami (Lapps) lead a seminomadic existence inside the Arctic Circle. A majority of women go out to work, continuing a long tradition of equality between the sexes. Families tend to be close-knit, though divorce rates are high.

THE ECONOMY

Strong engineering and electronics sectors. World leader in pulp and paper production.

◆ **INSIGHT:** *Finland has Europe's largest inland waterway system*

FACTFILE

OFFICIAL NAME: Republic of Finland
DATE OF FORMATION: 1917
CAPITAL: Helsinki
POPULATION: 5.2 million
TOTAL AREA: 130,127 sq. miles (337,030 sq. km)
DENSITY: 44 people per sq. mile

LANGUAGES: Finnish*, Swedish*, Sami
RELIGIONS: Evangelical Lutheran 89%, other 9%, Orthodox Christian 1%, Roman Catholic 1%
ETHNIC MIX: Finnish 93%, other (including Sami) 7%
GOVERNMENT: Parliamentary system
CURRENCY: Euro = 100 cents

France

Stretching across western Europe, from the English Channel (la Manche) to the Mediterranean Sea, France was Europe's first modern republic, and is now a leading industrial power.

GEOGRAPHY

Broad plain covers northern half of the country. Tall mountain ranges in the east and southwest, with a mountainous plateau in the center.

CLIMATE

Three main climates: temperate and damp northwest; continental east; and Mediterranean south.

PEOPLE & SOCIETY

Strong French national identity coexists with pronounced regional differences, including local languages. Immigration laws have been tightened since the 1970s. The far right is active, but negated by an inclusivist and liberal youth culture. Women are not well represented in politics.

◆ **INSIGHT:** *France is the most popular tourist destination in the world, with over 76 million visitors a year*

THE ECONOMY

Steel, chemicals, electronics, heavy engineering, and aircraft typify a strong and diversified export sector. World leader in cosmetics, perfumes, and quality wines.

FACTFILE

OFFICIAL NAME: French Republic
DATE OF FORMATION: 987
CAPITAL: Paris
POPULATION: 59.7 million
TOTAL AREA: 211,208 sq. miles (547,030 sq. km)
DENSITY: 281 people per sq. mile

LANGUAGES: French*, Provençal, other
RELIGIONS: Catholic 88%, Muslim 8%, Protestant 2%, Jewish 1%, Buddhist 1%
ETHNIC MIX: French 90%, North African 6%, German 2%, Breton 1%, other 1%
GOVERNMENT: Mixed presidential–parliamentary system
CURRENCY: Euro = 100 cents

Gabon

Gabon is a former French colony straddling the equator on Africa's west coast. Independent since 1960, it returned to multiparty politics in 1990, after 22 years of one-party rule.

GEOGRAPHY
Low plateaus and mountains lie beyond the coastal strip. Two-thirds of the land is covered by rainforest.

CLIMATE
Hot and tropical, with little distinction between seasons. Cold Benguela current cools the coast.

PEOPLE & SOCIETY
Some 40 different languages are spoken. The Fang, who live mainly in the north, are the largest ethnic group, but have yet to gain control of the government. Oil wealth has led to the growth of an affluent middle class. Menial jobs are done by immigrant workers. Education follows the French system. With over 80% of people living in towns, Gabon is one of Africa's most urbanized countries. The government is encouraging population growth.

THE ECONOMY
Oil is the main source of revenue. Tropical hardwoods are being exploited. Cocoa beans, coffee, and rice are grown for export.

◆ **INSIGHT:** *Libreville was founded as a settlement for freed French slaves in 1849*

FACTFILE
OFFICIAL NAME: Gabonese Republic
DATE OF FORMATION: 1960
CAPITAL: Libreville
POPULATION: 1.3 million
TOTAL AREA: 103,346 sq. miles (267,667 sq. km)
DENSITY: 13 people per sq. mile

LANGUAGES: Fang, French*, Punu, other
RELIGIONS: Christian (predominantly Roman Catholic) 55%, traditional beliefs 40%, other 4%, Muslim 1%
ETHNIC MIX: Fang 35%, other Bantu 29%, Eshira 25%, other 9%, French 2%
GOVERNMENT: Presidential system
CURRENCY: CFA franc = 100 centimes

Gambia

Gambia is a narrow state on the west coast of Africa, almost entirely surrounded by Senegal. It was renowned for its stability until its government was overthrown in a coup in 1994.

GEOGRAPHY
Located on the narrow strip of land bordering the Gambia River. Long, sandy beaches are backed by mangrove swamps along the river. Savanna and tropical forests higher up.

CLIMATE
Subtropical, with wet, humid months July–October, and warm, dry season November–May.

PEOPLE & SOCIETY
Little tension between various ethnic groups. The largest group, the Mandinka, has traditionally held power. Islam is a strong social influence, though there is no official state religion. A small expatriate community from the UK lives on the coast. Each year seasonal migrants come from neighboring states to farm groundnuts. Women are very active as traders.

THE ECONOMY
Around 80% of the labor force is involved in agriculture. Groundnuts are the principal crop. Fish stocks are declining. "Eco-tourism" is promoted, though most visitors come for the beaches. Smuggling problems. Banjul is one of west Africa's finest deepwater ports.

INSIGHT: *Overfishing in the waters off the Gambia and Senegal, mainly by foreign vessels, is a growing problem*

FACTFILE
OFFICIAL NAME: Republic of the Gambia
DATE OF FORMATION: 1965
CAPITAL: Banjul
POPULATION: 1.4 million
TOTAL AREA: 4363 sq. miles (11,300 sq. km)
DENSITY: 363 people per sq. mile

LANGUAGES: Mandinka, Fulani, Wolof, Jola, Soninke, English*
RELIGIONS: Sunni Muslim 90%, Christian 9%, traditional beliefs 1%
ETHNIC MIX: Mandinka 42%, Fulani 18%, Wolof 16%, Jola 10%, Serahuli 9%, other 5%
GOVERNMENT: Presidential system
CURRENCY: Dalasi = 100 butut

Georgia

Located on the eastern shore of the Black Sea, Georgia has been torn by civil war and ethnic disputes since achieving independence from the Soviet Union in 1991.

GEOGRAPHY

Kura Valley lies between Caucasus Mountains in the north and Lesser Caucasus range in south. Lowlands along the Black Sea coast.

CLIMATE

Subtropical along the coast, changing to continental extremes at high altitudes. Rainfall is moderate.

PEOPLE & SOCIETY

Paternalistic society, with strong family, cultural, and literary traditions. Georgia was converted to Christianity in 326 CE. Civil conflict and wars against Abkhaz and Osset separatists in the early 1990s displaced over 300,000 people. Abkhazia and South Ossetia now effectively operate as separate states. A small, wealthy elite is found in Tbilisi while the ethnic Armenians of the south are among the poorest people in society.

THE ECONOMY

Georgia is a gateway to the West for Azeri oil. It has a long-established and booming wine industry, exporting mostly to Russia. Political instability deters investment.

◆ **INSIGHT:** *Western Georgia was the land of the legendary Golden Fleece of Greek mythology*

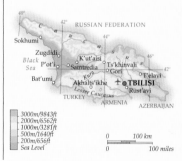

| 3000m/9843ft |
| 2000m/6562ft |
| 1000m/3281ft |
| 500m/1640ft |
| 200m/656ft |
| Sea Level |

0   100 km
0   100 miles

FACTFILE

OFFICIAL NAME: Georgia
DATE OF FORMATION: 1991
CAPITAL: Tbilisi
POPULATION: 4.6 million
TOTAL AREA: 26,911 sq. miles (69,700 sq. km)
DENSITY: 171 people per sq. mile

LANGUAGES: Georgian*, Russian, other
RELIGIONS: Georgian Orthodox 65%, Muslim 11%, Russian Orthodox 10%, Armenian Orthodox 8%, other 6%
ETHNIC MIX: Georgian 70%, Armenian 8%, other 10%, Russian 6%, Azeri 6%
GOVERNMENT: Presidential system
CURRENCY: Lari = 100 tetri

Germany

Europe's strongest economic and industrial power, Germany was divided into a democratic west and a communist east in 1945. It was reunified in 1990, after the fall of the Berlin Wall.

GEOGRAPHY
Coastal plains in the north, rising to rolling hills of central region. Alpine region in the south.

CLIMATE
Damp, temperate in northern and central regions. Continental extremes in mountainous south.

PEOPLE & SOCIETY
Regionalism is strong. The north is mainly Protestant while the south is staunchly Roman Catholic. Social and economic differences still exist between east and west. Turks are the largest single ethnic minority; many came as guest workers in the 1950s–1970s. Immigration now focuses on skilled workers. Feminism is strong.

◆ **INSIGHT:** *Germany's rivers and canals carry as much freight as its busy toll-free roads*

THE ECONOMY
Massive exports of electronics, heavy engineering, chemicals, and cars. Global slowdown from 2001 boosted unemployment levels.

2000m/6562ft
1000m/3281ft
500m/1640ft
200m/656ft
Sea Level

0   100 km
0   100 miles

FACTFILE
OFFICIAL NAME: Federal Republic of Germany
DATE OF FORMATION: 1871
CAPITAL: Berlin
POPULATION: 82 million
TOTAL AREA: 137,846 sq. miles (357,021 sq. km)

DENSITY: 608 people per sq. mile
LANGUAGES: German*, Turkish
RELIGIONS: Protestant 34%, Roman Catholic 33%, other 30%, Muslim 3%
ETHNIC MIX: German 92%, other 3%, other European 3%, Turkish 2%
GOVERNMENT: Parliamentary system
CURRENCY: Euro = 100 cents

Ghana

The heartland of the ancient Ashanti kingdom, Ghana in west Africa was once known as the Gold Coast. It has experienced intermittent periods of military rule since independence in 1957.

GEOGRAPHY

Mostly low-lying. The west is covered by rainforest. The world's third-largest artificial lake – Lake Volta – was created by damming the White Volta River.

CLIMATE

Tropical. There are two wet seasons in the south, but the north is drier, and has just one.

PEOPLE & SOCIETY

Around 75 cultural-linguistic groups. The largest is the Akan, who include the Ashanti and Fanti peoples. Over 100 languages and dialects are spoken. Southern peoples are richer and more urban than those of the north. There are few tribal tensions. Family ties are strong. The election of John Kufuor in 2000 marked Ghana's first peaceful handover of power since independence.

THE ECONOMY

Produces 14% of the world's cocoa. Gold is now the major export. Hardwood trees such as maple and sapele. Hydropower is exported.

INSIGHT: Ghana was the first colony in west Africa to gain independence

FACTFILE

OFFICIAL NAME: Republic of Ghana
DATE OF FORMATION: 1957
CAPITAL: Accra
POPULATION: 20.2 million
TOTAL AREA: 92,100 sq. miles (238,540 sq. km)
DENSITY: 227 people per sq. mile

LANGUAGES: Twi, Fanti, Ewe, Ga, Adangbe, Gurma, Dagomba, English*
RELIGIONS: Christian 43%, traditional beliefs 38%, Muslim 11%, other 8%
ETHNIC MIX: Ashanti and Fanti 52%, Moshi 16%, Ewe 12%, other 12%, Ga 8%
GOVERNMENT: Presidential system
CURRENCY: Cedi = 100 psewas

Greece

The Balkan state of Greece is bounded on three sides by the Mediterranean, Aegean, and Ionian Seas. It has a strong seafaring tradition, with some of the world's richest shipowners.

 GEOGRAPHY
Mountainous peninsula and over 2000 islands. Large plain along the mainland's Aegean coast.

 CLIMATE
Mainly Mediterranean with dry, hot summers. Alpine climate in northern mountain areas.

PEOPLE & SOCIETY
Postwar industrial development altered the dominance of agriculture and seafaring. The rural exodus to industrial cities has been stemmed but over half the population now live in the two largest cities. Age-old culture and Greek Orthodox Church balance social mobility. Civil marriage and divorce only became legal in 1982.

◆ **INSIGHT:** *Classical sights have made tourism one of the most important industries in Greece*

THE ECONOMY
One of Europe's leading tourist destinations. The world's largest beneficially owned shipping fleets. Thriving black economy. Public debt and unemployment remain high.

 FACTFILE

OFFICIAL NAME: Hellenic Republic
DATE OF FORMATION: 1829
CAPITAL: Athens
POPULATION: 10.6 million
TOTAL AREA: 50,942 sq. miles
(131,940 sq. km)
DENSITY: 210 people per sq. mile

LANGUAGES: Greek*, Turkish, Macedonian, Albanian
RELIGIONS: Orthodox Christian 98%, Muslim 1%, other 1%
ETHNIC MIX: Greek 98%, other 2%
GOVERNMENT: Parliamentary system
CURRENCY: Euro = 100 cents

Grenada

The southernmost of the Windward Islands, Grenada became a focus of world attention in 1983 when the US and Caribbean allies mounted an invasion to sever links with Castro's Cuba.

 GEOGRAPHY
Volcanic in origin, with densely forested central mountains. Its territory also includes the islands of Carriacou and Petite Martinique.

 CLIMATE
Tropical, tempered by trade winds. Hurricanes are a hazard in the July–November wet season.

PEOPLE & SOCIETY
Grenadians are mainly of African origin; their traditions remain strong, especially on Carriacou. Inter-ethnic marriage has reduced tensions between the groups. Extended families, often headed by women, are the norm. Wealth disparities are not marked, but levels of poverty are growing.

◆ **INSIGHT:** *Known as "the spice island of the Caribbean," it is the world's second-largest nutmeg producer*

 THE ECONOMY
Nutmeg, the most important crop, is affected by fluctuating world prices. Mace, cocoa, saffron, and cloves are also exported. Smuggling is a serious problem.

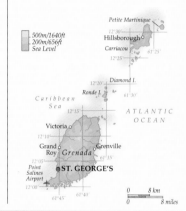

FACTFILE

OFFICIAL NAME: Grenada
DATE OF FORMATION: 1974
CAPITAL: St. George's
POPULATION: 89,211
TOTAL AREA: 131 sq. miles (340 sq. km)
DENSITY: 681 people per sq. mile

LANGUAGES: English*, English Creole
RELIGIONS: Roman Catholic 68%, Anglican 17%, other 15%
ETHNIC MIX: Black African 82%, Mulatto 13%, East Indian 3%, other 2%
GOVERNMENT: Parliamentary system
CURRENCY: East Caribbean $ = 100 cents

Guatemala

The largest and most populous nation on the Central American isthmus, Guatemala returned to civilian rule in 1986 after 32 years of violent and repressive military rule.

GEOGRAPHY
Narrow Pacific coastal plain. Central highlands with volcanoes. Short coast on the Caribbean Sea. Tropical rainforests in the north.

CLIMATE
Tropical: hot and humid in coastal regions and north. More temperate in central highlands.

PEOPLE & SOCIETY
Amerindians, concentrated in the highlands, form a majority. Power, wealth, and land are controlled by a *ladino* elite. Since civilian rule, the level of violence has diminished, but extreme poverty is increasing; almost 40% of the population live below the UN's poverty line of $2 a day.

◆ **INSIGHT:** *Guatemala, which means "land of trees," was the* center of the ancient Mayan civilization

THE ECONOMY
Agriculture is the key sector. Sugar, coffee, beef, bananas, and cardamom are top exports. Wealth inequalities inhibit domestic market.

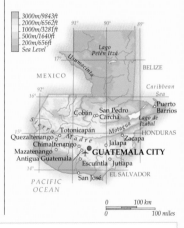

FACTFILE

OFFICIAL NAME: Republic of Guatemala

DATE OF FORMATION: 1838

CAPITAL: Guatemala City

POPULATION: 12 million

TOTAL AREA: 42,042 sq. miles (108,890 sq. km)

DENSITY: 287 people per sq. mile

LANGUAGES: Quiché, Mam, Cakchiquel, Kekchí, Spanish*

RELIGIONS: Roman Catholic 65%, Protestant 33%, other 2%

ETHNIC MIX: Amerindian 60%, Mestizo 30%, other 10%

GOVERNMENT: Presidential system

CURRENCY: Quetzal = 100 centavos

Guinea

Facing the Atlantic Ocean, on the west coast of Africa, Guinea became the first French colony in Africa to gain independence, in 1958. The country was under military rule from 1984 to 1995.

GEOGRAPHY
Coastal plains and mangrove swamps in west rise to forested or savanna highlands in the south. Semidesert in the north.

CLIMATE
Tropical, with a wet season April–October. Conakry is especially rainy. Hot, dry *harmattan* wind blows from Sahara during dry season.

PEOPLE & SOCIETY
Malinke and Fulani make up most of the population, but rivalries between them have allowed coastal peoples such as the Soussou to come to dominate politics. Daily life revolves around the extended family. Women acquired influence under Marxist party rule between 1958 and 1984, but the Muslim revival since then has reversed the trend. Private enterprise has created a business class.

THE ECONOMY
Two-thirds of people are farmers. Cash crops include bananas and palm oil. Substantial gold, diamond, and especially bauxite reserves.

INSIGHT: *The colors of Guinea's flag represent the three words of the country's motto: work (red), justice (yellow), and solidarity (green)*

1000m/3281ft
500m/1640ft
200m/656ft
Sea Level

0   100 km
0   100 miles

FACTFILE

OFFICIAL NAME: Republic of Guinea
DATE OF FORMATION: 1958
CAPITAL: Conakry
POPULATION: 8.4 million
TOTAL AREA: 94,925 sq. miles
(245,857 sq. km)
DENSITY: 88 people per sq. mile

LANGUAGES: Fulani, Malinke, Soussou, French*
RELIGIONS: Muslim 65%, traditional beliefs 33%, Christian 2%
ETHNIC MIX: Fulani 30%, Malinke 30%, Soussou 15%, Kissi 10%, other 15%
GOVERNMENT: Presidential system
CURRENCY: Guinea franc = 100 centimes

Guinea-Bissau

Known as Portuguese Guinea during its days as a colony, Guinea-Bissau is situated on Africa's west coast. There are plans to mover the capital east to Buba.

GEOGRAPHY
Low-lying, apart from savanna highlands in northeast. Rainforests and swamps are found along coastal areas.

CLIMATE
Tropical, with wet season May–November and dry season December–April. Hot, dry *harmattan* desert wind blows during dry season.

PEOPLE & SOCIETY
The largest ethnic group is the Balante, who live in the south. Though less than 2% of the population, the mixed Portuguese–African *mestiços* dominate the top ranks of government and bureaucracy. Most people live and work on small family farms, grouped in self-contained villages. The bulk of the urban population live in the capital, Bissau, where they face economic hardship and increasing political instability.

THE ECONOMY
Mostly subsistence farming – maize, sweet potatoes, cassava. Lack of sufficiency in rice staple. Main cash crops are cashews and groundnuts. Offshore oil as yet untapped. Fisheries and timber potential.

◆ **INSIGHT:** *In 1974, Guinea-Bissau became the first Portuguese colony to gain independence*

FACTFILE

OFFICIAL NAME: Rep. of Guinea-Bissau
DATE OF FORMATION: 1974
CAPITAL: Bissau
POPULATION: 1.3 million
TOTAL AREA: 13,946 sq. miles (36,120 sq. km)
DENSITY: 120 people per sq. mile

LANGUAGES: Portuguese Creole, Balante, Fulani, Malinke, Portuguese*
RELIGIONS: Indigenous beliefs 52%, Muslim 40%, Christian 8%
ETHNIC MIX: Other tribes 41%, Balante 25%, Fula 20%, Mandinka 12%, other 2%
GOVERNMENT: Transitional regime
CURRENCY: CFA franc = 100 centimes

Guyana

On the northeast coast of the continent, Guyana is South America's only English-speaking country. Independent since 1966, it has close ties with the anglophone Caribbean.

GEOGRAPHY
Mainly artificial coast, reclaimed by dikes and dams from swamps and tidal marshes. Forests cover 85% of the interior, rising to savanna uplands and mountains.

CLIMATE
Tropical. Coast cooled by sea breezes. Lowlands are hot, wet, and humid. Highlands are a little cooler.

PEOPLE & SOCIETY
Guyana is a complex multiracial society. Tension exists between the Afro-Guyanese, descended from slaves, and the Indo-Guyanese, descendants of laborers brought over after slavery was abolished. Politics is highly polarized around this split and often spills over into violence on the streets. Amerindian subsistence farmers are the poorest people in society and have little representation.

THE ECONOMY
Diverse exports: bauxite, gold, timber, sugar, rice, and diamonds. High foreign debt and unemployment.

INSIGHT: *Guyana means "land of many waters" – it has 3666 miles (5900 km) of navigable waterways*

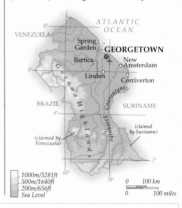

FACTFILE
OFFICIAL NAME: Cooperative Republic of Guyana
DATE OF FORMATION: 1966
CAPITAL: Georgetown
POPULATION: 765,000
TOTAL AREA: 83,000 sq. miles (214,970 sq. km)

DENSITY: 10 people per sq. mile
LANGUAGES: Creole, Hindi, English*
RELIGIONS: Christian 57%, Hindu 33%, Muslim 9%, other 1%
ETHNIC MIX: East Indian 52%, Black African 38%, other 6%, Amerindian 4%
GOVERNMENT: Presidential system
CURRENCY: Guyana dollar = 100 cents

Haiti

Formerly a French colony, Haiti shares the Caribbean island of Hispaniola with the Dominican Republic. At independence in 1804, it became the world's first black republic.

GEOGRAPHY
Predominantly mountainous, with forests and fertile plains.

CLIMATE
Tropical, with rain throughout the year. Humid in coastal areas, much cooler in the mountains.

PEOPLE & SOCIETY
Most Haitians are of African descent. A few have European roots, primarily French. The rigid class structure maintains vast disparities of wealth. The majority of the population live in extreme poverty; Haiti is one of the poorest countries in the Americas. A combination of political oppression and a collapsing economy has led thousands to seek asylum in the US or the Dominican Republic. As well as being Christians, many Haitians practice Voodoo, which was recognized as an official religion in 2003.

THE ECONOMY
Few natural resources. Transshipment of narcotics to the US provides a large source of income to smugglers. 70% unemployment.

INSIGHT: *A slave rebellion headed by Toussaint Louverture in 1791 led to Haiti's independence*

FACTFILE

OFFICIAL NAME: Republic of Haiti
DATE OF FORMATION: 1804
CAPITAL: Port-au-Prince
POPULATION: 8.4 million
TOTAL AREA: 10,714 sq. miles (27,750 sq. km)
DENSITY: 789 people per sq. mile

LANGUAGES: French Creole*, French*
RELIGIONS: Roman Catholic 80%, Protestant 16%, other 3%, nonreligious 1%; Voodoo is widely practiced
ETHNIC MIX: Black African 95%, Mulatto and European 5%
GOVERNMENT: Presidential system
CURRENCY: Gourde = 100 centimes

Honduras

Straddling the Central American isthmus, Honduras returned to democratic civilian rule in 1984, after a period of military government. Hurricane Mitch devastated the country in 1998.

GEOGRAPHY
Narrow plains along both coasts, with a mountainous interior, cut by river valleys. Tropical forests, swamps, and lagoons in the east.

CLIMATE
Tropical coastal lowlands are hot and humid, with May–October rains. Interior is cooler and drier.

PEOPLE & SOCIETY
The majority of the population is *mestizo* (mixed race). The estimated 45,000 Miskito Amerindians, and an English-speaking *garífuna* (black) community are united in their struggle to preserve their rights to land along the remote Caribbean coast. Women's status remains low. Hurricane Mitch killed 5600 people and impoverished 85% of the population in 1998. Poverty is at the root of social tension.

THE ECONOMY
Coffee, flowers, and fruit are the main exports, but the banana crop, a traditional mainstay of the economy, was devastated by Hurricane Mitch. Corruption and high unemployment.

◆ **INSIGHT:** *The Honduran currency is named after a Lenca Indian chief who was the main leader of resistance to the Spanish conquest in the 16th century*

FACTFILE

OFFICIAL NAME: Republic of Honduras
DATE OF FORMATION: 1838
CAPITAL: Tegucigalpa
POPULATION: 6.7 million
TOTAL AREA: 43,278 sq. miles (112,090 sq. km)
DENSITY: 155 people per sq. mile

LANGUAGES: Spanish*, Garífuna, English Creole
RELIGIONS: Roman Catholic 97%, Protestant 3%
ETHNIC MIX: Mestizo 90%, Black African 5%, Amerindian 4%, White 1%
GOVERNMENT: Presidential system
CURRENCY: Lempira = 100 centavos

Hungary

Landlocked in central Europe, Hungary was once the heart of the powerful Habsburg Empire. It lost two-thirds of its historical territory for supporting Germany in World War I.

GEOGRAPHY
Landlocked. Fertile plains in east and northwest; west and north are hilly. The Danube River cuts through the country and the capital.

CLIMATE
Continental, with wet springs, late but very hot summers, and cold, cloudy winters. The transition between seasons tends to be sudden.

PEOPLE & SOCIETY
Hungary's population is shrinking. Mostly ethnic Hungarian (Magyar), there are small minorities of Germans, Jews, and neighboring peoples. Roma face particular discrimination. The government is greatly concerned about the fate of ethnic Hungarians in Romania, Serbia, and Slovakia. Living standards are high, though working hours are longer than in Western Europe.

THE ECONOMY
High industrial production, open access for foreign investors, and strong exports, including high-tech goods and wine, have boosted the economy over the last decade.

◆ **INSIGHT:** *The Hungarian language is Asian in origin and is most closely related to Finnish*

FACTFILE

OFFICIAL NAME: Republic of Hungary
DATE OF FORMATION: 1918
CAPITAL: Budapest
POPULATION: 10.2 million
TOTAL AREA: 35,919 sq. miles (93,030 sq. km)
DENSITY: 286 people per sq. mile

LANGUAGES: Hungarian*
RELIGIONS: Catholic 52%, Calvinist 16%, other 15%, nonreligious 14%, Lutheran 3%
ETHNIC MIX: Magyar 90%, other 7%, Roma 2%, German 1%
GOVERNMENT: Parliamentary system
CURRENCY: Forint = 100 fillér

Iceland

Europe's westernmost country, Iceland has a strategic location in the north Atlantic, straddling the Mid-Atlantic Ridge. Its spectacular landscape is largely uninhabited.

GEOGRAPHY

Grassy coastal lowlands, with fjords in the north. Central plateau of cold lava desert, geothermal springs, and glaciers. Around 200 volcanoes, with numerous geysers and solfataras.

CLIMATE

Its location in the middle of the Gulf Stream moderates the climate. Mild winters and brief, cool summers.

PEOPLE & SOCIETY

Prosperous and homogeneous, Icelandic society includes only a few thousand foreign residents. There is high social mobility, free health care, and low-cost heating (geothermal and hydropower). Longevity rates are among the highest in the world. Strong emphasis on education and literacy. The Icelandic language has changed little in 700 years, in part due to the country's isolation.

THE ECONOMY

The high-tech fishing industry dominates export earnings. Tourism is growing. Geothermal and hydro-electric energy are abundant.

◆ INSIGHT: *The word geyser is taken from Geysir (the "gusher") in southwest Iceland*

■	1000m/3281ft
■	500m/1640ft
■	200m/656ft
□	Sea Level
□	Ice Cap

0   50 km
0   50 miles

FACTFILE

OFFICIAL NAME: Republic of Iceland
DATE OF FORMATION: 1944
CAPITAL: Reykjavík
POPULATION: 283,000
TOTAL AREA: 39,768 sq. miles (103,000 sq. km)
DENSITY: 7 people per sq. mile

LANGUAGES: Icelandic*
RELIGIONS: Evangelical Lutheran 93%, nonreligious 6%, other (mostly Christian) 1%
ETHNIC MIX: Icelandic 94%, other 5%, Danish 1%
GOVERNMENT: Parliamentary system
CURRENCY: Icelandic króna = 100 aurar

India

India is the world's second most populous country. The birth-rate has recently been falling, but even at its current level India's population will probably overtake China's by 2030.

GEOGRAPHY

Separated from northern Asia by the Himalaya mountain range, India forms a subcontinent. As well as the Himalayas, there are two other main geographical regions, the Indo-Gangetic plain, which lies between the foothills of the Himalayas and the Vindhya Mountains, and the central-southern Deccan plateau. The Ghats are smaller mountain ranges located on the east and west coasts.

CLIMATE

Varies greatly according to latitude, altitude, and season. Most of India has three seasons: hot, wet, and cool. In summer, temperatures in the north can reach 104°F (40°C). The monsoon breaks in June and peters out in September to October. In the cool season, the weather is mainly dry. The climate in the warmer south is less variable than in the north.

PEOPLE & SOCIETY

Cultural and religious pressures encourage large families. Nationwide awareness campaigns aim to promote the idea of smaller families. India's planners consider the rise in the population the most significant brake on development. Despite a major birth control program, the decrease in population growth has been marginal. The population officially passed the one-billion mark in 2000. The majority of Indians are Hindu. Various attempts to reform the Hindu caste system, which determines social standing and even marriage, have met with violent opposition. Severe tensions exist between Hindus and the Muslim minority, especially in Kashmir and Gujarat. Smaller ethnic groups exist in the northeast, and many struggle for greater autonomy. Almost 80% of Indians live in poverty. Rural deprivation encourages urban growth.

FACTFILE

OFFICIAL NAME: Republic of India
DATE OF FORMATION: 1947
CAPITAL: New Delhi
POPULATION: 1.04 billion
TOTAL AREA: 1,269,338 sq. miles (3,287,590 sq. km)
DENSITY: 907 people per sq. mile

LANGUAGES: Hindi*, English*, Urdu, Bengali, Marathi, Telugu, Tamil, other
RELIGIONS: Hindu 83%, Muslim 11%, Christian 2%, Sikh 2%, other 2%
ETHNIC MIX: Indo-Aryan 72%, Dravidian 25%, Mongoloid and other 3%
GOVERNMENT: Parliamentary system
CURRENCY: Indian rupee = 100 paise

THE ECONOMY
India has the fastest-growing economy in Asia after China. Protectionism has given way to free-market economics. The success of "Bollywood" films and high-tech industries contrast with massive levels of poverty.

◆ **INSIGHT:** *India's national animal, the tiger, was worshipped as early as 4000 years ago by the Mohenjo-Daro civilization*

5000m/16405ft
4000m/13124ft
3000m/9843ft
2000m/6562ft
1000m/3281ft
500m/1640ft
200m/656ft
Sea Level

A 'line of control' was agreed between India and Pakistan in 1972

Aksai Chin - administered by China, claimed by India

Demchok/Dêmqog - administered by China, claimed by India

Much of Arunāchal Pradesh is claimed by China

Srinagar
Jammu &
Kashmir
Amritsar
Jalandhar
Ludhiāna
Chandigarh
CHINA
Meerut
Delhi
NEW DELHI
PAKISTAN
Thar Desert
Jodhpur
Jaipur
Agra
Bareilly
Lucknow
NEPAL
Shiliguri
BHUTAN
Brahmaputra
MYANMAR
(BURMA)
Assam
Kānpur
Gwalior
Kota
Ganges
Patna
Imphāl
BANGLADESH
Varanāsi
Gulf
of
Kachchh
Ahmadābād
Indore
Bhopāl
Dhanbād
Jābalpur
Ranchi
Kolkata
(Calcutta)
Jāmnagar
Rājkot
Vadodara
Narmada
Nāgpur
Jamshedpur
Haora
Mouths
of the Ganges
Sūrat
Gulf
of
Khambhāt
Kalyān
Nānded
Cuttack
Mahānadi
Mumbai
(Bombay)
Pune
Deccan
Godāvari
Visākhapatnam
Bay
of
Bengal
Arabian
Sea
Solāpur
Hyderābād
Western Ghats
Krishna
Eastern Ghats
Hubli
Panāji
Andaman Islands
North
Andaman
Middle
Andaman
Chennai
(Madras)
INDIAN
OCEAN
South
Andaman
Port Blair
Little
Andaman
Bangalore
Mysore
Salem
Coimbatore
Cochin
Madurai
Lakshadweep
(Laccadive Is.)
Nicobar Islands
Indira Point
Great
Nicobar

0   200 km
0   200 miles

Indonesia

Formerly known as the Dutch East Indies, Indonesia is the world's largest archipelago. Its 18,108 islands stretch 3000 miles (5000 km) eastward from the Indian Ocean to the Pacific.

GEOGRAPHY

Indonesia is highly mountainous with numerous tropical swamps. The land is covered with dense rainforest, especially on New Guinea, where it remains largely unexplored. There are more than 200 volcanoes in the region, many of which are still active. The land masses of Java, Bali, Sumatra, Lombok, and Borneo were once joined together by dry land, which has since been submerged by rising sea levels. Some of the islands are large enough to have formed coastal lowlands.

CLIMATE

The climate of Indonesia is predominantly tropical monsoon. Variations relate mainly to differences in latitude and altitude; hilly areas are cooler overall. Rain falls throughout the year, often in thunderstorms, but there is a relatively dry season from June to September.

THE ECONOMY

Varied resources, especially energy. Cheap and plentiful labor pool. Bureaucracy and corruption damages investor confidence. Large foreign debt has been rescheduled. Piracy is a serious problem.

Bandaaceh
Strait of Malacca
100°
Langsa
Aceh
Medan
Pematangsiantar
Pulau Nias
Pakanbaru
Sumatra
Singkawang
Pontianak
Padang
Jambi
Bangka
Pangkalpinang
Ketapang
Palembang
Pulau Belitung
Bengkulu
Bandarlampung
JAKARTA
Kepulauan Natuna
Kepulauan Mentawai
Pegunungan Barisan

	4000m/13124ft
	3000m/9843ft
	2000m/6562ft
	1000m/3281ft
	500m/1640ft
	Sea Level

INDIAN
OCEAN
Bogor
Bandung
Semarang
Java
Yogyakarta
Suraka

FACTFILE

OFFICIAL NAME: Republic of Indonesia
DATE OF FORMATION: 1949
CAPITAL: Jakarta
POPULATION: 218 million
TOTAL AREA: 741,096 sq. miles
(1,919,440 sq. km)
DENSITY: 314 people per sq. mile

LANGUAGES: Javanese, Sundanese, Madurese, Bahasa Indonesia*, Dutch
RELIGIONS: Sunni Muslim 87%, Christian 9%, Hindu 2%, other 2%
ETHNIC MIX: Javanese 45%, other 33%, Sundanese 14%, coastal Malays 8%
GOVERNMENT: Parliamentary system
CURRENCY: Rupiah = 100 sen

Indonesia

PEOPLE & SOCIETY

The basic Melanesian–Malay ethnic division disguises a diverse society. Bahasa Indonesia, the national language, coexists with at least 250 other spoken languages or dialects. Attempts by the Javanese political elite to suppress local cultures have been vigorously opposed, especially by the East Timorese (who have now attained independence), the Aceh of northern Sumatra, and the Papuans. Religious and interethnic hostility is increasing. There have been clashes between Christians and Muslims in many areas, and discrimination against ethnic Chinese has encouraged vicious attacks on their businesses. Gender equality is enshrined in law, and women are active in public life.

◆ **INSIGHT:** *Indonesia has a very youthful population; almost 45% of its people are under 20 years of age*

Iran

Since the 1979 Islamic fundamentalist revolution led by Ayatollah Khomeini, the Middle Eastern country of Iran has become the world's largest theocracy.

GEOGRAPHY
High desert plateau with large salt pans in the east. West and north are mountainous. Coastal land bordering Caspian Sea is rainy and forested.

CLIMATE
Desert climate. Hot summers, and bitterly cold winters. Area around the Caspian Sea is more temperate.

PEOPLE & SOCIETY
Many ethnic groups, including Persians, Azaris (ethnically related to Azeris), and Kurds. Militant Shi'a Islamism has dominated since the 1979 revolution. The mullahs' belief that adherence to religious values is more important than economic welfare has resulted in declining living standards. Female emancipation has also been reversed. Liberal attitudes, particularly prevalent among students, have led to clashes.

THE ECONOMY
One of the world's biggest oil producers. Government restricts contact with the West, blocking acquisition of vital technology. High unemployment and inflation.

◆ **INSIGHT:** *More than a hundred offenses carry the death penalty*

3000m/9843ft
2000m/6562ft
1000m/3281ft
500m/1640ft
200m/656ft
Sea Level

0   200 km
0   200 miles

FACTFILE

OFFICIAL NAME: Islamic Republic of Iran
DATE OF FORMATION: 1502
CAPITAL: Tehran
POPULATION: 72.4 million
TOTAL AREA: 636,293 sq. miles
(1,648,000 sq. km)
DENSITY: 115 people per sq. mile

LANGUAGES: Farsi*, Azeri, Luri, Gilaki, Mazanderani, Kurdish, Turkmen, Arabic
RELIGIONS: Shi'a Muslim 95%, Sunni Muslim 4%, other 1%
ETHNIC MIX: Persian 50%, Azari 24%, other 10%, Kurd 8%, Lur and Bakhtiari 8%
GOVERNMENT: Islamic theocracy
CURRENCY: Iranian rial = 100 dinars

Iraq

Oil-rich Iraq is situated in the central Middle East. The last 50 years have been dominated by periods of war and civil conflict. It has been occupied by the US-led Coalition since April 2003.

GEOGRAPHY
Mainly desert. The Tigris and Euphrates Rivers water fertile regions and create the southern marshland. Mountains along northeast border.

CLIMATE
Southern deserts have hot, dry summers and mild winters. North has dry summers, but winters can be harsh in the mountains. Rainfall is low.

PEOPLE & SOCIETY
Carved out of remnants of the Ottoman Empire, Iraq is home to three distinct ethnic groups, as well as smaller minorities. The Arab Muslims are divided between Shi'a and Sunni. Some religious tension exists. The Kurds of the north were persecuted by the regime of Saddam Hussein which was ousted by a US-led invasion in 2003. Poverty is widespread after years of war and sanctions.

THE ECONOMY
The country's infrastructure was destroyed by a decade of sanctions and war. Hopes of recovery rest on massive oil reserves and aid.

◆ **INSIGHT:** *As Mesopotamia, Iraq was the site where the Sumerians established the world's first civilization*

FACTFILE
OFFICIAL NAME: Republic of Iraq
DATE OF FORMATION: 1932
CAPITAL: Baghdad
POPULATION: 24.2 million
TOTAL AREA: 168,753 sq. miles (437,072 sq. km)
DENSITY: 143 people per sq. mile

LANGUAGES: Arabic*, Kurdish, Turkic languages, Armenian, Assyrian
RELIGIONS: Shi'a Muslim 62%, Sunni Muslim 33%, other 5%
ETHNIC MIX: Arab 79%, Kurdish 16%, Persian 3%, Turkman 2%
GOVERNMENT: Transitional regime
CURRENCY: Dinar = 20 dirhams = 1000 fils

Ireland

Lying in the Atlantic Ocean, off the west coast of Britain, the Irish republic occupies about 85% of the island of Ireland, with the remainder (Northern Ireland) being part of the UK.

GEOGRAPHY
Low mountain ranges along an irregular coastline surround an inland plain punctuated by lakes, undulating hills, and peat bogs.

CLIMATE
The Gulf Stream accounts for the mild and wet climate. Snow is rare, except in the mountains.

PEOPLE & SOCIETY
Though homogeneous in ethnicity and Roman Catholic religion, the population show signs of change. The younger Irish question teachings on birth control, divorce, and abortion. Traditionally an emigrant nation, there is now net immigration. Living standards have improved greatly. The Good Friday peace agreement over Northern Ireland was reached in 1998, though a definitive peace remains elusive.

THE ECONOMY
High unemployment tarnishes high-tech export successes and trade surplus. The workforce is highly educated. Efficient agriculture and food-processing industries.

◆ **INSIGHT:** *About 260,000 people speak Irish Gaelic fluently*

FACTFILE

OFFICIAL NAME: Ireland
DATE OF FORMATION: 1922
CAPITAL: Dublin
POPULATION: 3.9 million
TOTAL AREA: 27,135 sq. miles (70,280 sq. km)
DENSITY: 147 people per sq. mile

LANGUAGES: English*, Irish Gaelic*
RELIGIONS: Roman Catholic 88%, other and nonreligious 8%, Anglican 3%, Jewish 1%
ETHNIC MIX: Irish 95%, other 5%
GOVERNMENT: Parliamentary system
CURRENCY: Euro = 100 cents

Israel

 Created as a new state in 1948, Israel lies in the eastern Mediterranean. The Palestinian population launched the latest *intifada* (armed struggle) against Israeli occupation in 2000.

 GEOGRAPHY
Coastal plain. Desert in the south. In the east lie the Great Rift Valley and the Dead Sea – the lowest point on the Earth's land surface.

 CLIMATE
Summers are hot and dry. Wet season, March–November, is mild.

PEOPLE & SOCIETY
Large numbers of Jews settled in Palestine before Israel was founded in 1948. After World War II, there was a massive increase in immigration. Sephardi Jews from the Middle East and Mediterranean are now in the majority, but Ashkenazi Jews from central Europe still dominate business and politics. Palestinians in Gaza and Jericho gained limited autonomy in 1994 but their desire, backed by most of the world, for a separate state has led to years of fierce violence.

 THE ECONOMY
The benefits of a modern infrastructure and educated labor force are overshadowed by conflict.

 INSIGHT: *All Jews worldwide have the right to Israeli citizenship*

 FACTFILE

OFFICIAL NAME: State of Israel
DATE OF FORMATION: 1948
CAPITAL: Jerusalem (unrecognized by UN)
POPULATION: 6.6 million
TOTAL AREA: 8019 sq. miles (20,770 sq. km)
DENSITY: 841 people per sq. mile

LANGUAGES: Hebrew*, Arabic*, Yiddish, German, Russian, Polish, other
RELIGIONS: Jewish 80%, Muslim (mainly Sunni) 16%, other 2%, Christian 2%
ETHNIC MIX: Jewish 80%, other (mostly Arab) 20%
GOVERNMENT: Parliamentary system
CURRENCY: Shekel = 100 agorot

Italy

The Italian peninsula was home to the Roman Empire, one of the greatest ancient civilizations. The south has two famous volcanoes, Vesuvius and Etna.

GEOGRAPHY
The Appennino form the backbone of a rugged peninsula, extending from the Alps into the Mediterranean Sea. Alluvial plain in the north.

CLIMATE
Mediterranean in the south. Seasonal extremes in the mountains and on the northern alluvial plain.

PEOPLE & SOCIETY
Ethnically homogeneous, but with a gulf between the prosperous, industrial north and the poorer, agricultural south. Strong regional identities persist, especially on the islands of Sicily and Sardinia. Allegiance to the family survives the lessened influence of the Church.

◆ **INSIGHT:** *Italy was a collection of dukedoms, monarchies, and city-states before unification in the 1860s*

THE ECONOMY
World leader in industrial and product design, as well as textiles. Strong tourism and agriculture sectors. Large public sector debt.

FACTFILE
OFFICIAL NAME: Italian Republic
DATE OF FORMATION: 1861
CAPITAL: Rome
POPULATION: 57.4 million
TOTAL AREA: 116,305 sq. miles (301,230 sq. km)
DENSITY: 506 people per sq. mile

LANGUAGES: Italian*, German, French, Rhaeto-Romanic, Sardinian
RELIGIONS: Roman Catholic 83%, other and nonreligious 17%
ETHNIC MIX: Italian 94%, other 4%, Sardinian 2%
GOVERNMENT: Parliamentary system
CURRENCY: Euro = 100 cents

Jamaica

First colonized by the Spanish and then by the English, the Caribbean island of Jamaica achieved independence in 1962. It remains an influential force in Caribbean politics.

GEOGRAPHY

Mainly mountainous, with lush tropical vegetation. Inaccessible limestone area in the northwest. Low, irregular coastal plains are broken by hills and plateaus.

CLIMATE
Tropical. Hot and humid at sea level, with temperate mountain areas. Hurricanes are likely June–November.

PEOPLE & SOCIETY

Social tensions result from vast disparities in wealth, rather than race. Economic and political life is dominated by a few wealthy, long-established families. Many women hold senior positions in public life. Armed crime, much of it narcotics-related, is a problem. Large areas of Kingston, which have their own *patois*, are ruled by violent gangs. Jamaican music styles are influential worldwide.

THE ECONOMY
Major producer of bauxite (aluminum ore). Tourism well developed. Light industry and data processing for US companies. Sugar, coffee, and rum are exported.

INSIGHT: *Jamaica's Rastafarians look to the late emperor of Ethiopia, Haile Selassie, as their spiritual leader, and Africa as their spiritual home*

Montego Bay · St. Ann's Bay · *Caribbean Sea* · The Cockpit Country · Ocho Rios · Savanna-la-Mar · Ewarton · Port Antonio · Portmore · **KINGSTON** · Mandeville · Spanish Town · May Pen · Old Harbour · *Caribbean Sea* · 18° · 78° · 77°

2000m/6562ft
1000m/3281ft
500m/1640ft
200m/656ft
Sea Level

0   40 km
0   40 miles

FACTFILE

OFFICIAL NAME: Jamaica
DATE OF FORMATION: 1962
CAPITAL: Kingston
POPULATION: 2.6 million
TOTAL AREA: 4243 sq. miles (10,990 sq. km)
DENSITY: 622 people per sq. mile

LANGUAGES: English Creole, English*
RELIGIONS: Protestant 55%, other and nonreligious 45%
ETHNIC MIX: Black African 75%, Mulatto 13%, European and Chinese 11%, East Indian 1%
GOVERNMENT: Parliamentary system
CURRENCY: Jamaican dollar = 100 cents

Japan

Japan is located off the east Asian coast and comprises four principal islands and over 3000 smaller ones. A powerful economy, it has an emperor as ceremonial head of state.

GEOGRAPHY

The terrain is predominantly mountainous, with fertile coastal plains; over two-thirds is woodland. There is no single continuous mountain range; the mountains divide into many small land blocks separated by lowlands and dissected by numerous river valleys. The islands lie on the Pacific "Ring of Fire," and earthquakes and volcanic eruptions are frequent. The Pacific coast is vulnerable to *tsunamis* – tidal waves triggered by submarine earthquakes.

CLIMATE

Generally temperate–oceanic. Spring is warm and sunny, while summer is hot and humid, with high rainfall. In western Hokkaido and northwest Honshu, winters are very cold, with heavy snowfall. Freak storms and damaging floods in recent years have raised concern over global climate changes.

PEOPLE & SOCIETY

One of the most racially homogeneous societies in the world. Its sense of order is reflected in the phenomenon of the lifetime employer. People define themselves by the company they work for, not the job they do. Employers organize social activities and even encourage and approve marriages. Women traditionally run the home; though, some are beginning to take up long-term careers. Social form remains very important. Respect for elders and social and business superiors is strongly ingrained. There is little tradition of generation rebellion, but the youth market is powerful and current fashions focus on teenagers. The education system is highly pressurized. Nongraduates have difficulty reaching management-level jobs, so competition for university places is intense.

FACTFILE

OFFICIAL NAME: Japan
DATE OF FORMATION: 1590
CAPITAL: Tokyo
POPULATION: 128 million
TOTAL AREA: 145,882 sq. miles (377,835 sq. km)
DENSITY: 877 people per sq. mile

LANGUAGES: Japanese*, Korean, Chinese
RELIGIONS: Shinto and Buddhist 76%, Buddhist 16%, other (including Christian) 8%
ETHNIC MIX: Japanese 99%, other (mainly Korean) 1%
GOVERNMENT: Parliamentary system
CURRENCY: Yen = 100 sen

THE ECONOMY
The world's most competitive producer of high-tech electronic products and cars. Talent for developing ideas from overseas. Once-revolutionary management and production methods. Global spread of business, especially to the EU and the US. Commitment to long-term research and development. The trade surplus is a source of international tension. Desperately needed reform of the financial sector is obstructed by traditional economic power brokers.

INSIGHT: The Japanese are among the world's most avid newspaper readers, with daily sales exceeding 70 million copies

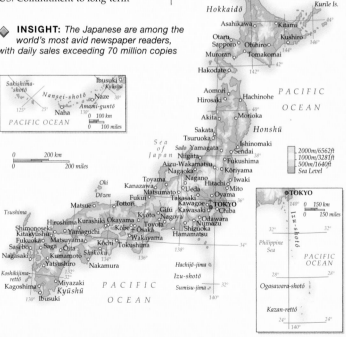

Jordan

The Kingdom of Jordan lies east of Israel, and borders the Palestinian West Bank. Its relations with its Arab neighbors are troubled by its relatively close ties to the US.

GEOGRAPHY
Mostly desert plateaus, with occasional salt pans. Lowest parts lie along the eastern shores of the Dead Sea and the Jordan River.

CLIMATE
Hot, dry summers. Cool, wet winters. Areas below sea level very hot in summer, and warm in winter.

PEOPLE & SOCIETY
A predominantly Muslim country with a strong national identity, Jordan's population has Bedouin roots. There is a Christian minority while half of the population are Palestinians who emigrated from Israeli-occupied territory. Jordan ceded its claim to the West Bank to the aspiring Palestinian state in 1988. The monarchy's power base lies among the rural tribes, which also provide the backbone of the military.

THE ECONOMY
Phosphates, chemicals, and fertilizers are principal exports. Skilled workforce hit by high unemployment.

◆ **INSIGHT:** *The Nabataean ruins of the ancient city of Petra attract thousands of tourists every year*

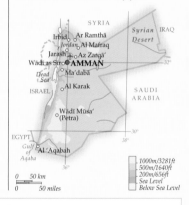

FACTFILE
OFFICIAL NAME: Hashemite Kingdom of Jordan
DATE OF FORMATION: 1946
CAPITAL: Amman
POPULATION: 5.2 million
TOTAL AREA: 35,637 sq. miles (92,300 sq. km)

DENSITY: 151 people per sq. mile
LANGUAGES: Arabic
RELIGIONS: Muslim (mainly Sunni) 92%, other (mostly Christian) 8%
ETHNIC MIX: Arab 98%, Circassian 1%, Armenian 1%
GOVERNMENT: Monarchy
CURRENCY: Jordanian dinar = 1000 fils

Kazakhstan

Mineral-rich Kazakhstan was the last of the former Soviet republics to declare independence. It has the potential to become a major regional economic power.

GEOGRAPHY

Mainly steppe. Volga delta and Caspian Sea in the west. Central plateau. Inhospitable Altai Mountains in the east. Semidesert in the south.

CLIMATE

Dry continental. Temperature variations between desert south and northern steppes are large. Winters are mildest near the Caspian Sea.

PEOPLE & SOCIETY

Kazakhstan's ethnic diversity arose mainly from forced settlements there during Soviet times. The proportion of ethnic Russians has dropped considerably since independence. Many emigrated, while ethnic Kazakhs arrived from neighboring states. Very few Kazakhs maintain a nomadic lifestyle, but Islam and loyalty to traditional clans remain strong.

THE ECONOMY

Vast mineral resources: gas, oil, bismuth, and cadmium. Increasing foreign investment, but living standards have fallen. The sale of farm land has only been allowed since 2003.

INSIGHT: The Soviet-built Baikonur space center is still an important launch site for international missions

FACTFILE

OFFICIAL NAME: Republic of Kazakhstan
DATE OF FORMATION: 1991
CAPITAL: Astana
POPULATION: 16 million
TOTAL AREA: 1,049,150 sq. miles (2,717,300 sq. km)
DENSITY: 15 people per sq. mile

LANGUAGES: Kazakh*, Russian, Ukrainian, Tatar, Uzbek, Uighur, other
RELIGIONS: Muslim (mainly Sunni) 50%, other 37%, Orthodox Christian 13%
ETHNIC MIX: Kazakh 53%, Russian 30%, other 11%, Ukrainian 4%, Tatar 2%
GOVERNMENT: Presidential system
CURRENCY: Tenge = 100 tiyn

Kenya

Kenya straddles the equator on Africa's east coast. After nearly 40 years in power the KANU party was soundly defeated in elections in 2002. Corruption is a serious issue.

GEOGRAPHY

A central plateau is divided by the Great Rift Valley. North of the equator is mainly semidesert. To the east lies a fertile coastal belt.

CLIMATE

The coast and the Great Rift Valley are hot and humid. The plateau interior is temperate. The northeastern desert is hot and dry. Rain usually falls April–May and October–November.

PEOPLE & SOCIETY

70 ethnic groups share about 40 languages. Strong clan and family links in rural areas are being weakened by urban migration. Poverty, severe drought, and a high population growth rate exacerbate ethnic tensions.

◆ INSIGHT: *Kenya has more than 30 game reserves, national parks, and marine reservations*

THE ECONOMY

Tourism is the leading foreign exchange earner. Tea and coffee are grown as cash crops. There is a large and diversified manufacturing sector.

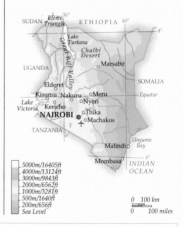

SUDAN — Elemi Triangle — ETHIOPIA
Lake Turkana
Chalbi Desert
Marsabit
UGANDA
SOMALIA
Eldoret
Kisumu Nakuru — Meru — Equator
Lake Victoria — Kericho — Nyeri
NAIROBI
Thika
Machakos
TANZANIA
Malindi — Ungama Bay
Mombasa — INDIAN OCEAN

5000m/16405ft
4000m/13124ft
3000m/9843ft
2000m/6562ft
1000m/3281ft
500m/1640ft
200m/656ft
Sea Level

0   100 km
0   100 miles

FACTFILE

OFFICIAL NAME: Republic of Kenya
DATE OF FORMATION: 1963
CAPITAL: Nairobi
POPULATION: 31.9 million
TOTAL AREA: 224,961 sq. miles (582,650 sq. km)
DENSITY: 146 people per sq. mile

LANGUAGES: Kiswahili*, English*, Kikuyu, Luo, Kalenjin, Kamba
RELIGIONS: Christian 60%, traditional beliefs 25%, other 9%, Muslim 6%
ETHNIC MIX: Other 41%, Kikuyu 21%, Luhya 14%, Luo 13%, Kalenjin 11%
GOVERNMENT: Presidential system
CURRENCY: Kenya shilling = 100 cents

Kiribati

Part of the British colony of the Gilbert and Ellice Islands in the mid-Pacific, the Gilberts adopted the name Kiribati (pronounced "Keer-ee-bus") at independence in 1979.

GEOGRAPHY

Kiribati consists of three groups of tiny, very low-lying coral atolls scattered across 1,930,000 sq. miles (5 million sq. km) of ocean. Most of the 33 atolls have central lagoons.

CLIMATE

Central islands have a maritime equatorial climate. Those to north and south are tropical, with constant high temperatures. There is little rainfall.

PEOPLE & SOCIETY

Officially I-Kiribati, many local people still refer to themselves as Gilbertese. Almost all are Micronesian, apart from the inhabitants of the island of Banaba, who employed anthropologists to establish their racial distinction. Most people are poor subsistence farmers and many travel abroad to work. The islands are effectively ruled by traditional chiefs.

THE ECONOMY

Since Banaba's phosphate deposits were exhausted in 1980, coconuts, copra, and fish have become the main exports. Foreign aid is vital to compensate for the country's isolation and the lack of resources.

◆ **INSIGHT:** *In 1981, the UK paid A$10 million to Banabans for the destruction of their island by mining*

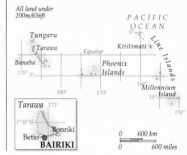

FACTFILE

OFFICIAL NAME: Republic of Kiribati
DATE OF FORMATION: 1979
CAPITAL: Bairiki (Tarawa Atoll)
POPULATION: 96,335
TOTAL AREA: 277 sq. miles (717 sq. km)
DENSITY: 352 people per sq. mile

LANGUAGES: English*, Kiribati
RELIGIONS: Roman Catholic 53%, Kiribati Protestant Church 39%, other 8%
ETHNIC MIX: Micronesian 96%, other 4%
GOVERNMENT: Nonparty system
CURRENCY: Australian dollar = 100 cents

North Korea

Separated from the democratic South by the world's most heavily defended border, the Stalinist North Korean state has been isolated from the outside world since its creation in 1948.

GEOGRAPHY
Mostly mountainous, with fertile plains in the southwest.

CLIMATE
Continental. Warm summers and cold winters, especially in the north, where snow is common.

PEOPLE & SOCIETY
Life is heavily regulated; divorce is nonexistent, extramarital sex is highly frowned upon, and religion, including Korea's own Chondogyo, is strictly regulated. Women make up over half of the workforce, but are also expected to run the home. Children are looked after in state-run crèches. The Korean Worker's Party is the sole political party. The 200,000-strong political elite lead a privileged lifestyle.

◆ **INSIGHT:** *Telephones and private cars are forbidden in North Korea*

THE ECONOMY
Other than minerals, North Korea's economy has few strengths and suffers badly from international isolation. Vital aid streams were lost with the global collapse of communism after 1989.

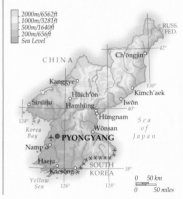

2000m/6562ft
1000m/3281ft
500m/1640ft
200m/656ft
Sea Level

RUSS. FED.

CHINA

Ch'ŏngjin

Kanggye
Kimch'aek
Sinŭiju
Hŭich'ŏn
Iwŏn
Hamhŭng
Korea
Bay
Hŭngnam
Wŏnsan
Sea of Japan
●PYONGYANG
Namp'o
Haeju
SOUTH
KOREA
Kaesŏng
Yellow
Sea

0   50 km
0   50 miles

FACTFILE
OFFICIAL NAME: Democratic People's Republic of Korea
DATE OF FORMATION: 1948
CAPITAL: Pyongyang
POPULATION: 22.6 million
TOTAL AREA: 46,540 sq. miles (120,540 sq. km)

DENSITY: 486 people per sq. mile
LANGUAGES: Korean*, Chinese
RELIGIONS: Government-controlled religions include Chondogyo, Buddhism, and Christianity
ETHNIC MIX: Korean 100%
GOVERNMENT: One-party state
CURRENCY: N. Korean won = 100 chon

South Korea

South Korea occupies the southern half of the Korean peninsula Under US sponsorship, it was separated from the communist North in 1948, and is now a successful capitalist economy.

GEOGRAPHY
Over 80% is mountainous and two-thirds is forested. The flattest and most populous parts lie along the west coast and in the extreme south.

CLIMATE
There are four distinct seasons. Winters are dry, and bitterly cold. Summers are hot and humid.

PEOPLE & SOCIETY
Inhabited by a single ethnic group for the last 2000 years. The nuclear family is replacing traditional extended households. Since the 1953 armistice, North and South Korea have remained technically at war. Reunification is still the ultimate goal. New links have been opened since 2000, but diplomatic progress is slow.

◆ **INSIGHT:** *Half of all Koreans are named Kim, Lee, Park, or Choi*

THE ECONOMY
World's biggest shipbuilder. High demand in China for Korean goods, especially cars. There is very strong competition from Japan.

1000m/3281ft
500m/1640ft
200m/656ft
Sea Level

NORTH KOREA

Sea of Japan

SEOUL
Inch'ŏn
Sŏngnam
Suwŏn

Kangnŭng
Tonghae

Yellow Sea

Taejŏn

Kunsan
Taegu
Ulsan

Kwangju
Masan
Pusan

Mokp'o
Yŏsu

Korea Strait

Cheju Strait

Cheju
Cheju-do

0   50 km
0   50 miles

FACTFILE
OFFICIAL NAME: Republic of Korea
DATE OF FORMATION: 1948
CAPITAL: Seoul
POPULATION: 47.4 million
TOTAL AREA: 38,023 sq. miles (98,480 sq. km)
DENSITY: 1243 people per sq. mile

LANGUAGES: Korean*, Chinese
RELIGIONS: Mahayana Buddhist 47%, Protestant 38%, Roman Catholic 11%, Confucianist 3%, other 1%
ETHNIC MIX: Korean 100%
GOVERNMENT: Presidential system
CURRENCY: South Korean won = 100 chon

Kuwait

Kuwait lies at the northwest extreme of the Gulf, dwarfed by its neighbors Iraq, Iran, and Saudi Arabia. It was a British protectorate until 1961, when full independence was granted.

GEOGRAPHY
Terrain is low-lying desert. The lowest land is in the north. Cultivation is only possible along the coast.

CLIMATE
Summers are very hot and dry. Winters are cooler, with some rain and occasional frost at night.

PEOPLE & SOCIETY
An oil-rich monarchy, ruled by the al-Sabah family. Oil wealth has attracted workers from India, Pakistan, and other Arab states, and immigrants now outnumber native Kuwaitis. Though it is a very conservative Sunni Muslim society, women are relatively free. Nonetheless, they are persistently denied the right to vote by Islamic traditionalists in parliament. Kuwait was invaded by Iraq in 1990 and was used as the launching pad for the 2003 invasion of its northern neighbor.

THE ECONOMY
Oil and gas production dominates the economy. Skilled labor, raw materials, and food are imported. Strategic vulnerability has deterred significant foreign investment.

INSIGHT: *During the 1991 Gulf War, 800 of Kuwait's 950 oil wells were deliberately set on fire*

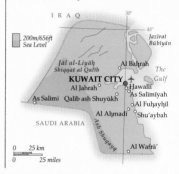

FACTFILE

OFFICIAL NAME: State of Kuwait
DATE OF FORMATION: 1961
CAPITAL: Kuwait City
POPULATION: 2 million
TOTAL AREA: 6880 sq. miles (17,820 sq. km)
DENSITY: 291 people per sq. mile

LANGUAGES: Arabic*, English
RELIGIONS: Sunni Muslim 45%, Shi'a Muslim 40%, Christian, Hindu, and other 15%
ETHNIC MIX: Kuwaiti 45%, other Arab 35%, South Asian 9%, other 11%
GOVERNMENT: Monarchy
CURRENCY: Kuwaiti dinar = 1000 fils

Kyrgyzstan

A small and very mountainous landlocked state in central Asia, Kyrgyzstan is one of the least urbanized of the ex-Soviet republics, and was slow to develop its own cultural nationalism.

GEOGRAPHY

The mountainous spurs of the Tien Shan range contain glaciers, alpine meadows, forests, and narrow valleys. Semidesert in the west.

CLIMATE

Varies from permanent snow and cold deserts at high altitudes, to hot deserts in low regions.

PEOPLE & SOCIETY

Ethnic Kyrgyz have only been in the majority since the late 1980s – due to a high birthrate and the emigration of ethnic Russians. Wary of losing skills vital to the economy, the government has attempted to deter Russians from leaving; concessions include making Russian an official language. There are tensions between Kyrgyz and Uzbeks. The trend in politics is toward greater Islamization, and the rural population is growing.

THE ECONOMY

The economy remains under state control and is dominated by agriculture. Small quantities of commercially exploitable coal, oil, and gas. There is great potential for hydroelectric power generation.

◆ **INSIGHT:** *Kyrgyz folklore is based around the 1000-year-old poem,* Manas, *which takes a week to recite*

4000m/13124ft
3000m/9843ft
2000m/6562ft
1000m/3281ft
500m/1640ft

FACTFILE

OFFICIAL NAME: Kyrgyz Republic
DATE OF FORMATION: 1991
CAPITAL: Bishkek
POPULATION: 5 million
TOTAL AREA: 76,641 sq. miles (198,500 sq. km)
DENSITY: 65 people per sq. mile

LANGUAGES: Kyrgyz*, Russian*, other
RELIGIONS: Muslim (mainly Sunni) 70%, Orthodox Christian 30%
ETHNIC MIX: Kyrgyz 57%, Russian 19%, Uzbek 13%, other 7%, Tatar 2%, Ukrainian 2%
GOVERNMENT: Presidential system
CURRENCY: Som = 100 tyyn

Laos

A former French colony, independent in 1953, Laos lies landlocked in southeast Asia. Heavily bombed during the Vietnam War, it has been under communist rule since 1975.

GEOGRAPHY
Largely forested mountains, broadening in the north to a plateau. Lowlands along the Mekong valley.

CLIMATE
Monsoon rains September–May. The rest of the year is hot and dry.

PEOPLE & SOCIETY
There are over 60 ethnic groups. Lowland Laotians (Lao Loum) live along the Mekong River and are rice farmers. Upland Laotians (Lao Theung) and highland Laotians (Lao Soung) traditionally employ environmentally damaging slash-and-burn farming and grow illegal cash crops. Government efforts to reform these practices are resisted.

◆ **INSIGHT:** *Three small Laotian kingdoms were unified under French control in 1899*

THE ECONOMY
One of the world's least developed nations. Levels of foreign investment are rising. There is potential for timber, mining, and garment manufacturing.

FACTFILE

OFFICIAL NAME: Lao People's Democratic Republic
DATE OF FORMATION: 1953
CAPITAL: Vientiane
POPULATION: 5.5 million
TOTAL AREA: 91,428 sq. miles (236,800 sq. km)

DENSITY: 62 people per sq. mile
LANGUAGES: Lao*, Mon-Khmer, other
RELIGIONS: Buddhist 85%, other (including animist) 15%
ETHNIC MIX: Lao Loum 66%, Lao Theung 30%, Lao Soung 2%, other 2%
GOVERNMENT: One-party state
CURRENCY: New kip = 100 at

Latvia

Latvia lies on the east coast of the Baltic Sea, between Estonia and Lithuania. Like its Baltic neighbors, it became independent from Moscow in 1991. It retains a large Russian population.

GEOGRAPHY

A flat coastal plain which is deeply indented by the Gulf of Riga. Poor drainage creates many bogs and swamps in the forested interior.

CLIMATE

Temperate, with warm summers and cold winters. There is steady rainfall throughout the year.

PEOPLE & SOCIETY

Latvians make up just over half of the population and are mostly Lutheran. They have been officially favored by the state since 1991 over the largely Orthodox Christian Russian minority. Latvian was declared the only official language in 2000 and will be used exclusively in schools from 2004. This discrimination has strained relations with neighboring Russia. Women enjoy full equality. The divorce rate is high.

THE ECONOMY

The thriving services sector now accounts for over 70% of GDP: tourism is growing. Manufacturing industry remains buoyant. Germany has replaced Russia as the main trading partner as Latvia turns increasingly to the West.

◆ **INSIGHT:** *Ethnic Latvians form a minority of the population in Riga*

200m/656ft
Sea Level

0   50 km
0   50 miles

FACTFILE

OFFICIAL NAME: Republic of Latvia
DATE OF FORMATION: 1991
CAPITAL: Riga
POPULATION: 2.4 million
TOTAL AREA: 24,938 sq. miles (64,589 sq. km)
DENSITY: 96 people per sq. mile

LANGUAGES: Latvian*, Russian
RELIGIONS: Lutheran 55%, Catholic 24%, other 12%, Orthodox Christian 9%
ETHNIC MIX: Latvian 57%, Russian 32%, Belarussian 4%, Ukrainian 3%, Polish 2%, other 2%
GOVERNMENT: Parliamentary system
CURRENCY: Lats = 100 santims

Lebanon

Living in the shadow of its two powerful, and antagonistic neighbors, Syria and Israel, Lebanon has largely recovered from a devastating 14-year civil war which ended in 1989.

GEOGRAPHY
Behind a narrow coastal plain, two parallel mountain ranges run the entire length of the country, separated by the fertile Beqaa Valley.

CLIMATE
Winters are mild and summers are hot, with high coastal humidity. Snow falls on high ground in winter.

PEOPLE & SOCIETY
The population is split between Christians and Muslims, but retains a strong sense of national identity. Though in the minority, Christians have been the traditional rulers. In 1975, civil war broke out between the two groups. A settlement, which gave the Muslims more power, was reached in 1989, but has left Syria as the main power broker. A huge economic gulf exists between the poor and a small, immensely rich elite.

THE ECONOMY
Lebanon has regained its position as an important regional financial center. Wine and fruit production show much potential.

◆ **INSIGHT:** *The Cedar of Lebanon has been the nation's symbol for more than 2000 years*

FACTFILE
OFFICIAL NAME: Republic of Lebanon
DATE OF FORMATION: 1941
CAPITAL: Beirut
POPULATION: 3.6 million
TOTAL AREA: 4015 sq. miles (10,400 sq. km)
DENSITY: 911 people per sq. mile

LANGUAGES: Arabic*, French, Armenian, Assyrian
RELIGIONS: Muslim 70%, Christian 30%
ETHNIC MIX: Arab 94%, Armenian 4%, other 2%
GOVERNMENT: Parliamentary system
CURRENCY: Lebanese pound = 100 piastres

Lesotho

The landlocked Kingdom of Lesotho is entirely surrounded by – and economically dependent on – South Africa, which even sent in troops to restore calm after rioting in 1998.

GEOGRAPHY

A high mountainous plateau, cut by valleys and ravines. The Maluti range runs through the center. The Drakensberg range lies to the east.

CLIMATE

Temperate. Summers are hot with torrential rain storms. Snow is frequent in the mountains in winter.

PEOPLE & SOCIETY

The overwhelming majority of people are Sotho, though there are some South Asians, Europeans, and Chinese. A strong sense of national identity has tended to minimize ethnic tensions. Many men work as migrant laborers in South Africa, leaving a majority of households run by women.

◆ **INSIGHT:** *Lesotho has one of the highest literacy rates in Africa, and the highest female literacy rate – 94%*

THE ECONOMY

Few natural resources; dependent on South Africa. Subsistence farming is the main activity. Water and energy are being exported from the new Highlands Water Scheme.

3000m/9843ft
2000m/6562ft
1000m/3281ft

0   50 km
0   50 miles

FACTFILE

OFFICIAL NAME: Kingdom of Lesotho
DATE OF FORMATION: 1966
CAPITAL: Maseru
POPULATION: 2.1 million
TOTAL AREA: 11,720 sq. miles (30,355 sq. km)
DENSITY: 179 people per sq. mile

LANGUAGES: English*, Sesotho*, isiZulu
RELIGIONS: Christian 90%, traditional beliefs 10%
ETHNIC MIX: Sotho 97%, European and Asian 3%
GOVERNMENT: Parliamentary system
CURRENCY: Loti = 100 lisente

Liberia

Liberia, Africa's oldest republic, faces the Atlantic Ocean. Today Liberia is mired in a long-running, and often brutal, civil war. A tentative peace deal was signed in 2003.

GEOGRAPHY
A coastline of beaches and mangrove swamps rises to forested plateaus and highlands inland.

CLIMATE
High temperatures. There is only one wet season, from May to October, Except in the extreme southeast.

PEOPLE & SOCIETY
The key social distinction used to be between Americo-Liberians – descendants of freed slaves – and the indigenous tribal peoples. However, political assimilation and intermarriage have eased tensions. Intertribal tension is now a much more serious problem, fueling the civil war which has ravaged the country since 1990.

◆ **INSIGHT:** *Liberia is named after the people liberated from slavery who arrived from the US in the 1800s*

THE ECONOMY
Civil war has led to the collapse of the economy – there is very little commercial activity. Only 1% of the land is suitable for cultivation. There are an estimated one billion tonnes of iron ore reserves at Mount Nimba.

FACTFILE

OFFICIAL NAME: Republic of Liberia
DATE OF FORMATION: 1847
CAPITAL: Monrovia
POPULATION: 3.3 million
TOTAL AREA: 43,000 sq. miles (111,370 sq. km)
DENSITY: 89 people per sq. mile

LANGUAGES: Kpelle, Vai, Bassa, Kru, Grebo, Kissi, Gola, Loma, English*
RELIGIONS: Christian 68%, traditional beliefs 18%, Muslim 14%
ETHNIC MIX: Indigenous tribes (16 main groups) 95%, Americo-Liberians 5%
GOVERNMENT: Transitional regime
CURRENCY: Liberian dollar = 100 cents

Libya

Situated on the Mediterranean coast of north Africa, Libya is a Muslim dictatorship, politically marginalized by the West for its terrorist links. UN sanctions were lifted in 2003.

GEOGRAPHY

Apart from the coastal strip and a mountain range in the south, Libya is desert or semidesert. Natural oases provide the agricultural land.

CLIMATE

Hot and arid. The coastal area has a temperate climate, with mild, wet winters and hot, dry summers.

PEOPLE & SOCIETY

Most Libyans are of Arab and Berber origin. A revolution in 1969 brought Colonel Gaddafi to power. He represents independence, Islamic faith, belief in communal lifestyle, and hatred of the urban rich. Revolution wiped out private enterprise and the middle classes. Jews and European settlers were banished. Since then, Libya has changed from being largely a nation of nomads and livestock herders to almost 90% city dwellers.

THE ECONOMY

Almost all export earnings come from oil, which is subject to fluctuating world prices. Dates, olives, peaches, and grapes are grown in the oases.

INSIGHT: 90% of Libya is still desert, despite grand irrigation schemes

FACTFILE

OFFICIAL NAME: Great Socialist People's Libyan Arab Jamahariyah

DATE OF FORMATION: 1951

CAPITAL: Tripoli

POPULATION: 5.5 million

TOTAL AREA: 679,358 sq. miles (1,759,540 sq. km)

DENSITY: 8 people per sq. mile

LANGUAGES: Arabic*, Tuareg

RELIGIONS: Muslim (mainly Sunni) 97%, other 3%

ETHNIC MIX: Arab and Berber 95%, other 5%

GOVERNMENT: One-party state

CURRENCY: Libyan dinar = 1000 dirhams

Liechtenstein

Perched in the Alps between Switzerland and Austria, the small state of Liechtenstein became an independent principality of the Holy Roman Empire in 1719. It has close links with Switzerland.

GEOGRAPHY

The upper Rhine Valley covers the western third of the country. The mountains and narrow valleys of the eastern Alps make up the remainder.

CLIMATE

Warm, dry summers. Winters are cold, with heavy snow in the mountains from December to March.

PEOPLE & SOCIETY

The country's role as a financial center accounts for its many foreign residents (38% of the population), of whom half are Swiss and the rest mostly German. A high standard of living results in few social or ethnic tensions. There is a close alliance with Switzerland, which handles its foreign relations and defense policies.

◆ **INSIGHT:** *Women in Liechtenstein only received the vote in 1984*

THE ECONOMY

Banking secrecy and low taxes help to attract foreign investment. A well-diversified export market includes dental products, furniture, chemicals, and precision instruments.

2000m/6562ft
1000m/3281ft
500m/1640ft
200m/656ft
Sea Level

Ruggell
Mauren
Bendern
Planken
Schaan
AUSTRIA
VADUZ
SWITZERLAND
Triesenberg
Triesen
Balzers

47°15'
47°10'
47°05'
9°30'
9°35'

0   4 km
0   4 miles

FACTFILE

OFFICIAL NAME: Principality of Liechtenstein
DATE OF FORMATION: 1719
CAPITAL: Vaduz
POPULATION: 32,842
TOTAL AREA: 62 sq. miles (160 sq. km)

DENSITY: 530 people per sq. mile
LANGUAGES: German*, Alemannish dialect, Italian
RELIGIONS: Catholic 81%, other 19%
ETHNIC MIX: Liechtensteiner 62%, other 38%
GOVERNMENT: Parliamentary system
CURRENCY: Swiss franc = 100 centimes

Lithuania

Lying on the eastern coast of the Baltic Sea, Lithuania is the largest and most powerful of the Baltic states. It was the first Soviet republic to declare independence from Moscow in 1991.

GEOGRAPHY

Mostly flat with moors, bogs, and an intensively farmed central lowland. Numerous lakes and forested sandy ridges in the east.

CLIMATE

Coastal location moderates continental extremes. Cold winters, cool summers, and steady rainfall.

PEOPLE & SOCIETY

Homogeneous population, with Lithuanians forming a large majority. Strong Roman Catholic tradition and historic links with Poland. There are better relations among ethnic groups than in other Baltic states and inter-ethnic marriages are fairly common. However, ethnic Russians and Poles see a threat from "Lithuanianization," and relations with the Jewish minority remain strained. A large income gap has grown since independence.

THE ECONOMY

A wide range of high-tech and heavy industries includes textiles, engineering, shipbuilding, and food processing. The euro is legal tender.

INSIGHT: *The "amber coasts" of the Baltic states, particularly Lithuania, produce most of the world's amber – fossilized resin*

FACTFILE

OFFICIAL NAME: Republic of Lithuania
DATE OF FORMATION: 1991
CAPITAL: Vilnius
POPULATION: 3.7 million
TOTAL AREA: 25,174 sq. miles
(65,200 sq. km)
DENSITY: 147 people per sq. mile

LANGUAGES: Lithuanian*, Russian
RELIGIONS: Roman Catholic 83%, other 12%, Protestant 5%
ETHNIC MIX: Lithuanian 80%, Russian 9%, Polish 7%, Belarussian 2%, other 2%
GOVERNMENT: Parliamentary system
CURRENCY: Litas = 100 centu

Luxembourg

Making up part of the plateau of the Ardennes in western Europe, Luxembourg is one of Europe's richest states. A tax haven and banking center, it is also home to key EU institutions.

GEOGRAPHY
Dense Ardennes forests in the north, with a low, open plateau to the south. Undulating terrain throughout.

CLIMATE
The climate is moist, with warm summers and mild winters. Snow is common only in the Ardennes.

PEOPLE & SOCIETY
Ethnic tensions are rare, despite a large proportion of foreigners (half the workforce and just over a quarter of residents). Integration has been straightforward; most are fellow western Europeans and Catholics, mainly from Italy and Portugal. Very low unemployment and high salaries promote stability.

◆ **INSIGHT:** *Luxembourg's capital is home to around 1000 investment funds and over 200 banks*

THE ECONOMY
Traditional industries such as steelmaking have given way in recent years to a thriving banking and service sector. Its banking and secrecy laws attract foreign companies.

500m/1640ft
200m/656ft
Sea Level

Clervaux

GERMANY

Ettelbrück

Echternach

Mersch

BELGIUM

●LUXEMBOURG

Pétange

Differdange
Esch-sur-Alzette
Dudelange

FRANCE

0   10 km
0   10 miles

FACTFILE

OFFICIAL NAME: Grand Duchy of Luxembourg
DATE OF FORMATION: 1867
CAPITAL: Luxembourg-Ville
POPULATION: 448,000
TOTAL AREA: 998 sq. miles (2586 sq. km)
DENSITY: 449 people per sq. mile

LANGUAGES: Luxembourgish*, German*, French*
RELIGIONS: Roman Catholic 97%, Jewish Greek Orthodox, and Protestant 3%
ETHNIC MIX: Luxembourger 73%, foreign residents 27%
GOVERNMENT: Parliamentary system
CURRENCY: Euro = 100 cents

Macedonia

Landlocked in the southern Balkans, Macedonia was troubled by the sanctions placed on its northern trading partners in the mid-1990s, and by violent conflict with ethnic Albanians in 2001.

GEOGRAPHY

Mainly mountainous or hilly, with deep river basins in the center. Plains in the northeast and southwest.

CLIMATE

Continental climate with wet springs and dry autumns. Heavy snowfalls in northern mountains.

PEOPLE & SOCIETY

Slav Macedonians comprise two-thirds of the population; they are mostly Orthodox Christians, with some Muslims. Officially 20% of the population are Muslim Albanians, though they claim to account for a third. Albanian militants fought a bitter war against the government in 2001. A peace deal promises greater equality. The Greek government is still wary that Macedonia may try to absorb historic "Macedonian" lands in northern Greece.

THE ECONOMY

Though there has been a growth in internal and foreign investment, the country is held back by a legacy of regional instability and a dependence on industrial imports.

◆ **INSIGHT:** *Ohrid is the deepest lake in Europe at 964 ft (294 m)*

FACTFILE

OFFICIAL NAME: Republic of Macedonia
DATE OF FORMATION: 1991
CAPITAL: Skopje
POPULATION: 2.1 million
TOTAL AREA: 9781 sq. miles (25,333 sq. km)
DENSITY: 212 people per sq. mile

LANGUAGES: Macedonian*, Albanian*
RELIGIONS: Orthodox Christian 59%, Muslim 26%, other 11%, Catholic 4%
ETHNIC MIX: Macedonian 67%, Albanian 23%, Turkish 4%, other 4%, Serb 2%
GOVERNMENT: Mixed presidential–parliamentary system
CURRENCY: Macedonian denar = 100 deni

Madagascar

Lying off the east African coast in the Indian Ocean, the former French colony of Madagascar is the world's fourth-largest island. An electoral dispute spilled over into civil conflict in 2002.

GEOGRAPHY
More than two-thirds of the country forms a savanna-covered plateau, which drops sharply to a narrow coastal belt in the east.

CLIMATE
Tropical and often hit by cyclones. Monsoons affect the east coast. The southwest is much drier.

PEOPLE & SOCIETY
People are Malay-Indonesian in origin, intermixed with later migrants from the African mainland. The main ethnic division is between the Merina of the central plateau and the poorer *côtier* (coastal) peoples. The Merina were the country's historic rulers, and remain the social elite.

◆ **INSIGHT:** *80% of Madagascar's plants and many of its animal species are found nowhere else*

THE ECONOMY
The majority of people are farmers. Vanilla and coffee are the most important cash crops. Prawns are a valuable export.

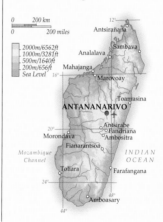

2000m/6562ft	
1000m/3281ft	
500m/1640ft	
200m/656ft	
Sea Level	

FACTFILE

OFFICIAL NAME: Republic of Madagascar

DATE OF FORMATION: 1960

CAPITAL: Antananarivo

POPULATION: 16.9 million

TOTAL AREA: 226,656 sq. miles (587,040 sq. km)

DENSITY: 75 people per sq. mile

LANGUAGES: Malagasy*, French*

RELIGIONS: Traditional beliefs 52%, Christian 41%, Muslim 7%

ETHNIC MIX: Other Malay 46%, Merina 26%, Betsimisaraka 15%, Betsileo 12%, other 1%

GOVERNMENT: Presidential system

CURRENCY: Ariayry = 500 centimes

Malawi

A former colony of the UK, Malawi lies landlocked in southeast Africa, following the Great Rift Valley. Its name means "the land where the sun is reflected in the water like fire."

GEOGRAPHY
Lake Nyasa takes up one-fifth of the landscape. Highlands lie west of the lake. Much of the land is covered by forests and savanna.

CLIMATE
Mainly subtropical. The south is hot and humid. Highlands are cooler.

PEOPLE & SOCIETY
Ethnicity has not been exploited for political ends in Malawi as has been the case in neighboring states. Most Malawians share a common Bantu origin. The 1994 election of President Bakili Muluzi, a member of the Muslim minority, signaled the failure of previous attempts to enforce Protestant dominance.

◆ **INSIGHT:** *Lake Nyasa is 353 miles (568 km) in length and contains at least 500 species of fish*

THE ECONOMY
Tobacco accounts for 76% of export earnings. Tea and sugar production. Drought is a serious problem.

2000m/6562ft	
1000m/3281ft	
500m/1640ft	
200m/656ft	
Sea Level	

FACTFILE
OFFICIAL NAME: Republic of Malawi
DATE OF FORMATION: 1964
CAPITAL: Lilongwe
POPULATION: 11.8 million
TOTAL AREA: 45,745 sq. miles (118,480 sq. km)
DENSITY: 325 people per sq. mile

LANGUAGES: Chewa, Lomwe, Yao, Ngoni, English*
RELIGIONS: Protestant 55%, Muslim 20%, Catholic 20%, traditional beliefs 5%
ETHNIC MIX: Bantu 99%, other 1%
GOVERNMENT: Presidential system
CURRENCY: Malawi kwacha = 100 tambala

Malaysia

Comprising the three territories of Peninsular Malaysia, Sarawak, and Sabah, Malaysia stretches 1240 miles (2000 km) from the Malay peninsula to eastern Borneo.

GEOGRAPHY

Almost three-quarters of the land is tropical rainforest or swamp forest. A central mountain chain, the Banjaran Titiwangsa, divides Peninsular Malaysia, separating a narrow eastern coastal belt from fertile western plains and sheltered beaches and bays. The territories of Sarawak and Sabah share the island of Borneo with Indonesia, and surround Brunei. They are characterized by swampy coastal plains rising to mountains along the southern border.

CLIMATE

Warm equatorial. Rainfall is heavy throughout the year, but with distinct rainy seasons from March to May and from September to November. Coastal areas are subject to the alternating southwest and northeast monsoon winds.

INSIGHT: *Malaysia is southeast Asia's major tourist destination, with over 13 million visitors a year. Most come for the beaches and highlands of Malaya, or the ancient rainforests of Borneo*

2000m/6562ft	
1000m/3281ft	
500m/1640ft	
200m/656ft	
Sea Level	

FACTFILE

OFFICIAL NAME: Federation of Malaysia
DATE OF FORMATION: 1963
CAPITALS: Kuala Lumpur and Putrajaya
POPULATION: 23 million
TOTAL AREA: 127,316 sq. miles (329,750 sq. km)
DENSITY: 181 people per sq. mile

LANGUAGES: Bahasa Malaysia*, Malay, Chinese, Tamil, English
RELIGIONS: Muslim 53%, Buddhist 19%, Chinese faiths 12%, other 9%, Christian 7%
ETHNIC MIX: Malay 48%, Chinese 29%, indigenous tribes 12%, other 11%
GOVERNMENT: Parliamentary system
CURRENCY: Ringgit = 100 sen

Malaysia

PEOPLE & SOCIETY

The key distinction in Malaysian society is between the indigenous Malays, termed the "Bumiputras" (literally, sons of the soil), and the Chinese. The Malays form the larger group, accounting for just under half of the population. However, the smaller Chinese population has traditionally controlled most economic activity. Malays have been favored in the education system and job market since the 1970s, in order to address this imbalance. There are estimated to be more than one million Indonesian and Filipino immigrants in Malaysia, attracted by its labor shortages and a dearth of employment in their own countries. Gender discrimination was only outlawed in 2001. In an attempt to promote Islamic tradition, Muslim women are encouraged to wear veils.

THE ECONOMY

Rapid growth since late 1980s, largely state-directed and under-pinned by a push for foreign investment and privatization of state assets. Successful car and electronics industries – the *Proton* car is regarded as a national success, while the new capital Putrajaya is being promoted as a high-tech center. Tourism is a major earner. Heavy industries such as steel. Leading producer of palm oil, pepper, tin, and tropical hardwoods. High level of debt. Shortage of skilled labor. Asian financial crisis of 1997–1998 forced Malaysia to adopt economic austerity measures, and revise plans for industrialization.

Maldives

The Maldives is an archipelago of 1190 small coral islands, or atolls, set in the Indian Ocean, southwest of Sri Lanka. The word atoll comes from the Dhivehi word "atolu."

GEOGRAPHY
Consists of low-lying islands and coral atolls. The larger ones are covered in lush, tropical vegetation.

CLIMATE
Tropical. Rain falls throughout the year, but is heaviest June–November, during the monsoon. Violent storms occasionally hit the northern islands.

PEOPLE & SOCIETY
Maldivians, who are all Sunni Muslim, are descended from Sinhalese, Dravidian, Arab, and black ancestors. About 25% of the population live on Male'. Tourism has grown on separate resort islands away from residents. Politics is restricted to a small group of influential families, and is based around family and clan loyalties rather than formal political parties. A new, young elite is pressing for a more liberal political system.

THE ECONOMY
Too dependent on the fluctuating tourist industry, which is the economic mainstay. Fish, especially tuna, are the leading exports.

INSIGHT:
The islands, which all lie below 4 ft (1.2 m), are threatened by rising sea levels, brought about by global warming and climatic changes

Ihavandippolhu Atoll

6°

Faadhippolhu Atoll

Horsburgh Atoll

Male' Atoll

MALE'

Ari Atoll

Felidhu Atoll

Mulaku Atoll

Kolhumadulu Atoll

Hadhdhunmathi Atoll

One and Half Degree Channel

INDIAN OCEAN

North Huvadhu Atoll

South Huvadhu Atoll

Equator

73°

Addu Atoll
Gan

0   100 km
0   100 miles

☐ Sea Level

FACTFILE
OFFICIAL NAME: Republic of Maldives
DATE OF FORMATION: 1965
CAPITAL: Male'
POPULATION: 309,000
TOTAL AREA: 116 sq. miles (300 sq. km)

DENSITY: 2664 people per sq. mile
LANGUAGES: Dhivehi* (Maldivian), Sinhala, Tamil, Arabic
RELIGIONS: Sunni Muslim 100%
ETHNIC MIX: All Maldivians are of mixed ethnic descent
GOVERNMENT: Nonparty system
CURRENCY: Rufiyaa = 100 lari

Mali

A former French colony, Mali is landlocked in the heart of west Africa. Multiparty democratic elections held since 1992 under a new constitution, have provoked accusations of irregularities.

GEOGRAPHY

The northern half of the country lies in the Sahara. The inland delta of the Niger River flows through a grassy savanna region in the south.

CLIMATE

In the south, intensely hot, dry weather precedes the westerly rains. The north is almost rainless.

PEOPLE & SOCIETY

Most people live in southern savanna region. The Bambara tribe are politically dominant. A few nomadic Fulani and Tuareg herders travel the northern plains. There is tension between the peoples of the south and Tuareg in the north. Malian women have little status.

◆ **INSIGHT:** *Tombouctou (Timbuktu) was the center of the 14th-century Malinke trading empire*

THE ECONOMY

One of the poorest countries in the world. Less than 2% of land can be cultivated. Most people are farmers, herders, or river fishermen. Gold deposits are now being mined.

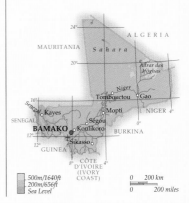

500m/1640ft
200m/656ft
Sea Level

0   200 km
0   200 miles

FACTFILE

OFFICIAL NAME: Republic of Mali
DATE OF FORMATION: 1960
CAPITAL: Bamako
POPULATION: 12 million
TOTAL AREA: 478,764 sq. miles
(1,240,000 sq. km)
DENSITY: 25 people per sq. mile

LANGUAGES: Bambara, Fulani, Senufo, Soninke, French*
RELIGIONS: Muslim 80%, traditional beliefs 18%, Christian 1%, other 1%
ETHNIC MIX: Bambara 32%, other 33%, Fulani 14%, Senufu 12%, Soninka 9%
GOVERNMENT: Presidential system
CURRENCY: CFA franc = 100 centimes

Malta

The Maltese archipelago lies midway between Europe and Africa. Controlled throughout its history by successive colonial powers, it gained independence from the UK in 1964.

GEOGRAPHY

The main island of Malta has low hills and a ragged coastline with numerous harbors, bays, sandy beaches, and rocky coves. The island of Gozo is more densely vegetated.

CLIMATE

Mediterranean climate. There are many hours of sunshine all year round, with very little rainfall.

PEOPLE & SOCIETY

Over the centuries, the Maltese have been subject to Arab, Sicilian, Spanish, French, and British influences. Today, the population is socially conservative and devoutly Roman Catholic – on a percentage basis more so than virtually any other nation. Divorce is illegal. Many young Maltese go abroad to find work – notably to the US and Australia – as opportunities for them on the islands are few.

THE ECONOMY

Tourism is the chief source of income. Offshore banking potential. Schemes have been set up to attract foreign high-tech industry. Almost all requirements have to be imported.

INSIGHT: *The Maltese language has Phoenician origins but features Arabic etymology and intonation*

FACTFILE

OFFICIAL NAME: Republic of Malta
DATE OF FORMATION: 1964
CAPITAL: Valletta
POPULATION: 393,000
TOTAL AREA: 122 sq. miles (316 sq. km)
DENSITY: 3169 people per sq. mile

LANGUAGES: Maltese*, English*
RELIGIONS: Roman Catholic 98%, other and nonreligious 2%
ETHNIC MIX: Maltese 96%, other 4%
GOVERNMENT: Parliamentary system
CURRENCY: Maltese lira = 100 cents

Marshall Islands

Under US rule as part of the UN Trust Territory of the Pacific Islands until independence in 1986, the Marshall Islands comprises a group of 34 widely scattered atolls.

GEOGRAPHY

Narrow coral rings with sandy beaches enclosing lagoons. Those in the south have thicker vegetation. Kwajalein is the world's largest atoll.

CLIMATE

Tropical oceanic, cooled year round by northeast trade winds.

PEOPLE & SOCIETY

Majuro, the capital city and commercial center, is home to almost half the population. Tensions are high due to poor living conditions. Life on the outlying islands is still traditional, based around subsistence agriculture and fishing. Marshallese society is matrilineal: titles are chiefly handed down from the mother's side.

◆ **INSIGHT:** *In 1954, Bikini Atoll was the site for the testing of the largest US H-bomb – the 18–22 megaton Bravo*

THE ECONOMY

Almost totally dependent on US aid and the rent paid by the US for its missile base on Kwajalein Atoll. Revenue from Japan for the use of Marshallese waters for tuna fishing. Copra and coconut oil are the only significant agricultural exports.

FACTFILE

OFFICIAL NAME: Republic of the Marshall Islands

DATE OF FORMATION: 1986

CAPITAL: Majuro

POPULATION: 73,630

TOTAL AREA: 70 sq. miles (181 sq. km)

DENSITY: 1052 people per sq. mile

LANGUAGES: Marshallese*, English*, Japanese, German

RELIGIONS: Protestant 90%, Roman Catholic 8%, other 2%

ETHNIC MIX: Micronesian 97%, other 3%

GOVERNMENT: Parliamentary system

CURRENCY: US dollar = 100 cents

Mauritania

Two-thirds of Mauritania's territory is desert – the only productive land is that drained by the Senegal River. The country has taken a strongly Arab direction since 1964.

GEOGRAPHY
The Sahara, barren except for some scattered oases, covers the north. Savanna lands lie to the south.

CLIMATE
The climate is generally hot and dry, aggravated by the dusty *harmattan* wind. Summer rain in the south, virtually none in the north.

PEOPLE & SOCIETY
The majority Maures control political life. There is a sizable black minority. Ethnic tension centers on the oppression of blacks by Maures. Tens of thousands of blacks are estimated to be in illegal slavery. Family solidarity among nomadic peoples is particularly strong.

INSIGHT: *Slavery officially became illegal in Mauritania in 1980, but de facto slavery still persists*

THE ECONOMY
Agriculture and herding. Iron and copper mining. World's largest gypsum deposits. Some of the best fishing grounds in west Africa.

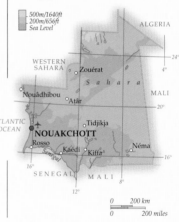

FACTFILE

OFFICIAL NAME: Islamic Republic of Mauritania
DATE OF FORMATION: 1960
CAPITAL: Nouakchott
POPULATION: 2.8 million
TOTAL AREA: 397,953 sq. miles (1,030,700 sq. km)

DENSITY: 7 people per sq. mile
LANGUAGES: Hassaniyah Arabic*, Wolof, French
RELIGIONS: Sunni Muslim 100%
ETHNIC MIX: Maure 81%, Wolof 7%, Tukolor 5%, other 4%, Soninka 3%
GOVERNMENT: Presidential system
CURRENCY: Ouguiya = 5 khoums

Mauritius

The islands that make up Mauritius lie in the Indian Ocean east of Madagascar. They have enjoyed considerable economic success following recent industrial diversification and expansion.

 GEOGRAPHY

The volcanic main island of Mauritius is ringed by coral reefs, and rises from the coast to a fertile central plateau. The outer islands – Rodriguez, the Agalega Islands, and the Cargados Carajos Shoals – lie some 300 miles (500 km) to the north.

CLIMATE

Warm and humid. Tropical storms are frequent December–March, the hottest and wettest months.

PEOPLE & SOCIETY

Most people are descendants of laborers brought over from India in the 19th century. A small minority of French descent form the wealthiest group. The Creole community complains of discrimination. Crime rates on the main island are fairly low; the outer islands are virtually free from crime altogether.

 THE ECONOMY

Sugar, tourism, and clothing manufacture are main sources of income. Potential as an offshore financial center is being developed. Most food has to be imported.

◆ **INSIGHT:** *The islands lie on the Mascarene Archipelago – once a land bridge between Asia and Africa*

Ile Plate
500m/1640ft
200m/656ft
Sea Level
57°30'
20°
Triolet • Grand Baie
• Pamplemousses
PORT LOUIS
Curepipe •
Mahébourg
Bel Ombre
20°30'
Souillac

Rodrigues
Port Mathurin
19°45'
63°25'

INDIAN OCEAN

0   10 km
0   10 miles

 FACTFILE

OFFICIAL NAME: Republic of Mauritius
DATE OF FORMATION: 1968
CAPITAL: Port Louis
POPULATION: 1.2 million
TOTAL AREA: 718 sq. miles (1860 sq. km)
DENSITY: 1671 people per sq. mile

LANGUAGES: French Creole, Hindi, Urdu, Tamil, Chinese, English*, French
RELIGIONS: Hindu 52%, Catholic 26%, Muslim 17%, other 3%, Protestant 2%
ETHNIC MIX: Indo-Mauritian 68%, Creole 27%, other 5%
GOVERNMENT: Parliamentary system
CURRENCY: Mauritian rupee = 100 cents

Mexico

Increasingly considered a part of North rather than Central America, Mexico reaches south into the ancient Aztec and Mayan heartlands. Independence from Spain came in 1836.

GEOGRAPHY

Coastal plains along the Pacific and Atlantic seaboards rise to a high arid central plateau. To the east and west are the Sierra Madre mountain ranges. Limestone lowlands form the projecting Yucatan peninsula.

CLIMATE

The plateau and high mountains are warm for much of the year. Pacific coast is tropical: storms occur mostly March–December. Northwest is dry.

THE ECONOMY

One of the world's largest oil producers. Exotic fruits and vegetables are grown as cash crops. Population growth is outstripping job creation. The North American Free Trade Agreement, signed with the US and Canada, came into force in 1994. Austerity measures introduced in the late 1990s please investors but hold up social spending.

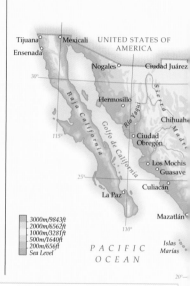

Tijuana
Ensenada
Mexicali
UNITED STATES OF AMERICA
Nogales
Ciudad Juárez
30°
Hermosillo
Baja California
Sierra Madre
Río Yaqui
Chihuahua
115°
Ciudad Obregón
Golfo de California
Los Mochis
Guasave
25°
Culiacán
La Paz
Mazatlán

3000m/9843ft
2000m/6562ft
1000m/3281ft
500m/1640ft
200m/656ft
Sea Level

110°

*P A C I F I C
O C E A N*

Islas Marías

20°

📖 FACTFILE

OFFICIAL NAME: United Mexican States

DATE OF FORMATION: 1836

CAPITAL: Mexico City

POPULATION: 102 million

TOTAL AREA: 761,602 sq. miles (1,972,550 sq. km)

DENSITY: 138 people per sq. mile

LANGUAGES: Spanish*, Nahuatl, Mayan, Zapotec, Mixtec, Otomi, Totonac, other

RELIGIONS: Roman Catholic 95%, other 4%, Protestant 1%

ETHNIC MIX: Mestizo 55%, Amerindian 20%, European 16%, other 9%

GOVERNMENT: Presidential system

CURRENCY: Mexican peso = 100 centavos

Mexico

PEOPLE & SOCIETY

Most Mexicans are *mestizos* of mixed Spanish and Amerindian descent. Though their culture is promoted by the state, rural Amerindians are largely segregated from Hispanic society and most live in poverty. The situation dates back to the Spanish colonial period, and only recently has it been seriously challenged in the form of intermittent rebellions by landless Amerindians. A lackluster Indigenous Rights and Culture Bill was rejected by Zapatista guerrillas in 2001. The small black community is well integrated. Men remain dominant in business and few women take part in the political process. The left-wing Institutional Revolutionary Party was defeated in elections in 2000 after more than 70 years in power since the Mexican Revolution. Migration to towns, and high unemployment are major problems.

INSIGHT: *More people emigrate from Mexico than any other state in the world. Hundreds of thousands of Mexicans cross into the US each year, many of them staying as illegal immigrants*

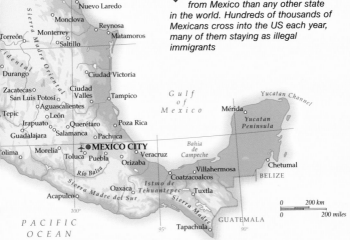

Micronesia

The Federated States of Micronesia (FSM), situated in the western Pacific, comprise 607 islands and atolls grouped into four main island states: Pohnpei, Kosrae, Chuuk, and Yap.

GEOGRAPHY

Mixture of high volcanic islands with forested interiors, and low-lying coral atolls. Some of the islands have coastal mangrove swamps.

CLIMATE

Tropical, with high humidity. There is very heavy rainfall outside the January–March dry season.

◆ **INSIGHT:** *Chuuk's lagoon contains the sunken wrecks of over 100 Japanese ships and 270 planes from World War II*

PEOPLE & SOCIETY

Micronesians are physically, culturally, and linguistically diverse. Melanesians live on Yap and Polynesians in Pohnpei. Most islanders live without electricity or running water. Society is traditionally matrilineal.

THE ECONOMY

Tourism, fishing, and copra are economic mainstays. The construction industry is the largest private sector activity. Unemployment is high.

FACTFILE

OFFICIAL NAME: Federated States of Micronesia

DATE OF FORMATION: 1986

CAPITAL: Palikir (Pohnpei Island)

POPULATION: 135,869

TOTAL AREA: 271 sq. miles (702 sq. km)

DENSITY: 501 people per sq. mile

LANGUAGES: Trukese, Pohnpeian, Mortlockese, Kosraean, English*

RELIGIONS: Roman Catholic 50%, Protestant 48%, other 2%

ETHNIC MIX: Micronesian 100%

GOVERNMENT: Nonparty system

CURRENCY: US dollar = 100 cents

Moldova

The smallest and most densely populated of the former Soviet republics, Moldova has strong ethnic, linguistic, and cultural links with Romania to the west.

GEOGRAPHY

The steppes and hilly plains are drained by Dniester and Prut Rivers.

CLIMATE

Warm summers and relatively mild winters. Moderate rainfall is evenly spread throughout the year.

PEOPLE & SOCIETY

A shared heritage with Romania defines national identity, though in 1994 Moldovans voted against possible reunification with Romania. Most of the population is engaged in intensive agriculture. Transdniestria is a breakaway state along the east bank of the Dniester, home to a largely ethnic Slav population. The Gagauz, in the south, have accepted autonomy.

◆ **INSIGHT:** *Vast underground wine vaults contain entire "streets" of bottles built into rock quarries*

THE ECONOMY

Well-developed agricultural sector: wine, tobacco, cotton, food processing. Light manufacturing. Chronic instability deters investors. High unemployment and foreign debt.

FACTFILE

OFFICIAL NAME: Republic of Moldova
DATE OF FORMATION: 1991
CAPITAL: Chisinau
POPULATION: 4.3 million
TOTAL AREA: 13,067 sq. miles (33,843 sq. km)
DENSITY: 330 people per sq. mile

LANGUAGES: Moldovan*, Ukrainian, Russian
RELIGIONS: Orthodox Christian 98%, Jewish 2%
ETHNIC MIX: Moldovan 65%, Ukrainian 14%, Russian 13%, Gagauz 4%, other 4%,
GOVERNMENT: Parliamentary system
CURRENCY: Moldovan leu = 100 bani

Monaco

Monaco is a tiny enclave on the Côte d'Azur. Its destiny changed radically when the casino was opened in 1863. Today, it promotes its image as an upmarket, glamorous destination.

GEOGRAPHY
A rocky promontory overlooking a narrow coastal strip that has been enlarged through land reclamation.

CLIMATE
Mediterranean. Summers are hot and dry; days with 12 hours of sunshine are not uncommon. Winters are mild and sunny.

PEOPLE & SOCIETY
Less than 20% of residents are Monégasques. Around half are French, the rest Italian, American, British, and Belgian. Nationals enjoy considerable privileges, including housing subsidies to protect them from Monaco's high property prices, and the right of first refusal before a job can be offered to a foreigner. Women have equal status but only acquired the vote in 1962.

THE ECONOMY
Tourism and gambling are the mainstays. Banking secrecy laws and tax-haven conditions are attractive to foreign investment. Monaco is almost totally dependent on imports due to its lack of natural resources.

INSIGHT: *High-profile social and sporting events attract large crowds each spring, including the Rose Ball, Tennis Open, and Grand Prix*

FACTFILE

OFFICIAL NAME: Principality of Monaco
DATE OF FORMATION: 1861
CAPITAL: Monaco-Ville
POPULATION: 31,987
TOTAL AREA: 0.75 sq. miles (1.95 sq. km)
DENSITY: 42,649 people per sq. mile

LANGUAGES: French*, Italian, Monégasque, English
RELIGIONS: Roman Catholic 89%, Protestant 6%, other 5%
ETHNIC MIX: French 47%, other 20%, Monégasque 17%, Italian 16%
GOVERNMENT: Monarchy
CURRENCY: Euro = 100 cents

Mongolia

Landlocked between Russia and China, Mongolia is a vast and isolated country with a large nomadic population. Over two-thirds of the country is part of the vast Gobi Desert.

GEOGRAPHY

A mountainous steppe plateau in the north, with lakes in the north and west. The desert region of the Gobi dominates the south.

CLIMATE

Continental. Mild summers and long, dry, very cold winters, with heavy snowfall. Temperatures can drop as low as −22°F (−30°C).

PEOPLE & SOCIETY

Mongolia was unified by Genghis Khan in 1206 and was later absorbed into Manchu China. A majority of ethnic Mongolians live over the border in Inner Mongolia. Tibetan Buddhism dominates. The traditional, nomadic way of life has been eroded as urban migration continues, spurred by recent ferocious winters, known as *zud*, which have devastated the rural economy.

THE ECONOMY

Rich deposits of oil, coal, copper, uranium, and other minerals remain largely untapped. Democracy, from 1990, has brought a shift toward a market economy, but also rising poverty and a decay in infrastructure. Harsh winters ravaged livestock between 1999 and 2001.

◆ **INSIGHT:** *Horseracing, wrestling, and archery are the national sports*

3000m/9843ft	
2000m/6562ft	
1000m/3281ft	
500m/1640ft	

0   400 km

0   400 miles

FACTFILE

OFFICIAL NAME: Mongolia
DATE OF FORMATION: 1924
CAPITAL: Ulan Bator
POPULATION: 2.6 million
TOTAL AREA: 604,247 sq. miles (1,565,000 sq. km)
DENSITY: 4 people per sq. mile

LANGUAGES: Khalkha Mongolian*, other
RELIGIONS: Tibetan Buddhist 96%, Muslim 4%
ETHNIC MIX: Mongol 90%, Kazakh 4%, other 2%, Chinese 2%, Russian 2%
GOVERNMENT: Mixed presidential–parliamentary system
CURRENCY: Tugrik (tögrög) = 100 möngö

Morocco

Morocco is a former French colony in northwest Africa. Since 1975 it has occupied the territory of Western Sahara, the future of which is yet to be determined by UN-supervised referendum.

GEOGRAPHY
Fertile coastal plain is interrupted in the east by the Rif Mountains. Atlas Mountain ranges to the south. Beyond lies the outer fringe of the Sahara.

CLIMATE
Ranges from temperate and warm in the north, to semiarid in the south. Cooler in the mountains.

PEOPLE & SOCIETY
About 35% of the population are descendants of original Berber inhabitants of north Africa, and live mainly in mountain villages. The Arab majority inhabits the lowlands. Morocco is unusual among Arab states in granting Jews religious freedom and civil rights. The government is pressured by Islamic traditionalists who fear the loss of Arab identity. The king is spiritual leader and head of state.

THE ECONOMY
A leading world exporter of phosphates. Tourism and agriculture have great potential. Production of cannabis complicates closer EU links.

◆ **INSIGHT:** *Karueein University in Fès, founded in 859 CE, is the world's oldest existing educational institution*

FACTFILE
OFFICIAL NAME: Kingdom of Morocco
DATE OF FORMATION: 1956
CAPITAL: Rabat
POPULATION: 31 million
TOTAL AREA: 172,316 sq. miles (446,300 sq. km)
DENSITY: 180 people per sq. mile

LANGUAGES: Arabic*, Tamazight (Berber), French, Spanish
RELIGIONS: Muslim (mainly Sunni) 99%, other (mostly Christian) 1%
ETHNIC MIX: Arab 70%, Berber 29%, European 1%
GOVERNMENT: Monarchy
CURRENCY: Dirham = 100 centimes

Mozambique

Mozambique lies on the southeast African coast. It was torn apart by a savage and devastating civil war between the Marxist government and a rebel faction between 1977 and 1992.

GEOGRAPHY

Largely a savanna-covered plateau. The coast is fringed by coral reefs and lagoons. The Zambezi River bisects the country.

CLIMATE

Tropical. Temperatures are hottest on the coast. Extremes of rainfall: drought and flood.

PEOPLE & SOCIETY

Tensions exist between north and south, rather than ethnic groups. Life is centered on the extended family. Polygamy is fairly common. The country is struggling with the legacy of a war which killed over one million people, and the effects of terrible flooding in 2000 and 2001. Around 80% of people live in poverty.

◆ INSIGHT: *Maputo, the capital, has Africa's second-largest harbor*

THE ECONOMY

Mozambique is almost entirely dependent on foreign aid. Mineral resources have yet to be fully exploited.

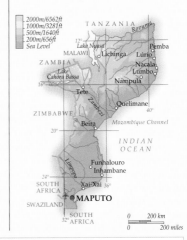

FACTFILE

OFFICIAL NAME: Rep. of Mozambique
DATE OF FORMATION: 1975
CAPITAL: Maputo
POPULATION: 19 million
TOTAL AREA: 309,494 sq. miles (801,590 sq. km)
DENSITY: 63 people per sq. mile

LANGUAGES: Makua, Xitsonga, Sena, Lomwe, Portuguese*
RELIGIONS: Traditional beliefs 60%, Christian 30%, Muslim 10%
ETHNIC MIX: Makua Lomwe 47%, Tsonga 23%, Malawi 12%, Shona 11% other 7%
GOVERNMENT: Presidential system
CURRENCY: Metical = 100 centavos

Myanmar (Burma)

Forming the eastern shores of the Bay of Bengal and the Andaman Sea in southeast Asia, Myanmar suffers from extensive political repression and ethnic conflict.

GEOGRAPHY

The fertile Irrawaddy basin lies at the center. Mountains to the west, Shan plateau to the east. Tropical rainforest covers much of the land.

CLIMATE

Tropical. Hot summers, with high humidity, and warm winters.

PEOPLE & SOCIETY

The military, in power since 1962, rules Myanmar with little regard to human rights. Opposition is not tolerated. The National League for Democracy won elections in 1990, but was kept from power. Its leader, Aung San Suu Kyi, is frequently detained. Minority groups maintain low-level guerrilla activity against the state.

◆ INSIGHT: *Myanmar is the one of the world's biggest teak exporters, though reserves are diminishing rapidly*

THE ECONOMY

The ruling junta has encouraged investment from foreign companies. There is a nationwide black market, on which prices are soaring. Main products are gems, teak, and rice.

■	4000m/13124ft
■	2000m/6562ft
■	1000m/3281ft
■	500m/1640ft
■	200m/656ft
	Sea Level

0   200 km

0   200 miles

FACTFILE

OFFICIAL NAME: Union of Myanmar
DATE OF FORMATION: 1948
CAPITAL: Rangoon (Yangon)
POPULATION: 49 million
TOTAL AREA: 261,969 sq. miles (678,500 sq. km)
DENSITY: 193 people per sq. mile

LANGUAGES: Burmese*, Shan, Karen, Rakhine, Chin, Yangbye, Kachin, Mon
RELIGIONS: Buddhist 87%, Christian 6%, Muslim 4%, other 2%, Hindu 1%
ETHNIC MIX: Burman 68%, other 13%, Shan 9%, Karen 6%, Rakhine 4%
GOVERNMENT: Military-based regime
CURRENCY: Kyat = 100 pyas

Namibia

Located in southwestern Africa, Namibia gained independence from South Africa in 1990, after 24 years of armed struggle. It regained the territory of Walvis Bay in 1994.

GEOGRAPHY

The Namib Desert stretches along the coastal strip. Inland, a ridge of mountains rises to 8000 ft (2500 m). The Kalahari Desert lies in the east.

CLIMATE

Almost rainless. The coast is usually shrouded in thick fog, unless the hot, dry *berg* wind is blowing.

PEOPLE & SOCIETY

The largest ethnic group, the Ovambo, live mainly in the north. Whites, including a large German community, are centered around Windhoek. Whites still control the economy. The minority San and Khoi bushmen are among the oldest human communities in the world. Homosexuality is not tolerated.

◆ **INSIGHT:** *The Namib is the Earth's oldest, and one of its driest, deserts*

THE ECONOMY

Varied mineral resources, including uranium and diamonds. Rich offshore fishing grounds. Lack of skilled labor, and a growing AIDS epidemic.

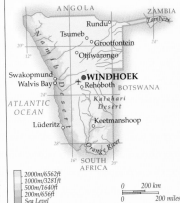

2000m/6562ft
1000m/3281ft
500m/1640ft
200m/656ft
Sea Level

0   200 km
0   200 miles

FACTFILE

OFFICIAL NAME: Republic of Namibia
DATE OF FORMATION: 1990
CAPITAL: Windhoek
POPULATION: 1.8 million
TOTAL AREA: 318,694 sq. miles (825,418 sq. km)
DENSITY: 6 people per sq. mile

LANGUAGES: Ovambo, Kavango, English*, Bergdama, German, Afrikaans
RELIGIONS: Christian 90%, traditional beliefs 10%
ETHNIC MIX: Ovambo 50%, other tribes 25%, Kavango 9%, Damara 8%, Herero 8%
GOVERNMENT: Presidential system
CURRENCY: Namibian dollar = 100 cents

Nauru

Nauru lies in the Pacific, northeast of Australia. Phosphate deposits made its citizens among the wealthiest in the world, but economic mismanagement has left it facing ruin.

GEOGRAPHY

A single low-lying coral atoll, with a fertile coastal belt. Coral cliffs encircle an elevated interior plateau.

CLIMATE

Equatorial, moderated by sea breezes. Occasional long droughts.

PEOPLE & SOCIETY

Native Nauruans are of mixed Micronesian and Polynesian origin. Most live in simple, traditional houses and spend their money on luxury cars and consumer goods. The government provides free welfare and education. A diet of imported processed foods has caused widespread obesity and diabetes. Mining is left to an imported labor force, mainly from Kiribati, who live in enclaves of male-only barracks and have few rights. Many of the young attend boarding schools in Australia and New Zealand.

THE ECONOMY

Phosphate revenues all but dried up in 2003. Nauru has no other resources but considerable investments overseas. Offshore banking facilities were closed after international pressure.

◆ **INSIGHT:** *Phosphate mining has left 80% of the island uninhabitable*

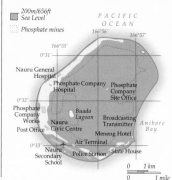

FACTFILE

OFFICIAL NAME: Republic of Nauru
DATE OF FORMATION: 1968
CAPITAL: None
POPULATION: 12,329
TOTAL AREA: 8.1 sq. miles
(21 sq. km)
DENSITY: 1522 people per sq. mile

LANGUAGES: Nauruan*, Kiribati, Chinese, Tuvaluan, English
RELIGIONS: Nauruan Congregational Church 60%, Catholic 35%, other 5%
ETHNIC MIX: Nauruan 62%, other Pacific islanders 25%, other 13%
GOVERNMENT: Parliamentary system
CURRENCY: Australian $ = 100 cents

Nepal

Nepal, lying between India and China on the southern shoulder of the Himalayas, is one of the world's poorest countries. Its agricultural economy is heavily dependent on the monsoon.

GEOGRAPHY
Mainly mountainous. The area includes some of the highest mountains in the world, such as Everest. Flat, fertile river plains form the south.

CLIMATE
Warm monsoon season from July to October. The rest of the year is dry, sunny, and mild. Winter temperatures in the Himalayas average 14°F (−10°C).

PEOPLE & SOCIETY
There are few tensions between the diverse ethnic groups. Sherpa women, like other Buddhists, face fewer social restrictions than Hindus. The monarchy exercised absolute power until 1990. Despite democratization, politics has become increasingly turbulent. A Maoist insurgency, seeking a socialist republic, began in 1999 and has thrown the country into a state of virtual civil war.

THE ECONOMY
Agriculture accounts for almost all of GDP. Crops include rice, maize, and millet. Previously healthy tourist sector has been ravaged by conflict. There is potential for hydropower.

◆ **INSIGHT:** *Southern Nepal was the birthplace of Buddha (Prince Siddhartha Gautama) in 563 BCE*

Dadeldhura
Jumla
CHINA
Baglung
Pokhara
Mt. Everest
29,035ft (8850m)
(Sagarmatha)
KATHMANDU
Bhaktapur
Lalitpur
INDIA
Janakpur
Ilam
Biratnagar

4000m/13124ft
3000m/9843ft
2000m/6562ft
1000m/3281ft
500m/1640ft
200m/656ft
Sea Level

0   100 km
0   100 miles

FACTFILE

OFFICIAL NAME: Kingdom of Nepal
DATE OF FORMATION: 1769
CAPITAL: Kathmandu
POPULATION: 24.2 million
TOTAL AREA: 54,363 sq. miles (140,800 sq. km)
DENSITY: 458 people per sq. mile

LANGUAGES: Nepali*, Maithili, Bhojpuri
RELIGIONS: Hindu 90%, Buddhist 5%, Muslim 3%, other 2%
ETHNIC MIX: Nepalese 52%, other 19%, Maithili 11%, Tibeto-Burmese 10%, Bhojpuri 8%
GOVERNMENT: Parliamentary system
CURRENCY: Nepalese rupee = 100 paise

Netherlands

Astride the delta of five major rivers in northwest Europe, the Netherlands was one of the world's first confederative republics. The main port, Rotterdam, is also the world's largest.

GEOGRAPHY

Mainly flat, with 27% of the land below sea level and protected by dunes, dikes, and canals. There are a few low hills in the south and east.

CLIMATE

Mild, rainy winters and cool summers. Gales from the North Sea are common in fall and winter.

PEOPLE & SOCIETY

The Dutch see their country as the most tolerant in Europe. This reflects a long history of welcoming immigrants from former colonies and refugees seeking religious and political asylum. Population density is high and there is a large urban concentration. The state does not try to impose a particular morality on its citizens. Laws concerning issues such as drug-taking, sexuality, and euthanasia, are among the world's most liberal.

THE ECONOMY

Diverse industrial sector exports metals, machinery, electronics, and chemicals. High-profile multinationals. The social welfare system is costly.

◆ **INSIGHT:** *In 2002 the Netherlands became the first country in the world to legalize euthanasia*

Sea Level
Below Sea Level

North Sea

Waddeneilanden

Wadden

Hisselmeer

Groningen — 53°

Haarlem ● **AMSTERDAM**
'S-GRAVENHAGE ● Apeldoorn Enschede
(THE HAGUE) ● Leiden Utrecht
Delft ● *Neder Rijn* ● Arnhem — 52°
Rotterdam ● Nijmegen
Maas
Breda ● Tilburg GERMANY
Eindhoven —

5°

B E L G I U M

0 40 km
0 40 miles

Maastricht — 51°

4° 6°

FACTFILE

OFFICIAL NAME: Kingdom of the Netherlands
DATE OF FORMATION: 1648
CAPITALS: Amsterdam and The Hague
POPULATION: 16.2 million
TOTAL AREA: 16,033 sq. miles (41,526 sq. km)

DENSITY: 1237 people per sq. mile
LANGUAGES: Dutch*, Frisian
RELIGIONS: Roman Catholic 36%, other 34%, Protestant 27%, Muslim 3%
ETHNIC MIX: Dutch 82%, other 12%, Surinamese, Turkish, and Moroccan 6%
GOVERNMENT: Parliamentary system
CURRENCY: Euro = 100 cents

New Zealand

Lying in the South Pacific, 990 miles (1600 km) southeast of Australia, New Zealand comprises North and South Island, separated by the Cook Strait, and many smaller islands.

GEOGRAPHY
North Island contains hot springs and geysers, and the bulk of the population. South Island is mostly mountainous, with eastern lowlands.

CLIMATE
Generally temperate and damp. The far north is almost subtropical, whereas southern winters are cold.

PEOPLE & SOCIETY
Maoris were the first settlers, 1200 years ago. Today's majority European population is descended mainly from British migrants who settled after 1840. Maoris' living and education standards are generally lower than average. The government is currently attempting to negotiate the settlement of Maori land claims.

INSIGHT: *New Zealand women were the first to get the vote (1893)*

THE ECONOMY
Modern agricultural sector; one of the world's five biggest exporters of dairy products. Manufacturing and tourism industries growing. Very high debt.

2000m/6562ft
1000m/3281ft
500m/1640ft
200m/656ft
Sea Level

North Island

36°

Auckland
Manurewa
Hamilton   Tauranga
Rotorua
New   Taupo
Plymouth   Napier
Hastings
Palmerston
North
Lower Hutt
WELLINGTON
Tasman
Sea   Blenheim
40°
176°
Cook Strait

South Island

44°   Christchurch

Timaru
172°

Southern Alps

PACIFIC
OCEAN

Dunedin

Invercargill
Stewart Island
168°

0   200 km
0   200 miles

FACTFILE

OFFICIAL NAME: New Zealand
DATE OF FORMATION: 1947
CAPITAL: Wellington
POPULATION: 4 million
TOTAL AREA: 103,737 sq. miles (268,680 sq. km)
DENSITY: 39 people per sq. mile

LANGUAGES: English*, Maori*
RELIGIONS: Anglican 24%, other 22%, Presbyterian 18%, nonreligious 16%, Roman Catholic 15%, Methodist 5%
ETHNIC MIX: European 77%, Maori 12%, other immigrant 6%, Pacific islanders 5%
GOVERNMENT: Parliamentary system
CURRENCY: New Zealand $ = 100 cents

Nicaragua

Nicaragua lies at the heart of Central America. The Sandinista revolution of 1978 led to 11 years of civil war between the left-wing Sandinistas and the right-wing US-backed, Contras.

GEOGRAPHY

Extensive forested plains in the east. Central mountain region with many active volcanoes. The Pacific coastlands are dominated by lakes.

CLIMATE

Tropical. The lowlands are hot all year round. The mountains are cooler. Prone to occasional hurricanes.

PEOPLE & SOCIETY

Most of the population is mixed race, and there is a large white elite. The Caribbean regions are home to communities of Miskito Amerindians and blacks, who gained autonomy in 1987. The revolution improved the status of women, but these gains have been undone by rampant poverty.

◆ **INSIGHT:** *Lake Nicaragua is the only freshwater lake in the world to contain ocean animals*

THE ECONOMY

Coffee, sugar, and cotton are the main exports. All are affected by world price fluctuations. A heavy debt burden, high unemployment, and a lack of investment hold back growth.

1000m/3281ft
500m/1640ft
200m/656ft
Sea Level

HONDURAS

Coco

14°

Ocotal

Jinotega
Esteli Matagalpa
Chinandega Telica
Corinto Matiguas
Leon Nagarote
San Rafael del Sur MANAGUA
Granada Juigalpa
Nandaime
Diriamba *Lago de Nicaragua*
Jinotepe Rivas *(Lake Nicaragua)*

Mosquito Coast

Caribbean Sea

Bluefields

12°

86° COSTA RICA San Juan 84°

0 ____ 100 km
0 ____ 100 miles

FACTFILE

OFFICIAL NAME: Republic of Nicaragua
DATE OF FORMATION: 1838
CAPITAL: Managua
POPULATION: 5.3 million
TOTAL AREA: 49,998 sq. miles (129,494 sq. km)
DENSITY: 116 people per sq. mile

LANGUAGES: Spanish*, English Creole, Miskito
RELIGIONS: Roman Catholic 80%, Protestant Evangelical 17%, other 3%
ETHNIC MIX: Mestizo 69%, White 14%, Black 8%, Amerindian 5%, Zambo 4%
GOVERNMENT: Presidential system
CURRENCY: Córdoba oro = 100 centavos

Niger

Landlocked in the west of Africa, Niger is linked to the sea by the Niger River. It was ruled by one-party or military regimes until 1992, when a multiparty constitution was introduced.

GEOGRAPHY
The north and northeast regions are part of the Sahara. The Aïr Mountains in the center rise high above the desert. Savanna lies to the south.

CLIMATE
High temperatures persist for most of the year at around 95°F (35°C). The north is virtually rainless.

PEOPLE & SOCIETY
Considerable tensions exist between Tuareg nomads in the north and groups in the south. Tuareg have felt alienated from mainstream politics. A five-year rebellion by northern Tuareg ended in 1995 with a peace agreement. A sense of community and egalitarianism among the southern peoples helps to combat economic difficulties. Niger is largely Islamic. Women have limited rights, and restricted access to education.

THE ECONOMY
Niger has vast uranium deposits. Frequent droughts and the southwest expansion of the Sahara are problems.

◆ **INSIGHT:** *Niger's name is derived from the Tuareg word* n'eghirren, *which means "flowing water"*

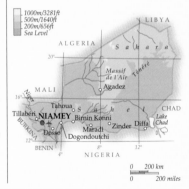

FACTFILE

OFFICIAL NAME: Republic of Niger
DATE OF FORMATION: 1960
CAPITAL: Niamey
POPULATION: 11.6 million
TOTAL AREA: 489,188 sq. miles
(1,267,000 sq. km)
DENSITY: 24 people per sq. mile

LANGUAGES: Hausa, French*, other
RELIGIONS: Muslim 85%, traditional beliefs 14%, other 1%
ETHNIC MIX: Hausa 54%, Djerma and Songhai 21%, Fulani 10%, Tuareg 9%, other 6%
GOVERNMENT: Presidential system
CURRENCY: CFA franc = 100 centimes

Nigeria

Lying in west Africa, Nigeria (a former UK colony) is now a federation of 36 states and the capital, Abuja. Dominated by military governments since 1966, democracy returned in 1999.

GEOGRAPHY
Coastal area of beaches, swamps, and lagoons gives way to rainforest, and then to savanna on the high plateaus. Semidesert to the north.

CLIMATE
The south is hot, rainy and humid for most of the year. The arid north has one very humid wet season. The Jos Plateau and highlands are cooler.

PEOPLE & SOCIETY
Some 250 ethnic groups: the largest are the Hausa, Yoruba, Ibo, and Fulani. Tensions between groups threaten national unity, and fierce intercommunal violence is common. The northern states have introduced *sharia* (Islamic law) for their majority Muslim populations. In the south, women are allowed economic independence; in the north they are restricted by conservative Islam.

THE ECONOMY
Nigeria has been overdependent on oil, its principal export, since the 1970s. Corruption is a serious issue.

◆ **INSIGHT:** *Nigeria is Africa's most populous state – one in every seven Africans is Nigerian*

1000m/3281ft
500m/1640ft
200m/656ft
Sea Level

FACTFILE
OFFICIAL NAME: Federal Republic of Nigeria
DATE OF FORMATION: 1960
CAPITAL: Abuja
POPULATION: 120 million
TOTAL AREA: 356,667 sq. miles (923,768 sq. km)

DENSITY: 341 people per sq. mile
LANGUAGES: Hausa, English*, Yoruba, Ibo
RELIGIONS: Muslim 50%, Christian 40%, traditional beliefs 10%
ETHNIC MIX: Hausa 21%, Yoruba 21%, Ibo 18%, Fulani 11%, other 29%
GOVERNMENT: Presidential system
CURRENCY: Naira = 100 kobo

Norway

The Kingdom of Norway traces the rugged western coast of Scandinavia. Settlements are largely restricted to southern and coastal areas. Vast oil and gas revenues bring prosperity.

GEOGRAPHY

The western coast is indented with numerous fjords and features tens of thousands of islands. Mountains and plateaus cover most of the country.

CLIMATE

Mild coastal climate. Inland, weather is more extreme, with warm summers and cold, snowy winters.

PEOPLE & SOCIETY

Fairly homogeneous, with some recent refugees from the Bosnian conflict. There is a strong family tradition despite the high divorce rate. Fair-minded consensus promotes female equality, boosted by the generous child-care provision. Wealth is more evenly distributed than in most developed countries.

◆ **INSIGHT:** *Near Narvik, mainland Norway is only 4 miles (7 km) wide*

THE ECONOMY

Europe's largest producer and exporter of oil and gas. Metal, engineering, and chemical industries.

2000m/6562ft
1000m/3281ft
500m/1640ft
200m/656ft
Sea Level

 FACTFILE

OFFICIAL NAME: Kingdom of Norway

DATE OF FORMATION: 1905

CAPITAL: Oslo

POPULATION: 4.5 million

TOTAL AREA: 125,181 sq. miles
(324,220 sq. km)

DENSITY: 38 people per sq. mile

LANGUAGES: Norwegian* (Bokmål and Nynorsk), Sami

RELIGIONS: Evangelical Lutheran 89%, other 10%, Roman Catholic 1%

ETHNIC MIX: Norwegian 93%, other 6%, Sami 1%

GOVERNMENT: Parliamentary system

CURRENCY: Norwegian krone = 100 øre

Oman

Situated on the eastern coast of the Arabian Peninsula, Oman occupies a strategic position at the entrance to the Persian Gulf. It is the least developed Gulf state, despite modest oil exports.

 GEOGRAPHY
Mostly gravelly desert, with mountains in the north and south. Some narrow fertile coastal strips.

 CLIMATE
Blistering heat in the west. Summer temperatures often climb above 113°F (45°C). Southern uplands receive rains June–September.

 PEOPLE & SOCIETY
Urban drift has seen most Omanis move to northern towns. The majority are Ibadi Muslims who follow an appointed leader, the imam. Ibadism is not opposed to freedom for women, and a few women hold positions of authority. Baluchi from Pakistan are the largest group of foreign workers.

◆ **INSIGHT:** *Until the late 1980s, Oman was closed to all but business or official visitors*

 THE ECONOMY
Oil accounts for most export revenue. Other exports include fish, dates, limes, and coconuts. Foreign workers are needed in all sectors.

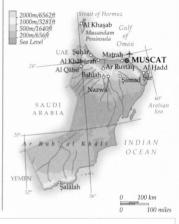

FACTFILE

OFFICIAL NAME: Sultanate of Oman
DATE OF FORMATION: 1951
CAPITAL: Muscat
POPULATION: 2.7 million
TOTAL AREA: 82,031 sq. miles
(212,460 sq. km)
DENSITY: 33 people per sq. mile

LANGUAGES: Arabic*, Baluchi, other
RELIGIONS: Ibadi Muslim 75%, other Muslim and Hindu 25%
ETHNIC MIX: Arab 88%, Baluchi 4%, Persian 3%, Indian and Pakistani 3%, African 2%
GOVERNMENT: Monarchy
CURRENCY: Omani rial = 1000 baizas

Pakistan

Once a part of British India, Pakistan was created in 1947 in response to demands for an independent, largely Muslim state. Bangladesh (former East Pakistan) gained independence in 1971.

GEOGRAPHY
The floodplain of the Indus River dominates east and south. Hindu Kush mountains in the north. The west is semidesert plateau and mountains.

CLIMATE
Temperatures can soar to 122°F (50°C) in south and west, and fall to −4°F (−20°C) in the Hindu Kush.

PEOPLE & SOCIETY
Punjabis dominate government and the army. There are many tensions with minority groups, exacerbated by the vast gap between rich and poor. Strong family ties are reflected in a dynastic and nepotistic political system. Relations with India are very tense over the issue of Kashmir.

◆ **INSIGHT:** *In 1988, Pakistan elected the first female prime minister in the Muslim world*

THE ECONOMY
Leading producer of cotton and rice, but unpredictable weather conditions often affect the crop. Oil and gas reserves. Weak and over-stretched infrastructure.

■	5000m/16405ft
■	4000m/13124ft
■	3000m/9843ft
■	2000m/6562ft
■	1000m/3281ft
■	500m/1640ft
■	200m/656ft
	Sea Level

CHINA

Hindu Kush — Karakoram Range
72° 76°
Indus

ISLĀMĀBĀD
Khyber Pass 34°
Peshāwar
Rāwalpindi Siālkot
AFGHANISTAN Sargodha Gujrānwāla
68° Faisalābād Lahore
64° *Punjab*
Quetta Multān 30°
Bahāwalpur
Baluchistan Indus
IRAN Sukkur INDIA
Thar Desert
26°
Sindh
Karāchi Hyderābād
Arabian Sea

0 200 km
0 200 miles

FACTFILE
OFFICIAL NAME: Islamic Rep. of Pakistan
DATE OF FORMATION: 1947
CAPITAL: Islamabad
POPULATION: 149 million
TOTAL AREA: 310,401 sq. miles (803,940 sq. km)
DENSITY: 500 people per sq. mile

LANGUAGES: Punjabi, Sindhi, Pashtu, Urdu*, Baluchi, Brahui
RELIGIONS: Sunni Muslim 77%, Shi'a Muslim 20%, Hindu 2%, Christian 1%
ETHNIC MIX: Punjabi 50%, Sindhi 15%, Pathan 15%, Mohajir 8%, other 12%
GOVERNMENT: Presidential system
CURRENCY: Pakistani rupee = 100 paisa

Palau

The 300-island Palau archipelago (known locally as Belau) lies in the western Pacific Ocean. It achieved independence in 1994, but continues to be heavily dependent on US aid.

GEOGRAPHY

Terrain varies from thickly forested mountains to limestone and coral reefs. Babelthuap, the largest island, is volcanic, with many rivers and waterfalls.

CLIMATE

Hot and wet. Little variation in daily and seasonal temperatures. February–April is the dry season.

PEOPLE & SOCIETY

Native Palauans are a mix of the original southeast Asian migrants and Pacific settlers. A modern influx from Asia has led to tension. 70% of the population live on the island-city of Koror, prompting the construction of a new capital on Babelthuap. Native culture is preserved on outer islands despite strong influence from the US and Japan. Modekngei is a blend of Christianity and local beliefs.

THE ECONOMY

Subsistence level. Main crops are coconuts and cassava. Revenue from fishing licenses and tourism.

◆ **INSIGHT:** *Palau's reefs contain 1500 species of fish and 700 types of coral*

FACTFILE

OFFICIAL NAME: Republic of Palau
DATE OF FORMATION: 1994
CAPITAL: Koror
POPULATION: 19,409
TOTAL AREA: 177 sq. miles (458 sq. km)
DENSITY: 99 people per sq. mile

LANGUAGES: Palauan*, English*, Japanese, Angaur, Tobi, Sonsorolese
RELIGIONS: Christian 66%, Modekngei 34%
ETHNIC MIX: Micronesian 87%, Filipino 8%, Chinese and other Asian 5%
GOVERNMENT: Nonparty system
CURRENCY: US dollar = 100 cents

Panama

Panama is the southernmost country in Central America.
The colossal Panama Canal (which was under US-control
until 2000) links the Pacific and Atlantic Oceans.

GEOGRAPHY

Lowlands along both coasts,
with savanna-covered plains and
rolling hills. Mountainous interior.
Swamps and rainforests in the east.

CLIMATE

Hot and humid, with heavy
rainfall in the May–December wet
season. Cooler at high altitudes.

PEOPLE & SOCIETY

A multiethnic society,
dominated by people of
Spanish origin. Amerindians
live in remote areas. The
Panama Canal and former
US military bases (the last of
which closed in 1999) have
given society a cosmopolitan
outlook, but Catholicism and the
extended family remain strong. In
1989, US troops arrested dictator Gen.
Noriega and restored civilian rule.

THE ECONOMY

Colón Free Trade Zone: second-
largest in the world. Income from the
canal. Earnings from merchant ships
sailing under Panamanian flag.
Banana and shrimp exports.

INSIGHT: *The Panama Canal
shortens the sea route between
the east coast of the US and Japan
by 3000 miles (4800 km)*

	2000m/6562ft
	1000m/3281ft
	500m/1640ft
	200m/656ft
	Sea Level

FACTFILE

OFFICIAL NAME: Republic of Panama
DATE OF FORMATION: 1903
CAPITAL: Panama City
POPULATION: 2.9 million
TOTAL AREA: 30,193 sq. miles
(78,200 sq. km)
DENSITY: 99 people per sq. mile

LANGUAGES: English Creole, Spanish*,
Amerindian languages
RELIGIONS: Roman Catholic 86%,
other 8%, Protestant 6%
ETHNIC MIX: Mestizo 60%, White 14%,
Black 12%, Amerindian 8%, other 6%
GOVERNMENT: Presidential system
CURRENCY: Balboa = 100 centesimos

Papua New Guinea

A former Australian colony, Papua New Guinea (PNG) occupies the eastern section of the island of New Guinea and several other island groups. Much of the country is isolated.

GEOGRAPHY

Mountainous and forested mainland, with broad, swampy river valleys. 40 active volcanoes in the north. Around 600 outer islands.

CLIMATE

Hot and humid in lowlands, cooling toward highlands, where snow can fall on highest peaks.

PEOPLE & SOCIETY

Around 750 language groups and even more tribes. The main social distinction is between lowlanders, who have frequent contact with the outside world, and the very isolated, but increasingly threatened, highlanders. Great tensions exist between highland tribes, and vendettas can often last several generations. The island of Bougainville has been granted autonomy and an eventual referendum on independence.

THE ECONOMY

Minerals: significant quantities of gold, copper, oil, and natural gas. High government spending almost led to national bankruptcy in 2002.

INSIGHT: *PNG is home to the only known poisonous birds; contact with the feathers of some species of pitohui produce skin blisters*

FACTFILE

OFFICIAL NAME: Independent State of Papua New Guinea
DATE OF FORMATION: 1975
CAPITAL: Port Moresby
POPULATION: 5 million
TOTAL AREA: 178,703 sq. miles (462,840 sq. km)

DENSITY: 29 people per sq. mile
LANGUAGES: Pidgin English, Papuan, English*, Motu, c.750 native languages
RELIGIONS: Protestant 60%, Roman Catholic 37%, other 3%
ETHNIC MIX: Melanesian and mixed 100%
GOVERNMENT: Parliamentary system
CURRENCY: Kina = 100 toeas

Paraguay

Landlocked in central South America, and once a Spanish colony, Paraguay's postindependence history has included periods of military rule. Free elections were held in 1993.

GEOGRAPHY

The Paraguay River divides hilly and forested east from a flat alluvial plain with marsh and semidesert scrub land in the west.

CLIMATE

Subtropical. The Gran Chaco is generally hotter and drier. All areas experience floods and droughts.

PEOPLE & SOCIETY

Population mainly of mixed Spanish and native Guaraní origin. Most people are bilingual, though in rural areas Guaraní is more widely heard. Cattle-ranchers populate the Chaco, along with communities of the German-origin Mennonite Church. The army is politically active.

◈ **INSIGHT:** *The War of the Triple Alliance (1864–1870) killed almost 90% of Paraguay's male population*

THE ECONOMY

Agriculture: soybeans and cotton are main exports. Large hydroelectric dams allow Paraguay to export electricity – covering the cost of oil imports. Political instability deters investment.

FACTFILE

OFFICIAL NAME: Republic of Paraguay

DATE OF FORMATION: 1811

CAPITAL: Asunción

POPULATION: 5.8 million

TOTAL AREA: 157,046 sq. miles (406,750 sq. km)

DENSITY: 38 people per sq. mile

LANGUAGES: Guaraní, Spanish*, German

RELIGIONS: Roman Catholic 96%, Protestant (including Mennonite) 4%

ETHNIC MIX: Mestizo 90%, other 8%, Amerindian 2%

GOVERNMENT: Presidential system

CURRENCY: Guaraní = 100 centimos

Peru

Once the heart of the Inca empire, before the Spanish conquest in the 16th century, Peru lies on the Pacific coast of South America, just south of the equator.

GEOGRAPHY
Coastal plain rises to Andes mountains. Uplands, dissected by fertile valleys, lie east of the Andes. Tropical forest in extreme east.

CLIMATE
Coast is mainly arid. Middle slopes of the Andes are temperate; higher peaks are snow-covered. East is hot, humid, and very wet.

PEOPLE & SOCIETY
Though populated mainly by Amerindians or mixed-race *mestizos*, society is dominated by a small group of Spanish descendants. Amerindians, together with the small black community, suffer discrimination in the towns, but access to information and political representation is growing. Clashes with left-wing militants killed almost 70,000 people between 1980 and 2000, mostly Amerindians.

THE ECONOMY
The economy is overreliant on, albeit abundant, mineral resources. Rich Pacific fish stocks. Weak banks.

INSIGHT: *Lake Titicaca is the world's highest navigable lake*

■	4000m/13124ft
■	2000m/6562ft
■	500m/1640ft
	Sea Level

0   200 km
0   200 miles

FACTFILE

OFFICIAL NAME: Republic of Peru
DATE OF FORMATION: 1824
CAPITAL: Lima
POPULATION: 26.5 million
TOTAL AREA: 496,223 sq. miles (1,285,200 sq. km)
DENSITY: 54 people per sq. mile

LANGUAGES: Spanish*, Quechua*, Aymara
RELIGIONS: Roman Catholic 95%, other 5%
ETHNIC MIX: Amerindian 54%, Mestizo 32%, White 12%, other 2%
GOVERNMENT: Presidential system
CURRENCY: New sol = 100 centimos

Philippines

Lying in the western Pacific Ocean, the Philippines is the world's second-largest archipelago. It comprises 7107 islands, of which 4600 are named and 1000 inhabited.

GEOGRAPHY
Larger islands are forested and mountainous. Over 20 active volcanoes. Frequent earthquakes.

CLIMATE
Tropical. Warm and humid all year round. Typhoons occur in the rainy season: June–October.

PEOPLE & SOCIETY
Over 100 ethnic groups; most are of Malay origin and Roman Catholic. The Church is a dominant cultural force; it opposes family-planning programs, despite the accelerating population growth. The Chinese minority has been established for 400 years. Women play a prominent part in society. San Carlos University was founded in 1595 by the Spanish.

◆ **INSIGHT:** *Mass "People Power" demonstrations have brought down two presidents, in 1986 and 2001*

THE ECONOMY
Agricultural productivity is rising; pineapples and bananas are major exports. Poor infrastructure limits room for growth.

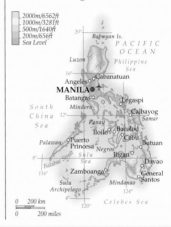

FACTFILE

OFFICIAL NAME: Rep. of the Philippines
DATE OF FORMATION: 1946
CAPITAL: Manila
POPULATION: 78.6 million
TOTAL AREA: 115,830 sq. miles (300,000 sq. km)
DENSITY: 683 people per sq. mile

LANGUAGES: Filipino*, Tagalog, Cebuano, Hiligaynon, other including English*
RELIGIONS: Roman Catholic 83%, Protestant 9%, Muslim 5%, other 3%
ETHNIC MIX: Malay 95%, other 3%, Chinese 2%
GOVERNMENT: Presidential system
CURRENCY: Philippine peso = 100 centavos

Poland

Located in the heart of Europe, Poland has undergone massive social, economic, and political change since the collapse of communism in 1989. It is set to join the EU in 2004.

GEOGRAPHY

Lowlands, part of the North European Plain, cover most of the country. The Tatra mountains run along the southern border.

CLIMATE

Rainfall peaks during the hot summers. Cold winters with snow, especially in mountains.

PEOPLE & SOCIETY

Ethnic homogeneity masks a number of tensions. Secular liberals criticize the semiofficial status of the Roman Catholic Church, and emerging wealth disparities are resented by those unaffected by free-market reforms. The German minority in the west is growing more assertive.

INSIGHT: *Poland was the second country in Europe to have a written constitution*

THE ECONOMY

Foreign investment is linked to government privatization program and reflects status as central Europe's largest market. Heavy industries still dominate, though services growing.

1000m/3281ft
500m/1640ft
200m/656ft
Sea Level

0   100 km
0   100 miles

FACTFILE

OFFICIAL NAME: Republic of Poland
DATE OF FORMATION: 1918
CAPITAL: Warsaw
POPULATION: 38.2 million
TOTAL AREA: 120,728 sq. miles (312,685 sq. km)
DENSITY: 325 people per sq. mile

LANGUAGES: Polish
RELIGIONS: Roman Catholic 93%, other and nonreligious 5%, Orthodox Christian 2%
ETHNIC MIX: Polish 97%, other 2%, Silesian 1%
GOVERNMENT: Parliamentary system
CURRENCY: Zloty = 100 groszy

Portugal

Portugal, with its long Atlantic coast, lies on the western side of the Iberian Peninsula, which it shares with Spain. It is the most westerly country on the European mainland.

GEOGRAPHY
The Tagus River bisects the country roughly east to west, dividing mountainous north from lower and more undulating south.

CLIMATE
North is cool and moist. South is warmer with dry, mild winters.

PEOPLE & SOCIETY
A homogeneous and stable society, which is losing some of its conservative traditions. A small, well-assimilated immigrant population, mainly from former colonies. Urban areas and the south are more socially liberal. The north is more responsive to traditional Roman Catholic values. Family ties remain important.

◆ **INSIGHT:** *Portugal is the world's leading producer of cork, which comes from the bark of the cork oak*

THE ECONOMY
Agricultural exports: vegetables, fruits, and wine – though methods are outdated. Clothing and car exports. Strong banking and tourism sectors.

FACTFILE

OFFICIAL NAME: Republic of Portugal
DATE OF FORMATION: 1139
CAPITAL: Lisbon
POPULATION: 10 million
TOTAL AREA: 35,672 sq. miles (92,391 sq. km)
DENSITY: 282 people per sq. mile

LANGUAGES: Portuguese
RELIGIONS: Roman Catholic 97%, other 2%, Protestant 1%
ETHNIC MIX: Portuguese 98%, African and other 2%
GOVERNMENT: Parliamentary system
CURRENCY: Euro = 100 cents

Qatar

Projecting north from the Arabian Peninsula into the Gulf, Qatar was a founder member of OPEC. Its plentiful reserves of oil and gas make it one of the wealthiest states in the region.

GEOGRAPHY

Flat, semiarid desert with dunes and salt pans. Vegetation is limited to small patches of scrub.

CLIMATE

Hot and humid. Temperatures in summer can soar to over 104°F (40°C). Rainfall is rare.

PEOPLE & SOCIETY

Only one in five residents are native-born; the rest are guest workers from the Indian subcontinent, Iran, and north Africa. Qataris were once nomadic Bedouins, but since the advent of oil wealth around 90% now live in Doha. As a result, the north is dotted with abandoned villages. Women enjoy relative freedom and don't have to wear the veil.

◆ **INSIGHT:** *There are over 700 mosques in the capital, Doha*

THE ECONOMY

Steady supply of crude oil and huge gas reserves, plus related industries. Economy is heavily dependent on foreign workforce. All raw materials and most foods, except vegetables, are imported.

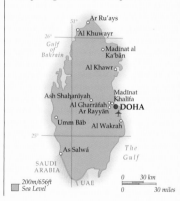

FACTFILE

OFFICIAL NAME: State of Qatar

DATE OF FORMATION: 1971

CAPITAL: Doha

POPULATION: 584,000

TOTAL AREA: 4416 sq. miles (11,437 sq. km)

DENSITY: 138 people per sq. mile

LANGUAGES: Arabic

RELIGIONS: Muslim (mainly Sunni) 95%, other 5%

ETHNIC MIX: Arab 40%, Indian 18%, Pakistani 18%, other 14%, Iranian 10%

GOVERNMENT: Monarchy

CURRENCY: Qatar riyal = 100 dirhams

Romania

Once dominated by Poles, Hungarians, and Ottomans, Romania has been slowly converting to a free-market economy since the overthrow of its communist regime in 1989.

 GEOGRAPHY
Carpathian Mountains encircle the Transylvanian plateau. Wide plains to the south and east. Danube River forms southern border.

 CLIMATE
Continental. Summers are hot and humid, winters are cold and snowy. Very heavy spring rains.

 PEOPLE & SOCIETY
Romanians are ethnically distinct from their Slav and Hungarian (Magyra) neighbors. Hungarians are the largest minority and are based in Transylvania. They are protected by the influence of Hungary, unlike the Roma, who suffer from discrimination. The overall population is shrinking.

 INSIGHT: *In 2001, Romania became the last country in Europe to lift its ban on homosexuality*

THE ECONOMY

Pollution-spreading, outdated heavy industries and unmechanized agricultural sector. Textiles and metals are main exports which have helped pull the country out of years of recession. Privatization continues.

FACTFILE

OFFICIAL NAME: Romania
DATE OF FORMATION: 1878
CAPITAL: Bucharest
POPULATION: 21.7 million
TOTAL AREA: 91,699 sq. miles
(237,500 sq. km)
DENSITY: 244 people per sq. mile

LANGUAGES: Romanian*, Hungarian
RELIGIONS: Romanian Orthodox 87%, Roman Catholic 5%, Protestant 4%, other 2%, Greek Orthodox 1%, Uniate 1%
ETHNIC MIX: Romanian 89%, Magyar 7%, Roma 3%, other 1%
GOVERNMENT: Presidential system
CURRENCY: Romanian leu

Russian Federation

The Russian Federation is still the world's largest state, despite the breakup of the Soviet Union in 1991. It is currently struggling to capitalize on its diversity.

GEOGRAPHY

The Ural Mountains divide the European steppes and forests from the tundra and forests of Siberia. South-central deserts and mountains.

CLIMATE

Continental in European Russia. Elsewhere climate ranges from sub-arctic to Mediterranean and hot desert.

PEOPLE & SOCIETY

Ethnic Russians make up over 80% of the population, but there are many minorities; 57 "nationalities" have territorial status, while a further 95 lack their own region. Most ethnic republics are concentrated in European Russia. There are around 20 million Muslims in Russia. The ongoing war with Chechnya highlights the potential for ethnic crisis. Wealth disparities, rising crime, and black-market activities have accompanied reforms.

◆ **INSIGHT:** *The Trans-Siberian Railroad, which runs 5800 miles (9335 km) from Moscow to Vladivostok, is the longest in the world, passing through seven time zones*

📖 FACTFILE

OFFICIAL NAME: Russian Federation
DATE OF FORMATION: 1480
CAPITAL: Moscow
POPULATION: 143 million
TOTAL AREA: 6,592,735 sq. miles (17,075,200 sq. km)
DENSITY: 22 people per sq. mile

LANGUAGES: Russian*, Tatar, Ukrainian, Chavash, other national languages
RELIGIONS: Orthodox Christian 75%, Muslim 14%, other 11%
ETHNIC MIX: Russian 82%, other 10%, Tatar 4%, Ukrainian 3%, Chavash 1%
GOVERNMENT: Presidential system
CURRENCY: Russian rouble = 100 kopeks

Russian Federation

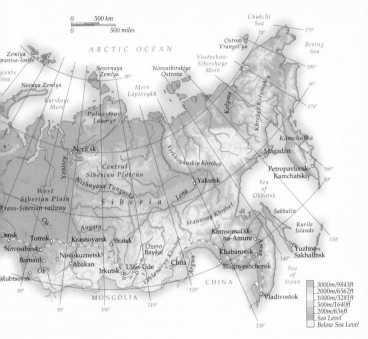

0 ___ 500 km
0 ___ 500 miles

Chukchi Sea
Ostrov Vrangel'ya
Bering Sea
ARCTIC OCEAN
Vostochno-Sibirshoye More
Zemlya Frantsa-Iosifa
rents Sea
Novaya Zemlya
Karskoye More
Severnaya Zemlya
Novosibirskiye Ostrova
More Laptevykh
Poluostrov Taymyr
Khrebet Kolymskiy
Kolyma
Kamchatka
Noril'sk
Magadan
Yenisey
Central Siberian Plateau
Verkhoyanskiy Khrebet
Petropavlovsk-Kamchatskiy
West Siberian Plain
Nizhnyaya Tunguska
Yakutsk
Sea of Okhotsk
Trans-Siberian railway
S i b e r i a
Lena
Sakhalin
Kurile Islands
Omsk
Angara
Stanovoy Khrebet
Yuzhno-Sakhalinsk
Tomsk
Krasnoyarsk
Bratsk
Komsomol'sk-na-Amure
Novosibirsk
Amur
Ob'
Novokuznetsk
Abakan
Khabarovsk
Barnaul
Ozero Baykal
Yablonovyy Khrebet
Chita
Blagoveshchensk
Sea of Japan
Rubtsovsk
Ob'
Irkutsk
Ulan-Ude
Argun'
CHINA
MONGOLIA
Vladivostok

3000m/9843ft
2000m/6562ft
1000m/3281ft
500m/1640ft
200m/656ft
Sea Level
Below Sea Level

$ THE ECONOMY

Lingering inefficiencies since transition to market economy sap Russia's obvious strengths: huge natural resources, in particular oil and gas, precious metals, timber, and hydrocarbons. Important engineering, military, and scientific base.

Privatization, which is proceeding fast, and foreign investment could transform industry and agriculture. Many postcommunist gains were wiped out by financial crisis in 1998. Organized crime syndicates own huge areas of the economy, and the black market accounts for 50% of trade.

Rwanda

Rwanda lies just south of the equator in east central Africa, far from the nearest sea port. Since independence from France in 1962, ethnic tensions have dominated politics.

GEOGRAPHY

A series of plateaus descend from the ridge of volcanic peaks in the west to the Akagera River on the eastern border. The Great Rift Valley also passes through this region.

CLIMATE

Tropical, though tempered by the altitude. Two wet seasons are separated by a dry season, from June to August. Heaviest rain in the west.

PEOPLE & SOCIETY

For over 500 years the cattle-owning Tutsi minority were politically dominant over the land-owning Hutu. In 1959, violent revolt led to a reversal of the roles. Ethnic tensions are fierce; in the most recent violence, in 1994, over 800,000 people, mostly Tutsi, were massacred in an act of state-backed genocide; trials are ongoing. Rwandans live a subsistence existence.

THE ECONOMY

Rwanda has few resources, but if it could achieve lasting stability, it could become a key producer of coffee and tea. The potential from possible oil and gas reserves is offset by the high cost of transportation.

◆ **INSIGHT:** *Rwanda is the most densely populated country in mainland Africa*

FACTFILE

OFFICIAL NAME: Republic of Rwanda

DATE OF FORMATION: 1962

CAPITAL: Kigali

POPULATION: 8.16 million

TOTAL AREA: 10,169 sq. miles (26,338 sq. km)

DENSITY: 847 people per sq. mile

LANGUAGES: Kinyarwanda*, French*, Kiswahili, English*

RELIGIONS: Catholic 65%, traditional beliefs 25%, Protestant 9%, Muslim 1%

ETHNIC MIX: Hutu 90%, Tutsi 9%, other (including Twa) 1%

GOVERNMENT: Transitional regime

CURRENCY: Rwanda franc = 100 centimes

St. Kitts & Nevis

One of the Caribbean's most popular tourist destinations, St. Kitts and Nevis lies in the northern part of the Leeward Island chain. Nevis is the less developed of the two islands.

GEOGRAPHY
Volcanic in origin, with forested, mountainous interiors. Nevis has hot and cold springs.

CLIMATE
Tropical, tempered by trade winds. Little seasonal variation in temperature. Moderate rainfall.

PEOPLE & SOCIETY
The majority of the population are descended from former African slaves. There are small numbers of Europeans, South Asians, and a community of Lebanese. Levels of emigration are high, and overseas remittances are an important source of national income. Native professionals have largely replaced the former expatriate elite. They are the best paid group, but wealth disparities are not great. The secessionist movement on Nevis remains an issue.

THE ECONOMY
Successful and still expanding tourist industry is vulnerable to downturns in key US and UK markets. Sugar industry is in terminal decline.

INSIGHT: *Nevis has been renowned as a spa since the 18th century, and is known as the "Queen of the Caribbean"*

FACTFILE
OFFICIAL NAME: Federation of Saint Christopher and Nevis
DATE OF FORMATION: 1983
CAPITAL: Basseterre
POPULATION: 38,736
TOTAL AREA: 101 sq. miles (261 sq. km)
DENSITY: 279 people per sq. mile

LANGUAGES: English*, English Creole
RELIGIONS: Anglican 33%, Methodist 29%, other 22%, Moravian 9%, Roman Catholic 7%
ETHNIC MIX: Black 94%, mixed 3%, other and Amerindian 2%, White 1%
GOVERNMENT: Parliamentary system
CURRENCY: East Caribbean $ = 100 cents

St. Lucia

St. Lucia is one of the most beautiful of the Caribbean Windward Islands. Ruled by France and the UK at different times in its past, the island retains the character of both.

GEOGRAPHY
Volcanic and mountainous, with some broad fertile valleys. The Pitons, ancient lava cones, rise from the sea on the forested west coast.

CLIMATE
Tropical, moderated by trade winds. May–October wet season brings daily warm showers. Rainfall is highest in the mountains.

PEOPLE & SOCIETY
Population is a tension-free mixture of descendants of Africans, Caribs, and Europeans. Family life and the Roman Catholic Church are important to most St. Lucians. In rural areas women often head the households, and run much of the farming. Plantation and hotel owners are the richest group. There is growing local resistance to overdevelopment of the island for tourism.

THE ECONOMY
Mainly agricultural, with some light industry. Bananas are biggest export. Successful tourist industry, but most resorts are foreign-owned.

INSIGHT: St. Lucia has two Nobel laureates, the most per capita in the world

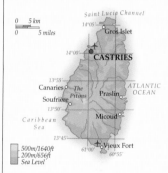

FACTFILE

OFFICIAL NAME: Saint Lucia
DATE OF FORMATION: 1979
CAPITAL: Castries
POPULATION: 160,145
TOTAL AREA: 239 sq. miles (620 sq. km)
DENSITY: 679 people per sq. mile

LANGUAGES: English*, French Creole
RELIGIONS: Roman Catholic 90%, other 10%
ETHNIC MIX: Black 90%, Mulatto (mixed race) 6%, Asian 3%, White 1%
GOVERNMENT: Parliamentary system
CURRENCY: East Caribbean $ = 100 cents

St. Vincent & the Grenadines

The islands of St. Vincent and the Grenadines form part of the Windward group in the Caribbean. St. Vincent is mostly volcanic, while the Grenadines are flat, mainly bare, coral reefs.

GEOGRAPHY

St. Vincent is mountainous and forested, with one of two active volcanoes in the Caribbean, La Soufrière. The Grenadines are 32 islands and cays fringed by beaches.

CLIMATE

Tropical, with constant trade winds. Hurricanes are likely during July–November wet season.

PEOPLE & SOCIETY

Population is racially diverse; intermarriage has reduced tensions. Society is informal and relaxed, but family life is strongly influenced by the Church. Locals fear that their traditional lifestyle is being threatened by the expanding tourist industry.

◆ **INSIGHT:** *The islands' precolonial inhabitants, the Carib, named them "Harioun" – home of the blessed*

THE ECONOMY

Dependent on agriculture and tourism. Bananas are the main cash crop. Tourism, targeted at the jet-set and cruise-ship markets, is concentrated on the Grenadines.

FACTFILE

OFFICIAL NAME: Saint Vincent and the Grenadines
DATE OF FORMATION: 1979
CAPITAL: Kingstown
POPULATION: 116,394
TOTAL AREA: 150 sq. miles (389 sq. km)

DENSITY: 889 people per sq. mile
LANGUAGES: English*, English Creole
RELIGIONS: Anglican 42%, Methodist 20%, other 19%, Roman Catholic 19%
ETHNIC MIX: Black 66%, Mulatto (mixed race) 19%, Asian 6%, other 5%, White 4%
GOVERNMENT: Parliamentary system
CURRENCY: East Caribbean $ = 100 cents

Samoa

The southern Pacific islands of Samoa gained independence from New Zealand in 1962. Four of the nine volcanic islands are inhabited – Apolima, Manono, Savai'i, and Upolu.

GEOGRAPHY

Comprises two large islands and seven smaller ones. The two largest islands have rainforested, mountainous interiors surrounded by coastal lowlands and coral reefs.

CLIMATE

Tropical, with high humidity. Cooler May–November. Hurricane season December–March.

PEOPLE & SOCIETY

Ethnic Samoans are the world's second-largest Polynesian group, after the Maoris. Their way of life is communal and formalized. Extended family groups own 80% of the land. Each family has an elected chief, who looks after its political and social interests. Large-scale migration to the US and New Zealand reflects the country's lack of jobs and the attractions of a Western lifestyle.

THE ECONOMY

Agricultural products include taro, coconut cream, cocoa, and copra. Growth of the service sector since launch of offshore banking in 1989. Dependent on aid and expatriate remittances. Rainforests are increasingly exploited for timber.

◆ **INSIGHT:** *Samoa was named for the sacred (sa) chickens (moa) of Lu, son of Tagaloa, the god of creation*

FACTFILE

OFFICIAL NAME: Independent State of Samoa
DATE OF FORMATION: 1962
CAPITAL: Apia
POPULATION: 176,848
TOTAL AREA: 1104 sq. miles (2860 sq. km)

DENSITY: 162 people per sq. mile
LANGUAGES: Samoan*, English*
RELIGIONS: Christian 99%, other 1%
ETHNIC MIX: Polynesian 90%, Euronesian (mixed European and Polynesian) 9%, other 1%
GOVERNMENT: Parliamentary system
CURRENCY: Tala = 100 sene

San Marino

Perched on the slopes of Monte Titano in the Italian Appennino, San Marino has maintained its independence since the 4th century CE, but Italy effectively controls most of its affairs.

GEOGRAPHY

Distinctive limestone outcrop of Monte Titano dominates wooded hills and pastures near Italy's Adriatic coast.

CLIMATE

High altitude and sea breezes moderate a Mediterranean climate. Hot summers and cool, wet winters.

PEOPLE & SOCIETY

Territory is divided into nine "castles," or districts. Tightly knit society, with 16 centuries of tradition. Strict immigration rules require 30-year residence before applying for citizenship. Living standards are similar to those in northern Italy. About 20,000 Sammarinesi live abroad, most in Italy.

◆ **INSIGHT:** *Sales of postage stamps contribute 10% of the national income*

THE ECONOMY

Tourism provides 60% of total government income. Light industries – led by mechanical engineering and high-quality clothing – generate export revenue. Italian infrastructure is a boon.

500m/1640ft
200m/656ft
Sea Level

44°

Dogana
Serravalle
Fiorina
Cailungo
Gualdicciolo
Borgo
Maggiore ● **SAN MARINO**
ITALY
Monte Titano ▲
739m
Faetano
Murata
ITALY
A p p e n n i n o
Chiesanuova
Montegiardino

12°30'

0 ___ 4 km
0 ___ 4 miles

FACTFILE

OFFICIAL NAME: Republic of San Marino

DATE OF FORMATION: 1631

CAPITAL: San Marino

POPULATION: 27,730

TOTAL AREA: 23.6 sq. miles (61 sq. km)

DENSITY: 1155 people per sq. mile

LANGUAGES: Italian

RELIGIONS: Roman Catholic 93%, other and nonreligious 7%

ETHNIC MIX: Sammarinese 80%, Italian 19%, other 1%

GOVERNMENT: Parliamentary system

CURRENCY: Euro = 100 cents

São Tomé & Príncipe

A former Portuguese colony São Tomé and Príncipe lies off the west coast of Africa, comprising two main islands and the surrounding islets. Elections in 1991 ended 15 years of Marxism.

GEOGRAPHY
Islands scattered across the equator. São Tomé and Príncipe are heavily forested and mountainous.

CLIMATE
Hot and humid, but cooled by the Benguela Current. Plentiful rainfall.

PEOPLE & SOCIETY
Population is mostly black, though Portuguese culture predominates. Blacks run the political parties. Society is well integrated and free of racial prejudice. Wealth disparities are not great, though there is a growing business class. Extended family offers main form of social security. Príncipe assumed autonomous status in 1995.

◆ **INSIGHT:** *The population is entirely of immigrant descent: the islands were uninhabited when colonized in 1470*

THE ECONOMY
Cocoa provides 90% of export earnings. Palm oil, pepper, and coffee are farmed. One of Africa's highest aid-to-population ratios.

FACTFILE

OFFICIAL NAME: Democratic Republic of São Tomé and Príncipe
DATE OF FORMATION: 1975
CAPITAL: São Tomé
POPULATION: 170,372
TOTAL AREA: 386 sq. miles (1001 sq. km)
DENSITY: 459 people per sq. mile

LANGUAGES: Portuguese Creole, Portuguese*
RELIGIONS: Roman Catholic 84%, other 16%
ETHNIC MIX: Black 90%, Portuguese and Creole 10%
GOVERNMENT: Presidential system
CURRENCY: Dobra = 100 centimos

Saudi Arabia

Occupying most of the Arabian Peninsula, Saudi Arabia covers an area the size of western Europe. It has the world's largest oil and gas reserves and a major petrochemicals industry.

GEOGRAPHY

Mostly desert or semidesert plateau. Mountain ranges in the west run parallel to the Red Sea and drop steeply to a coastal plain.

CLIMATE

In summer, temperatures often soar above 118°F (48°C), but in winter they may fall below freezing. Rainfall is rare.

PEOPLE & SOCIETY

Most Saudis are Sunni Muslims who follow the strictly orthodox Wahhabi interpretation of Islam and embrace *sharia* (Islamic law) in their daily lives. Women are obliged to wear the veil, cannot hold driving licenses, and have no role in public life. The al-Sa'ud family have been absolutist rulers since 1932. With the support of the religious establishment, they control all political life.

THE ECONOMY

Vast oil and gas reserves. Other minerals include coal, iron, and gold. Most food is imported.

INSIGHT: *Over two million Muslims a year make the* haj *(pilgrimage) to the holy city of Mecca. Only practicing Muslims are allowed inside the city*

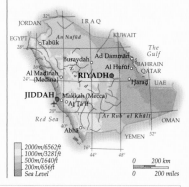

FACTFILE

OFFICIAL NAME: Kingdom of Saudi Arabia
DATE OF FORMATION: 1932
CAPITALS: Riyadh and Jiddah
POPULATION: 21.7 million
TOTAL AREA: 756,981 sq. miles (1,960,582 sq. km)

DENSITY: 27 people per sq. mile
LANGUAGES: Arabic
RELIGIONS: Sunni Muslim 85%, Shi'a Muslim 15%
ETHNIC MIX: Arab 90%, Afro-Asian 10%
GOVERNMENT: Monarchy
CURRENCY: Saudi riyal = 100 halalat

Senegal

Senegal's capital, Dakar, stands on the westernmost cape of Africa. After independence from France, Senegal became a single-party state. Multiparty elections were first held in 1981.

GEOGRAPHY
Arid semidesert in the north. The south is mainly savanna bushland. Plains in the southeast.

CLIMATE
Tropical, with humid rainy conditions June–October, and a drier season December–May. The coast is cooled by northern trade winds.

PEOPLE & SOCIETY
Interethnic marriage has reduced ethnic tensions. Groups can be identified regionally. Dakar is a Wolof area, the Senegal River is dominated by the Toucouleur, and the Malinke mostly live in the east. The Diola (Jola) in Casamance have felt politically excluded, prompting a long-running secessionist struggle. A large diaspora has raised global awareness of Senegalese culture, particularly its music.

THE ECONOMY
Good infrastructure, particularly the key port at Dakar, assist the strong industrial sector. Access to oil in Casamance is hampered by conflict.

◆ **INSIGHT:** *Senegal's name derives from the Zenega Berbers who invaded in the 1300s, bringing Islam with them*

200m/656ft Sea Level
0   100 km
0   100 miles

FACTFILE
OFFICIAL NAME: Republic of Senegal
DATE OF FORMATION: 1960
CAPITAL: Dakar
POPULATION: 9.9 million
TOTAL AREA: 75,749 sq. miles (196,190 sq. km)
DENSITY: 133 people per sq. mile

LANGUAGES: Wolof, Pulaar, Serer, Diola, Mandinka, Malinke, Soninke, French*
RELIGIONS: Sunni Muslim 90%, traditional beliefs 5%, Christian 5%
ETHNIC MIX: Wolof 43%, Toucouleur 24%, Serer 15%, Diola 4%, other 14%
GOVERNMENT: Presidential system
CURRENCY: CFA franc = 100 centimes

Serbia & Montenegro

In a new constitution in 2003, Serbia and Montenegro redefined their relationship after emerging from the wreckage of Yugoslavia. Montenegro may choose independence in 2006.

GEOGRAPHY

Fertile Danube plain in the north, rolling uplands in center. Mountains in south, and behind narrow Adriatic coastal plain.

CLIMATE

Mediterranean along coast, continental inland. Hot summers and cold winters, with heavy snow.

PEOPLE & SOCIETY

Serbs and Montenegrins share a language and the Orthodox Christian faith. The two republics run their affairs separately. The main ethnic minorities are the Muslim Albanians of Kosovo and the Hungarians (Magyars) in Vojvodina. Kosovo has been run by the UN since NATO intervention over oppression in 1999.

 INSIGHT: *The two republics use different currencies*

THE ECONOMY

The ouster of former dictator Slobodan Milosevic in 2000 opened the way for renewed trade and an end to sanctions.

FACTFILE

OFFICIAL NAME: Serbia and Montenegro
DATE OF FORMATION: 1992
CAPITAL: Belgrade
POPULATION: 10.5 million
TOTAL AREA: 39,517 sq. miles
(102,350 sq. km)
DENSITY: 266 people per sq. mile

LANGUAGES: Serbo-Croat*, other
RELIGIONS: Orthodox Christian 65%, Muslim 19%, other 12%, Catholic 4%
ETHNIC MIX: Serb 62%, Albanian 17%, other 13%, Montenegrin 5%, Magyar 3%
GOVERNMENT: Parliamentary system
CURRENCIES: Dinar = 100 para (Serbia); euro = 100 cents (Montenegro)

Seychelles

The Seychelles comprises 115 islands in the Indian Ocean. Formerly a UK colony, multiparty elections were held in 1993 after 14 years as a one-party state.

GEOGRAPHY

Mostly low-lying coral atolls, but 40, including the largest, Mahé, are mountainous and are the only granitic midocean islands in the world.

CLIMATE

Tropical oceanic climate. Hot and humid. Rainy season December–May.

PEOPLE & SOCIETY

The islands were uninhabited when French settlers arrived in the 18th century. Today, the population is homogeneous – a result of inter-marriage between ethnic groups. Almost 90% of people live on Mahé. Living standards are among Africa's highest. Poverty is rare and the welfare system caters for all.

◆ INSIGHT: *The Seychelles' unique species include the giant tortoise and the world's largest seed, the coco-de-mer*

THE ECONOMY

Tourism is the main source of income, based on the appeal of beaches and exotic plants and animals. Tuna is fished and canned for export. There are virtually no mineral resources. All domestic requirements are imported.

FACTFILE

OFFICIAL NAME: Republic of Seychelles
DATE OF FORMATION: 1976
CAPITAL: Victoria
POPULATION: 80,098
TOTAL AREA: 176 sq. miles (455 sq. km)
DENSITY: 770 people per sq. mile

LANGUAGES: Creole*, English*, French*
RELIGIONS: Roman Catholic 90%, Anglican 8%, other (including Muslim) 2%
ETHNIC MIX: Creole 89%, Indian 5%, other 4%, Chinese 2%
GOVERNMENT: Presidential system
CURRENCY: Seychelles rupee = 100 cents

Sierra Leone

The west African state of Sierra Leone achieved independence from the UK in 1961. Today, it is still trying to recover from a devastating civil war, and is one of the world's poorest nations.

GEOGRAPHY

Flat plain, running the length of the coast, stretches inland for 83 miles (133 km). Beyond, forests rise to highlands near neighboring Guinea in the northeast.

CLIMATE

Hot tropical weather, with very high rainfall and humidity. The dusty, northeastern *harmattan* wind blows November–April.

PEOPLE & SOCIETY

Mende and Temne are the major ethnic groups. Freetown's citizens are largely descended from slaves freed from Britain and the US, resulting in a strongly Anglicized Creole culture in the capital. The countryside is less developed. A brutal civil war broke out in 1991 and was not properly resolved until a 2001 peace agreement. Two million people were displaced.

THE ECONOMY

Palm products are exported, though most people live by subsistence farming or are dependent on aid. Diamonds are the key resource, though smuggling is rife.

 INSIGHT: *The British philanthropist Granville Sharp set up a settlement for freed slaves in Freetown in 1787*

FACTFILE

OFFICIAL NAME: Republic of Sierra Leone
DATE OF FORMATION: 1961
CAPITAL: Freetown
POPULATION: 4.8 million
TOTAL AREA: 27,698 sq. miles (71,740 sq. km)
DENSITY: 174 people per sq. mile

LANGUAGES: Mende, Temne, Krio, English*
RELIGIONS: Muslim 30%, traditional beliefs 30%, other 30%, Christian 10%
ETHNIC MIX: Mende 35%, Temne 32%, other 21%, Limba 8%, Kuranko 4%
GOVERNMENT: Presidential system
CURRENCY: Leone = 100 cents

Singapore

Linked to the southernmost tip of the Malay peninsula by a causeway, Singapore was established as a trading settlement in 1819. It is one of Asia's most important commercial centers.

GEOGRAPHY

Little remains of the original vegetation on Singapore Island. The other 54 much smaller islands are little more than swampy jungle.

CLIMATE

Equatorial. Hot and humid, with heavy rainfall all year round.

PEOPLE & SOCIETY

Dominated by the Chinese, who make up three-quarters of the community. The old English-speaking Straits Chinese and newer Mandarin-speakers are now well integrated. Malays are generally the poorest group. There is a significant foreign workforce. Society is highly regulated and government campaigns to improve public behavior are frequent. Crime is limited and punishment can be severe.

THE ECONOMY

Massive accumulated wealth is derived from success as an entrepôt and as a center of high-tech industries; Singapore leads the field in producing disk drives and new biotechnologies. All food, energy, and water imported.

INSIGHT: *Chewing gum was banned outright from 1992 to 2002*

FACTFILE

OFFICIAL NAME: Republic of Singapore
DATE OF FORMATION: 1965
CAPITAL: Singapore
POPULATION: 4.2 million
TOTAL AREA: 250 sq. miles
(648 sq. km)
DENSITY: 17,797 people per sq. mile

LANGUAGES: Mandarin*, Malay*, Tamil*, English*
RELIGIONS: Buddhist 55%, Taoist 22%, Muslim 16%, Hindu, Christian, Sikh 7%
ETHNIC MIX: Chinese 77%, Malay 14%, Indian 8%, other 1%
GOVERNMENT: Parliamentary system
CURRENCY: Singapore dollar = 100 cents

Slovakia

Landlocked in central Europe, Slovakia became an independent state in 1993. It is the less developed half of the former Czechoslovakia, with high levels of international debt.

GEOGRAPHY
The Tatra Mountains stretch along the northern border with Poland. Southern lowlands include the fertile Danube plain.

CLIMATE
Continental. Moderately warm summers and steady rainfall. Cold winters with heavy snowfalls.

PEOPLE & SOCIETY
Slovaks are the largest and most dominant group. The largest minority, the Magyars, seek protection of their language and culture, and are backed by Hungary. Tensions are eased by the existence of Magyar parties in the political mainstream. Ethnic Czechs have dual citizenship. Roma are unrepresented and face significant discrimination. The rural eastern regions are the least developed.

THE ECONOMY
Emphasis on heavy industry: dogged by low productivity. High inflation and unemployment. Links with EU, the main trading partner; membership is due in 2004.

◆ **INSIGHT:** *Bratislava was known as Pozsony when it served as the capital of Hungary from 1526 to 1784*

FACTFILE
OFFICIAL NAME: Slovak Republic
DATE OF FORMATION: 1993
CAPITAL: Bratislava
POPULATION: 5.4 million
TOTAL AREA: 18,859 sq. miles (48,845 sq. km)
DENSITY: 285 people per sq. mile

LANGUAGES: Slovak*, Hungarian (Magyar), Czech
RELIGIONS: Roman Catholic 60%, other 22%, Atheist 10%, Protestant 8%
ETHNIC MIX: Slovak 85%, Magyar 11%, other 2%, Roma 1%, Czech 1%
GOVERNMENT: Parliamentary system
CURRENCY: Slovak koruna = 100 halierov

Slovenia

The northernmost of the former Yugoslav republics, Slovenia
has close links with western Europe. Transition to independence
in 1991 avoided the violence of the breakup of Yugoslavia.

GEOGRAPHY
Alpine terrain with hills and
mountains. Forests cover almost half
the country's area. There is a short
coastline on the Adriatic Sea.

CLIMATE
Mediterranean climate on
the small coastal strip. The alpine
interior has continental extremes.

PEOPLE & SOCIETY
Slovenia's long historical
association with western Europe,
accounts for its "Alpine," rather
than "Balkan," outlook, despite
close similarities to other former
Yugoslavs. The lack of sizable
Serb or Croat minorities made for
a relatively peaceful secession
from Yugoslavia. There are
small communities of Italians
and Magyars (Hungarians) in the
southwest and east respectively.

THE ECONOMY
Competitive manufacturing
industry and healthy exports. There
are prospects for growth from EU
membership (due in 2004).

INSIGHT: *Slovenia has the
highest standard of living of
any former Soviet bloc country*

FACTFILE

OFFICIAL NAME: Republic of Slovenia
DATE OF FORMATION: 1991
CAPITAL: Ljubljana
POPULATION: 1.96 million
TOTAL AREA: 7820 sq. miles
(20,253 sq. km)
DENSITY: 251 people per sq. mile

LANGUAGES: Slovene*, Serbo-Croat
RELIGIONS: Roman Catholic 96%,
other 3%, Muslim 1%
ETHNIC MIX: Slovene 83%, other 12%,
Serb 2%, Croat 2%, Bosniak 1%
GOVERNMENT: Parliamentary
system
CURRENCY: Tolar = 100 stotinov

Solomon Islands

The Solomons archipelago comprises several hundred coral reef islands scattered in the southwestern Pacific. Most of the population live on the six largest islands.

GEOGRAPHY

The six largest islands are volcanic, mountainous, and thickly forested. Flat coastal plains provide the only cultivable land.

CLIMATE

Northern islands are hot and humid all year round; further south a cool season develops. November–April wet season brings cyclones.

PEOPLE & SOCIETY

Almost all Solomon Islanders are Melanesian. Tensions are regional; Guadalcanal natives (Isatabu) fought against immigrant Malaitan workers in the 1998–2000 conflict, displacing thousands and ruining the economy. In 2003 Australian-led peacekeepers arrived to restore the rule of law. Outlying islands have pressed for autonomy. Animist beliefs exist alongside Christianity.

THE ECONOMY

Main products are agricultural, though there are significant deposits of gold, copper, and bauxite. Civil conflict bankrupted the government, closed the main gold mine, and severed trade links.

INSIGHT: *The Solomons have no local television service; the islanders oppose TV, fearing cultural dilution*

FACTFILE

OFFICIAL NAME: Solomon Islands
DATE OF FORMATION: 1978
CAPITAL: Honiara
POPULATION: 479,000
TOTAL AREA: 10,985 sq. miles
(28,450 sq. km)
DENSITY: 44 people per sq. mile

LANGUAGES: English*, Pidgin English, Melanesian Pidgin
RELIGIONS: Anglican 34%, Catholic 19%, other Protestant 38%, other 9%
ETHNIC MIX: Melanesian 94%, Polynesian 4%, other 2%
GOVERNMENT: Parliamentary system
CURRENCY: Solomon Is $ = 100 cents

Somalia

Somalia is a semiarid state occupying the Horn of Africa. The colonies of Italian Somaliland and British Somaliland were united in 1960 to form an independent Somalia.

GEOGRAPHY

Highlands in the north, flatter scrub-covered land to the south. Coastal areas are more fertile.

CLIMATE

Very dry, except for the north coast, which is hot and humid. The interior has among the world's highest average annual temperatures.

PEOPLE & SOCIETY

The clan system forms the basis of all commercial, political, and social activities. The majority of people are ethnic Somali. The minority Bantu community is traditionally seen as socially inferior. The government collapsed altogether in 1991, since when Somalia has been without a central authority. The northern regions of Somaliland and Puntland have declared their independence. Talks between various factions continue.

THE ECONOMY

Every commodity, except arms, is in short supply. The south has few natural strengths, while trade for the relatively stable northern breakaway republics is hampered by a lack of international recognition.

◆ **INSIGHT:** *Until 1973 Somali was an unwritten language*

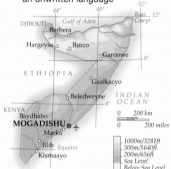

	1000m/3281ft	
	500m/1640ft	
	200m/656ft	
	Sea Level	
	Below Sea Level	

FACTFILE

OFFICIAL NAME: Somalia
DATE OF FORMATION: 1960
CAPITAL: Mogadishu
POPULATION: 9.6 million
TOTAL AREA: 246,199 sq. miles
(637,657 sq. km)
DENSITY: 40 people per sq. mile

LANGUAGES: Somali*, Arabic*, English, Italian
RELIGIONS: Sunni Muslim 98%, Christian 2%
ETHNIC MIX: Somali 85%, other 15%
GOVERNMENT: Transitional regime
CURRENCY: Somali shilling = 100 centesimi

South Africa

South Africa is the southernmost nation on the African continent. After 80 years of white minority rule, the country held its first multiracial, multiparty elections in 1994.

GEOGRAPHY

Much of the interior is grassy *veld*. Desert in the west and far north. Mountains east, south, and west.

CLIMATE

Warm, temperate, and dry. Cape Town has a Mediterranean climate. Semiarid in the west.

PEOPLE & SOCIETY

The majority black population now dominates politically, but the minority white community still controls the economy. A small black middle class is growing, but unemployment among blacks is as high as 40%. Wealth disparities are widening. Over five million suffer from AIDS and the fight against it is hampered by social attitudes.

◆ **INSIGHT:** *Over the last century, South Africa have produced over half of the world's gold.*

THE ECONOMY

Africa's largest and most developed economy. Rich in mineral resources, particularly metals. Insecurity deters investment. Wealth gap and AIDS epidemic worsening.

FACTFILE

OFFICIAL NAME: Republic of South Africa
DATE OF FORMATION: 1934
CAPITAL: Pretoria; Cape Town; Bloemfontein
POPULATION: 44.8 million
TOTAL AREA: 471,008 sq. miles (1,219,912 sq. km)
DENSITY: 95 people per sq. mile

LANGUAGES: English*, isiZulu*, isiXhosa*, 8 other languages* (including Afrikaans)
RELIGIONS: Christian 68%, animist and traditional beliefs 29%, other 3%
ETHNIC MIX: Black 79%, White 10%, Colored 9%, Asian 2%
GOVERNMENT: Presidential system
CURRENCY: Rand = 100 cents

Spain

 Lodged between Europe, Africa, the North Atlantic, and the Mediterranean, Spain has occupied a pivotal global position since unification under Ferdinand and Isabella in 1492.

GEOGRAPHY

Mountain ranges in the north, center, and south, with a huge central plateau. Mediterranean lowlands. Verdant valleys in the northwest.

CLIMATE

Maritime in north. Hotter and drier in south. The central plateau has an extreme climate.

PEOPLE & SOCIETY

A vigorous ethnic regionalism, long suppressed under Franco's regime, now flourishes. There are now 17 autonomous regions. People remain churchgoing, though Roman Catholic teachings on social issues are often flouted. Spanish women are increasingly emancipated, with strong political representation.

◆ **INSIGHT:** *Over 3000 festivals and feasts take place each year in Spain*

THE ECONOMY

One of the fastest-growing economies in the West with a well-qualified workforce. There are few natural resources. Spain has one of the world's largest fishing fleets. South American investments hit by 2001 Argentine crisis.

FACTFILE

OFFICIAL NAME: Kingdom of Spain
DATE OF FORMATION: 1492
CAPITAL: Madrid
POPULATION: 39.9 million
TOTAL AREA: 194,896 sq. miles
(504,782 sq. km)
DENSITY: 207 people per sq. mile

LANGUAGES: Spanish*, Catalan*, Galician*, Basque*
RELIGIONS: Roman Catholic 96%, other 4%
ETHNIC MIX: Spanish 72%, Catalan 17%, Galician 6%, other 3%, Basque 2%
GOVERNMENT: Parliamentary system
CURRENCY: Euro = 100 cents

Sri Lanka

The teardrop-shaped island of Sri Lanka is separated from India by the Palk Strait. Nineteen years of civil war between the government and ethnic Tamil rebels finally ended in 2002.

 GEOGRAPHY
The main island is dominated by rugged central highlands. Fertile northern plains are dissected by rivers. Much of the land is tropical jungle.

 CLIMATE
Tropical, with breezes on the coast and cooler air in highlands. Northeast is driest and hottest.

PEOPLE & SOCIETY
The Sinhalese are mostly Buddhist, while Tamils are mostly Hindu. Tamils were the minority group favored by the British colonists. Majority-Sinhalese power since independence in 1948 fueled tensions, erupting into civil war in 1983. A peace deal was secured in 2002, and the Tamil Tiger rebels accepted autonomy in the north and east. Moors are the Muslim descendants of Arab traders.

 THE ECONOMY
World's largest tea exporter. Civil war seriously drained government funds, while insecurity continues to deter investors and tourists.

 INSIGHT: *Sri Lanka elected the world's first woman prime minister in 1960*

 FACTFILE

OFFICIAL NAME: Democratic Socialist Republic of Sri Lanka
DATE OF FORMATION: 1948
CAPITAL: Colombo
POPULATION: 19.3 million
TOTAL AREA: 25,332 sq. miles (65,610 sq. km)

DENSITY: 772 people per sq. mile
LANGUAGES: Sinhala*, Tamil*, English
RELIGIONS: Buddhist 69%, Hindu 15%, Muslim 8%, Christian 8%
ETHNIC MIX: Sinhalese 74%, Tamil 18%, Moor 7%, other 1%
GOVERNMENT: Parliamentary system
CURRENCY: Sri Lanka rupee = 100 cents

Sudan

The largest country in Africa, Sudan borders the Red Sea. Tensions between Arab north and black African south have led to two civil wars since independence from the UK and Egypt.

GEOGRAPHY
Lies within the upper Nile basin. Mostly arid plains, with marshes in the south. Highlands border the Red Sea in the northeast.

CLIMATE
North is hot, arid desert with constant dry winds. Rainy season ranging from two months in the center to eight in the south.

PEOPLE & SOCIETY
Large number of ethnic and linguistic groups. Two million people are nomads. Major social division is between Arabized Muslims in the north, and the mostly black African, largely Christian or animist peoples in the south. Attempts to impose Arab and Islamic values throughout Sudan were the root cause of the civil war that ravaged the south during 1983-2005. Women's rights are restricted.

THE ECONOMY
Oil exports began in 1999. War and drought hamper farming; sesame and gum arabic are among key crops.

◆ **INSIGHT:** *Sudan's Sudd is the world's largest swamp*

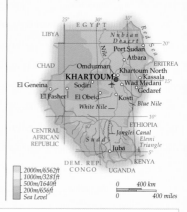

2000m/6562ft
1000m/3281ft
500m/1640ft
200m/656ft
Sea Level

0 — 400 km
0 — 400 miles

FACTFILE
OFFICIAL NAME: Republic of the Sudan
DATE OF FORMATION: 1956
CAPITAL: Khartoum
POPULATION: 32.6 million
TOTAL AREA: 967,493 sq. miles
(2,505,810 sq. km)
DENSITY: 34 people per sq. mile

LANGUAGES: Arabic*, African languages
RELIGIONS: Muslim 70%, Traditional beliefs 20%, Christian 9%, Other 1%
ETHNIC MIX: Black 59% (of which Beja 6%), Arab 40%, other 1%
GOVERNMENT: Presidential system
CURRENCY: Sudanese pound or dinar = 100 piastres

Suriname

Suriname is a former Dutch colony on the north coast of South America. Democracy was restored in 1991, after almost 11 years of military rule. The Netherlands is still the main supplier of aid.

GEOGRAPHY

Mostly covered by tropical rainforest. Coastal plain rises to central plateaus and the Guiana Highlands.

CLIMATE

Tropical. Hot and humid, but cooled by trade winds. High rainfall, especially in the interior.

PEOPLE & SOCIETY

About 250,000 people have emigrated to the Netherlands since independence. Of those left, 90% live near the coast; the rest live in scattered rainforest communities. Around 7000 are indigenous Amerindians. *Bosnegers* – descendants of runaway African slaves – fought the Creole-dominated government in the 1980s. Many South Asians and Javanese work in farming. Since return to civilian rule, each group has had a political party representing its interests.

THE ECONOMY

Aluminum and bauxite are the leading exports. Rice and fruit are main cash crops, though Suriname is a net importer of food.

◆ **INSIGHT:** *Suriname was ceded to Holland by the English, in exchange for what is now New York state, in 1667*

1000m/3281ft	
500m/1640ft	
200m/656ft	
Sea Level	

0   200 km
0   200 miles

FACTFILE

OFFICIAL NAME: Republic of Suriname
DATE OF FORMATION: 1975
CAPITAL: Paramaribo
POPULATION: 421,000
TOTAL AREA: 63,039 sq. miles (163,270 sq. km)
DENSITY: 7 people per sq. mile

LANGUAGES: Sranan (creole), Dutch*, Javanese, Hindi, Saramaccan, other
RELIGIONS: Christian 48%, Hindu 27%, Muslim 20%, traditional beliefs 5%
ETHNIC MIX: Creole 34%, South Asian 34%, Javanese 18%, Black 9%, Other 5%
GOVERNMENT: Parliamentary system
CURRENCY: Guilder or florin = 100 cents

Swaziland

The tiny southern African kingdom of Swaziland is economically dependent on South Africa. The strong hereditary monarchy is being challenged by demands for a multiparty government.

GEOGRAPHY
Mainly high plateaus and mountains. Rolling grasslands and low scrub plains to the east. Pine forests on western border.

CLIMATE
Temperatures rise and rainfall declines as the land descends eastward, from high to low grassy *veld*.

PEOPLE & SOCIETY
One of the most conservative states in Africa, though there is pressure from urban-based modernizers. The political system promotes Swazi tradition and is dominated by a powerful monarchy. Women face discrimination and chastity is promoted to combat AIDS.

◆ **INSIGHT:** *Polygamy is practiced in Swaziland – when King Sobhuza died in 1982, he left 100 widows*

THE ECONOMY
Sugarcane is the main cash crop. Wood pulp and coal are also exported. Agricultural modernization is hindered by lack of land title and small plot size. AIDS epidemic.

FACTFILE
OFFICIAL NAME: Kingdom of Swaziland
DATE OF FORMATION: 1968
CAPITAL: Mbabane
POPULATION: 948,000
TOTAL AREA: 6704 sq. miles (17,363 sq. km)
DENSITY: 143 people per sq. mile

LANGUAGES: English*, siSwati*, isiZulu, Xitsonga
RELIGIONS: Christian 60%, traditional beliefs 40%
ETHNIC MIX: Swazi 97%, other 3%
GOVERNMENT: Monarchy
CURRENCY: Lilangeni = 100 cents

Sweden

The largest Scandinavian country in both population and area, Sweden has one of the world's most extensive welfare systems, and is among the leading proponents of equal rights for women.

GEOGRAPHY

Heavily forested, with many lakes. Northern plateau extends beyond the Arctic Circle. Southern lowlands are widely cultivated.

CLIMATE

Southern coasts warmed by Gulf Stream. Northern areas have more extreme continental climate.

PEOPLE & SOCIETY

The nuclear family forms the basis of society, though the rates of births and marriages are declining and cohabitation is now common. The comprehensive welfare system was cut back during recession in the 1990s, but remains generous. Women are well represented at all levels. A 15,000-strong minority of Sami lives in the far north. Most industries and the bulk of the population are based in and around the southern cities.

THE ECONOMY

Companies of global importance, including Volvo, Saab, SFK, Ericsson. Highly developed infrastructure. Up-to-date technology. Skilled labor force.

INSIGHT:

Sweden has maintained a position of armed neutrality since 1815

1000m/3281ft
500m/1640ft
200m/656ft
Sea Level

0   100 km
0   100 miles

FINLAND
Lapland
Arctic Circle
NORWAY
Luleå
Umeå
Gulf of Bothnia
Östersund
Sundsvall
Uppsala
Västerås
Örebro
Vänern
Trollhättan
Göteborg
Borås
Vättern
Jönköping
Linköping
Norrköping
STOCKHOLM
Gotland
Öland
Kattegat
Helsingborg
Karlskrona
Malmö
Baltic Sea
20°
24°
16°
12°
68°
66°
64°
62°
60°
58°
56°

FACTFILE

OFFICIAL NAME: Kingdom of Sweden
DATE OF FORMATION: 1523
CAPITAL: Stockholm
POPULATION: 8.8 million
TOTAL AREA: 173,731 sq. miles (449,964 sq. km)
DENSITY: 55 people per sq. mile

LANGUAGES: Swedish*, Finnish, Sami
RELIGIONS: Evangelical Lutheran 82%, other 13%, Roman Catholic 2%, Muslim 2%, Orthodox Christian 1%
ETHNIC MIX: Swedish 88%, recent immigrant 10%, Finnish and Sami 2%
GOVERNMENT: Parliamentary system
CURRENCY: Swedish krona = 100 öre

Switzerland

One of the world's most prosperous countries, Switzerland lies at the center of western Europe. It has managed to retain its neutral status through every major European conflict since 1815.

GEOGRAPHY

Mostly mountainous, with river valleys. The Alps cover 60% of its area; the Jura in the west cover 10%. Lowlands lie along the east–west axis.

CLIMATE

Most rain falls in the warm summer months. Winters are snowy, but milder and foggy away from the mountains. Avalanches are a problem.

PEOPLE & SOCIETY

Switzerland is composed of distinct German-Swiss, French-Swiss, and Italian-Swiss linguistic groups. Germans are in the majority and there is a 40,000-strong Romansch minority in the east. The country is divided into 26 autonomous cantons (states), each with control over housing and economic policy. Society is conservative; marriage is common and the divorce rate lower than the European average.

THE ECONOMY

Diversified economy relies on services – the banking sector manages one-third of the world's offshore private wealth – and specialized industries (engineering, watches, etc.).

◆ **INSIGHT:** *Famed for its neutrality, Switzerland only became a member of the UN in 2002*

3000m/9843ft
2000m/6562ft
1000m/3281ft
500m/1640ft
200m/656ft

| 0 | | 50 km |
| 0 | | 50 miles |

FACTFILE

OFFICIAL NAME: Swiss Confederation
DATE OF FORMATION: 1291
CAPITAL: Bern
POPULATION: 7.2 million
TOTAL AREA: 15,942 sq. miles
(41,290 sq. km)
DENSITY: 469 people per sq. mile

LANGUAGES: German*, Swiss-German, French*, Italian*, Romansch
RELIGIONS: Roman Catholic 46%, Protestant 40%, other 12%, Muslim 2%
ETHNIC MIX: German 65%, French 18%, Italian 10%, other 6%, Romansch 1%
GOVERNMENT: Parliamentary system
CURRENCY: Franc = 100 rappen/centimes

Syria

Stretching from the eastern Mediterranean to the Tigris River, Syria's borders are regarded as an artificial creation of French colonial rule by many Syrians. Foreign affairs are turbulent.

GEOGRAPHY

A coastal plain is backed by a low range of hills. The Euphrates River cuts through a vast interior desert plateau.

CLIMATE

Mediterranean coastal climate. Inland areas are arid. In winter, snow is common on the mountains.

PEOPLE & SOCIETY

Most Syrians live within 60 miles (100 km) of the coast, where the largest cities are sited. 90% are Muslim, including the politically dominant Alawis. In the north and west are groups of Kurds, Armenians, and Turkic-speaking peoples. Some 300,000 Palestinian refugees have also settled in Syria. They, together with the urban unemployed, are the poorest groups, with a growing gulf between rich and poor.

THE ECONOMY

High defense spending is a major drain on the economy. Exporter of crude oil. Agriculture is thriving: crops include cotton, wheat, and olives.

INSIGHT: *Syria is an ancient land; there are at least 3500 as yet unexcavated archaeological sites*

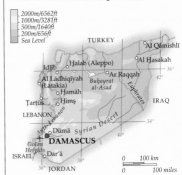

FACTFILE

OFFICIAL NAME: Syrian Arab Republic
DATE OF FORMATION: 1941
CAPITAL: Damascus
POPULATION: 17 million
TOTAL AREA: 71,498 sq. miles (184,180 sq. km)
DENSITY: 239 people per sq. mile

LANGUAGES: Arabic*, French, Kurdish, Armenian, Circassian, other
RELIGIONS: Sunni Muslim 74%, other Muslim 16%, Christian 10%
ETHNIC MIX: Arab 89%, Kurdish 6%, other 5%
GOVERNMENT: One-party state
CURRENCY: Syrian pound = 100 piasters

Taiwan

The island republic of Taiwan (formerly Formosa) lies 80 miles (130 km) off the southeast coast of mainland China. China still considers it to be a renegade province.

GEOGRAPHY

Mountain region covers two-thirds of the island. Highly fertile lowlands and coastal plains.

CLIMATE

Tropical monsoon. Hot and humid. Typhoons July–September. Snow falls in mountains in winter.

PEOPLE & SOCIETY

Most Taiwanese are Han Chinese, descendants of the 1644 migration of the Ming dynasty from the mainland. The modern republic was created in 1949, when the nationalist Kuomintang was expelled from the mainland following communist victory in the civil war. 100,000 emigrés established themselves as a ruling class. Initial resentment has subsided as a new, Taiwanese generation has taken over the reins of power. The aboriginal minority suffers discrimination.

THE ECONOMY

Successful economy based on small, adaptable manufacturing companies. Goods include footwear, televisions, and calculators.

◆ **INSIGHT:** *Taiwan lost its seat at the UN to Beijing in 1971: both claim to represent "China"*

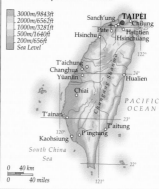

FACTFILE

OFFICIAL NAME: Republic of China (ROC)
DATE OF FORMATION: 1949
CAPITAL: Taipei
POPULATION: 22.5 million
TOTAL AREA: 13,892 sq. miles (35,980 sq. km)
DENSITY: 1810 people per sq. mile

LANGUAGES: Amoy Chinese, Mandarin Chinese*, Hakka Chinese
RELIGIONS: Buddhist, Confucian, and Taoist 93%, Christian 5%, other 2%
ETHNIC MIX: Indigenous Chinese 84%, mainland Chinese 14%, aborigine 2%
GOVERNMENT: Presidential system
CURRENCY: Taiwan dollar = 100 cents

Tajikistan

Tajikistan lies landlocked on the western slopes of the Pamirs in central Asia. The Tajik language and traditions are similar to those of Iran, rather than to those of Turkic Uzbekistan.

GEOGRAPHY
Mainly mountainous: the bare slopes of the Pamir ranges cover most of the country. Small but fertile Fergana Valley in northwest.

CLIMATE
Continental extremes in the valleys. Bitterly cold winters in the mountains. Rainfall is low.

PEOPLE & SOCIETY
Unlike the other former Soviet "-stans," Tajikistan is dominated by a people of Persian (Iranian) rather than Turkic origin. The main ethnic conflict is with the Turkic Uzbek minority. Russians are discriminated against and their population has halved since 1989. Civil war in the 1990s, between communists and Islamists, degraded the standard of living. Islamist militants are still active.

THE ECONOMY
The formal economy is precarious and relies heavily on bartering. Key resources are uranium and fast-flowing rivers which could provide hydroelectric power exports.

◆ **INSIGHT:** *Carpet-making, an ancient tradition learned from Persia, is still a major source of revenue*

4000m/13124ft
3000m/9843ft
2000m/6562ft
1000m/3281ft
500m/1640ft
200m/656ft

FACTFILE
OFFICIAL NAME: Republic of Tajikistan
DATE OF FORMATION: 1991
CAPITAL: Dushanbe
POPULATION: 6.2 million
TOTAL AREA: 55,251 sq. miles (143,100 sq. km)
DENSITY: 112 people per sq. mile

LANGUAGES: Tajik*, Uzbek, Russian
RELIGIONS: Sunni Muslim 80%, other 15%, Shi'a Muslim 5%
ETHNIC MIX: Tajik 62%, Uzbek 24%, Russian 8%, other 4%, Tatar 1%, Kyrgyz 1%
GOVERNMENT: Presidential system
CURRENCY: Somoni = 100 diram

Tanzania

The east African state of Tanzania was formed in 1964
by the union of Tanganyika and the Zanzibar islands.
A third of its area is game reserve or national park.

GEOGRAPHY
The mainland is mostly a high
plateau lying to the east of the Great
Rift Valley. Forested coastal plain.
Highlands in the north and south.

CLIMATE
Tropical on the coast and
Zanzibar. Semiarid on central
plateau, semitemperate in the
highlands. March–May rains.

PEOPLE & SOCIETY
99% of people belong to one of
120 small ethnic Bantu groups. Arabs,
Asians, and Europeans make up the
remaining population. Use of Kiswahili
as the lingua franca has eliminated
ethnic rivalries. The majority of
Tanzanians are subsistence famers.

◆ **INSIGHT:** At 19,340 ft (5895 m),
Kilimanjaro in northeast Tanzania
is Africa's highest mountain

THE ECONOMY
Heavily reliant on agriculture,
including forestry and livestock.
Cotton, coffee, tea, and cloves are cash
crops. Diamonds and gold are mined.
Boom in nontraditional exports.

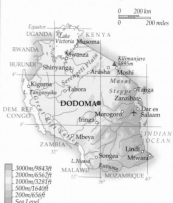

FACTFILE
OFFICIAL NAME: United Republic
of Tanzania
DATE OF FORMATION: 1964
CAPITAL: Dodoma
POPULATION: 36.8 million
TOTAL AREA: 364,898 sq. miles
(945,087 sq. km)

DENSITY: 108 people per sq. mile
LANGUAGES: Kiswahili*, English*, other
RELIGIONS: Muslim 33%, Christian 33%,
traditional beliefs 30%, other 4%
ETHNIC MIX: Native African (over 120
tribes) 99%, European and Asian 1%
GOVERNMENT: Presidential system
CURRENCY: Tanzanian shilling = 100 cents

Thailand

Thailand lies at the heart of mainland southeast Asia. Continuing rapid industrialization has resulted in massive congestion in the capital and a serious depletion of natural resources.

GEOGRAPHY
One-third of the country is occupied by a low plateau, drained by tributaries of the Mekong River. Central plain is the most fertile area.

CLIMATE
Tropical. Hot, humid March–May; monsoon rains May–October; cooler season November–March.

PEOPLE & SOCIETY
Buddhism is a national binding force. The north and northeast are home to about 600,000 hill tribespeople, with their own languages. The Chinese minority is the most assimilated in the region. There are tensions with the one million Muslim Malays living in the far south.

◆ **INSIGHT:** *Thailand, meaning "land of the free," is the only SE Asian nation never to have been colonized*

THE ECONOMY
Rapid economic growth. Successful manufacturing. Major world exporter of rice and rubber. Gas reserves. Sex tourism harms image.

FACTFILE
OFFICIAL NAME: Kingdom of Thailand
DATE OF FORMATION: 1238
CAPITAL: Bangkok
POPULATION: 64.3 million
TOTAL AREA: 198,455 sq. miles (514,000 sq. km)
DENSITY: 326 people per sq. mile

LANGUAGES: Thai*, Chinese, Malay, Khmer, Mon, Karen, Miao
RELIGIONS: Buddhist 95%, Muslim 4%, other (including Christian) 1%
ETHNIC MIX: Thai 83%, Chinese 12%, Malay 3%, Khmer and other 2%
GOVERNMENT: Parliamentary system
CURRENCY: Baht = 100 stang

Togo

Togo lies sandwiched between Ghana and Benin in west Africa. The president, General Eyadéma, has been in power since 1967. The port of Lomé is an important entrepôt for west African trade.

GEOGRAPHY

Central forested region bounded by savanna lands to the north and south. Mountain range stretches southwest to northeast.

CLIMATE

Coast hot and humid; drier inland. Rainy season March–July, with heaviest falls in the west.

PEOPLE & SOCIETY

Harsh resentment between Ewe in the south and Kabye in the north. Kabye control military, but the north is undeveloped compared with the south. Extended family is important. Tribalism and nepotism are key factors in everyday life. Some ethnic groups, such as the Mina, have matriarchal societies.

◆ **INSIGHT:** *The "Nana Benz," the market-women of Lomé, control Togo's retail trade*

THE ECONOMY

Most people are farmers. Self-sufficient in basic foodstuffs. Main export crops are coffee, cocoa, and cotton. Togo's phosphate deposits have the world's highest mineral content, though world prices remain low.

BURKINA

Dapaong

BENIN

Sansanné-Mango

Kara

Tchamba

GHANA

Mono

0 50 km
0 50 miles

Atakpamé

Mono

500m/1640ft
200m/656ft
Sea Level

Kpalimé

Tsévié
Aného

LOMÉ

ATLANTIC OCEAN

FACTFILE

OFFICIAL NAME: Republic of Togo
DATE OF FORMATION: 1960
CAPITAL: Lomé
POPULATION: 4.8 million
TOTAL AREA: 21,924 sq. miles (56,785 sq. km)
DENSITY: 229 people per sq. mile

LANGUAGES: Ewe, Kabye, Gurma, French*
RELIGIONS: Traditional beliefs 50%, Christian 35%, Muslim 15%
ETHNIC MIX: Ewe 46%, Kabye 27%, other African 26%, European 1%
GOVERNMENT: Presidential system
CURRENCY: CFA franc = 100 centimes

Tonga

Tonga is an archipelago of 170 islands in the South Pacific. Only 45 of these islands are inhabited. The economy is based on agriculture, and politics is effectively controlled by the king.

GEOGRAPHY
Easterly islands are generally low and fertile. Those in the west are higher and volcanic in origin.

CLIMATE
Tropical oceanic. Temperatures range between 68°F (20°C) and 86°F (30°C) all year round. Heavy rainfall, especially February–March.

PEOPLE & SOCIETY
The last remaining Polynesian monarchy, and the only Pacific state never brought under full foreign rule. All land is property of the crown, but is administered by nobles who allot it to the common people. Respect for traditional values remains high, though younger, Westernized Tongans are starting to question some attitudes.

◆ **INSIGHT:** *A self-appointed "court jester" stole US$20 million in 2001*

THE ECONOMY
Most people are subsistence farmers. Commercial production of coconuts, cassava, and passion fruit. Tourism is increasingly important.

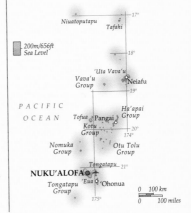

FACTFILE
OFFICIAL NAME: Kingdom of Tonga
DATE OF FORMATION: 1970
CAPITAL: Nuku'alofa
POPULATION: 106,137
TOTAL AREA: 289 sq. miles (748 sq. km)
DENSITY: 382 people per sq. mile

LANGUAGES: English*, Tongan*
RELIGIONS: Free Wesleyan 64%, other 21%, Roman Catholic 15%
ETHNIC MIX: Polynesian 99%, other 1%
GOVERNMENT: Monarchy
CURRENCY: Pa'anga (Tongan dollar) = 100 seniti

Trinidad & Tobago

The two islands of the former UK colony of Trinidad and Tobago are the most southerly of the Caribbean Windward Islands, lying just 9 miles (15 km) off the coast of Venezuela.

GEOGRAPHY
Both islands are hilly and wooded. Trinidad has a rugged mountain range in the north, and swamps on its east and west coasts.

CLIMATE
Tropical, with July–December wet season. Escapes the region's hurricanes, which pass to the north.

PEOPLE & SOCIETY
Trinidad's East Indian community is the largest in the Caribbean and holds on to its Muslim and Hindu heritage. There are muted ethnic tensions with the predominantly Christian blacks; political parties are divided along race lines. Blacks form the majority on Tobago.

◆ **INSIGHT:** *Trinidad and Tobago is the birthplace of steel bands and Calypso music*

THE ECONOMY
Oil accounts for 70% of export earnings. Gas is increasingly being exploited to support new industries. Tourism is particularly strong on wildlife-rich Tobago.

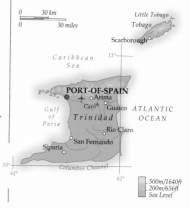

FACTFILE

OFFICIAL NAME: Republic of Trinidad and Tobago
DATE OF FORMATION: 1962
CAPITAL: Port-of-Spain
POPULATION: 1.3 million
TOTAL AREA: 1980 sq. miles (5128 sq. km)
DENSITY: 656 people per sq. mile

LANGUAGES: English Creole, English*, Hindi, French, Spanish
RELIGIONS: Catholic 32%, Hindu 24%, Protestant 28%, other 9%, Muslim 7%
ETHNIC MIX: East Indian 40%, Black 40%, mixed 19%, White and Chinese 1%
GOVERNMENT: Parliamentary system
CURRENCY: Trin. & Tob. dollar = 100 cents

Tunisia

Tunisia has traditionally been one of the more liberal Arab states, moving toward a multiparty democracy, but its government is now facing a challenge from Islamic fundamentalists.

GEOGRAPHY
Mountains in the north are surrounded by plains. Vast, low-lying salt pans in the center. To the south lies the Sahara Desert.

CLIMATE
Summer temperatures are high. The north is often wet and windy in winter. Far south is arid.

PEOPLE & SOCIETY
The population is almost entirely of Arab-Berber descent, with Jewish and Christian minorities. Many still live in extended family groups, in which three or four generations are represented. Women have better rights than in any other Arab country and make up 30% of the total workforce. Politics, however, remains a male preserve. A low birth-rate is a result of a long-standing family planning policy.

THE ECONOMY
Well-diversified, despite limited resources. Oil and gas exports. Expanding manufacturing. Tourism. European investment.

◆ **INSIGHT:** *Tunisia was the center of trading empires from the 9th century BCE*

FACTFILE
OFFICIAL NAME: Republic of Tunisia
DATE OF FORMATION: 1956
CAPITAL: Tunis
POPULATION: 9.7 million
TOTAL AREA: 63,169 sq. miles (163,610 sq. km)
DENSITY: 162 people per sq. mile

LANGUAGES: Arabic*, French
RELIGIONS: Muslim (mainly Sunni) 98%, Christian 1%, Jewish 1%
ETHNIC MIX: Arab and Berber 98%, Jewish 1%, European 1%
GOVERNMENT: Presidential system
CURRENCY: Tunisian dinar = 1000 millimes

Turkey

Lying partly in the region of eastern Thrace in Europe, but mostly in Asia, Turkey's position gives it significant influence in the Mediterranean, the Black Sea, and the Middle East.

GEOGRAPHY
Asian Turkey (Anatolia) is dominated by two mountain ranges, separated by a high, semidesert plateau. Coastal regions are fertile.

CLIMATE
Coast has a Mediterranean climate. Interior has cold, snowy winters and hot, dry summers.

PEOPLE & SOCIETY
The Turks are racially diverse. Many are refugees or descendants of refugees, often from the Balkans. However, the sense of national identity is strong. Turkey has close links with other Turkic states. Kurds, the largest minority, are based in the southeast and fought a violent campaign for greater autonomy from 1984 until a tentative cease-fire in 1999. Tensions remain high.

THE ECONOMY
The liberalized economy is boosted by self-sufficient agriculture and strong textiles, construction, tourism, and manufacturing sectors.

INSIGHT: *Turkey had two of the seven wonders of the ancient world: the tomb of King Mausolus at Halicarnassus (now Bodrum), and the temple of Artemis at Ephesus*

FACTFILE

OFFICIAL NAME: Republic of Turkey
DATE OF FORMATION: 1923
CAPITAL: Ankara
POPULATION: 68.6 million
TOTAL AREA: 301,382 sq. miles (780,580 sq. km)
DENSITY: 231 people per sq. mile

LANGUAGES: Turkish*, Kurdish, Arabic, Circassian, Armenian, Greek, other
RELIGIONS: Muslim (mainly Sunni) 99%, other 1%
ETHNIC MIX: Turkish 70%, Kurdish 20%, other 8%, Arab 2%
GOVERNMENT: Parliamentary system
CURRENCY: Turkish lira = 100 kurus

Turkmenistan

Stretching from the Caspian Sea into the deserts of central Asia, Turkmenistan adjusted better than most other former Soviet states to independence, but is now run as a dictatorship.

GEOGRAPHY
Low Karakumy Desert covers 80% of the country. Mountains on southern border with Iran. Fertile Amu Darya Valley in north.

CLIMATE
Arid desert climate with extreme summer heat, but sub-freezing winter temperatures.

PEOPLE & SOCIETY
Before czarist Russia annexed the country in 1884, the Turkmen were a largely nomadic tribal people. Today, the tribal unit remains strong, with most of the population clustered around desert oases. Relations between Turkmen and the Uzbek and Russian minorities are generally peaceful, but tribal conflicts are a source of strife. Political repression has grown under the dictatorship of President Niyazov.

THE ECONOMY
Cotton and gas are the main resources. Agriculture is opening up to private investment, but is still dominated by the cotton crop.

INSIGHT: *President Niyazov has created an elaborate personality cult, styling himself Turkmenbashi – father of all Turkmen*

FACTFILE
OFFICIAL NAME: Turkmenistan
DATE OF FORMATION: 1991
CAPITAL: Aşgabat
POPULATION: 4.9 million
TOTAL AREA: 188,455 sq. miles (488,100 sq. km)
DENSITY: 26 people per sq. mile

LANGUAGES: Turkmen*, Uzbek, Russian, Kazakh, other
RELIGIONS: Sunni Muslim 87%, Orthodox Christian 11%, other 2%
ETHNIC MIX: Turkmen 77%, Uzbek 9%, Russian 7%, other 5%, Kazakh 2%
GOVERNMENT: One-party state
CURRENCY: Manat = 100 tenga

Tuvalu

One of the world's smallest, most isolated states, Tuvalu lies in the central Pacific. The nine islands were linked to the Gilbert Islands (Kiribati) as a UK colony until independence.

GEOGRAPHY

A series of coral atolls, none more than 15 ft (4.6 m) above sea level. Poor soils restrict vegetation to bush, coconut palms, and breadfruit trees.

CLIMATE

Hot all year round. Heavy annual rainfall. Hurricane season brings many violent storms.

PEOPLE & SOCIETY

People are mostly Polynesian. Almost half the population live on Funafuti, where government jobs are based. Life is communal and traditional. Most people live by subsistence farming, digging pits out of the coral to grow crops. Fresh water is precious due to frequent droughts.

◆ **INSIGHT:** *Tuvaluans have a reputation as excellent sailors, many work overseas on merchant ships*

THE ECONOMY

World's smallest sovereign economy. Fishing licenses sold mostly to foreign boats. Exports are few: copra, stamps, and clothes. Income from trust fund and the lease of .tv Internet suffix.

FACTFILE

OFFICIAL NAME: Tuvalu
DATE OF FORMATION: 1978
CAPITAL: Fongafale, on Funafuti Atoll
POPULATION: 11,146
TOTAL AREA: 10 sq. miles (26 sq. km)
DENSITY: 1115 people per sq. mile

LANGUAGES: Tuvaluan, Kiribati, English*
RELIGIONS: Church of Tuvalu 97%, Seventh-day Adventist 1%, Baha'i 1% other 1%
ETHNIC MIX: Polynesian 96%, other 4%
GOVERNMENT: Nonparty system
CURRENCY: Australian dollar and Tuvaluan dollar = 100 cents each

Uganda

Landlocked in east Africa, Uganda has a history of ethnic strife. Under President Museveni, peace has been restored and steps taken to rebuild the economy and democracy.

GEOGRAPHY
Predominantly a large plateau with the Ruwenzori mountain range and the Great Rift Valley in the west. Lake Victoria lies to the southeast. Vegetation is of savanna type.

CLIMATE
Altitude and the influence of the lakes modify the equatorial climate. Rain falls throughout the year; spring is the wettest period.

PEOPLE & SOCIETY
The predominantly rural population comprises some 13 main ethnic groups. Since 1986, President Museveni has worked hard to break down traditional ethnic animosities, but a noticeable north–south divide persists, with economic development focused in the south. Nonetheless, Uganda now has one of the best human rights records in Africa.

THE ECONOMY
Coffee earns 93% of export income. Hydroelectric power is to be developed to replace 50% of oil imports. Great potential from the country's underused mines.

INSIGHT: *Lake Victoria is the world's third-largest lake*

FACTFILE
OFFICIAL NAME: Republic of Uganda
DATE OF FORMATION: 1962
CAPITAL: Kampala
POPULATION: 24.8 million
TOTAL AREA: 91,135 sq. miles (236,040 sq. km)
DENSITY: 322 people per sq. mile

LANGUAGES: Luganda, Nkole, Chiga, Lango, Acholi, Teso, Lugbara, English*
RELIGIONS: Roman Catholic 38%, Protestant 33%, traditional beliefs 13%, other (including Hindu) 11%, Muslim 5%
ETHNIC MIX: Bantu tribes 50%, other 50%
GOVERNMENT: Nonparty system
CURRENCY: New Ug. shilling = 100 cents

Ukraine

The former "breadbasket of the Soviet Union," Ukraine lies on the northern coast of the Black Sea. It balances assertive nationalism with concerns over its relations with Russia.

GEOGRAPHY

Mainly fertile steppes and forests. Carpathian Mountains in west, Crimean chain in south. Pripet Marshes in northwest.

CLIMATE

Mainly continental climate, with distinct seasons. Southern Crimea has Mediterranean climate.

PEOPLE & SOCIETY

Over 90% of the population in western Ukraine are Ukrainian. However, in several cities in the east and south, and in Crimea, Russians form a majority. The government is wary of Crimean separatism. Tatars have been returning there since the collapse of the Soviet Union and now comprise around 12% of the local population. Just under half of all Ukrainians live below the UN poverty line ($2 a day).

THE ECONOMY

Ukraine has 5% of global mineral reserves, and metals account for around 60% of export earnings. Slow reform of land laws has held back the revival of agriculture.

◆ **INSIGHT:** *Ukraine means "on the border," referring to its historic position on the edge of the old Russian Empire*

FACTFILE

OFFICIAL NAME: Ukraine
DATE OF FORMATION: 1991
CAPITAL: Kiev
POPULATION: 48.7 million
TOTAL AREA: 223,089 sq. miles (603,700 sq. km)
DENSITY: 209 people per sq. mile

LANGUAGES: Ukrainian*, Russian, Tatar
RELIGIONS: Christian (mainly Orthodox) 95%, other 4%, Jewish 1%
ETHNIC MIX: Ukrainian 73%, Russian 22%, other 4%, Jewish 1%
GOVERNMENT: Presidential system
CURRENCY: Hryvna = 100 kopiykas

United Arab Emirates

Bordering the Gulf on the northern coast of the Arabian Peninsula, the seven states of the United Arab Emirates form the Arab world's only working federation.

GEOGRAPHY

Mostly flat, semiarid desert with dunes, salt pans, and occasional oases. Cities are watered by extensive irrigation systems.

CLIMATE

Summers are humid, despite minimal rainfall. Sand-laden *shamal* winds blow in winter and spring.

PEOPLE & SOCIETY

Emirians, who make up just a quarter of the population, are mostly Sunni Muslims of Bedouin descent, and largely city dwellers. In theory, women enjoy equal rights with men. Poverty is rare and there is no income tax. The 1970s oil boom encouraged the immigration of workers, mostly from Asia. Western expatriates are permitted a virtually unrestricted lifestyle. Islamism, however, is a growing force among the young.

THE ECONOMY

Major exporter of oil and natural gas. Fish and shellfish are caught in the Gulf, as well as oysters for their pearls. Most food and raw materials are imported, and water is scarce.

◆ **INSIGHT:** *Mina Jabal Ali, in Dubai, is the largest man-made port in the world*

OMAN
56°
26°
RAS AL KHAYMAH
UMM AL QAYWAYN
SHARJAH ○ AJMAN
DUBAI ○ FUJAYRAH
The Gulf
52°
QATAR
54°
ABU DHABI ○ Al Maqta'
Ghuwayfat
Tarif ○ Al 'Ayn
24°
Habshan ○
OMAN
SAUDI ARABIA

500m/1640ft
200m/656ft
Sea Level

0 50 km
0 50 miles

DUBAI Emirate capital

FACTFILE

OFFICIAL NAME: United Arab Emirates
DATE OF FORMATION: 1971
CAPITAL: Abu Dhabi
POPULATION: 2.7 million
TOTAL AREA: 32,000 sq. miles (82,880 sq. km)
DENSITY: 84 people per sq. mile

LANGUAGES: Arabic*, Farsi, Indian and Pakistani languages, English
RELIGIONS: Muslim (mainly Sunni) 96%, Christian, Hindu, and other 4%
ETHNIC MIX: Asian 60%, Emirian 25%, other Arab 12%, European 3%
GOVERNMENT: Monarchy
CURRENCY: UAE dirham = 100 fils

United Kingdom

Separated from continental Europe by the English Channel, the United Kingdom controls Great Britain (England, Wales, and Scotland), a number of smaller islands, and Northern Ireland.

GEOGRAPHY

Rugged uplands dominate the landscape of Scotland, Wales, and northern England. All of the peaks in the United Kingdom over 4000 ft (1219 m) lie in highland Scotland. Known as the "backbone of England," the Pennine mountains run the length of northern England. Lowland England rises into several ranges of rolling hills, and there is an interconnected system of rivers and canals. Over 600 islands, mostly uninhabited, lie west and north of the Scottish mainland.

CLIMATE

Generally mild, temperate, and highly changeable. Rain is fairly well distributed throughout the year. The west is generally wetter than the east, and the south warmer than the north. Winter snow is common in upland areas.

PEOPLE & SOCIETY

The Welsh and Scottish nations remain recognizably distinct, despite forming a unified state. The creation of the Scottish Parliament and Welsh Assembly has given each country greater political autonomy. Ethnic minorities account for around 5% of the population, and over 50% were born in the UK. There are Asian and West Indian minorities in most cities, where they face deprivation and social stress. Immigrant women in particular can suffer from social isolation. In key areas such as policing, multiethnic recruitment has made little progress and prejudice persists. Marriage is in decline. A third of all births occur outside marriage, but most of them to cohabiting couples. Single-parent households account for one-fifth of all families with children under the age of 18. Income inequality is greater now than in 1884 when records began.

FACTFILE

OFFICIAL NAME: United Kingdom of Great Britain and Northern Ireland
DATE OF FORMATION: 1707
CAPITAL: London
POPULATION: 58.8 million
TOTAL AREA: 94,525 sq. miles (244,820 sq. km)

DENSITY: 630 people per sq. mile
LANGUAGES: English*, Welsh*, other
RELIGIONS: Anglican 45%, other 39%, Catholic 9%, Presbyterian 4% Muslim 3%
ETHNIC MIX: English 80%, Scottish 9%, Northern Irish 3%, Welsh 3%, other 5%
GOVERNMENT: Parliamentary system
CURRENCY: Pound sterling = 100 pence

United Kingdom

THE ECONOMY

World leader in financial services, pharmaceuticals, and defense industries. Strong multinationals. Precision engineering and high-tech industries, including biotechnology and telecommunications. Energy sector based on North Sea oil and gas production. Innovative in computer software development. Flexible working practices. Success in controlling inflationary tendencies. Decline of manufacturing sector, particularly heavy industries and car manufacture, matched by rise in financial and other services. High levels of government and consumer debt. Nonparticipation in euro threatens former status as EU's largest recipient of inward investment, and has prompted some major investors to close UK factories. The government is wary of holding a referendum on adopting the currency as a majority of the population remains hostile to the idea.

INSIGHT: *The UK has no formal written constitution; nevertheless Parliament has existed in its present form since the middle of the 14th century*

1000m/3281ft
500m/1640ft
200m/656ft
Sea Level

0   100 km
0   100 miles

United States of America

Stretching across the most temperate part of North America, and with many natural resources, the US is the world's leading economic power and third-largest country.

GEOGRAPHY

The US has a varied topography. Forested mountains stretch from New England in the far northeast, giving way to lowlands and swamps in the extreme south. The central plains are dominated by the Mississippi–Missouri River system and the Great Lakes on the Canadian border. The Rocky Mountains in the west contain active volcanoes and drop to the coast across the earthquake-prone San Andreas Fault. The southwest is arid desert. Mountainous Alaska is mostly Arctic tundra.

CLIMATE

There are four principal climatic zones. The north and east are continental and temperate, with heavy rainfall, warm summers, and cold winters. Southern California is Mediterranean, with hot summers and mild winters. The southwest is arid desert with searing summer heat and low rainfall. Florida and the Deep South are tropical.

United States of America

◆ **INSIGHT:** *The United States of America has the world's oldest constitution. Drafted in 1787, it has operated continuously ever since, albeit with numerous amendments*

	3000m/9843ft
	2000m/6562ft
	1000m/3281ft
	500m/1640ft
	200m/656ft
	Sea Level

United States of America

◆ **INSIGHT:** *By law, information collected in a United States census must remain confidential for 72 years*

PEOPLE & SOCIETY

Though the demographic, economic, and cultural dominance of the whites is firmly entrenched after almost 400 years of settlement, the ethnic balance is rapidly shifting. The Hispanic community is now the largest single minority, and is predicted to account for 25% of the population by 2050. Despite its growing size, it struggles to compete socially with the better established, and more politically sensitive black community. The original native Amerindians, meanwhile, were dispossessed in the 19th century and are now among the poorest people. Constitutionally, state and religion are clearly separated. Conservative Christianity, however, is increasingly dominant politically. Living standards are high, but bad diet and insufficient exercise have left 30% of Americans clinically obese.

THE ECONOMY

World's largest economy: massive resource base, well-established engineering and high-tech industries, global spread of US culture. Manufacturing is in decline as jobs are lost to low-wage economies. Imports are increasing despite weak US dollar, which now faces competition from the euro as the leading global currency. In 2001 a record nine-year boom came to an end, bringing large corporations crashing down and raising unemployment to new highs, in a serious economic downturn. Recovery efforts focus on promoting consumer spending, the engine which drives the whole US economy. Taxes have been slashed along with interest rates. A concurrent increase in government spending, however, notably on defense and the 2003 war on Iraq, has seen a huge budget surplus slump to a record deficit.

FACTFILE

OFFICIAL NAME: United States of America
DATE OF FORMATION: 1776
CAPITAL: Washington D.C.
POPULATION: 289 million
TOTAL AREA: 3,717,792 sq. miles (9,626,091 sq. km)
DENSITY: 82 people per sq. mile

LANGUAGES: English*, Spanish, other immigrant and Amerindian languages
RELIGIONS: Protestant 61%, Catholic 25%, other 10%, Muslim 2%, Jewish 2%
ETHNIC MIX: White 69%, Hispanic 13%, Black 13%, Asian 4%, Amerindian 1%
GOVERNMENT: Presidential system
CURRENCY: US dollar = 100 cents

Uruguay

Situated in southeastern South America, Uruguay returned to civilian government in 1985, after 12 years of military rule. Offshore banking brings in substantial foreign earnings.

GEOGRAPHY

Low, rolling grasslands cover 80% of the country. Narrow coastal plain. Alluvial floodplain in south-west. Five rivers flow westward and drain into the Uruguay River.

CLIMATE

Temperate throughout the country. Warm summers, mild winters, and moderate rainfall.

PEOPLE & SOCIETY

Uruguayans are largely second- or third- generation Italians or Spaniards. Wealth derived from cattle ranching enabled the country to become the first welfare state in South America. Despite economic decline since the 1950s, a large, if less prosperous, middle class remains. Though a Roman Catholic country, Uruguay is liberal in its attitude to religion and all forms are tolerated.

THE ECONOMY

Most land given over to crops and livestock. Wool, meat, and hides are exported. Buoyant tourism.

◆ **INSIGHT:** *Uruguay's rich pastures are ideal for raising livestock; animal products account for 30% of export earnings*

200m/656ft
Sea Level

0   100 km
0   100 miles

FACTFILE

OFFICIAL NAME: Eastern Republic of Uruguay
DATE OF FORMATION: 1828
CAPITAL: Montevideo
POPULATION: 3.4 million
TOTAL AREA: 68,039 sq. miles (176,220 sq. km)

DENSITY: 50 people per sq. mile
LANGUAGES: Spanish*
RELIGIONS: Roman Catholic 66%, other 30%, Jewish 2%, Protestant 2%
ETHNIC MIX: White 90%, Mestizo 6%, Black 4%
GOVERNMENT: Presidential system
CURRENCY: Peso = 100 centésimos

Uzbekistan

Sharing what is left of the Aral Sea with its northern neighbor, Kazakhstan, Uzbekistan lies on the ancient Silk Road between Asia and Europe. It is the most populous central Asian republic.

GEOGRAPHY
Arid and semiarid plains in much of the west. Fertile, irrigated farmland in the east lies below the peaks of the western Pamirs.

CLIMATE
Harsh continental climate. Summers can be extremely hot and dry; winters are cold.

PEOPLE & SOCIETY
Complex ethnic makeup, with potential for racial and regional conflict. Ex-communists are in firm control, but traditional social patterns based on family, religion, clan, and region have reemerged. Constitutional measures aim to control the influence of Islam.The population is concentrated in the fertile east. Birthrates are high, and the status of women continues to be low.

THE ECONOMY
Mostly agricultural outside Tashkent. Besides one of the world's largest gold mines, rich mineral deposits are largely underexploited. Dependent on grain imports.

◆ **INSIGHT:** *The Aral Sea has shrunk to less then half of the area it covered in the 1970s, due to diversion of rivers for irrigation*

	3000m/9843ft
	2000m/6562ft
	1000m/3281ft
	500m/1640ft
	200m/656ft
	Sea Level

KAZAKHSTAN

Nukus
Xo'jayli *Turan* Qizilqum
Lowland
Urganch
Amu Darya

TASHKENT Chirchiq
Angren
Aydarko'l Olmaliq Namangan
Ko'li Navoiy Farg'ona
Buxoro Samarqand
Qarshi TAJIKISTAN

TURKMENISTAN

KYRGY.
KYRGY.

0 100 km
0 100 miles

AFGHANISTAN

FACTFILE

OFFICIAL NAME: Republic of Uzbekistan
DATE OF FORMATION: 1991
CAPITAL: Tashkent
POPULATION: 25.6 million
TOTAL AREA: 172,741 sq. miles (447,400 sq. km)
DENSITY: 148 people per sq. mile

LANGUAGES: Uzbek*, Russian, Tajik, Kazakh
RELIGIONS: Sunni Muslim 88%, Orthodox Christian 9%, other 3%
ETHNIC MIX: Uzbek 71%, other 12%, Russian 8%, Tajik 5%, Kazakh 4%
GOVERNMENT: Presidential system
CURRENCY: Som = 100 tiyin

Vanuatu

An archipelago of 82 islands and islets in the South Pacific, Vanuatu was ruled jointly by the UK and France from 1906 until independence in 1980. Politics is democratic but volatile.

GEOGRAPHY
Mountainous and volcanic, with coral beaches and dense rainforest. Cultivated land along the coasts.

CLIMATE
Tropical. Temperatures and rainfall decline from north to south.

PEOPLE & SOCIETY
Indigenous Melanesians form a majority. Ni-Vanuatu culture is traditional; local social and religious customs are strong, despite centuries of missionary influence. Subsistence farming and fishing are the main activities. 80% of the population live on the 12 main islands. Women have lower social status than men and payment of bride-price is common.

◆ **INSIGHT:** *With 105 indigenous tongues, Vanuatu has the world's highest per capita density of languages*

THE ECONOMY
Copra and cocoa exports are declining. Tourism is growing. Offshore banking has been stopped after international pressure.

```
                    0      100 km
                    0      100 miles
       Torres Islands
14°         Banks Islands
       Espiritu              P A C I F I C
       Santo    Aoba  Maéwo  O C E A N
  Luganville
                      Pentecost
16°    Norsup    Ambrym
       Malekula  Epi
  C o r a l          Shepherd Islands
  S e a
18°           ✦ PORT VILA
              Efate
       168°        Erromango
                 Tanna
       Isangel
20°              Aneityum
                    170°

  1000m/3281ft
  500m/1640ft
  200m/656ft
  Sea Level
```

FACTFILE

OFFICIAL NAME: Republic of Vanuatu
DATE OF FORMATION: 1980
CAPITAL: Port Vila
POPULATION: 207,000
TOTAL AREA: 4710 sq. miles (12,200 sq. km)
DENSITY: 44 people per sq. mile

LANGUAGES: Bislama*, English*, French*
RELIGIONS: Presbyterian 37%, other 25%, Anglican 15%, Roman Catholic 15%, traditional beliefs 8%
ETHNIC MIX: Melanesian 94%, Polynesian 3%, other 3%
GOVERNMENT: Parliamentary system
CURRENCY: Vatu = 100 centimes

Vatican City

The Vatican City, or Holy See, the seat of the Roman Catholic Church, is a walled enclave in the city of Rome, Italy. It is the world's smallest fully independent state.

GEOGRAPHY

The Vatican's territory includes ten other buildings in Rome, plus the papal residence. The Vatican Gardens cover half the City's area.

CLIMATE

Mild winters with regular rainfall. Hot, dry summers with occasional thunderstorms.

PEOPLE & SOCIETY

The Vatican has about 900 permanent inhabitants, including over 100 lay persons. It also employs thousands of lay staff. Citizenship can be acquired through stable residence and holding a position within the City. The reigning pope has supreme legislative and judicial powers, and holds office for life. Though the Vatican City is officially neutral, papal opinion has a great influence on the world's one billion Roman Catholics.

THE ECONOMY

Investments and voluntary contributions made by Catholics worldwide (known as Peter's Pence) are backed up by tourist revenue and the issue of Vatican stamps and coins.

◆ **INSIGHT:** *The Vatican City is the spiritual center for 17% of the world's population*

FACTFILE

OFFICIAL NAME: State of the Vatican City
DATE OF FORMATION: 1929
CAPITAL: Vatican City
POPULATION: 900
TOTAL AREA: 0.17 sq. miles (0.44 sq. km)
DENSITY: 5294 people per sq. mile

LANGUAGES: Italian*, Latin*
RELIGIONS: Roman Catholic 100%
ETHNIC MIX: Cardinals are from many nationalities, but Italians form the largest group. The current pope is from Poland.
GOVERNMENT: Papal state
CURRENCY: Euro = 100 cents

Venezuela

Lying on the southern shores of the Caribbean, Venezuela was the first of Spain's colonies to seek independence. Despite large oil reserves, many Venezuelans still live in dire poverty.

GEOGRAPHY
Andes Mountains and the Maracaibo lowlands in the northwest. Central grassy plains are drained by the Orinoco River system. Forested Guiana Highlands in the southeast.

CLIMATE
Tropical. Hot and humid. Uplands are cooler. Orinoco plains are alternately parched or flooded.

PEOPLE & SOCIETY
Venezuela is historically a "melting pot," with immigrants from Europe and all over Latin America. The few indigenous Amerindians live in remote areas. Venezuela has one of the most urbanized societies in the region, with most of its population living in the northern cities. President Chávez's left-wing "Bolivarian revolution" faces stiff opposition, particularly from urban society.

THE ECONOMY
In addition to oil, Venezuela has vast reserves of coal, bauxite, iron, and gold. Government revenues dented by overmanned and often inefficient state sector, plus widespread tax evasion.

◆ **INSIGHT:** *Venezuela's Angel Falls is the world's highest waterfall at 3210 ft (979 m)*

FACTFILE
OFFICIAL NAME: Bolivarian Republic of Venezuela
DATE OF FORMATION: 1830
CAPITAL: Caracas
POPULATION: 25.1 million
TOTAL AREA: 352,143 sq. miles (912,050 sq. km)

DENSITY: 74 people per sq. mile
LANGUAGES: Spanish*, native languages
RELIGIONS: Roman Catholic 89%, Protestant and other 11%
ETHNIC MIX: Mestizo 69%, White 20%, Black 9%, Amerindian 2%
GOVERNMENT: Presidential system
CURRENCY: Bolívar = 100 centimos

Vietnam

Situated on the western edge of the South China Sea, Vietnam is run as a single-party Communist state. Since 1986 the regime has pursued a liberal economic policy known as *doi moi*.

GEOGRAPHY
A heavily forested mountain range separates the northern Red River delta lowlands from the Mekong River delta in the south.

CLIMATE
Cool winters in north; south is tropical, with even temperatures.

PEOPLE & SOCIETY
Ethnic Vietnamese dominate; the Chinese minority was viewed as a corrupt bourgeoisie by the victorious Communists after the war. Mountain-based minorities (*montagnards*) were also sidelined by the regime; tensions persist over the resettlement of the central highlands by lowlanders. Women play an active role in society.

◆ **INSIGHT:** The 1962–1975 Vietnam War was the longest conflict of the 20th century

THE ECONOMY
The potential for continued strong growth rests on a diverse resource base (including gas reserves), an educated workforce, and strong light industries.

FACTFILE

OFFICIAL NAME: Socialist Republic of Vietnam
DATE OF FORMATION: 1976
CAPITAL: Hanoi
POPULATION: 80.2 million
TOTAL AREA: 127,243 sq. miles (329,560 sq. km)

DENSITY: 638 people per sq. mile
LANGUAGES: Vietnamese*, Chinese, Thai, Khmer, Muong, Nung, Miao, other
RELIGIONS: Buddhist 55%, other 45%
ETHNIC MIX: Vietnamese 88%, other 6%, Chinese 4%, Thai 2%
GOVERNMENT: One-party state
CURRENCY: Dông = 10 hao = 100 xu

Yemen

Located in southern Arabia, Yemen was formerly two countries:
the People's Democratic Republic of Yemen (south and east)
and the Yemen Arab Republic (northwest), were united in 1990.

GEOGRAPHY
Mountainous west with a fertile
strip along the Red Sea. Arid desert
and mountains elsewhere.

CLIMATE
Desert climate, modified by
altitude, which affects temperatures
by as much as 54°F (30°C).

PEOPLE & SOCIETY
Yemenis are almost entirely
of Arab and Bedouin descent. The
majority are Sunni Muslims, of the
Shafi sect. In rural areas and in
the north, Islamic orthodoxy is
strong and most women wear
the veil. Tension continues to
exist between the south, led by
the cosmopolitan city of Aden,
and the more conservative
northwest. Clashes between
their former armies escalated
into a brief civil war in 1994.

THE ECONOMY
Instability deters investment.
Considerable oil and gas reserves.
Agriculture is the largest employer:
cotton, livestock, and fish.

INSIGHT: *Mokha, on the Red Sea,
gave its name to the first coffee
beans exported to Europe in the 1600s*

3000m/9843ft
2000m/6562ft
1000m/3281ft
500m/1640ft
200m/656ft
Sea Level

0   100 km
0   100 miles

FACTFILE

OFFICIAL NAME: Republic of Yemen
DATE OF FORMATION: 1990
CAPITAL: Sana
POPULATION: 19.9 million
TOTAL AREA: 203,849 sq. miles
(527,970 sq. km)
DENSITY: 92 people per sq. mile

LANGUAGES: Arabic*
RELIGIONS: Sunni Muslim 55%,
Shi'a Muslim 42%, Christian, Hindu,
and Jewish 3%
ETHNIC MIX: Arab 95%, Afro-Arab 3%,
Indian, Somali, and European 2%
GOVERNMENT: Presidential system
CURRENCY: Yemeni rial = 100 sene

Zambia

Bordered to the south by the Zambezi River, Zambia lies at the heart of southern Africa. In 1991, it made a peaceful transition from single-party rule to multiparty democracy.

 GEOGRAPHY
A high savanna plateau, broken by mountains in northeast. Vegetation mainly trees and scrub.

 CLIMATE
Tropical, with three seasons: cool and dry, hot and dry, and wet. Southwest is prone to drought.

 PEOPLE & SOCIETY
There are more than 70 different ethnic groups, but there are fewer ethnic tensions than in many African states. The largest group is the Bemba in the northeast. Other major groups are the Tonga in the south, the eastern Nyanja, and the Lozi in the west. There are also thousands of refugees, mostly from Angola. A National Gender Policy was issued in 2000 to redress inequalities between the sexes. The standard of living has fallen in real terms since independence.

 THE ECONOMY
World copper prices have fallen and Zambia's reserves have dwindled. New agricultural exports have boomed: notably flowers and cotton.

◆ **INSIGHT:** *Spray from Musi-o-Tunya (Victoria Falls) can be seen up to 20 miles away*

FACTFILE

OFFICIAL NAME: Republic of Zambia
DATE OF FORMATION: 1964
CAPITAL: Lusaka
POPULATION: 10.9 million
TOTAL AREA: 290,584 sq. miles (752,614 sq. km)
DENSITY: 38 people per sq. mile

LANGUAGES: Bemba, Tonga, Nyanja, Lozi, Lala-bisa, Nsenga, English*
RELIGIONS: Christian 63%, traditional beliefs 36%, Muslim and Hindu 1%
ETHNIC MIX: Bemba 34%, other 27%, Tonga 16%, Nyanja 14%, Lozi 9%
GOVERNMENT: Presidential system
CURRENCY: Kwacha = 100 ngwee

Zimbabwe

Situated in southern Africa, Zimbabwe achieved independence from the UK in 1980. President Robert Mugabe, in power since then, has become increasingly authoritarian.

GEOGRAPHY
High plateaus in center bordered by Zambezi River in the north and Limpopo in the south. Rivers crisscross central area.

CLIMATE
Tropical, though moderated by the high altitude. Wet season November–March. Drought is common in the eastern highlands.

PEOPLE & SOCIETY
There are two main ethnic groups, Shona in the north and east, and Ndebele in the south. Shona outnumber Ndebele by four to one. Whites are generally far more affluent than blacks. Government efforts to redress this imbalance have become increasingly more aggressive. Economic mismanagement and international isolation has destroyed the economy and prices have rocketed.

THE ECONOMY
The broad-based economy is undermined by drought, budget deficits, unemployment, and massive inflation. Food is increasingly scarce.

◆ **INSIGHT:** *The city of Great Zimbabwe, after which the country is named, was built in the 8th century, near Masvingo*

FACTFILE
OFFICIAL NAME: Republic of Zimbabwe
DATE OF FORMATION: 1980
CAPITAL: Harare
POPULATION: 13.1 million
TOTAL AREA: 150,803 sq. miles
(390,580 sq. km)
DENSITY: 88 people per sq. mile

LANGUAGES: Shona, isiNdebele, English*
RELIGIONS: Syncretic Christian/ traditional beliefs 50%, Christian 25%, traditional beliefs 24%, other 1%
ETHNIC MIX: Shona 71%, Ndebele 16%, other African 11%, White 1%, Asian 1%
GOVERNMENT: Presidential system
CURRENCY: Zimbabwe $ = 100 cents

Overseas territories

Despite the rapid process of global decolonization since World War II, around 10 million people in more than 50 territories around the world continue to live under the protection of France, Australia, Denmark, the Netherlands, Norway, New Zealand, the UK, or the USA. These remnants of former colonial empires may have persisted for economic, strategic, or political reasons and are administered by the protecting country in a variety of ways.

AUSTRALIA

Australia's overseas territories have not been an issue since Papua New Guinea became independent in 1975. Consequently there is no overriding policy toward them.
Norfolk Island is inhabited by descendants of the HMS Bounty mutineers and more recent Australian migrants. Phosphate is mined on Christmas Island.

ASHMORE & CARTIER IS. *Ref: 124 A3*

STATUS: External territory
CLAIMED: 1931
CAPITAL: Not applicable
POPULATION: None
AREA: 2 sq miles (5.2 sq km)

CHRISTMAS ISLAND *Ref: 123 E5*

STATUS: External territory
CLAIMED: 1958
CAPITAL: The Settlement
POPULATION: 474
AREA: 52 sq miles (135 sq km)

COCOS ISLANDS *Ref: 123 D5*

STATUS: External territory
CLAIMED: 1955
CAPITAL: Not applicable
POPULATION: 632
AREA: 5.5 sq miles (14 sq km)

CORAL SEA ISLANDS *Ref: 126 B4*

STATUS: External territory
CLAIMED: 1969
CAPITAL: Not applicable
POPULATION: 8 (Meteorologists)
AREA: 1.2 sq miles (3 sq km)

HEARD & MCDONALD IS. *Ref: 123 C7*

STATUS: External territory
CLAIMED: 1947
CAPITAL: Not applicable
POPULATION: None
AREA: 161 sq miles (417 sq km)

NORFOLK ISLAND *Ref: 124 D4*

STATUS: External territory
CLAIMED: 1774
CAPITAL: Kingston
POPULATION: 1866
AREA: 13 sq miles (34 sq km)

DENMARK

The Faeroe Islands have been under Danish administration since Queen Margreth I of Denmark inherited Norway in 1380. The Home Rule Act of 1948 gave the Faeroese control over all their internal affairs. Greenland first came under Danish rule in 1380. Denmark remains responsible for the island's foreign affairs.

Overseas territories

FAEROE ISLANDS *Ref: 65 F5*

STATUS: External territory
CLAIMED: 1380
CAPITAL: Tórshavn
POPULATION: 46,011
AREA: 540 sq miles (1399 sq km)

GREENLAND *Ref: 64 D3*

STATUS: External territory
CLAIMED: 1380
CAPITAL: Nuuk
POPULATION: 56,376
AREA: 840,000 sq miles (2,175,500 sq km)

FRANCE

France has developed economic ties with its *Territoires d'Outre–Mer*, thereby stressing interdependence over independence. Overseas *départements*, officially part of France, have their own governments. Territorial *collectivités* and overseas *territoires* have varying degrees of autonomy.

CLIPPERTON ISLAND *Ref: 135 F3*

STATUS: Dependency of French Polynesia
CLAIMED: 1935
CAPITAL: Not applicable
POPULATION: None
AREA: 2.7 sq miles (7 sq km)

FRENCH GUIANA *Ref: 41 H3*

STATUS: Overseas department
CLAIMED: 1817
CAPITAL: Cayenne
POPULATION: 182,333
AREA: 35,135 sq miles (91,000 sq km)

FRENCH POLYNESIA *Ref: 127 H4*

STATUS: Overseas territory
CLAIMED: 1843
CAPITAL: Papeete
POPULATION: 257,847
AREA: 1608 sq miles (4165 sq km)

GUADELOUPE *Ref: 37 G4*

STATUS: Overseas department
CLAIMED: 1635
CAPITAL: Basse-Terre
POPULATION: 435,739
AREA: 687 sq miles (1780 sq km)

MARTINIQUE *Ref: 37 G4*

STATUS: Overseas department
CLAIMED: 1635
CAPITAL: Fort-de-France
POPULATION: 422,277
AREA: 425 sq miles (1100 sq km)

MAYOTTE *Ref: 61 G2*

STATUS: Territorial collectivity
CLAIMED: 1843
CAPITAL: Mamoudzou
POPULATION: 170,879
AREA: 144 sq miles (374 sq km)

NEW CALEDONIA *Ref: 126 D5*

STATUS: Overseas territory
CLAIMED: 1853
CAPITAL: Nouméa
POPULATION: 207,858
AREA: 7347 sq miles (19,100 sq km)

RÉUNION *Ref: 61 H4*

STATUS: Overseas department
CLAIMED: 1638
CAPITAL: Saint-Denis
POPULATION: 743,981
AREA: 970 sq miles (2500 sq km)

Overseas territories

ST PIERRE & MIQUELON
Ref: 21 G4
STATUS: Territorial collectivity
CLAIMED: 1604
CAPITAL: Saint-Pierre
POPULATION: 6954
AREA: 93 sq miles (242 sq km)

WALLIS & FUTUNA
Ref: 127 E4
STATUS: Overseas territory
CLAIMED: 1842
CAPITAL: Matā'Utu
POPULATION: 15,585
AREA: 106 sq miles (274 sq km)

NETHERLANDS

The country's two remaining
territories were formerly part
of the Dutch West Indies. Both
are now self-governing, but the
Netherlands remains responsible
for their defense.

ARUBA *Ref: 37 E5*

STATUS: Autonomous part
of the Netherlands
CLAIMED: 1634
CAPITAL: Oranjestad
POPULATION: 70,441
AREA: 75 sq miles (194 sq km)

NETHERLANDS ANTILLES *Ref: 37 E5*

STATUS: Autonomous part
of the Netherlands
CLAIMED: 1816
CAPITAL: Willemstad
POPULATION: 214,258
AREA: 371 sq miles (960 sq km)

NEW ZEALAND

New Zealand's government has
no desire to retain any overseas
territories. However, the economic
weakness of Tokelau, Niue, and
the Cook Islands has forced it
to remain responsible for their
foreign policy and defense.

COOK ISLANDS *Ref: 127 G4*

STATUS: Associated
territory
CLAIMED: 1901
CAPITAL: Avarua
POPULATION: 20,811
AREA: 91 sq miles (235 sq km)

NIUE *Ref: 127 F5*

STATUS: Associated
territory
CLAIMED: 1901
CAPITAL: Alofi
POPULATION: 2134
AREA: 102 sq miles (264 sq km)

TOKELAU *Ref: 127 F3*
STATUS: Dependent territory
CLAIMED: 1926
CAPITAL: Not applicable
POPULATION: 1431
AREA: 4 sq miles (10 sq km)

NORWAY

In 1920, 41 nations signed the
Spits-bergen treaty recognizing
Norwegian sovereignty over
Svalbard. There is a Nato base
on Jan Mayen. Bouvet Island
is a nature reserve.

Overseas territories

BOUVET ISLAND *Ref: 49 D7*
STATUS: Dependency
CLAIMED: 1928
CAPITAL: Not applicable
POPULATION: None
AREA: 22 sq miles (58 sq km)

JAN MAYEN *Ref: 65 F3*
STATUS: Dependency
CLAIMED: 1929
CAPITAL: Not applicable
POPULATION: None
AREA: 147 sq miles (381 sq km)

PETER I. ISLAND *Ref: 136 A3*
STATUS: Dependency
CLAIMED: 1931
CAPITAL: Not applicable
POPULATION: None
AREA: 69 sq miles (180 sq km)

SVALBARD *Ref: 65 F2*
STATUS: Dependency CLAIMED: 1920
CAPITAL: Longyearbyen
POPULATION: 2868
AREA: 24,289 sq miles (62,906 sq km)

UNITED KINGDOM

The UK has the largest number of overseas territories. These are locally governed by a mixture of elected representatives and appointed officials.

ANGUILLA *Ref: 37 G3*

STATUS: Dependent territory
CLAIMED: 1650
CAPITAL: The Valley
POPULATION: 12,446
AREA: 37 sq miles (96 sq km)

ASCENSION ISLAND *Ref: 49 C5*
STATUS: Dependency of St Helena
CLAIMED: 1673
CAPITAL: Georgetown
POPULATION: 1177
AREA: 34 sq miles (88 sq km)

BERMUDA *Ref: 17 E6*

STATUS: Crown colony
CLAIMED: 1612
CAPITAL: Hamilton
POPULATION: 63,960
AREA: 20 sq miles (53 sq km)

BRITISH INDIAN OCEAN TERRITORY *Ref: 122 C4*

STATUS: Dependent territory
CLAIMED: 1814
CAPITAL: Diego Garcia
POPULATION: 930
AREA: 23 sq miles (60 sq km)

BRITISH VIRGIN IS. *Ref: 37 F3*

STATUS: Dependent territory
CLAIMED: 1672
CAPITAL: Road Town
POPULATION: 21,272
AREA: 59 sq miles (153 sq km)

CAYMAN ISLANDS *Ref: 36 B3*

STATUS: Dependent territory
CLAIMED: 1670
CAPITAL: George Town
POPULATION: 36,273
AREA: 100 sq miles (259 sq km)

FALKLAND ISLANDS *Ref: 47 D7*

STATUS: Dependent territory
CLAIMED: 1832
CAPITAL: Stanley
POPULATION: 2967
AREA: 4699 sq miles (12,173 sq km)

Overseas territories

GIBRALTAR *Ref: 74 D5*

STATUS: Crown colony
CLAIMED: 1713
CAPITAL: Gibraltar
POPULATION: 27,714
AREA: 2.5 sq miles (6.5 sq km)

GUERNSEY *Ref: 71 D8*

STATUS: Crown dependency
CLAIMED: 1066
CAPITAL: St. Peter Port
POPULATION: 64,587
AREA: 25 sq miles (65 sq km)

ISLE OF MAN *Ref: 71 C5*

STATUS: Crown dependency
CLAIMED: 1765
CAPITAL: Douglas
POPULATION: 73,873
AREA: 221 sq miles (572 sq km)

JERSEY *Ref: 71 D8*

STATUS: Crown dependency
CLAIMED: 1066
CAPITAL: St. Helier
POPULATION: 89,775
AREA: 45 sq miles (116 sq km)

MONTSERRAT *Ref: 37 G4*

STATUS: Dependent territory
CLAIMED: 1632
CAPITAL: Plymouth (uninhabitable)
POPULATION: 8437
AREA: 40 sq miles (102 sq km)

PITCAIRN ISLANDS *Ref: 125 G4*

STATUS: Dependent territory
CLAIMED: 1887
CAPITAL: Adamstown POPULATION: 47
AREA: 18 sq miles (47 sq km)

ST HELENA *Ref: 49 D5*

STATUS: Dependent territory
CLAIMED: 1673
CAPITAL: Jamestown
POPULATION: 7317
AREA: 47 sq miles (122 sq km)

SOUTH GEORGIA & THE SANDWICH ISLANDS *Ref: 49 C7*
STATUS: Dependent territory
CLAIMED: 1775 CAPITAL: Not applicable
POPULATION: None
AREA: 1387 sq miles (3592 sq km)

TRISTAN DA CUNHA *Ref: 49 D6*
STATUS: Dependency of St. Helena
CLAIMED: 1612 CAPITAL: Edinburgh
POPULATION: 313
AREA: 38 sq miles (98 sq km)

TURKS & CAICOS ISLANDS *Ref: 37 E2*

STATUS: Dependent territory
CLAIMED: 1766
CAPITAL: Cockburn Town
POPULATION: 18,738
AREA: 166 sq miles (430 sq km)

UNITED STATES

US Commonwealth territories are self-governing incorporated territories that are an integral part of the US. Unincorporated territories have varying degrees of autonomy.

AMERICAN SAMOA *Ref: 127 F4*

STATUS: Unincorporated territory
CLAIMED: 1900
CAPITAL: Pago Pago
POPULATION: 68,688
AREA: 75 sq miles (195 sq km)

Overseas territories

BAKER & HOWLAND ISLANDS
Ref: 127 E2

STATUS: Unincorporated territory
CAPITAL: Not applicable
CLAIMED: 1856 POPULATION: None
AREA: 0.5 sq miles (1.4 sq km)

GUAM *Ref: 126 B1*

STATUS: Unincorporated territory
CLAIMED: 1898
CAPITAL: Hagåtña
POPULATION: 160,796
AREA: 212 sq miles (549 sq km)

JARVIS ISLAND *Ref: 127 G2*

STATUS: Unincorporated territory
CLAIMED: 1856
CAPITAL: Not applicable
POPULATION: None
AREA: 1.7 sq miles (4.5 sq km)

JOHNSTON ATOLL *Ref: 125 E1*

STATUS: Unincorporated territory
CLAIMED: 1858
CAPITAL: Not applicable
POPULATION: 327
AREA: 1 sq miles (2.8 sq km)

KINGMAN REEF *Ref: 127 F2*

STATUS: Administered territory
CLAIMED: 1856
CAPITAL: Not applicable
POPULATION: None
AREA: 0.4 sq miles (1 sq km)

MIDWAY ISLANDS *Ref: 134 D2*

STATUS: Administered territory
CLAIMED: 1867
CAPITAL: Not applicable
POPULATION: 40
AREA: 2 sq miles (5.2 sq km)

NAVASSA ISLAND *Ref: 36 D3*

STATUS: Unincorporated territory
CLAIMED: 1856 CAPITAL: Not applicable
POPULATION: None
AREA: 2 sq miles (5.2 sq km)

NORTHERN MARIANA ISLANDS
Ref: 124 C1

STATUS: Commonwealth territory
CLAIMED: 1947
CAPITAL: Saipan POPULATION: 77,311
AREA: 177 sq miles (457 sq km)

PALMYRA ATOLL *Ref: 127 G2*

STATUS: Unincorporated territory
CLAIMED: 1898 CAPITAL: Not applicable
POPULATION: None
AREA: 5 sq miles (12 sq km)

PUERTO RICO *Ref: 37 F3*

STATUS: Commonwealth territory
CLAIMED: 1898
CAPITAL: San Juan
POPULATION: 4 million
AREA: 3515 sq miles (9104 sq km)

VIRGIN ISLANDS *Ref: 37 F3*

STATUS: Unincorporated territory
CLAIMED: 1917
CAPITAL: Charlotte Amalie
POPULATION: 123,498
AREA: 137 sq miles (355 sq km)

WAKE ISLAND *Ref: 124 D1*

STATUS: Unincorporated territory
CLAIMED: 1898
CAPITAL: Not applicable
POPULATION: 200
AREA: 2.5 sq miles (6.5 sq km)

International organizations

This listing provides acronym definitions for the main international organizations concerned with worldwide economics, trade and defense, plus an indication of membership.

ASEAN

Association of Southeast Asian Nations
ESTABLISHED: 1967
MEMBERS: Brunei, Cambodia, Thailand, Laos, Malaysia, Singapore, Ind., Philippines, Vietnam, Myanmar

CIS

Commonwealth of Independent States
ESTABLISHED: 1991
MEMBERS: Armenia, Az., Belarus, Kazakhstan, Kyrgyzstan, Moldova, Russia, Tajikistan, Turkmenistan, Ukraine, Uzbekistan, Georgia

COMM

The Commonwealth
ESTABLISHED: 1931; evolved out of the British Empire. Formerly known as the British Commonwealth of Nations.
MEMBERS: 54

EU

European Union
ESTABLISHED: 1965; formerly known as EEC (European Economic Community) and EC (Economic Community)
MEMBERS: Belgium, Denmark, France, Germany, Greece, Ireland, Italy, Luxembourg, Netherlands, Portugal, Spain, UK, Austria, Finland and Sweden

G8

Group of 8
ESTABLISHED: 1994
MEMBERS: Canada, France, Germany, Italy, Japan, Russia, UK, US

IMF

International Monetary Fund
(UN agency)
ESTABLISHED: 1945 MEMBERS: 184

NAFTA

North American Free Trade Agreement
ESTABLISHED: 1994
MEMBERS: Canada, Mexico, US

NATO

North Atlantic Treaty Organization
ESTABLISHED: 1949
MEMBERS: Belgium, Canada, Czech Rep., Denmark, Fr., Ger., Greece, Hung., Iceland, Italy, Lux., Neth., Norway, Poland, Port., Spain, Turkey, UK, US

OPEC

Organization of Petroleum Exporting Countries
ESTABLISHED: 1960 MEMBERS: Algeria, Indonesia, Iran, Iraq, Kuwait, Libya, Nigeria, Qatar, Saudi Arabia, United Arab Emirates, Venezuela

UN

United Nations
ESTABLISHED: 1945 MEMBERS: 191; all nations are represented, except Taiwan. The Vatican City has "observer status" only.

WHO

World Trade Organization
ESTABLISHED: 1995
MEMBERS: 143

Abbreviations

This glossary provides a comprehensive guide to the abbreviations used in this atlas.

abbrev. abbreviation
Afgh. Afghanistan
Amh. Amharic
anc. ancient
Ar. Arabic
Arm. Armenia/Armenian
Aus. Austria
Aust. Australia
Az. Azerbaijan

Bas. Basque
Bel. Belorussian
Belg. Belgium/Belgian
Bos. & Herz. Bosnia & Herzegovina
Bul. Bulgarian
Bulg. Bulgaria
Bur. Burmese

C Central
C. Cape
Cam. Cambodian
Cast. Castilian
Chin. Chinese
Cord. Cordillera (Sp. mts.)
Cz. Czech
Czech Rep. Czech Republic

D.C. District of Columbia
Dan. Danish
Dominican Rep. Dominican Republic

E East
Emb. Embalse
Eng. English
Eq. Guinea Equatorial Guinea
Est. Estonia/Estonian

Faer. Faeroese
Fin. Finnish
Flem. Flemish
Fr. France/French

Geo. Georgia
Geor. Georgian
Ger. Germany, German
Gk. Greek

Heb. Hebrew
Hung. Hungary/Hungarian

I. Island
Ind. Indonesia, Indonesian
Is. Islands
It. Italian

Kaz. Kazakh
Kep. Kepulauan (Ind. island group)
Kir. Kirghiz
Kor. Korean
Kurd. Kurdish
Kyrgy. Kyrgyzstan

L. Lake, Lago
Lat. Latvia
Latv. Latvian
Leb. Lebanon
Liech. Liechtenstein
Lith. Lithuania/Lithuanian
Lux. Luxembourg

m meters
Mac. Macedonia
Med. Sea Mediterranean Sea
Mold. Moldova
Mt. Mount/Mountain
Mts. Mountains

N North
N. Korea North Korea
Neth. Netherlands
NW Northwest
NZ New Zealand

P. Pulau (Ind. island)
Peg. Pegunungan (Ind. mountain range)
Per. Persian
Pol. Poland/Polish
Port. Portugal, Portuguese
prev. previously

R. River, Rio, Río
Res. Reservoir
Rom. Romania/Romanian
Rus. Russian
Russ. Fed. Russian Federation

S South
S. Korea South Korea
SA South Africa
SCr. Serbian and Croatian
Serb. & Mon. Serbia and Montenegro
Slvka. Slovakia
Slvna. Slovenia
Som. Somali
Sp. Spanish
St, St. Saint
Str. Strait
Swed. Swedish
Switz. Switzerland

Tajik. Tajikistan
Th. Thai
Turk. Turkish
Turkm. Turkmen
Turkmen. Turkmenistan

U.A.E. United Arab Emirates
UK United Kingdom
Ukr. Ukranian
US United States of America
Uzb. Uzbek
Uzbek. Uzbekistan

var. variant
Vdkhr. Vodokhranilishche (Rus. reservoir)
Vdskh. Vodoskhovyshche (Ukr. reservoir)
Ven. Venezuela

W West
W. Sahara Western Sahara
Wel. Welsh

Yugo. Yugoslavia

A

Aabenraa Denmark 67 A8

Aachen Germany 76 A4

Aalborg Denmark 67 B7

Aalst Belgium 69 B5

Aba Nigeria 57 G5

Ābādān Iran 102 C4

Abashiri Japan 112 D2

Abéché Chad 58 D3

Aberdeen Scotland, UK 70 D3

Aberdeen South Dakota, USA 25 E2

Aberdeen Washington, USA 26 A2

Aberystwyth Wales, UK 71 C6

Abhā Saudi Arabia 103 B6

Abidjan Côte d'Ivoire 56 D5

Abilene Texas, USA 29 F3

Abomey Benin 57 F4

Abu Dhabi *capital of* United Arab Emirates *var.* Abū Ẓaby 103 D5

Abuja *capital of* Nigeria 57 G4

Abū Ẓaby *see* Abu Dhabi

Acapulco Mexico 33 E5

Acarai Mountains *mountain range* Brazil/Guyana 41 F3

Acarigua Venezuela 40 D1

Accra *capital of* Ghana 57 E5

Acklins Island *island* Bahamas 36 D2

Aconcagua, Cerro *peak* Argentina 46 B4

A Coruña Spain *Cast.* La Coruña 74 C1

ACT *see* Australian Capital Territory

Adalia *see* Antalya

Adalia, Gulf of *see* Antalya Körfezi

'Adan Yemen *Eng.* Aden 103 B7

Adana Turkey *var.* Seyhan 98 D4

Adapazarı Turkey *var.* Sakarya 98 B2

Ad Dahnā' *desert* Saudi Arabia 103 C5

Ad Dakhla Western Sahara 52 A4

Ad Dawḥah *see* Doha

Addis Ababa *capital of* Ethiopia *Amh.* Ādīs Ābeba 55 C5

Adelaide Australia 131 B6

Adélie, Terre d' *territory* Antarctica 136 C4

Aden *see* 'Adan

Aden, Gulf of *sea feature* Indian Ocean 122 A3

Adige *river* Italy 78 C2

Ādīs Ābeba *see* Addis Ababa

Adıyaman Turkey 99 E4

Adriatic Sea Mediterranean Sea 78 D4

Aegean Sea Mediterranean Sea *Gk.* Aigaío Pélagos, *Turk.* Ege Denizi 87 D5

Aeolian Islands *see* Isole Eolie

Afghanistan *country* C Asia 104-105

Africa 50-51

Africa, Horn of *physical region* Ethiopia/Somalia 122 A3

Afyon Turkey *prev.* Afyonkarahisar 98 B3

Afyonkarahisar *see* Afyon

Agadez Niger 57 G3

Agadir Morocco 52 B2

Agassiz Fracture Zone *tectonic feature* Pacific Ocean 135 E4

Agen France 73 B6

Āgra India 116 D3

Agrigento Italy 79 C7

Agrinio Greece 87 B5

Aguarico *river* Ecuador/Peru 40 B4

Aguascalientes Mexico 32 D4

Ahaggar *mountains* Algeria *var.* Hoggar 53 E4

Ahmadābād India 116 C4

Ahvāz Iran 102 C4

Ahvenanmaa *see* Åland

Aigaío Pélagos *see* Aegean Sea

Aintab *see* Gaziantep

Aïr, Massif de l' *region* Niger 57 G2

Aix-en-Provence France 73 D6

Ajaccio Corse, France 73 E7

Ajdābiyā Libya 53 G2

Ajmer India 116 D3

Akaba *see* Al 'Aqabah

Akchâr *desert* Mauritania 56 C2

Akimiski Island *island* Canada 20 C3

Akita Japan 112 D3

Akjoujt Mauritania 56 C2

Akmola *see* Astana

Akmolinsk *see* Astana

Akpatok Island *island* Canada 21 E1

Akra Kanestron *see* Palioúri, Akrotírio

Akron Ohio, USA 22 D3

Aksai Chin *disputed region* China/India 108 B4

Aktau Kazakhstan *prev.* Shevchenko 96 A4

Akureyri Iceland 65 E4

Akyab *see* Sittwe

Alabama *state* USA 30 D3

Alajuela Costa Rica 34 D4

Alamogordo New Mexico, USA 28 D3

Åland *island group* Finland *Fin.* Ahvenanmaa 67 D6

Al 'Aqabah Jordan *var.* Akaba 101 B7

Alaska *state* USA 18

Alaska, Gulf of *sea feature* Pacific Ocean 16 C3

Alaska Range *mountain range* Alaska, USA 18 C3

Albacete Spain 75 E3

Alba Iulia Romania 90 B4

Albania *country* SE Europe 83

Albany Australia 129 B7

Albany Georgia, USA 31 E3

Albany New York, USA 23 F3

Albany Oregon, USA 26 A3

Albany *river* Canada 20 B3

Al Baṣrah Iraq *var.* Basra 102 C4

Al Baydā' Libya 53 G2

Albert, Lake *lake* Uganda/Dem. Rep. Congo 59 E5

Alberta *province* Canada 19 E4

Albi France 73 C6

Albuquerque New Mexico, USA 28 D2

Alcácer do Sal Portugal 74 C4

Aldabra Group *island group* Seychelles 61 G2

Aleg Mauritania 56 C3

Aleksandriya *see* Oleksandriya

Aleksandropol' *see* Gyumri

Aleksinac Serb. & Mon. (Yugo.) 82 E4

Alençon France 72 B3

Alessandria Italy 78 B2

Ålesund Norway 67 A5

Aleutian Basin *undersea feature* Bering Sea 134 D1

Aleutian Islands *islands* Alaska, USA 18 A3

Aleutian Trench *undersea feature* Pacific Ocean 134 D1

Alexander Island *island* Antarctica 136 A3

Alexandra New Zealand 133 B7

Alexandretta *see* İskenderun

Alexandria Egypt 54 B1

Alexandria Louisiana, USA 30 B3

Alexandroúpoli Greece 86 D3

Al Fāshir *see* El Fasher

Alföld *see* Great Hungarian Plain

Algarve *region* Portugal 74 C4

Algeciras Spain 74 D5

Algeria *country* N Africa 52-53

Alghero Italy 79 A5

Algiers *capital of* Algeria 52 D1

Al Ḥasakah Syria 100 D2

Al Ḥudaydah Yemen 103 B7

Al Hufūf Saudi Arabia 103 C5

Alicante Spain 75 F4

Alice Springs Australia 130 A4

Al Jawf Saudi Arabia 102 B4

Al Jazīrah *region* Iraq/Syria 100 E2

Al Jīzah *see* El Gîza

Al Karak Jordan 101 B6

Al Khalīl *see* Hebron

Al Khārijah *see* El Khârga

Al Khums Libya 53 F2

Al Khurṭūm *see* Khartoum

Alkmaar Netherlands 68 C2

Al Kufrah Libya 53 H4

Al Lādhiqīyah Syria *Eng.* Latakia 100 B3

Allahābād India 117 E4

Allenstein *see* Olsztyn

Allentown Pennsylvania, USA 23 F4

Alma-Ata *capital of* Kazakhstan *Rus./Kaz.* Almaty 96 C5

Al Madīnah Saudi Arabia *Eng.* Medina 102 A5

Al Mafraq Jordan 101 B5

Almalyk Uzbekistan *Uzb.* Olmaliq 105 C2

Al Manāmah *see* Manama

Al Marj Libya 53 G2

Almaty *see* Alma-Ata

Al Mawşil Iraq *Eng.* Mosul 102 B3

Almelo Netherlands 68 E3

Almería Spain 75 E5

Al Mukallā Yemen 103 C7

Alofi *capital of* Niue 127 F5

Alor, Kepulauan *island group* Indonesia 121 E5

Alps *mountain range* C Europe 62 D4

Al Qāhirah *see* Cairo

Al Qāmishlī Syria *var.* Kamishli 100 E1

Al Qunayṭirah Syria 100 B4

Altai Mountains *mountain range* C Asia 108 D2

Altamura Italy 79 E5

Altar, Desierto de *Desert* Mexico/USA *var.* Sonoran Desert 32 A1

Altay China 108 C2

Altay Mongolia 108 D2

Altun Shan *mountain range* China 108 C3

Alturas California, USA 26 B4

Alytus Lithuania *Pol.* Olita 89 B5

Amadeus, Lake *seasonal lake* Australia 129 E5

Amakusa-nada *island group* Japan 113 A6

Amami-Ō-shima *island* Japan 113 A8

Amarillo Texas, USA 29 E2

Amazon *river* South America 38 C3

Amazon Basin *region* C South America 42 D3

Ambanja Madagascar 61 G2

Ambarchik Russian Federation 97 G2

Ambato Ecuador 40 A4

Amboasary Madagascar 61 F4

Ambon Indonesia 121 F4

Ambositra Madagascar 61 G3

Ambriz Angola 60 B1

Amdo China 108 C4

Ameland *island* Netherlands 68 D1

American Falls Reservoir *Reservoir* Idaho, USA 26 E4

American Samoa *external territory* USA, Pacific Ocean 127 F4

Amersfoort Netherlands 68 D3

Amga *river* Russian Federation 95 F2

Amiens France 72 C3

Amindīvi Islands *island group* India 114 C2

Amirante Islands *island group* Seychelles 61 H1

Amman *capital of* Jordan 101 B5

Ammassalik Greenland *var.* Angmagssalik 64 D4

Ammochostos *see* Gazimağusa

Āmol Iran 102 C3

Amorgós *island* Greece 87 D6

Amritsar India 116 D2

Amsterdam *capital of* Netherlands 68 C3

Amsterdam Island *island* French Southern and Antarctic Territories 123 C6

Aral Sea *inland sea*
Kazakhstan/Uzbekistan 94 C3

Araouane Mali 57 E2

Ararat, Mount *peak* Turkey
var. Great Ararat, *Turk.*
Büyükağrı Dağ 94 F3

Aras *river* SW Asia *Arm.*
Arak's, *Per.* Rūd-e Aras, *Rus.*
Araks, *Turk.* Aras Nehri 99 G3

Aras Nehri *see* Aras

Arauca Colombia 40 C2

Arauca *river*
Colombia/Venezuela 40 C2

Arbīl Iraq *Kurd.* Hawlêr 102 B3

Arctic Ocean 18-19 137

Arda *river* Bulgaria/Greece
86 C3

Ardabīl Iran 102 C3

Ardennes *region* W Europe
69 D7

Arendal Norway 67 A6

Arensburg *see* Kuressaare

Arequipa Peru 42 B4

Arezzo Italy 78 C3

Argentina *country* S South
America 46-47

Argentine Basin *undersea
feature* Atlantic Ocean 49 B7

Argun *river* China/Russian
Federation 95 E3

Århus Denmark 67 A7

Arica Chile 46 B1

Arizona *state* USA 28 B2

Arkansas *state* USA 30 B1

Arkansas *river* C USA 17 C5

Arkhangel'sk Russian
Federation 92 C3 96 C2

Arles France 73 D6

Arlington Texas, USA 29 G3

Arlington Virginia, USA 23 E4

Arlon Belgium 69 D8

Armenia *country* SW Asia
99 G2

Armenia Colombia 40 B3

Armidale Australia 131 D5

Arnhem Netherlands 68 D4

Arnhem Land *region* Australia
128 E2

Arno *river* Italy 78 B3

Arran *island* Scotland, UK
70 C4

Ar Raqqah Syria 100 C2

Arras France 72 C3

Ar Riyāḍ *see* Riyadh

Ar Rub 'al Khālī *desert* Asia
Eng. Empty Quarter, Great
Sandy Desert 103 C6

Ar Rustāq Oman *var.* Rostak
103 D5

Artesia New Mexico, USA
28 D3

Artigas Uruguay 44 B4

Aru, Kepulauan *island group*
Indonesia 121 G5

Arua Uganda 55 B6

Aruba *external territory*
Netherlands, West Indies
37 E5

Arusha Tanzania 55 C7

Asad, Buḩayrat al *Lake* Syria
Eng. Lake Assad 100 C2

Asadābād Afghanistan 105 E4

Asahikawa Japan 112 D2

Asamankese Ghana 57 E5

Ascension *island* Atlantic
Ocean 49 C5

Ascoli Piceno Italy 78 C4

Aseb Eritrea *var.* Assab 54 D4

Ashburton New Zealand
133 C6

Asheville North Carolina, USA
31 E1

Aşgabat *capital of*
Turkmenistan *prev.*
Ashkhabad, Poltoratsk
104 C3

Ashkhabad *see* Aşgabat

Ashmore and Cartier Islands
Australian external territory
Indian Ocean 124 A3

Ash Shāriqah *see* Sharjah

Asia 94-95 106-107

Asmara *capital of* Eritrea *Amh.*
Asmera 54 C4

Asmera *see* Asmara

Assab *see* Aseb

As Salţ Jordan *var.* Salt 101 B5

Assamakka Niger 57 F2

Assen Netherlands 68 E2

Assad, Lake *see*
Asad, Buḩayrat al

As Sulayyil Saudi Arabia
103 B6

As Suwaydā' Syria 101 B5

Astana *country capital*
Kazakhstan *prev.* Akmola,
Akmolinsk, Tselinograd, Kaz.
Aqmola. 96 C4

Astoria Oregon, USA 26 A2

Astrakhan' Russian Federation
93 B7

Astypálaia *island* Greece 87 D6

Asunción *capital of* Paraguay
44 B4

Aswân Egypt 54 B2

Asyût Egypt 54 B2

Atacama Desert *desert* Chile
46 B2

Atamyrat *prev.* Kerki.
Turkmenistan 104 D3

Aṭâr Mauritania 56 C2

Atbara Sudan 54 C3

Athabasca, Lake *lake* Canada
19 F4

Athens *capital of* Greece *Gk.*
Athína, *prev.* Athínai 87 C5

Athens Georgia, USA 31 E2

Athína *see* Athens

Athínai *see* Athens

Athlone Ireland 71 B5

Ati Chad 58 C3

Atlanta Georgia, USA 30 D2

Atlantic City New Jersey, USA
23 F4

Atlantic Ocean 48-49

Atlantic-Indian Basin *undersea
feature* Atlantic Ocean 136 B1

Atlantic-Indian Ridge *undersea
feature* Atlantic Ocean 49 D7

Atlas Mountains *mountain
range* Morocco 52 C2

Aṭ Ţafilah Jordan 101 B6

Aṭ Ţā'if Saudi Arabia 102 B6

Attapu Laos 119 E5

Attawapiskat Canada 20 C3

Attawapiskat *river* Canada
20 B3

Attu Island *island* Alaska, USA
18 A2

Auch France 73 B6
Auckland New Zealand 132 D3
Auckland Islands *island group* New Zealand124 D5
Audijon Kyrgyzstan 105 F2
Augsburg Germany 77 C6
Augusta Australia 129 B7
Augusta Georgia, USA 31 E2
Augusta Maine, USA 23 G2
Aurillac France 73 C5
Aurora Colorado, USA 24 D4
Aurora Illinois, USA 22 B3
Aussig *see* Ústí nad Labem
Austin Texas, USA 29 G4
Australasia 124-125
Australes, Îles *island group* French Polynesia 125 F4
Austral Fracture Zone *tectonic feature* Pacific Ocean 125 H4
Australia *country* Pacific Ocean 124
Australian Alps Australia 131 D7
Australian Capital Territory *territory* Australia *abbrev.* A.C.T. *131* D6
Austria *country* C Europe 77
Auxerre France 72 C4
Avarua *capital of* Cook Islands 127 G5
Aveiro Portugal 74 C2
Avignon France 73 D6
Ávila Spain 74 D2
Avilés Spain 74 D1
Awbārī Libya 53 F3
Axel Heiberg Island *island* Canada 19 F1
Axios *see* Vardar
Ayacucho Peru 42 B4
Aydarkul', Ozero *lake* Uzbekistan 104 D2
Aydın Turkey 98 A3
Ayer's Rock *see* Uluru
Ayr Scotland, UK 70 C4
Ayutthaya Thailand 119 C5
Ayvalık Turkey 98 A3
Azaouâd *desert* Mali 57 E2
A'zāz Syria 100 B2

Azerbaijan *country* SW Asia 99 G2
Azores *islands* Portugal, Atlantic Ocean 48 C3
Azov, Sea of Black Sea *Ukr.* Azovs'ke More, *Rus.* Azovskoye More 93 A6 91 G4
Azovs'ke More *see* Azov, Sea of
Azovskoye More *see* Azov, Sea of
Azul Argentina 46 D4
Azur, Côte d' *coastal region* France 73 E6
Az Zarqā' Jordan 101 B5
Az Zāwiyah Libya 53 F2

B

Baalbek Lebanon *var.* Ba'labakk 100 B4
Babeldaob *island* Palau 124 B2
Babruysk Belarus *Rus.* Bobruysk 89 D6
Babuyan Channel *channel* Philippines 121 E1
Bacan, Pulau *island* Indonesia 121 F4
Bačka Topola Serb. & Mon. (Yugo.) 82 D3
Bacău Romania 90 C4
Badajoz Spain 74 C4
Baden Switzerland 77 E6
Bādiyat ash Shām *see* Syrian Desert
Baffin Bay *sea feature* Atlantic Ocean 48 B1
Baffin Island *island* Canada 19 G2
Bafing *river* Africa 56 C3
Bafoussam Cameroon 58 B4
Bagdad *see* Baghdad
Bagé Brazil 44 C5
Baghdad *capital of* Iraq *var.* Bagdad, *Ar.* Baghdād 102 B3
Baghdād *see* Baghdad
Baghlān Afghanistan 105 E3
Bagoé *river* Côte d'Ivoire/Mali 56 D4
Baguio Philippines 121 E1

Bahamas *country* West Indies, Atlantic Ocean 36
Baharden *see* Bäherden
Bahāwalpur Pakistan 116 C3
Bäherden Turkmenistan *prev.* Bakharden, *prev.* Bakherden, *var.* Baharden 104 B3
Bahía Blanca Argentina 47 C5
Bahía, Islas de la *islands* Honduras 34 D2
Bahir Dar Ethiopia 54 C4
Bahrain *country* SW Asia 103 C5
Baia Mare Romania 90 B3
Baikal, Lake *see* Baykal, Ozero
Bairiki *capital of* Kiribati 127 E2
Baja Hungary 81 C7
Baja California *peninsula* Mexico *Eng.* Lower California 32 B2
Bajo Nuevo *island* Colombia 35 F2
Baker Oregon, USA 26 C3
Baker & Howland Islands *external territory* USA, Pacific Ocean 125 E2
Bakersfield California, USA 27 C7
Bakharden *see* Bäherden
Bakherden *see* Bäherden
Bākhtarān Iran *prev.* Kermānshāh 102 C3
Bakı *see* Baku
Baku *capital of* Azerbaijan *Az.* Bakı, *var.* Baky 99 H2
Baky *see* Baku
Balabac Strait *sea feature* South China Sea/Sulu Sea 120 D2
Ba'labakk *see* Baalbek
Balakovo Russian Federation 93 C6
Bālā Morghāb Afghanistan 104 D4
Balaton *lake* Hungary *var.* Lake Balaton, *Ger.* Plattensee 81 C7
Balaton, Lake *see* Balaton

Balbina, Represa *Reservoir* Brazil 42 D2

Baleares, Islas *island group* Spain *Eng.* Balearic Islands 75 H3

Balearic Islands *see* Baleares, Islas.

Bali *island* Indonesia 120 D5

Balıkesir Turkey 98 A3

Balikpapan Indonesia 120 D4

Balkanabat Turkmenistan *prev.* Nebitdag 104 B2

Balkan Mountains *mountain range* Bulgaria *Bul.* Stara Planina 86 C2

Balkhash Kazakhstan 96 C5

Balkhash, Lake *see* Balkhash, Ozero

Balkhash, Ozero *lake* Kazakhstan *Eng.* Lake Balkhash 94 C3

Ballarat Australia 131 C7

Balsas *river* Mexico 33 E5

Bălți Moldova 90 D3

Baltic Port *see* Paldiski

Baltic Sea Atlantic Ocean 67 C7

Baltimore Maryland, USA 23 F4

Baltischport *see* Paldiski

Baltiski *see* Paldiski

Bamako *capital of* Mali 56 D3

Bambari Central African Republic 58 D4

Bamenda Cameroon 58 B4

Banaba *island* Kiribati *prev.* Ocean Island 127 E2

Bandaaceh Indonesia 120 A3

Banda, Laut *see* Banda Sea

Banda Sea *sea feature* Pacific Ocean *Ind.* Laut Banda 121 F4

Bandar-e ʿAbbās Iran 102 D4

Bandar-e Būshehr Iran 102 C4

Bandarlampung Indonesia *prev.* Tanjungkarang 120 C4

Bandarlampung Indonesia 120 C4

Bandar Seri Begawan *capital of* Brunei 120 D3

Bandon Oregon, USA 26 A3

Bandundu Dem. Rep. Congo 59 C6

Bandung Indonesia 120 C5

Bangalore India 114 D2

Banggai, Kepulauan *island group* Indonesia 121 E4

Banghāzī Libya *Eng.* Benghazi 53 G2

Bangka, Palau *island* Indonesia 120 C4

Bangkok *capital of* Thailand *Th.* Krung Thep 119 C5

Bangladesh *country* S Asia 117

Bangor Northern Ireland, UK 71 B5

Bangor Maine, USA 23 G2

Bangui *capital of* Central African Republic 59 C5

Bani *river* Mali 56 D3

Banī Suwayf *see* Beni Suef

Banja Luka Bosnia & Herzegovina 82 B3

Banjarmasin Indonesia 120 D4

Banjul *capital of* Gambia 56 B3

Banks Island *island* Canada 19 E2

Banks Islands *island group* Vanuatu, Pacific Ocean 126 D4

Banks Peninsula *peninsula* New Zealand 133 C6

Banks Strait *sea feature* Tasman Sea 131 C7

Banská Bystrica Slovakia *Ger.* Neusohl, *Hung.* Besztercebánya 81 C6

Bantry Bay *sea feature* Ireland 71 A6

Banyo Cameroon 58 B4

Banzare Seamounts *undersea feature* Indian Ocean 123 C7

Baotou China 109 F3

Baranavichy Belarus *Rus.* Baranovichi, *Pol.* Baranowicze 89 C6

Baranovichi *see* Baranavichy

Baranowicze *see* Baranavichy

Barbados *country* West Indies 37 H4

Barbuda *island* Antigua & Barbuda 37 G3

Barcaldine Australia 130 C4

Barcelona Spain 75 G2

Barcelona Venezuela 41 E1

Barcolod City Philippines 121 E2

Bareilly India 117 E3

Barentsburg Svalbard 65 F2

Barentsøya *island* Svalbard 65 G2

Barents Sea Arctic Ocean 137 H5

Bari Italy 79 E5

Barinas Venezuela 40 D2

Barisan, Pegunungan *mountains* Indonesia 120 B4

Barkly Tableland *plateau* Australia 130 B3

Barlavento, Ilhas de *island group* Cape Verde *var.* Windward Islands 56 A2

Bar-le-Duc France 72 D3

Barlee, Lake *lake* Australia 129 B 5

Barlee Range *mountain range* Australia 128 B4

Barnaul Russian Federation 96 D4

Barnstaple England, UK 71 C7

Barquisimeto Venezuela 40 D1

Barra *island* Scotland, UK 70 B3

Barranquilla Colombia 40 B1

Barrier Range *mountain range* Australia 131 C5

Barrow *river* Ireland 71 B6

Barstow California, USA 27 C7

Bartang *river* Tajikistan 105 F3

Bartica Guyana 41 G2

Baruun-Urt Mongolia 109 F2

Barwon River *river* Australia 131 D5

Barysaw Belarus *Rus.* Borisov 89 D5

Basarabeasca Moldova 90 D4

Basel Switzerland 77 B6

Basra *see* Al Baṣrah

Bassein Myanmar 118 A4

Basse-Terre *capital of* Guadeloupe 37 G4

Basseterre *capital of* St Kitts & Nevis 37 G3

Bass Strait *sea feature* Australia 131 C7

Bastia Corse, France 73 E7

Bastogne Belgium 69 D7

Bata Equatorial Guinea 58 A5

Batangas Philippines 121 E2

Bătdâmbâng Cambodia 119 D5

Bath England, UK 71 D6

Bathurst Canada 21 F4

Bathurst Island *island* Australia 128 D2

Bathurst Island *island* Canada 19 F2

Bāţin, Wādī al *dry watercourse* Asia 102 C4

Batman Turkey *var.* İluh 99 E4

Batna Algeria 53 E1

Baton Rouge Louisiana, USA 30 B3

Batticaloa Sri Lanka 115 E3

Bat'umi Georgia 99 F2

Bauru Brazil 44 D2

Bavarian Alps *mountains* Austria/Germany 77 C6

Bayamo Cuba 36 C2

Bayan Har Shan *mountain range* China 108 D4

Bayanhongor Mongolia 108 D2

Bay City Michigan, USA 22 C3

Baydhabo Somalia 55 D6

Baykal, Ozero *lake* Russian Federation *Eng.* Lake Baikal 95 E3

Bayonne France 73 A6

Baýramaly Turkmenistan 104 C3

Bayrūt *see* Beirut

Beaufort Sea Arctic Ocean 137 F2

Beaufort West South Africa 60 D5

Beaumont Texas, USA 29 H4

Beauvais France 72 C3

Béchar Algeria 53 E2

Be'ér Sheva' Israel 101 A6

Beijing *capital of* China *var.* Peking 110 C4

Beira Mozambique 61 E3

Beirut *capital of* Lebanon *var.* Beyrouth, Bayrūt 100 B4

Beja Portugal 74 C4

Béjaïa Algeria 53 E1

Bek-Budi *see* Karshi

Békéscsaba Hungary 81 D7

Belarus *country* E Europe *var.* Belorusia 89

Belau *see* Palau

Belcher Islands *islands* Canada 20 C2

Beledweyne Somalia 55 D5

Belém Brazil 43 F2

Belfast Northern Ireland, UK 71 B5

Belfort France 72 E4

Belgaum India 114 C1

Belgium *country* W Europe 69

Belgorod Russian Federation 93 A5

Belgrade *capital of* Serb. & Mon. (Yugo.) *SCr.* Beograd 82 D3

Belitung, Pulau *island* Indonesia 120 C4

Belize *country* Central America 34

Belize City Belize 34 C1

Belle Île *island* France 72 A4

Belle Isle, Strait of *sea feature* Canada 21 G3

Bellevue Washington, USA 26 B2

Bellingham Washington, USA 26 B1

Bellingshausen Sea Antarctica 136 A3

Bello Colombia 40 B2

Bellville South Africa 60 C5

Belmopan *capital of* Belize 34 C1

Belo Horizonte Brazil 45 F1

Belorussia *see* Belarus

Belostok *see* Białystok

Beloye More Arctic Ocean *Eng.* White Sea 163 F1

Belyy, Ostrov *island* Russian Federation 137 H4

Bend Oregon, USA 26 B3

Bendery *see* Tighina

Bendigo Australia 131 C7

Benevento Italy 79 D5

Bengal, Bay of *sea feature* Indian Ocean 122 D3

Bengbu China 111 D5

Benghazi *see* Banghāzī

Bengkulu Indonesia 120 B4

Benguela Angola 60 B2

Beni *river* Bolivia 42 C4

Benidorm Spain 75 F4

Beni Mellal Morocco 52 C2

Benin *country* N Africa *prev.* Dahomey 57

Benin, Bight of *sea feature* W Africa 57 F5

Benin City Nigeria 57 F5

Beni Suef Egypt *var.* Banī Suwayf 54 B1

Ben Nevis *mountain* Scotland, UK 70 C3

Benue *river* Cameroon/Nigeria 57 G4

Beograd *see* Belgrade

Berat Albania 83 D6

Berbera Somalia 54 D4

Berbérati Central African Republic 58 C5

Berdyans'k Ukraine 91 G4

Bereket Turkmenistan *prev.* Gazandzhyk, *var.* Kazandzhik, *Turkm.* Gazanjyk 104 B2

Berezina *see* Byerazino

Bergamo Italy 78 B2

Bergen Norway 67 A5

Bergse Maas *river* Netherlands 68 D4

Bering Sea Pacific Ocean 134 D1

Bering Strait *sea feature* Bering Sea/Chukchi Sea 134 D1

Berkeley California, USA 27 B6

Berlin *capital of* Germany 76 D3

Bermejo *river* Argentina 46 D2

Bermuda *external territory* UK, Atlantic Ocean 48 B3

Bern *capital of* Switzerland *Fr.* Berne 77 B7

Berne *see* Bern
Berner Alpen *mountain range* Switzerland 77 B7
Bertoua Cameroon 59 B5
Besançon France 72 D4
Besztercebánya *see* Banská Bystrica
Bethlehem West Bank 101 A5
Beyrouth *see* Beirut
Béziers France 73 C6
Bezmein *see* Büzmeýin
Bhamo Myanmar 118 B2
Bhāvnagar India 116 C4
Bhôpal India 116 D4
Bhutan *country* S Asia 117
Biak, Pulau *island* Indonesia 121 G4
Białystok Poland *Rus.* Belostok 80 E3
Biel Switzerland 77 B7
Bielefeld Germany 76 B4
Bielitz-Biala *see* Bielsko-Biala
Bielsko-Biała Poland *Ger.* Bielitz-Biala 81 C5
Bié Plateau *upland* Angola 51 C6
Bighorn Mountains *mountains* C USA 24 C2
Bignona Senegal 56 B3
Big Spring Texas, USA 29 E3
Bihać Bosnia & Herzegovina 82 B3
Bihār *state* India 117 F3
Bijelo Polje Serb. & Mon. (Yugo.) 82 D4
Bikāner India 116 C3
Bila Tserkva Ukraine 91 E2
Bilbao Spain 75 E1
Billings Montana, USA 24 C2
Bilma, Grand Erg de *desert* Niger 57 G3
Biloela Australia 130 D4
Biloxi Mississippi, USA 30 C3
Biltine Chad 58 D3
Binghamton New York, USA 23 F3
Birāk Libya 53 F3
Biratnagar Nepal 117 F3
Birmingham England, UK 71 D6

Birmingham Alabama, USA 30 D2
Bîr Mogreïn Mauritania 56 C1
Birsen *see* Biržai
Biržai Lithuania *Ger.* Birsen 88 C4
Biscay, Bay of *sea feature* Atlantic Ocean 62 C4
Bishkek *capital of* Kyrgyzstan *prev.* Frunze, Pishpek 105 F2
Bishop California, USA 27 C6
Biskra Algeria 53 E2
Bismarck North Dakota, USA 25 E2
Bismarck Archipelago *island group* Papua New Guinea 126 B3
Bismarck Sea *sea* Pacific Ocean 124 B2
Bissau *capital of* Guinea-Bissau 56 B4
Bitola Macedonia 83 E6
Bitterroot Range *mountains* NW USA 26 D2
Biwa-ko *lake* Japan 113 C5
Bizerte Tunisia 53 E1
Bjelovar Croatia 82 B2
Bjørnøya *Island* N Norway *Eng.* Bear Island 65 G3
Black Drin *river* Albania/Macedonia 83 D5
Black Forest *see* Schwarzwald
Black Hills *mountains* C USA 24 D3
Blackpool England, UK 71 D5
Black River *river* China/Vietnam 118 D3
Black Sea Asia/Europe 63 F4
Black Volta *river* Ghana/Côte d'Ivoire 57 E4
Blackwater *river* Ireland 71 A6
Blagoevgrad Bulgaria 86 C3
Blagoveshchensk Russian Federation 97 G4
Blanca, Bahía *sea feature* Argentina 39 D5
Blanche, Lake *lake* Australia 131 B5
Blantyre Malawi 61 E2
Blenheim New Zealand 133 D5

Blida Algeria 52 D1
Bloemfontein South Africa 60 D4
Blois France 72 C4
Bloomington Indiana, USA 22 C4
Bluefields Nicaragua 35 E3
Blue Mountains *mountains* W USA 26 C2
Blue Nile *river* Ethiopia/Sudan 54 C4
Blumenau Brazil 44 D3
Bo Sierra Leone 56 C4
Boa Vista Brazil 42 D1
Boa Vista *island* Cape Verde 56 A3
Bobo-Dioulasso Burkina 56 D4
Bobruysk *see* Babruysk
Boca de la Serpiente *see* Serpent's Mouth, The
Bochum Germany 76 B4
Bodø Norway 66 C3
Bodrum Turkey 98 A4
Bogor Indonesia 120 C5
Bogotá *capital of* Colombia 40 B3
Bo Hai *sea feature* Yellow Sea 110 D4
Bohemian Forest *region* Germany 77 D5
Bohol Sea *Sea* Philippines 121 E2
Boise Idaho, USA 26 D3
Boké Guinea 56 C4
Bokhara *see* Buxoro
Bol Chad 58 B3
Bolivia *country* C South America 42-43
Bologna Italy 78 C3
Bolton England, UK 71 D5
Bolzano Italy *Ger.* Bozen 78 C2
Boma Dem. Rep. Congo 59 B7
Bombay *see* Mumbai
Bomu *river* Central African Republic/Dem. Rep. Congo 59 D5
Bongo, Massif des *upland* Central African Republic 58 D4

Bongor Chad 58 C3
Bonn Germany 76 B4
Boosaaso Somalia 54 E4
Borås Sweden 67 B7
Bordeaux France 73 B5
Borger Texas, USA 29 E2
Borisov *see* Barysaw
Borlänge Sweden 67 C6
Borneo *island* SE Asia 120-121
Bornholm *island* Denmark 67 C8
Bosanski Šamac Bosnia & Herzegovina 82 C3
Bosna *river* Bosnia & Herzegovina 82 C3
Bosna I Hercegovina, Federacija Admin. region *republic* Bosnia and Herzegovina 82 C4
Bosnia & Herzegovina *country* SE Europe 82-83
Bosporus *sea feature* Turkey *Turk.* İstanbul Boğazı 98 B2
Bossangoa Central African Republic 58 C4
Bosten Hu *Lake* China 108 C3
Boston Massachusetts, USA 23 G3
Bothnia, Gulf of *sea feature* Baltic Sea 67 C5
Botoşani Romania 90 C3
Botswana *country* southern Africa 60
Bouar Central African Republic 58 C4
Bougainville Island *island* Papua New Guinea 126 C3
Bougouni Mali 56 D4
Boulder Colorado, USA 24 C4
Boulogne-sur-Mer France 72 C2
Bourges France 72 C4
Bourgogne *region* France *Eng.* Burgundy 72 D4
Bourke Australia 131 C5
Bournemouth England, UK 71 D7
Bouvet Island *external territory* Norway, Atlantic Ocean 49 D7
Bowen Australia 130 D3
Bowling Green Kentucky, USA 22 C5

Bozeman Montana, USA 24 B2
Bozen *see* Bolzano
Brač *island* Croatia 82 B4
Bradford England, UK 71 D5
Braga Portugal 74 C2
Bragança Portugal 74 C2
Brahmaputra *river* Asia 117 G3
Brăila Romania 90 D4
Brainerd Minnesota, USA 25 F2
Brandon Canada 19 F5
Brasília *capital of* Brazil 43 F4
Braşov Romania 90 C4
Bratislava *capital of* Slovakia *Ger.* Pressburg, *Hung.* Pozsony 81 C6
Bratsk Russian Federation 97 E4
Braunau am Inn Austria 77 D6
Braunschweig Germany *Eng.* Brunswick 76 C4
Brazil *country* South America 42-43
Brazil Basin *undersea feature* Atlantic Ocean 49 C5
Brazilian Highlands *upland* Brazil 43 G4
Brazos *river* SW USA 29 G3
Brazzaville *capital of* Congo 59 B6
Brecon Beacons *hills* Wales, UK 71 C6
Breda Netherlands 68 C4
Bregenz Austria 77 B7
Bremen Germany 76 B3
Bremerhaven Germany 76 B3
Brescia Italy 78 B2
Breslau *see* Wrocław
Brest Belarus *Pol.* Brześć nad Bugiem, *prev.* Brześć Litewski, *Rus.* Brest-Litovsk 89 B6
Brest France 72 A3
Brest-Litovsk *see* Brest
Bretagne *region* France *Eng.* Brittany 72 A3
Brezhnev *see* Naberezhnyye Chelny
Bria Central African Republic 58 D4

Bridgetown *capital of* Barbados 37 H4
Brig Switzerland 77 B5
Brighton England, UK 71 E7
Brindisi Italy 79 E5
Brisbane Australia 131 E5
Bristol England, UK 71 D6
British Columbia *province* Canada 18-19
British Indian Ocean Territory *external territory* UK, Indian Ocean 122 C4
British Isles *islands* W Europe 70-71
British Virgin Islands *external territory* UK, West Indies 37
Brittany *see* Bretagne
Brno Czech Republic *Ger.* Brünn 81 B5
Broken Arrow Oklahoma, USA 29 G1
Broken Hill Australia 131 B6
Broken Ridge *undersea feature* Indian Ocean 123 D6
Bromberg *see* Bydgoszcz
Brooks Range *mountains* Alaska, USA 18 D2
Brookton Australia 129 B6
Broome Australia 128 C3
Brownfield Texas, USA 29 E2
Brownsville Texas, USA 29 G5
Bruges *see* Brugge
Brugge Belgium *Fr.* Bruges 69 A5
Brunei *country* E Asia 120 D3
Brünn *see* Brno
Brunswick Georgia, USA 31 E3
Brunswick *see* Braunschweig
Brusa *see* Bursa
Brussel *see* Brussels
Brussels *capital of* Belgium *Fr.* Bruxelles, *Flem.* Brussel 69 C6
Brüx *see* Most
Bruxelles *see* Brussels
Bryan Texas, USA 29 G3
Bryansk Russian Federation 93 A5 96 A2
Brześć Litewski *see* Brest
Brześć nad Bugiem *see* Brest

Bucaramanga Colombia 40 C2

Buchanan Liberia 56 C5

Bucharest *capital of* Romania 90 C5

Budapest *capital of* Hungary 81 C6

Budweis *see* České Budějovice

Buenaventura Colombia 40 B3

Buenos Aires *capital of* Argentina 46 D4

Buenos Aires, Lago *lake* Argentina/Chile 47 B6

Buffalo New York, USA 23 E3

Bug *river* E Europe 90 C1

Bujumbura *capital of* Burundi *prev.* Usumbura 55 B7

Bukavu Dem. Rep. Congo 59 E6

Bukhara *see* Buxoro

Bulawayo Zimbabwe 60 D3

Bulgan Mongolia 109 E2

Bulgaria *country* E Europe 86

Bumba Dem. Rep. Congo 59 D5

Bunbury Australia 129 B6

Bundaberg Australia 130 E4

Bunia Dem. Rep. Congo 59 E5

Buraydah Saudi Arabia 103 B5

Burë Ethiopia 54 C4

Burgas Bulgaria 86 E2

Burgos Spain 75 E2

Burgundy *see* Bourgogne

Burketown Australia 130 B3

Burkina *country* W Africa 57

Burlington Iowa, USA 25 G4

Burlington Vermont, USA 23 F2

Burma *see* Myanmar

Burnie Tasmania 131 C8

Burns Oregon, USA 26 C3

Bursa Turkey *prev.* Brusa 98 B3

Burtnieku Ezers *lake* Latvia 88 C3

Buru, Pulau *island* Indonesia 121 E4

Burundi *country* C Africa 55

Busselton Australia 129 B7

Butembo Dem. Rep. Congo 59 E5

Buton, Pulau *island* Indonesia 121 E4

Butte Montana, USA 24 B2

Butuan Philippines 121 F2

Buxoro Uzbekistan *var.* Bokhara, *Rus.* Bukhara 104 D2

Büyükağrı Dağı *see* Ararat, Mount

Buzău Romania 90 C4

Bydgoszcz Poland *Ger.* Bromberg 80 C3

Byerazino *river* Belarus *Rus.* Berezina 89 D6

Büzmeýin Turkmenistan *prev.* Bezmein 104 B3

Byzantium *see* İstanbul

C

Caazapá Paraguay 44 C3

Cabanatuan Philippines 121 E1

Cabimas Venezuela 40 C1

Cabinda *exclave* Angola 60 B1

Cabot Strait *sea feature* Atlantic Ocean 21 G4

Čačak Serb. & Mon. (Yugo.) 82 D4

Cáceres Spain 74 D3

Cachoeiro de Itapemirim Brazil 45 F4

Cadiz Philippines 121 E2

Cádiz Spain 74 D5

Caen France 72 B3

Cagayan de Oro Philippines 121 F2

Cagliari Italy 79 A5

Cahors France 73 B5

Cairns Australia 130 D3

Cairo *capital of* Egypt *Ar.* Al Qāhirah, *var.* El Qâhira 54 B1

Čakovec Croatia 82 B2

Calabar Nigeria 57 G5

Calabria *region* Italy 79 D6

Calafate *see* El Calafate

Calais France 72 C2

Calais Maine, USA 23 H1

Calama Chile 46 B2

Calbayog Philippines 121 F2

Calcutta *see* Kolkata

Caldas da Rainha Portugal 74 B3

Caldwell Idaho, USA 27 C3

Caleta Olivia Argentina 47 C6

Calgary Canada 19 E5

Cali Colombia 40 A3

Calicut India *var.* Kozhikode 114 D2

California *state* USA 26-27

California, Golfo de *sea feature* Pacific Ocean *Eng.* California, Gulf of 32 B2 123 F2

Callabonna, Lake *lake* Australia 131 B5

Callao Peru 42 A3

Caltanissetta Italy 79 C7

Camagüey Cuba 36 C2

Cambodia *country* SE Asia *Cam.* Kampuchea 119

Cambridge England, UK 71 E6

Cambridge New Zealand 132 D2

Cameroon *country* W Africa 58-59

Campbell Plateau *undersea feature* Pacific Ocean 134 C5

Campeche Mexico 33 G4

Campeche, Bahía de *sea feature* Mexico *Eng.* Gulf of Campeche 33 G4

Campina Grande Brazil 43 H3

Campinas Brazil 45 E2

Campo Grande Brazil 44 C1

Campos Brazil 45 F2

Canada *country* North America 16-17

Canada Basin *undersea feature* Arctic Ocean *var.* Laurentian Basin 137 F2

Canadian River *river* SW USA 29 E2

Çanakkale Turkey 98 A3

Çanakkale Boğazı *see* Dardanelles

Canarias, Islas *islands* Spain *Eng.* Canary Islands 50 A2

Canary Basin *undersea feature* Atlantic Ocean 48 C4

Canary Islands see Canarias, Islas

Canaveral, Cape coastal feature Florida, USA 31 F4

Canberra capital of Australia 131 D6

Cancún Mexico 33 H3

Caniapiscau river Canada 21 E2

Caniapiscau, Réservoir Reservoir Canada 21 E3

Canik Dağları mountains Turkey 98 D2

Çankırı Turkey 98 C2

Cannes France 73 D6

Canoas Brazil 44 D4

Canterbury England, UK 71 E6

Canterbury Bight sea feature Pacific Ocean 133 C6

Canterbury Plains plain New Zealand 133 B6

Cần Thơ Vietnam 119 D6

Canton Ohio, USA 22 D4

Canton see Guangzhou

Cape Basin undersea feature Atlantic Ocean 49 D6

Cape Town South Africa 60 C5

Cape Verde country Atlantic Ocean 56 A2

Cape Verde Basin undersea feature Atlantic Ocean 48 C4

Cape York Peninsula peninsula Australia 124 B3

Cap-Haïtien Haiti 36 D3

Capri, Isola di island Italy 79 D5

Caquetá river Colombia 40 C4

CAR see Central African Republic

Caracas capital of Venezuela 40 D1

Carazinho Brazil 44 C3

Carbondale Illinois, USA 22 B5

Carcassonne France 73 C6

Cardiff Wales, UK 71 C6

Cardigan Bay sea feature Wales, UK 71 C6

Carey, Lake lake Australia 129 C5

Caribbean Sea Atlantic Ocean 36-37

Carlisle England, UK 70 D4

Carlsbad New Mexico, USA 28 D3

Carlsberg Ridge undersea feature Indian Ocean 122 B4

Carnarvon Australia 128 A5

Carnegie, Lake lake Australia 129 C5

Carolina Brazil 43 F3

Caroline Island see Millennium Island

Caroline Islands island group Micronesia 126 B1

Caroní river Venezuela 41 F2

Carpathian Mountains mountain range E Europe var. Carpathians 63 E4

Carpathians see Carpathian Mountains

Carpaţii Meridionali mountain range Romania Eng. South Carpathians, Transylvanian Alps 90 B4

Carpentaria, Gulf of sea feature Australia 130 B2

Carson City Nevada, USA 27 B5

Cartagena Colombia 40 B1

Cartagena Spain 75 F4

Cartago Costa Rica 35 E4

Cartwright Canada 21 G2

Carúpano Venezuela 41 E1

Casablanca Morocco 52 C2

Casa Grande Arizona, USA 28 B3

Cascade Range mountain range Canada/USA 26 B2

Cascais Portugal 74 B3

Casper Wyoming, USA 24 C3

Caspian Sea inland sea Asia/Europe 94 B4

Castelló de la Plana Spain 75 F3

Castelo Branco Portugal 74 C3

Castries capital of St Lucia 37 G4

Castro Chile 47 B6

Cat Island island Bahamas 36 D1

Catania Italy 79 D7

Catanzaro Italy 79 D6

Cauca river Colombia 40 B2

Caucasus mountains Asia/Europe 93 A7

Caura river Venezuela 41 E2

Caviana, Ilha island Brazil 43 F1

Cawnpore see Känpur

Caxias do Sul Brazil 44 D4

Cayenne capital of French Guiana 41 H3

Cayman Islands external territory UK, West Indies 36

Cebu Philippines 121 E2

Cedar Rapids Iowa, USA 25 G3

Cedros, Isla island Mexico 32 A2

Ceduna Australia 131 A6

Cefalù Italy 79 C6

Celebes see Sulawesi

Celebes Sea Pacific Ocean Ind. Laut Sulawesi 134 B3

Celje Slovenia 77 E7

Central African Republic country C Africa abbrev. CAR 58-59

Central, Cordillera mountain range Philippines 121 E1

Central Makrān Range mountains Pakistan 116 A3

Central Pacific Basin undersea feature Pacific Ocean 125 E1

Central Russian Upland upland Russian Federation 94 B3

Central Siberian Plateau see Srednesibirskoye Ploskogor'ye

Central Siberian Uplands see Srednesibirskoye Ploskogor'ye

Central, Sistema mountain range Spain 74 D3

Cephalonia see Kefalliniá

Ceram Sea Pacific Ocean 121 F4

Cernăuţi see Chernivtsi

Cēsis Latvia Ger. Wenden 88 C3

České Budějovice Czech Republic Ger. Budweis 81 B5

Ceuta external territory Spain, N Africa 52 C1

Cévennes *mountains* France 73 C6

Ceylon *see* Sri Lanka

Ceylon Plain *undersea feature* Indian Ocean 122 C4

Chad *country* C Africa 58

Chad, Lake *lake* C Africa 58 B3

Chăgai Hills *mountains* Pakistan 116 A2

Chagos-Laccadive Plateau *undersea feature* Indian Ocean 122 C4

Chagos Trench *undersea feature* Indian Ocean 122 C4

Chalkída Greece 87 C5

Challenger Deep *undersea feature* Pacific Ocean 134 B3

Châlons-en-Champagne France 72 D3

Chambéry France 73 D5

Champaign Illinois, USA 22 B4

Chañaral Chile 46 B2

Chandīgarh India 116 D2

Chang, Ko *island* Thailand 119 C5

Changchun China 110 D3

Chang Jiang *river* China *var.* Yangtze 111 B6

Changsha China 111 C6

Chaniá Greece 87 C7

Channel Islands *island group* California, USA 27 B8

Channel Islands *islands* UK 71 D8

Channel-Port-aux-Basques Canada 21 G4

Channel Tunnel France/UK 71 E7

Chapala, Lago de *lake* Mexico 32 D4

Chardzhev *see* Türkmenabat

Chardzhou *see* Türkmenabat

Chari *river* C Africa 58 C3

Chārīkār Afghanistan 105 E4

Chärjew *see* Türkmenabat

Charleroi Belgium 69 C6

Charleston South Carolina, USA 31 F2

Charleston West Virginia, USA 22 D5

Charleville Australia 130 C4

Charlotte North Carolina, USA 31 F1

Charlotte Amalie *capital of* Virgin Islands 37 F3

Charlottesville Virginia, USA 23 E5

Charlottetown Canada 21 G4

Charters Towers Australia 130 D3

Chartres France 72 C3

Charus Nuur *lake* Mongolia 108 C2

Châteauroux France 72 C4

Chatham Islands *islands* New Zealand 134 D4

Chattanooga Tennessee, USA 30 D1

Chauk Myanmar 118 A3

Chaves Portugal 74 C2

Cheboksary Russian Federation 93 C5

Cheboygan Michigan, USA 22 C2

Chech, Erg *desert* Algeria/Mali 56 D1

Che-chiang *see* Zhejiang

Cheju-do *island* South Korea 111 E5

Cheju Strait *sea feature* South Korea 111 E5

Chekiang *see* Zhejiang

Cheleken *see* Hazar

Chelyabinsk Russian Federation 96 C3

Chemnitz Germany *prev.* Karl-Marx-Stadt 76 D4

Chenāb *river* Pakistan 116 C2

Chengdu China 111 B5

Chennai India *prev.* Madras 115 E2

Cherbourg France 72 B3

Cherepovets Russian Federation 92 B4

Cherkasy Ukraine 91 E2

Cherkessk Russian Federation 93 A7

Chernigov *see* Chernihiv

Chernihiv Ukraine *Rus.* Chernigov 91 E1

Chernivtsi Ukraine *Rus.* Chernovtsy, *Rom.* Cernăuți 90 C3

Chernobyl' *see* Chornobyl'

Chernovtsy *see* Chernivtsi

Chernyakhovsk Kaliningrad, Russian Federation 88 B4

Chesapeake Bay *sea feature* USA 23 F5

Chester England, UK 71 D5

Cheyenne Wyoming, USA 24 D4

Chiang-hsi *see* Jiangxi

Chiang Mai Thailand 118 B4

Chiang-su *see* Jiangsu

Chiba Japan 113 D5

Chicago Illinois, USA 22 B3

Chiclayo Peru 42 A3

Chico California, USA 27 B5

Chicoutimi Canada 21 E4

Chifeng China 109 F2

Chihli *see* Hebei

Chihuahua Mexico 32 C2

Chile *country* S South America 46-47

Chile Basin *undersea feature* Pacific Ocean 135 G4

Chile Chico Chile 47 B6

Chile Rise *undersea feature* Pacific Ocean 135 G4

Chi-lin *see* Jilin

Chillán Chile 46 B4

Chiloé, Isla de *island* Chile 47 B6

Chimborazo *peak* Ecuador 38 A3

Chimbote Peru 42 A3

Chimkent *see* Shymkent

Chimoio Mozambique 61 E3

China *country* E Asia 108-109

Chinandega Nicaragua 34 C3

Chindwin *river* Myanmar 118 A2

Chinghai *see* Qinghai

Chingola Zambia 60 D2

Chinook Trough *undersea feature* Pacific Ocean 134 D1

Chíos Greece 87 D5

Chíos *island* Greece *prev.* Khíos 87 D5

Chirchik Uzbekistan *Uzb.* Chirchiq 105 E2

Chirchiq *see* Chirchik

Chiriquí, Golfo de *sea feature* Panama 35 E5

Chişinău *capital of* Moldova, *var.* Kishinev 90 D3

Chita Russian Federation 97 F4

Chitré Panama 35 F5

Chittagong Bangladesh 117 G4

Chitungwiza Zimbabwe 60 D3

Choluteca Honduras 34 C3

Choma Zambia 60 D3

Chona *river* Russian Federation 95 E2

Chon Buri Thailand 119 C5

Ch'ŏngjin North Korea 110 E3

Chongqing *province* China *var.* Chungking 111 B5

Chonos, Archipiélago de los *island group* Chile 47 B6

Chornobyl' Ukraine *Rus.* Chernobyl' 91 E1

Choûm Mauritania 56 C2

Choybalsan Mongolia 109 F2

Christchurch New Zealand 133 C6

Christmas Island *external territory* Australia, Indian Ocean 122 D5

Christmas Island *see* Kiritimati

Christmas Ridge *undersea feature* Pacific Ocean 125 F1

Chuan *see* Sichuan

Chubut *river* Argentina 47 B6

Chudskoye Ozero *see* Peipus, Lake

Chuí *see* Chuy

Chukchi Plain *undersea feature* Arctic Ocean 137 G2

Chukchi Sea Arctic Ocean *Rus.* Chukotskoye More 137 F1

Chukotskoye More *see* Chukchi Sea

Chula Vista California, USA 27 C8

Chulym *river* Russian Federation 94 D3

Chumphon Thailand 119 C6

Chungking *see* Chongqing

Chuquicamata Chile 46 B2

Chur Switzerland 77 B7

Churchill Canada 19 G4

Chuuk Islands *island group* Micronesia 126 B1

Chuy Brazil *var.* Chuí 44 C5

Cienfuegos Cuba 36 B2

Cieza Spain 75 E4

Cilacap Indonesia 120 C5

Cincinnati Ohio, USA 22 C4

Cirebon Indonesia 120 C5

Ciudad Bolívar Venezuela 41 E2

Ciudad del Este Paraguay 44 C3

Ciudad de México *see* Mexico City

Ciudad Guayana Venezuela 41 E2

Ciudad Juárez Mexico 32 C1

Ciudad Obregón Mexico 32 B2

Ciudad Ojeda Venezuela 40 C1

Ciudad Real Spain 75 E3

Ciudad Valles Mexico 33 E3

Ciudad Victoria Mexico 33 E3

Clarence *river* New Zealand 133 C5

Clarion Fracture Zone *tectonic feature* Pacific Ocean 125 G1

Clarksville Tennessee, USA 30 D1

Clearwater Florida, USA 31 E4

Clermont Australia 130 D4

Clermont-Ferrand France 73 C5

Cleveland Ohio, USA 22 D3

Clipperton Fracture Zone *tectonic feature* Pacific Ocean 125 G2

Clipperton Island *external territory* France, Pacific Ocean 135 F3

Cloncurry Australia 130 C3

Clovis New Mexico, USA 29 E2

Cluj-Napoca Romania 90 B3

Clutha *river* New Zealand 133 B7

Coast Ranges *mountain range* W USA 26 A5

Coats Island *island* Canada 20 C1

Coats Land *physical region* Antarctica 136 B2

Coatzacoalcos Mexico 33 G4

Cobán Guatemala 34 B2

Cochabamba Bolivia 42 C4

Cochin India 114 D3

Cochrane Canada 20 C4

Cochrane Chile 47 B6

Coco *river* Honduras/Nicaragua 34 D2

Cocos Basin *undersea feature* Indian Ocean 122 D4

Cocos Islands *external territory* Australia, Indian Ocean 122 D5

Cod, Cape *coastal feature* NE USA 23 G3

Coeur d'Alene Idaho, USA 26 C2

Coffs Harbour Australia 131 E6

Coihaique Chile 47 B6

Coimbatore India 114 D3

Coimbra Portugal 74 C3

Colchester England, UK 71 E6

Colmar France 72 E4

Cologne *see* Köln

Colombia *country* N South America 40-41

Colombo *capital of* Sri Lanka 115 E4

Colón Panama 35 F4

Colón, Archipiélago de *see* Galapagos Islands

Colorado *state* USA 24 C4

Colorado *river* USA 16 B5

Colorado *river* Argentina 47 C5

Colorado Plateau *upland region* S USA 28 B1

Colorado Springs Colorado, USA 24 D4

Columbia South Carolina, USA 31 F2

Columbia *river* NW USA 26 C1

Columbus Georgia, USA 30 D3

Columbus Mississippi, USA 30 C2

Columbus Nebraska, USA 25 E4

Columbus Ohio, USA 22 D4

Comayagua Honduras 34 C2

Comilla Bangladesh 117 G4

Communism Peak *peak* Tajikistan *Rus.* Pik Kommunizma, *prev.* Stalin Peak, Garmo Peak 105 F3

Como, Lago di *lake* Italy 78 B2

Comodoro Rivadavia Argentina 47 C6

Comoros *country* Indian Ocean 61

Conakry *capital of* Guinea 56 C4

Concepción Chile 47 B5

Concepción Paraguay 44 B2

Conchos *river* Mexico 32 C2

Concord New Hampshire, USA 22 G2

Concordia E Argentina 46 D3

Congo *country* C Africa 59

Congo *river* C Africa *var.* Zaire 51 C5

Congo Basin *drainage basin* C Africa 59 C5

Congo, Democratic Republic of *country* C Africa 59

Connecticut *state* USA 23 G3

Constance, Lake *river* C Europe 77 B6

Constantine Algeria 53 E1

Constantinople *see* İstanbul

Constanţa Romania 90 D5

Coober Pedy Australia 131 A5

Cook, Mount *see* Aoraki

Cook Islands *external territory* New Zealand, Pacific Ocean 127 G4

Cook Strait *sea feature* New Zealand 133 D5

Cooktown Australia 130 D2

Cooma Australia 131 D7

Coos Bay Oregon, USA 26 A3

Cootamundra Australia 131 D6

Copenhagen *capital of* Denmark 67 B7

Copiapó Chile 46 B3

Coppermine *see* Kuglukutuk

Coquimbo Chile 46 B3

Corabia Romania 90 B5

Coral Sea Pacific Ocean 130 E3

Coral Sea Islands *external territory* Australia, Coral Sea 130 E3

Corantijn *see* Courantyne

Cordillera Cantábrica *mountain range* Spain 74 D1

Córdoba Argentina 46 C3

Córdoba Spain 74 D4

Cordova Alaska, USA 18 D3

Corfu *see* Kérkyra

Corinth *see* Kórinthos

Corinth, Gulf of *see* Korinthiakós Kólpos

Corinto Nicaragua 34 C3

Cork Ireland 71 B6

Corner Brook Canada 21 G3

Coro Venezuela 40 D1

Coronel Oviedo Paraguay 44 B2

Corpus Christi Texas, USA 29 G5

Corrib, Lough *lake* Ireland 71 A5

Corrientes Argentina 46 D3

Corse *island* France *Eng.* Corsica 73 E7 84 D2

Corsica *see* Corse

Çorum Turkey 98 D2

Corvallis Oregon, USA 26 A3

Cosenza Italy 79 D6

Costa Blanca *coastal region* Spain 75 F4

Costa Brava *coastal region* Spain 75 H2

Costa Rica *country* Central America 34-35

Côte d'Ivoire *country* W Africa *Eng.* Ivory Coast 56 D4

Cottbus Germany 76 D4

Council Bluffs Iowa, USA 25 F4

Courantyne *river* Guyana /Suriname *var.* Corantijn 41 G3

Courland Lagoon *sea feature* Baltic Sea 88 B4

Coventry England, UK 71 D6

Covilhã Portugal 74 C3

Cowan, Lake *lake* Australia 129 C6

Cozumel, Isla de *island* Mexico 33 H3

Cracow *see* Kraków

Craiova Romania 90 B5

Cremona Italy 78 B2

Cres *island* Croatia 82 A3

Crescent City California, USA 26 A4

Crete *see* Kríti

Crete, Sea of *Mediterranean Sea Gk.* Kritikó Pélagos 87 D7

Crimea *see* Krym

Cristóbal Panama 48 A4

Croatia *country* SE Europe 82

Croker Island *island* Australia 128 E2

Crotone Italy 79 E6

Crozet Basin *undersea feature* Indian Ocean 123 B6

Crozet Islands *island group* Indian Ocean 123 B7

Crystal Brook Australia 131 B6

Cuanza *river* Angola 60 B2

Cuba *country* West Indies 36

Cubango *see* Okavango

Cúcuta Colombia 40 C2

Cuenca Ecuador 40 A5

Cuenca Spain 75 E3

Cuernavaca Mexico 33 E4

Cuiabá Brazil 43 E4

Culiacán Mexico 32 C3

Cumaná Venezuela 41 E1

Cumberland Maryland, USA 23 E4

Cunene *river* Angola/Namibia 60 B3

Cunnamulla Australia 131 C5

Curicó Chile 46 B4

Curitiba Brazil 44 D3

Cusco Peru *prev.* Cuzco 42 B4

Cuttack India 117 F5

Cuxhaven Germany 76 B3

Cuyuni *river* Guyana/Venezuela 41 F2

Cuzco *see* Cusco

Cyclades *see* Kykládes

Cymru *see* Wales

Cyprus *country* Mediterranean Sea 98 C5

Dhaka *capital of* Bangladesh *var.* Dacca 117 G4

Dhanbād India 117 F4

Dhrepano, Ákra *see* Drépano, Akrotírio

Diamantina Fracture Zone *tectonic feature* Indian Ocean 123 E6

Dickinson North Dakota, USA 24 D2

Diekirch Luxembourg 69 D7

Dieppe France 72 C3

Digul *River* Indonesia 121 H5

Dijon France 72 D4

Dikson Taymyrskiy (Dolgano-Nenetskiy) Russian Federation 137 H4

Dili *capital of* East Timor 121 F5

Dilling Sudan 54 B4

Dilolo Dem. Rep. Congo 59 D8

Dimashq *see* Damascus

Dimitrovo *see* Pernik

Dinant Belgium 69 C7

Dinaric Alps *mountains* Bosnia & Herzegovina/Croatia 82 B4

Diourbel Senegal 56 B3

Dirê Dawa Ethiopia 55 D5

Dirk Hartog *island* Australia 129 A5

Disappointment, Lake *salt lake* Australia 128 C4

Dispur India 117 G3

Divinópolis Brazil 45 F1

Diyarbakır Turkey 99 E4

Dkaraganda *see* Zhezkazgan

Djambala Congo 59 B6

Djibouti *country* E Africa 54

Djibouti *capital of* Djibouti *var.* Jibuti 54 D4

Dnieper *river* E Europe 63 F4

Dniester *river* Moldova/Ukraine 90 D3

Dnipropetrovs'k Ukraine 91 F3

Dobele Latvia *Ger.* Doblen 88 C3

Doberai, Jazirah *Peninsula* Indonesia 121 G4

Doblen *see* Dobele

Doboj Bosnia & Herzegovina 82 C3

Dobrich Bulgaria 86 E1

Dodecanese *see* Dodekánisos

Dodekánisos *islands* Greece *Eng.* Dodecanese 87 E6

Dodge City Kansas, USA 25 E5

Dodoma *capital of* Tanzania 55 C7

Doğu Karadeniz Dağları *mountains* Turkey *var.* Anadolu Dağları 99 E2

Doha *capital of* Qatar *Ar.* Ad Dawḥah 103 C5

Dolisie Congo 59 B6

Dolomites *see* Dolomitiche, Alpi

Dolomitiche, Alpi *mountains* Italy *Eng.* Dolomites 78 C2

Dolores Argentina 46 D4

Dolores Hidalgo Mexico 33 E4

Dominica *country* West Indies 37

Dominican Republic *country* West Indies 37

Don *river* Russian Federation 93 B6 96 A3

Donegal Bay *sea feature* Ireland 71 A5

Donets *river* Russian Federation/Ukraine 93 A6

Donets'k Ukraine 91 G3

Dongguan China 111 C6

Dongola Sudan 54 B3

Donostia *see* San Sebastián

Dordogne *river* France 73 B5

Dordrecht Netherlands 68 C4

Dorpat *see* Tartu

Dortmund Germany 76 B4

Dothan Alabama, USA 30 D3

Douai France 72 D3

Douala Cameroon 59 A5

Douglas UK 71 C5

Douglas Arizona, USA 28 C3

Dourados Brazil 44 C2

Douro *river* Portugal/Spain *Sp.* Duero 74 C2

Dover England, UK 71 E7

Dover Delaware, USA 23 F4

Drakensberg *mountain range* Lesotho/South Africa 60 D5

Drake Passage *sea feature* Atlantic Ocean/Pacific Ocean 39 C8

Dráma Greece 86 C3

Drammen Norway 67 B6

Drau *river* C Europe *var.* Drava 77 D7 82 C3

Drava *river* C Europe *var.* Drau 81 C7

Drépano, Akrotírio *coastal feature* Greece *var.* Dhrepano Ákra 86 C4

Dresden Germany 76 D4

Drina *river* Bosnia & Herzegovina/Serb. & Mon. (Yugo.) 82 D4

Drobeta-Turnu Severin Romania *prev.* Turnu Severin 90 B4

Dronning Maud Land *region* Antarctica 137 B1

Druskieniki *see* Druskininkai

Druskininkai Lithuania *Pol.* Druskieniki 89 B5

Dubayy United Arab Emirates 103 D5

Dubăsari Moldova 90 D3

Dubawnt *river* Canada 19 F4

Dubbo Australia 131 D6

Dublin *capital of* Ireland 71 B5

Dubrovnik Croatia 83 C5

Dubuque Iowa, USA 25 G3

Duero *river* Portugal/Spain *Port.* Douro 74 C2

Dugi Otok *island* Croatia 82 A4

Duisburg Germany 76 A4

Dulan China 108 D4

Duluth Minnesota, USA 25 F2

Dumfries Scotland, UK 70 C4

Düna *see* Western Dvina

Dünaburg *see* Daugavpils

Dundalk Ireland 71 B5

Dundee Scotland, UK 70 D3

Dunedin New Zealand 133 B7

Dunkerque France *Eng.* Dunkirk 72 C2

Dunkirk *see* Dunkerque

Duqm Oman 103 E6
Durango Mexico 32 D3
Durango Colorado, USA 24 C5
Durazno Uruguay 44 C5
Durban South Africa 60 E4
Durham North Carolina, USA 31 F1
Durrës Albania 83 C5
Dushanbe *capital of* Tajikistan *var.* Dyushambe, *prev.* Stalinabad 105 E3
Düsseldorf Germany 76 A4
Dutch Harbor Alaska, USA 18 B3
Dutch West Indies *see* Netherland Antilles
Dvinsk *see* Daugavpils
Dyushambe *see* Dushanbe
Dzaudzhikau *see* Vladikavkaz
Dzhalal-Abad Kyrgyzstan *Kir.* Jalal-Abad 105 F2
Dzhambul *see* Taraz
Dzhezkazgan *see* Zhezkazgan
Dzvina *see* Western Dvina

E

Eagle Pass Texas, USA 29 F4
East Cape *coastal feature* New Zealand 132 E2
East China Sea Pacific Ocean 111 E5
Easter Fracture Zone *tectonic feature* Pacific Ocean 135 G4
Easter Island *island* Pacific Ocean 135 F4
Eastern Ghats *mountain range* India 117 B5
Eastern Sierra Madre *see* Sierra Madre Oriental
East Falkland *island* Falkland Islands 47 D7
East Indiaman Ridge *undersea feature* Indian Ocean 23 D5
East Indies *island group* Asia 122 F4
East London South Africa 60 D5

Eastmain *river* Canada 20 D3
East Pacific Rise *undersea feature* Pacific Ocean 135 F4
East Siberian Sea *see* Vostochno-Sibirskoye More
East St Louis Illinois, USA 22 B4
East Timor *country* SE Asia 121
East Novaya Zemlya Trench *var.* Novaya Zemlya Trench. *Undersea feature* Kara Sea 137 H4
Eau Claire Wisconsin, USA 22 A2
Ebolowa Cameroon 59 B5
Ebro *river* Spain 75 F2
Ecuador *country* NW South America 40
Ede Netherlands 68 D3
Ede Nigeria 57 F4
Edgeøya *island* Svalbard 65 G2
Edinburgh Scotland, UK 70 C4
Edirne Turkey 98 A2
Edmonton Canada 19 E5
Edward, Lake *lake* Uganda/Dem. Rep. Congo 59 E6
Edwards Plateau *upland* S USA 29 F4
Efate *island* Vanuatu *prev.* Sandwich Island 124 D4
Effingham Illinois, USA 22 B4
Eforie-Sud Romania 90 D5
Egadi, Isole *island group* Italy 79 B6
Ege Denizi *see* Aegean Sea
Eger *see* Ohře
Egypt *country* NE Africa 54
Eighty Mile Beach *beach* Australia 128 C3
Eindhoven Netherlands 69 D5
Eisenstadt Austria 77 E6
Eivissa *island* Spain *Cast.* Ibiza 75 G4
Ejin Qi China 108 D3
Elat Israel 101 A7
Elâzığ Turkey 99 E3
Elba, Isola d' *island* Italy 78 B4
Elbasan Albania 83 D6
Elbe *river* Czech Republic/Germany 81 B5

Elbing *see* Elbląg
Elbląg Poland *Ger.* Elbing 80 D2
El'brus *peak* Russian Federation 93 A7
El Calafate Argentina *var.* Calafate 47 B7
Elche Spain 75 F4
Elda Spain 75 F4
Eldoret Kenya 55 C6
Eleuthera *island* Bahamas 36 C1
El Fasher Sudan *var.* Al Fāshir 54 A4
El Geneina Sudan 54 A4
Elgin Scotland, UK 70 C3
El Gîza Egypt *var.* Al Jīzah 54 B1
El Hank *cliff* Mauritania 56 D1
Elista Russian Federation 93 B6
El Khalîl *see* Hebron
El Khârga Egypt *var.* Al Khārijah 54 B2
Elko Nevada, USA 27 D5
Ellensburg Washington, USA 26 B2
Ellesmere Island *island* Canada 19 F1
Ellsworth Land *region* Antarctica 136 A3
El Minya Egypt 54 B2
Elmira New York, USA 23 E3
El Mreyyé *desert* Mauritania 56 D2
El Obeid Sudan 54 B4
El Paso Texas, USA 28 D3
El Puerto de Santa María Spain 74 D5
El Qâhira *see* Cairo
El Salvador *country* Central America 34
Eltanin Fracture Zone *tectonic feature* Pacific Ocean 135 E5
El Tigre Venezuela 41 E2
Ely Nevada USA 27 D5
Emden Germany 76 B3
Emerald Australia 130 D4
Emmen Netherlands 68 E2

F

Faxaflói *bay* Iceland 64 D5
Faya Chad 58 C2
Fayetteville Arkansas, USA 30 A1
Fayetteville North Carolina, USA 31 F1
Fdérik Mauritania 56 C1
Fear, Cape *coastal feature* North Carolina, USA 31 G2
Fehmarn *island* Germany 76 C2
Fehmarn Belt *sea feature* Germany 76 C2
Feira de Santana Brazil 43 G3
Fellin *see* Viljandi
Fénérive *see* Fenoarivo
Fengtien *see* Liaoning
Fenoarivo Madagascar *prev.* Fénérive 61 G3
Fens, The *wetland* England, UK 71 E6
Fergana *see* Farg'ona
Ferrara Italy 78 C3
Ferrol Spain 74 C1
Fès Morocco *Eng.* Fez 52 C2
Feyzäbäd Afghanistan *var.* Faizabad 105 E3
Fez *see* Fès
Fianarantsoa Madagascar 61 G3
Fier Albania 83 D6
Figueira da Foz Portugal 74 C3
Figueres Spain 75 G2
Figuig Morocco 52 D2
Fiji *country* Pacific Ocean 127
Finland *country* N Europe 66-67
Finland, Gulf of *sea feature* Baltic Sea 67 E6
Fiordland *physical region* New Zealand 133 A7
Firenze Italy *Eng.* Florence 78 C3
Fishguard Wales, UK 71 C6
Fitzroy *river* Australia 128 C3
Fitzroy Crossing Australia 128 D3
Fiume *see* Rijeka
Flagstaff Arizona, USA 28 B2
Flanders *region* Belgium 69 A5

Flensburg Germany 76 B2
Flinders Island *island* Australia 131 C7
Flinders Ranges *mountain range* Australia 131 B6
Flinders River *river* Australia 130 C3
Flin Flon Canada 19 F5
Flint Michigan, USA 22 C3
Flint Island *island* Kiribati 127 H4
Florence Alabama, USA 30 C2
Florence South Carolina, USA 31 F2
Florence *see* Firenze
Florencia Colombia 40 B3
Flores Guatemala 34 B1
Flores *island* Indonesia 121 E5
Flores, Laut *see* Flores Sea
Flores Sea Pacific Ocean *Ind.* Laut Flores 121 E5
Florianópolis Brazil 44 D3
Florida *state* USA 31 E4
Florida, Straits of *sea feature* Bahamas/USA 31 F5 36 B1
Florida Keys *island chain* Florida, USA 31 F5
Flórina Greece 86 B3
Flushing *see* Vlissingen
Foča Bosnia & Herzegovina 82 C4
Focşani Romania 90 C4
Foggia Italy 79 D5
Fogo *island* Cape Verde 56 A3
Foligno Italy 78 C4
Fongafale *capital of* Tuvalu 127 E3
Fonseca, Gulf of *sea feature* El Salvador/Honduras 34 C3
Forlì Italy 78 C3
Formentera *island* Spain 75 G4
Former Yugoslav Republic of Macedonia *see* Macedonia
Formosa Argentina 46 D2
Formosa *see* Taiwan
Formosa Strait *see* Taiwan Strait
Fóroyar *see* Faeroe Islands

Fortaleza Brazil 43 H2
Fortescue River *river* Australia 128 B4
Fort Collins Colorado, USA 24 D4
Fort-de-France *capital of* Martinique 37 G4
Forth *river* Scotland, UK 70 C4
Forth, Firth of *inlet* Scotland, UK 70 D4
Fort Lauderdale Florida, USA 31 F5
Fort McMurray Canada 19 F4
Fort Myers Florida, USA 31 E4
Fort Peck Lake *lake* Montana, USA 24 C1
Fort Saint John Canada 19 E4
Fort Smith Canada 19 E4
Fort Smith Arkansas, USA 30 A1
Fort Wayne Indiana, USA 22 C4
Fort William Scotland, UK 70 C4
Fort Worth Texas, USA 29 G3
Foveaux Strait *sea feature* New Zealand 133 A7
Fox Glacier New Zealand 133 B6
Franca Brazil 45 E1
France *country* W Europe 72-73
Francistown Botswana 60 D3
Frankfort Kentucky, USA 22 C5
Frankfurt *see* Frankfurt am Main
Frankfurt am Main Germany *Eng.* Frankfurt 77 B5
Frankfurt an der Oder Germany 76 D5
Fränkische Alb *mountains* Germany 77 C6
Frantsa-Iosifa, Zemlya *islands* Russian Federation *Eng.* Franz Josef Land 137 G4
Franz Josef Land *see* Frantsa-Iosifa, Zemlya
Fraser Island *island* Australia 130 E4
Frauenburg *see* Saldus
Fray Bentos Uruguay 44 B5
Fredericksburg Virginia, USA 23 E4

Fredericton Canada 21 F4
Frederikshavn Denmark 67 B7
Fredrikstad Norway 67 B6
Freeport Bahamas 36 C1
Freeport Texas, USA 29 G4
Freetown *capital of*
Sierra Leone 56 C4
Freiburg im Breisgau Germany
77 B6
Fremantle Australia 129 B6
French Guiana *external*
territory France, N South
America 41
French Polynesia *external*
territory France, Pacific
Ocean 135 E3
French Southern and Antarctic
Territories *French overseas*
territory Indian Ocean *Fr.*
Terres Australes et
Antarctiques Françaises 123 C7
Fresnillo Mexico 32 D1
Fresno California, USA 27 B6
Frome, Lake *salt lake* Australia
131 B5
Frunze *see* Bishkek
Fu-chien *see* Fujian
Fuerte Olimpo Paraguay 44 B1
Fuerteventura *island* Spain
52 A3
Fuhkien *see* Fujian
Fujian *province* China *var.* Fu-
chien, Fuhkien, Fukien, Min
111 D6
Fukien *see* Fujian
Fukui Japan 113 C5
Fukuoka Japan 113 A6
Fukushima Japan 112 D4
Fulda Germany 77 C5
Fünfkirchen *see* Pécs
Fushun China 110 D3
Furnas, Represa de *Reservoir*
Brazil 45 E1
Fuxin China 110 D3
Fuzhou China 111 D6
FYR Macedonia *see* Macedonia

––––––– **G** –––––––

Gaalkacyo Somalia 55 E5
Gabès Tunisia 53 E2

Gabon *country* W Africa 59
Gaborone *capital of* Botswana
60 D4
Gabrovo Bulgaria 86 D2
Gadsden Alabama, USA 30 D2
Gaeta, Golfo di *sea feature*
Italy 79 C5
Gafsa Tunisia 53 E2
Gagnoa Côte d'Ivoire 56 D5
Gagra Georgia 99 E1
Gairdner, Lake *lake* Australia
131 B6
Galapagos Fracture Zone
tectonic feature Pacific Ocean
135 F3
Galapagos Islands *islands*
Ecuador, Pacific Ocean *var.*
Tortoise Islands, *Sp.*
Archipiélago de Colón
135 G3
Galapagos Rise *undersea*
feature Pacific Ocean 135 G3
Galaţi Romania 90 D4
Galesburg Illinois, USA 22 B4
Galicia *region* Spain 74 C1
Galilee, Sea of *see* Tiberias, Lake
Galle Sri Lanka 115 E4
Gallego Rise *undersea feature*
Pacific Ocean 135 F3
Gallipoli Italy 79 E5
Gällivare Sweden 66 D3
Gallup New Mexico, USA
28 C2
Galveston Texas, USA 29 G4
Galway Ireland 71 A5
Gambia *country* W Africa 56
Gambia *River* Africa 56 C3
Gambier, Îles *island group*
French Polynesia 135 E4
Gan *see* Gansu
Gan *see* Jiangxi
Gäncä Azerbaijan *Rus.*
Gyandzha, *prev.* Kirovabad,
Yelisavetpol 99 G2
Gand *see* Gent
Gander Canada 21 H3
Gandia Spain 75 F3
Ganges *river* S Asia 116 F4
Ganges Fan *Undersea feature*
Bay of Bengal 122 D3

Ganges, Mouths of the
wetlands Bangladesh/India
117 G4
Gangtok India 117 G3
Gansu *province* China *var.* Gan,
Kansu 111 B5
Gao Mali 57 E3
Gaoual Guinea 56 C4
Gar China 108 A4
Garagum Kanaly *canal*
Turkmenistan *prev.*
Karakumskiy Kanal 104 C3
Garagum *desert* Turkmenistan
var. Kara Kum, Karakumy
104 C2
Garda, Lago di *lake* Italy 78 B2
Gardēz Afghanistan 105 E4
Garissa Kenya 55 C6
Garmo Peak *see* Communism
Peak
Garonne *river* France 73 B5
Garoowe Somalia 55 E5
Garoua Cameroon 58 B4
Gary Indiana, USA 22 B3
Gaspé Canada 21 F4
Gastonia North Carolina, USA
31 E1
Gävle Sweden 67 C5
Gaya India 117 F4
Gaza Gaza Strip 101 A6
Gazandzhyk *see* Bereket
Gazanjyk *see* Bereket
Gaza Strip *disputed territory*
SW Asia 101 A6
Gaziantep Turkey *prev.* Aintab
98 F4
Gazimağusa Cyprus *var.*
Famagusta *Gk.* Ammochostos
98 C5
Gdańsk Poland *Ger.* Danzig
80 C2
Gdingen *see* Gdynia
Gdynia Poland *Ger.* Gdingen
80 C2
Gedaref Sudan 54 C4
Geelong Australia 131 C7
Gēkdepe *see* Gökdepe
Gemena Dem. Rep. Congo
59 C5
General Eugenio A. Garay
Paraguay 44 A1

General Santos Philippines 121 F3
Geneva see Genève
Geneva, Lake lake France/ Switzerland Fr. Lac Léman, var. Le Léman, Ger. Genfer See 77 A7
Genève Switzerland Eng. Geneva 77 A7
Genfer See see Geneva, Lake
Genk Belgium 69 D5
Genoa see Genova
Genoa Italy see Genoa 78 B3
Genova Italy see Genoa 78 B3
Genova, Golfo di sea feature Italy 78 B3
Gent Belgium Fr. Gand, Eng. Ghent 69 B5
Geok-Tepe see Gökdepe
George South Africa 60 D5
George V Land physical region Antarctica 136 C4
Georgenburg see Jurbarkas
George Town capital of Cayman Islands 36 B3
Georgetown capital of Guyana 41 G2
George Town Malaysia 120 B3
Georgia country SW Asia 99 F2
Georgia state USA 31 E3
Gera Germany 76 C4
Geraldton Australia 129 A5
Gereshk Afghanistan 104 D5
Germany country W Europe 76-77
Gerona see Girona
Getafe Spain 75 E3
Gettysburg Pennsylvania, USA 23 E4
Gevgelija Macedonia 83 E6
Ghana country W Africa 57
Ghanzi Botswana 60 C3
Ghardaïa Algeria 52 D2
Gharyān Libya 53 F2
Ghaznī Afghanistan 105 E4
Ghent see Gent
Gibraltar external territory UK, SW Europe 74 D5
Gibson Desert desert region Australia 128 C4
Gijón Spain var. Xixón 74 D1

Gilbert Islands see Tungaru
Gilbert River river Australia 130 C3
Gillette Wyoming, USA 24 C3
Gingin Australia 129 B6
Girin see Jilin
Girne Cyprus var. Kyrenia 98 C5
Girona Spain var. Gerona 75 G2
Gisborne New Zealand 132 E3
Giurgiu Romania 90 C5
Gjirokastër Albania 83 D6
Gjøvik Norway 67 B5
Glasgow Scotland, UK 70 C4
Gleiwitz see Gliwice
Glendale Arizona, USA 28 B2
Glendive Montana, USA 24 D2
Gliwice Poland Ger. Gleiwitz 81 C5
Gloucester England, UK 71 D6
Glubokoye see Hlybokaye
Gobi desert China/Mongolia 108 D3
Godāveri river India 106 B3 115 E1
Godoy Cruz Argentina 46 B4
Godthåb see Nuuk
Godwin Austin, Mount see K2
Goiânia Brazil 43 F4
Gökdepe Turkmenistan prev. Geok-Tepe, prev. Gëkdepe 104 B3
Golan Heights disputed territory SW Asia 100 B4
Gold Coast coastal region Australia 131 E5
Goldingen see Kuldīga
Golmud China 108 D4
Goma Dem. Rep. Congo 59 E6
Gomel' see Homyel'
Gómez Palacio Mexico 32 D2
Gonaïves Haiti 36 D3
Gonder Ethiopia 54 C4
Gongola river Nigeria 57 G4
Good Hope, Cape of coastal feature South Africa 60 C5
Goondiwindi Australia 131 D5
Goose Lake lake W USA 26 B4
Goré Chad 58 C4

Gorē Ethiopia 55 C5
Gore New Zealand 133 B7
Gorgān Iran 102 D3
Gorki see Horki
Gor'kiy see Nizhniy Novgorod
Gorlovka see Horlivka
Gorontalo Indonesia 121 E4
Gorzów Wielkopolski Poland Ger. Landsberg 80 B3
Gospić Croatia 82 B3
Gosford Australia 131 D6
Gostivar Macedonia 83 D5
Göteborg Sweden 67 B7
Gotel Mountains mountain range Nigeria 57 G4
Gotland island Sweden 67 C7
Gotō-rettō island group Japan 113 A6
Göttingen Germany 76 C4
Gouda Netherlands 68 C4
Gough Island external territory UK, Atlantic Ocean 49 D7
Gouin, Réservoir Reservoir Canada 20 D4
Gouré Niger 57 G3
Governador Valadares Brazil 43 G4 45 F1
Govĭ Altayn Nuruu mountain range Mongolia 109 E3
Gozo island Malta 79 C7
Grafton Australia 131 E5
Grampian Mountains mountains Scotland, UK 70 C3
Granada Nicaragua 34 D3
Granada Spain 75 E4
Gran Canaria island Spain 52 A3
Gran Chaco region C South America 38 C4 44 A2 46 D2
Grand Bahama island Bahamas 36 C1
Grand Banks undersea feature Atlantic Ocean 48 B3
Grand Canyon valley SW USA 28 B1
Grande, Rio river Brazil 45 E1
Grande, Rio River Mexico/USA 17 B6

Grande Comore *island* Comoros 61 F2

Grande Prairie Canada 19 E4

Grand Erg Occidental *desert region* Algeria 52 D2

Grand Erg Oriental *desert region* Algeria/Tunisia 53 E3

Grand Falls Canada 21 G3

Grand Forks North Dakota, USA 25 E1

Grand Junction Colorado, USA 24 C4

Grand Rapids Michigan, USA 22 C3

Graudenz *see* Grudziądz

Graz Austria 77 E7

Great Abaco *island* Bahamas 36 C1

Great Ararat *see* Ararat, Mount

Great Australian Bight *sea feature* Australia 129 D6

Great Barrier Island *island* N NZ 132 D2

Great Barrier Reef *coral reef* Coral Sea 130 C4

Great Basin *region* USA 26 D4

Great Bear Lake *lake* Canada 19 E3

Great Dividing Range *mountain range* Australia 130-131

Great Exhibition Bay *inlet* New Zealand 132 C1

Great Wall of China *ancient monument* China 110 C4

Greater Antarctica *region* Antarctica 136 C3

Greater Antilles *island group* West Indies 36 C3

Great Exuma Island *island* Bahamas 36 C2

Great Falls Montana, USA 24 B1

Great Hungarian Plain *plain* SE Europe *Hung.* Alföld 81 D7

Great Inagua *island* Bahamas 36 D2

Great Khingan Range *see* Da Hinggan Ling

Great Lakes, The *lakes* N America *see* Erie, Huron, Michigan, Ontario, Superior 17 C5

Great Nicobar *island* India 115 H3

Great Plain of China *region* China 106 E2

Great Plains *region* N America 16-17 C5

Great Rift Valley *valley* E Africa/SW Asia 55 C6

Great Salt Desert *see* Kavīr, Dasht-e

Great Salt Lake *salt lake* Utah, USA 24 B3

Great Sand Sea *desert region* Egypt/Libya 53 H3

Great Sandy Desert *desert* Australia 128 C4

Great Sandy Desert *see* Ar Rub' al Khali

Great Slave Lake *lake* Canada 19 E4

Great Victoria Desert *desert* Australia 129 C5

Greece *country* SE Europe 86-87

Green Bay Wisconsin, USA 22 B2

Greenland *external territory* Denmark, Atlantic Ocean *var.* Grønland 64

Greenland Sea Atlantic Ocean 65 F2

Greenock Scotland, UK 70 C4

Greensboro North Carolina, USA 31 F1

Greenville South Carolina, USA 31 E2

Greifswald Germany 76 D2

Gregory Range *mountain range* Australia 130 C3

Grenada *country* West Indies 37 G5

Grenoble France 73 D5

Greymouth New Zealand 133 B5

Grey Range *mountain range* Australia 124 B4

Grimsby England, UK 71 E5

Groningen Netherlands 68 E1

Grønland *see* Greenland

Groote Eylandt *island* Australia 130 B2

Grootfontein Namibia 60 C3

Grosseto Italy 78 B4

Grosskanizsa *see* Nagykanizsa

Groznyy Russian Federation 93 B7 96 A4

Grudziądz Poland *Ger.* Graudenz 80 C3

Grünberg in Schlesien *see* Zielona Góra

Guadalajara Mexico 32 D4

Guadalcanal *island* Solomon Islands 124 C3

Guadalquivir *river* Spain 74 D4

Guadeloupe *external territory* France, West Indies 37 G4

Guadiana *river* Portugal/Spain 74 C4

Gualeguaychú Argentina 46 D4

Guam *external territory* USA, Pacific Ocean 126 B1

Guanare Venezuela 40 D1

Guanare *river* Venezuela 40 D2

Guangdong *province* China *var.* Kuang-tung, Kwangtung, Yue 111 C6

Guangxi *autonomous region* China *var.* Kwangsi 111 B6

Guangzhou China *Eng.* Canton 111 C6

Guantánamo Cuba 36 D3

Guaporé *River* Bolivia/Brazil 32 D3

Guarapuava Brazil 44 D3

Guatemala *country* Central America 34

Guatemala Basin *undersea feature* Pacific Ocean 135 G3

Guatemala City *capital of* Guatemala 34 B2

Guaviare *river* Colombia 40 D3

Guayaquil Ecuador 40 A4

Guayaquil, Golfo de *sea feature* Ecuador/Peru 40 A5

Guernsey *island* Channel Islands 71 D8

Güney Dogu Toroslar *mountain range* SE Turkey 99 F3

Guiana Highlands *upland* N South America 38 C2

Guider Cameroon 58 B4

Guimarães Portugal 74 C2

Guinea *country* W Africa 56
Guinea, Gulf of *sea feature* Atlantic Ocean 49 D5
Guinea-Bissau *country* W Africa 56
Guiyang China 111 B6
Guizhou *province* China *var.* Kuei-chou, Kweichow, Qian 111 B6
Gujarāt *state* India 116 C4
Gujrānwāla Pakistan 116 C2
Gujrāt Pakistan 116 C2
Gulf, The *sea feature* Arabian Sea *var.* Persian Gulf 122 B2
Gulfport Mississippi, USA 30 C3
Gulu Uganda 55 B6
Gumbinnen *see* Gusev
Gunnbjørn Fjeld *mountain* Greenland 64 D4
Gurbantünggüt Shamo *desert* China 108 C2
Guri, Embalse de *Reservoir* Venezuela 41 E2
Gusau Nigeria 57 F3
Gusev Kaliningrad, Russian Federation *prev.* Gumbinnen 88 B4
Gushgy Turkmenistan *prev.* Kushka 104 C4
Guwāhāti India 117 G3
Guyana *country* NE South America 41
Gwalior India 116 D3
Gyandzha *see* Gäncä
Gyangzê China 108 C5
Győr Hungary *Ger.* Raab 81 C6
Gyumri Armenia *Rus.* Kumayri, *prev.* Leninakan, Aleksandropol' 99 F2
Gyzylarbat *see* Serdar

——— **H** ———

Ha'apai Group *islands* Tonga 127 F5
Haapsalu Estonia *Ger.* Hapsal 88 C2
Haarlem Netherlands 68 C3

Haast New Zealand 133 B6
Hachijō-jima *island* Japan 113 D5
Hachinohe Japan 112 D3
Hadejia *river* Nigeria 57 G3
Ḥaḍramawt *Mountain range* Yemen 103 C7
Hagåtña Guam 126 B1
Hague, The *see* 's-Gravenhage
Haicheng China 110 D4
Haifa Israel *Heb.* Ḥefa 85 G4
Ḥā'il Saudi Arabia 102 B4
Hailar China 109 F1
Hainan *island* China *var.* Hainan Dao 106 D3 111 C8
Hainan *province* China *var.* Qiong 111 C7
Hainan Dao *see* Hainan Dao
Hai Phong Vietnam 118 D3
Haiti *country* West Indies 36
Hajdarken *see* Khaydarkan
Hakodate Japan 112 D3
Ḥalab Syria 100 B2
Ḥalāniyāt, Juzur al *Island group* Oman 103 D6
Halden Norway 67 B6
Halfmoon Bay New Zealand 133 A7
Halifax Canada 21 F4
Halle Germany 76 C4
Hallein Austria 77 D7
Halls Creek Australia 128 D3
Halmahera, Pulau *island* Indonesia 121 F3
Halmahera Sea *Sea* Indonesia 121 F4
Halmstad Sweden 67 B7
Hamada Japan 113 B5
Hamadān Iran 102 C3
Ḥamāh Syria 100 B3
Hamamatsu Japan 113 C5
Hamar Norway 67 B5
Hamburg Germany 76 C3
Hämeenlinna Finland 67 D5
HaMelaḥ, Yam *see* Dead Sea
Hamersley Range *mountain range* Australia 128 B4
Hamhŭng North Korea 110 E4

Hami China 108 C3
Hamilton Canada 20 D5
Hamilton New Zealand 132 D3
Hamm Germany 76 B4
Hammerfest Norway 66 D2
Handan China 110 C4
HaNegev *desert region* Israel *Eng.* Negev 101 A6
Hangayn Nuruu *mountain range* Mongolia 108 D2
Hangzhou China 111 D5
Hannover Germany *Eng.* Hanover 76 B4
Hanoi *capital of* Vietnam 118 D3
Hanover *see* Hannover
Hanzhong China 111 B5
Hapsal *see* Haapsalu
Ḥaraḍ Yemen 103 C5
Harare *capital of* Zimbabwe 61 E3
Harbin China 110 E3
Hargeysa Somalia 55 D5
Hari *river* Indonesia 120 B4
Harirūd *river* C Asia 104 D4
Harper Liberia 56 D5
Harrisburg Pennsylvania, USA 23 E4
Harstad Norway 66 C2
Hartford Connecticut, USA 23 G3
Hasselt Belgium 69 D5
Hastings New Zealand 132 E4
Hastings Nebraska, USA 24 D4
Hatay *see* Antakya
Hatteras, Cape *coastal feature* North Carolina, USA 31 G1
Hattiesburg Mississippi, USA 30 C3
Hat Yai Thailand 119 C7
Haugesund Norway 67 A6
Hauraki Gulf *gulf* New Zealand 132 D2
Havana *capital of* Cuba *Sp.* La Habana 36 B2
Havelock North Carolina, USA 31 G1
Havre Montana, USA 24 C1

Havre-Saint-Pierre Canada 21 F3

Hawaii *state* USA 135 E2

Hawaiian Islands *islands* USA 125 F1

Hawaiian Ridge *undersea feature* Pacific Ocean 134 D2

Hawera New Zealand 132 D4

Hawke Bay *bay* New Zealand 132 E4

Hawlēr *see* Arbīl

Hawthorne Nevada, USA 27 C6

Hay River Canada 19 E4

Hays Kansas, USA 25 E4

Hazar Turkmenistan *prev.* Cheleken 104 A2

Heard & McDonald Islands *islands* Indian Ocean 123 C7

Hebei *province* China *var.* Hopeh, Hopei, Ji; *prev.* Chihli 110 C4

Hebron West Bank *var.* Al Khalīl, El Khalil, *Heb.* Hevron 101 D7

Heerenveen Netherlands 68 D2

Heerlen Netherlands 69 D6

Hefa Israel *prev.* Haifa 101 A5

Hefei China 111 D5

Hei *see* Heilongjiang

Heidelberg Germany 77 B5

Heilbronn Germany 77 B5

Heilongjiang *province* China *var.* Hei, Hei-lung-chiang 110 E3

Hei-lung-chiang *see* Heilongjiang

Helena Montana, USA 24 B2

Hells Canyon *valley* Idaho/Oregon USA 26 C3

Helmand *river* Afghanistan 104 C5

Helmond Netherlands 69 D5

Helsingborg Sweden 67 B7

Helsinki *capital of* Finland 67 D6

Henan *province* China *var.* Honan, Yu 111 C5

Hengduan Shan *mountain range* China 111 A6

Hengelo Netherlands 68 E3

Hengyang China 111 C6

Henzada Myanmar 118 A4

Herāt Afghanistan 104 C4

Hermansverk Norway 67 A5

Hermosillo Mexico 32 B2

Herning Denmark 67 A7

Heywood Islands *island group* Australia 128 C3

Hiiumaa *island* Estonia *Ger.* Dagden, *Swed.* Dagö 88 C2

Hildesheim Germany 76 C4

Hilversum Netherlands 68 C3

Himalayas *mountain range* S Asia 106 B2

Himora Ethiopia 54 C4

Ḥimṣ Syria 100 B3

Hinchinbrook Island *island* Australia 130 D3

Hindu Kush *mountain range* C Asia 105 E4

Hiroshima Japan 113 B5

Hitachi Japan 112 D4

Hjørring Denmark 67 A7

Hlybokaye Belarus *Rus.* Glubokoye 89 D5

Hobart Tasmania 131 C8

Hobbs New Mexico, USA 29 E3

Hồ Chi Minh Vietnam *var.* Ho Chi Minh City, *prev.* Saigon 119 E6

Ho Chi Minh City *see* Hồ Chi Minh

Hodeida *see* Al Ḥudaydah

Hoek van Holland Netherlands 68 B4

Hoggar *see* Ahaggar

Hohe Tauern *mountain range* Austria 77 C7

Hohhot China 109 F3

Hokitika New Zealand 133 B5

Hokkaidō *island* Japan 112 D2

Holguín Cuba 36 C2

Holland *see* Netherlands

Hollabrunn Austria 77 E6

Holon Israel 101 A5

Holyhead Wales, UK 71 C5

Hombori Mopti, Mali 57 E3

Homyel' Belarus *Rus.* Gomel' 89 E7

Honan *see* Henan

Honduras *country* Central America 34-35

Honduras, Gulf of *sea feature* Caribbean Sea 34 C2

Hønefoss Norway 67 B6

Hồng Gai Vietnam 118 E3

Hong Kong China *var.* Xianggang 111 C6

Honiara *capital of* Solomon Islands 126 C3

Honshū *island* Japan 112 D3

Hoorn Netherlands 68 C2

Hopa Turkey 99 E2

Hopedale Canada 21 F2

Hopeh *see* Hebei

Hopei *see* Hebei

Hopkinsville Kentucky, USA 22 B5

Horki Belarus *Rus.* Gorki 89 E5

Horlivka Ukraine *Rus.* Gorlovka 90 G3

Horn, Cape *see* Hornos, Cabo

Hornos, Cabo *Eng* Cape Horn *coastal feature* Chile 47 C8

Horsham Australia 131 C7

Hospitalet *see* L'Hospitalet de Llobregat

Hot Springs Arkansas, USA 30 B2

Houston Texas, USA 29 G4

Hovd Mongolia 108 C2

Hövsgöl Nuur *lake* Mongolia 108 D1

Hradec Králové Czech Republic *Ger.* Königgrätz 81 B5

Hrodna Belarus *Rus.* Grodno 89 B5

Huacho Peru 42 A3

Huainan China 111 D5

Huambo Angola 60 B2

Huancayo Peru 42 B3

Huang He *river* China *Eng.* Yellow River 110 C4

Huánuco Peru 42 B3

Huaraz Peru 42 B3

Hubei *province* China 111 C5

Hubli India 114 C2

Hudson NE USA 23 F3

Hudson Bay *sea feature* Canada 16 C4

Hudson Strait *sea feature* Canada 19 H3

Huê Vietnam 118 E4

Huehuetenango Guatemala 34 B2

Huelva Spain 74 C4

Huesca Spain 75 F2

Hughenden Australia 130 C4

Hull *see* Kingston upon Hull

Hulun Nur *lake* China 109 F1

Humboldt *river* W USA 27 C5

Hunan *province* China var. Xiang 111 C6

Hungarian Plain *plain* C Europe 85 E2

Hungary *country* C Europe 81

Huntington Beach California, USA 27 C8

Huntington West Virginia, USA 22 D5

Huntsville Alabama, USA 30 D2

Hurghada Egypt 54 B2

Huron, Lake *lake* Canada/USA 22 D2

Hurunui *river* New Zealand 133 C5

Húsavík Iceland 65 E4

Huvadhu Atoll *island* Maldives 114 C5

Hvar *island* Croatia 82 B4

Hyargas Nuur *lake* Mongolia 108 D2

Hyderābād India 114 D1 116 B3

Hyères, Îles d' *islands* France 73 D6

──────── I ────────

Iaşi Romania 90 D3

Ibadan Nigeria 57 F4

Ibagué Colombia 40 B3

Ibarra Ecuador 40 A4

Iberian Peninsula *peninsula* SW Europe 84

Ibérico, Sistema *Mountain range* Spain 75 F2

Ibiza *see* Eivissa

Ica Peru 42 B4

İçel *see* Mersin

Iceland *country* Atlantic Ocean 65 E4

Idaho *state* USA 26

Idaho Falls Idaho, USA 26 E3

Idfu Egypt 54 B2

Idlib Syria 100 B2

Ieper Belgium *Fr.* Ypres 69 A6

Ifôghas, Adrar des *upland* Mali var. Adrar des Iforas 57 F2

Iforas, Adrar des *see* Ifôghas, Adrar des

Iglau *see* Jihlava

Iglesias Italy 79 A5

Iguaçu *River* Argentina/Brazil 44 C3

Iguîdi, 'Erg *Desert* Algeria/Mauritania 56 D1

Ihosy Madagascar 61 G4

Iisalmi Finland 66 E4

IJssel *river* Netherlands 68 D3

IJsselmeer *lake* Netherlands *prev.* Zuider Zee 68 D2

Ikaría *island* Greece 87 D5

Iki *island* Japan 113 A6

Ilagan Philippines 121 E1

Ilebo Dem. Rep. Congo 59 C6

Ili *River* China/Kazakhstan 94 D3

Iligan Philippines 121 F2

Illapel Chile 46 B3

Illinois *state* USA 22 B4

Iloilo Philippines 121 E2

Ilorin Nigeria 57 F4

İluh *see* Batman

Imatra Finland 67 E5

Imperatriz Brazil 43 F2

Impfondo Congo 59 C5

Imphāl India 117 H4

Independence Missouri, USA 25 F4

India *country* S Asia 114-115, 116-117

Indian Ocean 122-123

Indiana *state* USA 22 C4

Indianapolis Indiana, USA 22 C4

Indigirka *river* Russian Federation 95 F2

Indonesia *country* SE Asia 120-121

Indonesian Borneo *see* Kalimantan

Indore India 116 D4

Indus *river* S Asia 116 C1

Indus Cone *see.* Indus Fan

Indus Fan *var.* Indus Cone. *Undersea feature* Arabian Sea 122 B3

Indus, Mouths of the *wetlands* Pakistan 116 B4

Ingolstadt Germany 77 C6

Inguri *see* Enguri

Inhambane Mozambique 61 E4

Inn *river* C Europe 77 D6

Innaanganeq *headland* Greenland 64 C1

Inner Islands *islands* Seychelles 61 H1

Inner Mongolia *autonomous region* China 109 F3

Innsbruck Austria 77 C7

I-n-Sâkâne, Erg *Desert* Mali 57 E2

I-n-Salah Algeria 52 D3

Insein Myanmar 118 B4

Inukjuak Canada 20 D2

Inuvik Canada 19 E3

Invercargill New Zealand 133 A7

Inverness Scotland, UK 70 C3

Investigator Ridge *undersea feature* Indian Ocean 122 D4

Ioánnina Greece 86 A4

Ionian Islands *see* Iónioi Nísoi

Ionian Sea Mediterranean Sea 87 A6

Iónioi Nísoi *island group* Greece *Eng.* Ionian Islands 87 A5

Íos *island* Greece 87 D6

Iowa *state* USA 25 F3

Ipoh Malaysia 120 B3

Ipswich England, UK 71 E6

Iqaluit Canada 19 H3

Iquique Chile 46 B1

Iquitos Peru 42 B2

Irákleio Greece 87 D7

Iran *country* SW Asia 102-103

Jibuti see Djibouti
Jiddah Saudi Arabia *Eng.* Jedda 103 A5
Jiftlik Post West Bank 101 D7
Jihlava Czech Republic *Ger.* Iglau 81 B5
Jilin *province* China *var.* Chi-lin, Girin, Ji, Kirin 110 E3
Jilin China 110 E3
Jima Ethiopia 55 C5
Jin see Shanxi
Jinan China 111 C4
Jingdezhen China 111 D5
Jinhua China 111 D5
Jining China 109 F3
Jinotega Nicaragua 34 D3
Jinsha Jiang *river* China 108 D5
Jinzhou China 110 D4
Jīzān Saudi Arabia 103 B6
João Pessoa Brazil 43 H3
Jodhpur India 116 C3
Joensuu Finland 67 E5
Johannesburg South Africa 60 D4
Johnston Atoll *US unincorporated territory* Pacific Ocean 125 E1
Johor Bahru Malaysia 120 C3
Joinville Brazil 44 D3
Joliet Illinois, USA 22 B3
Jönköping Sweden 67 B7
Jonquière Canada 21 E4
Jordan *country* SW Asia 100–101
Jordan *river* SW Asia 101 B5
Joseph Bonaparte Gulf *gulf* Australia 128 D2
Jos Plateau *upland* Nigeria 57 G4
Juan Fernandez, Islas *islands* Chile 46 A4
Juàzeiro Brazil 43 G3
Juàzeiro do Norte Brazil 43 G3
Juba Sudan 55 B5
Júcar *river* Spain 75 E3
Judenburg Austria 77 D7
Juigalpa Nicaragua 34 D3
Juiz de Fora Brazil 43 G5 45 F2
Juneau Alaska, USA 18 D4

Junin Argentina 46 D4
Jura *mountains* France/Switzerland 77 A7
Jura *island* Scotland, UK 70 B4
Jurbarkas Lithuania *Ger.* Jurburg, *var.* Georgenburg 88 B4
Jurburg see Jurbarkas
Juruá *river* Brazil/Peru 42 C2
Juticalpa Honduras 34 D2
Jutland see Jylland
Juventud, Isla de la *island* Cuba 36 B2
Jylland *peninsula* Denmark *Eng.* Jutland 67 A7
Jyväskylä Finland 67 D5

K

K2 *peak* China/Pakistan *Eng.* Mount Godwin Austen 116 D1
Kaachka see Kaka
Kaahka see Kaka
Kabale Uganda 55 B6
Kabinda Dem. Rep. Congo 59 D7
Kābol see Kābul
Kābul *capital of* Afghanistan *Per.* Kābol 105 E4
Kachch, Gulf of *sea feature* Arabian Sea 116 B4
Kachch, Rann of *wetland* India/Pakistan *var.* Rann of Kutch 116 B4
Kadugli Sudan 54 B4
Kaduna Nigeria 57 G4
Kaédi Mauritania 56 C3
Kâghet *Physical region* Mauritania 56 D1
Kagoshima Japan 113 A6
Kahramanmaraş Turkey *var.* Marash, Maraş 98 D4
Kai, Kepulauan *island group* Indonesia 121 G4
Kaifeng China 111 C5
Kaikohe New Zealand 132 C2
Kaikoura New Zealand 133 C5
Kainji Reservoir *Reservoir* Nigeria 57 F4

Kairouan Tunisia 53 E1
Kaiserslautern Germany 77 B5
Kaitaia New Zealand 132 C2
Kajaani Finland 66 E4
Kaka Turkmenistan *prev.* Kaahka, *var.* Kaachka 104 C3
Kakhovka Ukraine 91 F4
Kakhovs'ka Vodoskhovyshche *Reservoir* Ukraine 91 F3
Kalahari Desert *desert* southern Africa 60 C4
Kalamariá Greece 86 C3
Kalámata Greece 87 B6
Kalāt Afghanistan 104 D5
Kalbarri Australia 129 A5
Kalemie Dem. Rep. Congo 59 E7
Kalgoorlie Australia 129 C6
Kalimantan *geopolitical region* Indonesia *Eng.* Indonesian Borneo 120 D4
Kaliningrad *external territory* Russian Federation 96 A2
Kaliningrad Kaliningrad, Russian Federation *prev.* Königsberg 88 A4
Kalinkavichy Belarus *Rus.* Kalinkovichi 89 D7
Kalinkovichi see Kalinkavichy
Kalisch see Kalisz
Kalispell Montana, USA 24 B1
Kalisz Poland *Ger.* Kalisch 80 C4
Kalmar Sweden 67 C7
Kalpeni Island *island* India 114 C3
Kama *river* Russian Federation 92 D4
Kamchatka *peninsula* Russian Federation 97 H3
Kamchiya *river* Bulgaria 86 E2
Kamina Dem. Rep. Congo 59 D7
Kamishli see Al Qāmishlī
Kamloops Canada 19 E5
Kampala *capital of* Uganda 55 B6
Kâmpóng Cham Cambodia 119 D6
Kâmpóng Chhnăng Cambodia 119 D5

Kâmpóng Saôm Cambodia 119 D6

Kâmpôt Cambodia 119 D6

Kampuchea *see* Cambodia

Kam"yanets'-Podil's'kyy Ukraine 90 C3

Kananga Dem. Rep. Congo 59 D7

Kanazawa Japan 112 C4

Kandahâr Afghanistan *var.* Qandahâr 104 D5

Kandi Benin 57 F4

Kanivs'ke Vodoskhovyshche *Reservoir* Ukraine 91 E2

Kandy Sri Lanka 115 E3

Kanestron, Ákra *see* Palioúri, Akrotírio

Kangaroo Island *island* Australia 131 B7

Kangertittivaq *region* Greenland 64 E3

Kangikajik *headland* Greenland 65 E4

Kanjiža Serb. & Mon. (Yugo.) 82 D2

Kankan Guinea 56 D4

Kano Nigeria 57 G4

Känpur India *prev.* Cawnpore 117 E3

Kansas *state* USA 24-25

Kansas City Kansas, USA 25 F4

Kansas City Missouri, USA 25 F4

Kansk Russian Federation 97 E4

Kansu *see* Gansu

Kaohsiung Taiwan 111 D7

Kaolack Senegal 56 B3

Kapfenberg Austria 77 E7

Kaposvár Hungary 81 C7

Kapsukas *see* Marijampolė

Kapuas *river* Indonesia 120 D4

Kara-Balta Kyrgyzstan 105 F2

Karabük Turkey 98 C2

Karãchi Pakistan 116 B4

Karaganda Kazakhstan 96 C4

Karakol Kyrgyzstan *prev.* Przheval'sk 105 G2

Kara Kum *see* Garagum

Karakumskiy Kanal *see* Garagum Kanaly

Karakumy *see* Garagum

Karamay China 108 C2

Karamea Bight *gulf* New Zealand 133 C5

Karasburg Namibia 60 C4

Kara Sea *see* Karskoye More

Karditsa Greece 86 B4

Kariba, Lake *lake* Zambia/Zimbabwe 60 D3

Karimata, Selat *strait* Indonesia 120 C4

Karkinits'ka Zatoka *sea feature* Black Sea 91 E4

Karl-Marx-Stadt *see* Chemnitz

Karlovac Croatia 82 B3

Karlovy Vary Czech Republic *Ger.* Karlsbad 81 A5

Karlsbad *see* Karlovy Vary

Karlskrona Sweden 67 C7

Karlsruhe Germany 77 B5

Karlstad Sweden 67 B6

Karnãtaka *state* India 114 D1

Kárpathos *island* Greece 87 E7

Kars Turkey 99 F2

Karshi Uzbekistan *prev.* Bek-Budi, *Uzb.* Qarshi 104 D3

Karskoye More Arctic Ocean *Eng.* Kara Sea 137 H3

Kasai *river* Dem. Rep. Congo 59 C6

Kasama Zambia 61 E2

Kaschau *see* Košice

Kãshãn Iran 102 C3

Kashi China 108 A3

Kasongo Dem. Rep. Congo 59 E6

Kassa *see* Košice

Kassala Sudan 54 C4

Kassel Germany 76 B4

Kastamonu Turkey 98 C2

Katanning Australia 129 B6

Kateríni Greece 86 B4

Katha Myanmar 118 B2

Katherine Australia 128 E2

Kathmandu *capital of* Nepal 117 F3

Katsina Nigeria 57 G3

Katowice Poland 81 C5

Kauen *see* Kaunas

Kaunas Lithuania *Ger.* Kauen, *Pol.* Kowno, *Rus.* Kovno 88 B4

Kavadarci Macedonia 82 E5

Kavála Greece 86 C3

Kavaratti Island *island* India 114 C3

Kavír, Dasht-e *Salt pan* Iran 102 D3

Kawasaki Japan 113 D5

Kayan *river* Indonesia 120 D3

Kayes Mali 56 C3

Kayseri Turkey 98 D3

Kazakhstan *country* C Asia 96

Kazan' Russian Federation 96 B3

Kazandzhik *see* Bereket

Kazanlŭk Bulgaria 86 D2

Kéa *island* Greece 87 C5

Kecskemét Hungary 81 D7

Kediri Indonesia 120 D5

Keetmanshoop Namibia 60 C4

Kefallinía *island* Greece *Eng.* Cephalonia 87 A5

Kelang *see* Klang

Kelmé Lithuania 88 B4

Kelowna Canada 19 E5

Kemerovo Russian Federation 96 D4

Kemi Finland 66 D4

Kemi *river* Finland 66 D3

Kemijärvi Finland 66 D3

Kendari Indonesia 121 E4

Këneurgench *see* Köneürgench

Kénitra Morocco 52 C2

Kennewick Washington, USA 26 C2

Kenora Canada 20 A3

Kentucky *state* USA 22 C5

Kenya *country* E Africa 55

Kerala *state* India 114 D3

Kerch Ukraine 91 G4

Kerguelen *island group* Indian Ocean 123 C7

Kerguelen Plateau *undersea feature* Indian Ocean 123 C7

Kerki *see* Atamyrat

Kérkira *see* Kérkyra

Kérkyra Greece 86 A4

Kérkyra *island* Greece *prev.* Kérkira, *Eng.* Corfu 86 A4

Kermadec Islands *island group* Pacific Ocean 125 E4

Kermadec Trench *undersea feature* Pacific Ocean 125 E4

Kermān Iran *var.* Kirman 102 D4

Kermānshāh *see* Bākhtarān

Kerulen *river* China/Mongolia 109 F3

Ketchikan Alaska, USA 18 D4

Key West Florida, USA 31 E5

Khabarovsk Russian Federation 97 G4

Khanka, Lake *lake* China/Russian Federation 110 E3

Khankendy *see* Xankāndi

Kharkiv Ukraine *Rus.* Khar'kov 91 G2

Khar'kov *see* Kharkiv

Khartoum *capital of* Sudan *var.* Al Khurṭūm 54 B4

Khāsh Iran 102 E4

Khaskovo Bulgaria 86 D2

Khaydarkan Kyrgyzstan *var.* Khaydarken, Hajdarken 105 E2

Khaydarken *see* Khaydarkan

Kherson Ukraine 91 E4

Kheta *river* Russian Federation 94 D2

Khíos *see* Chíos

Khirbet el 'Aujā et Tahtā West Bank 101 D6

Khmel 'nyts'kyy Ukraine 90 D2

Khodzhent *see* Khŭjand

Khojend *see* Khŭjand

Khokand *see* Qo'qon

Kholm Afghanistan 105 E3

Khon Kaen Thailand 118 C4

Khorog *see* Khorugh

Khorugh Tajikistan *Rus.* Khorog 105 F3

Khouribga Morocco 52 C2

Khudzhand *see* Khŭjand

Khŭjand Tajikistan *var.* Khodzheut, Khojend, *Rus.* Khudzhand *prev.* Leninabad 105 E2

Khulna Bangladesh 117 G4

Khvoy Iran 102 B3

Kiangsi *see* Jiangxi

Kiangsu *see* Jiangsu

Kičevo Macedonia 83 D5

Kiel Germany 76 C2

Kielce Poland 80 D4

Kiev *capital of* Ukraine *Ukr.* Kyyiv 91 E2

Kiffa Mauritania 56 C3

Kigali *capital of* Rwanda 55 B6

Kigoma Tanzania 55 B7

Kikládhes *see* Kyklades

Kikwit Dem. Rep. Congo 59 C6

Kilimanjaro *peak* Tanzania 55 C7

Kilkis Greece 86 B3

Killarney Ireland 71 A6

Kimberley South Africa 60 D4

Kimberley Plateau *upland* Australia 128 D3

Kindia Guinea 56 C4

Kindu Dem. Rep. Congo 59 D6

King Island *island* Australia 131 C7

Kingisepp *see* Kuressaare

Kingman Reef *external territory* USA, Pacific Ocean 125 F2

Kingsport Tennessee, USA 31 E1

Kingsville Texas, USA 29 G5

Kingston Canada 20 C5

Kingston *capital of* Jamaica 36 C3

Kingston upon Hull England, UK *var.* Hull 71 E5

Kingstown St Vincent & The Grenadines 36 G4

King William Island *island* Canada 19 F3

Kinneret, Yam *see* Tiberius, Lake

Kinshasa *capital of* Dem. Rep. Congo *prev.* Léopoldville 59 B6

Kirghizia *see* Kyrgyzstan

Kiribati *country* Pacific Ocean 127

Kirin *see* Jilin

Kiritimati *island* Kiribati *var.* Christmas Island 127 G2

Kirkenes Norway 66 E2

Kirklareli Turkey 98 A2

Kirksville Missouri, USA 25 F4

Kirkūk Iraq 102 B3

Kirkwall Scotland, UK 70 C2

Kirman *see* Kermān

Kirov Russian Federation 92 C4 96 B3

Kirovabad *see* Gäncä

Kirovakan *see* Vanadzor

Kirovohrad Ukraine 91 E3

Kiruna Sweden 66 C3

Kisangani Dem. Rep. Congo *prev.* Stanleyville 59 D5

Kishinev *see* Chişinău

Kismaayo Somalia 55 D6

Kisumu Kenya 55 C6

Kitakyūshū Japan 113 A5

Kitami Japan 112 D2

Kitchener Canada 20 C5

Kitwe Zambia 60 D2

Kivu, Lake *lake* Rwanda/Dem. Rep. Congo 55 B6 59 E6

Kızıl Irmak *river* Turkey 98 C2

Kizyl-Arvat *see* Serdar

Kladno Czech Republic 81 A5

Klagenfurt Austria 77 D7

Klaipėda Lithuania *Ger.* Memel 88 B4

Klamath Falls Oregon, USA 26 B4

Klang Malaysia *var.* Kelang 120 B2

Ključ Bosnia & Herzegovina 82 B3

Knin Croatia 82 B4

Knoxville Tennessee, USA 31 E1

Knud Rasmussen Land *region* Greenland 64 D1

Kōbe Japan 113 C5

Koblenz Germany 77 B5

Kobryn Belarus 89 B6

Kocaeli *see* İzmit

Kočani Macedonia 83 E5
Kōchi Japan 113 B6
Kodiak Alaska, USA 18 C3
Kodiak Island island Alaska, USA 18 C3
Koedoes see Kudus
Kohīma India 117 H3
Kohtla-Järve Estonia 88 D2
Kokand see Qo'qon
Kokchetav Kazakhstan 96 C4
Kokkola Finland 66 D4
Koko Nor see Qinghai
Koko Nor see Qinghai Hu
Kokshaal-Tau mountain range Kyrgyzstan 105 G2
Kola Peninsula see Kol'skiy Poluostrov
Kolguyev, Ostrov island Russian Federation 92 D2
Kolhumadulu Atoll island Maldives 114 C5
Kolka Latvia 88 C3
Kolkata India var. Calcutta 117 F4
Köln Germany Eng. Cologne 76 B4
Kol'skiy Poluostrov peninsula Russian Federation Eng. Kola Peninsula 63 F1 92 C2
Kolwezi Dem. Rep. Congo 59 D8
Kolyma river Russian Federation 95 G2
Kommunizma, Pik see Communism Peak
Komoé river Côte d'Ivoire 57 E4
Komotiní Greece 86 D3
Komsomol'sk-na-Amure Russian Federation 97 G4
Kondoz see Kunduz
Kondūz see Kunduz
Köneürgench Turkmenistan prev. Kunya-Urgench, prev. Këneurgench 104 C2
Kong Christian IX Land region Greenland 64 D4
Kong Christian X Land region Greenland 64 E3
Kong Frederik VI Kyst region Greenland 64 C4

Kong Frederik VIII Land region Greenland 64 E2
Kong Frederik IX Land region Greenland 64 C3
Kong Karls Land island group Svalbard 65 G2
Kong Oscar Fjord fjord Greenland 65 E3
Konia see Konya
Königgrätz see Hradec Králové
Königsberg see Kaliningrad
Konispol Albania 83 D7
Konjic Bosnia & Herzegovina 82 C4
Konya Turkey prev. Konia 98 C4
Kopaonik mountains Serb. & Mon. (Yugo.) 83 D4
Koper Slovenia 77 D8
Koprivnica Croatia 82 B2
Korçë Albania 83 D6
Korčula island Croatia 82 B4
Korea Bay bay China/North Korea 110 D4
Korea Strait sea feature Japan/South Korea 110-111 E5
Korinthiakós Kólpos sea feature Greece Eng. Gulf of Corinth 87 B5
Kórinthos Greece Eng. Corinth 87 B5
Kōriyama Japan 113 D4
Korla China 108 C3
Koror see Oreor
Korosten' Ukraine 90 D1
Kortrijk Belgium 69 A6
Kos island Greece 87 E6
Kosciusko, Mount peak Australia 131 D7
Košice Slovakia Ger. Kaschau, Hung. Kassa 81 D6
Köslin see Koszalin
Kosovo province Serb. & Mon. (Yugo.) 83 D5
Kosovska Mitrovica Serb. & Mon. (Yugo.) 82 D4
Kosrae island Micronesia 126 C2

Kossou, Lac de lake Côte d'Ivoire 56 D4
Kostanay Kazakhstan var. Kustanay 96 C4
Kostyantynivka Ukraine 91 G3
Koszalin Poland Ger. Köslin 80 B2
Kota India 116 D4
Kota Bharu Malaysia 120 B3
Kota Kinabalu Malaysia 120 D3
Kotka Finland 67 E5
Kotlas NW Russia 92 C4
Kotuy river Russian Federation 95 E2
Koudougou Burkina 57 E4
Kourou French Guiana 41 H2
Kousséri Cameroon 58 B3
Kouvola Finland 67 E5
Kovel' Ukraine 90 C1
Kovno see Kaunas
Kowno see Kaunas
Kozáni Greece 86 B4
Kozhikode see Calicut
Kra, Isthmus of coastal feature Myanmar/Thailand 119 B6
Kragujevac Serb. & Mon. (Yugo.) 82 D4
Krakau see Kraków
Kraków Poland Eng. Cracow, Ger. Krakau 81 D5
Kraljevo Serb. & Mon. (Yugo.) 82 D4
Kranj Slovenia 77 D7
Krasnodar Russian Federation 93 A6
Krasnovodsk see Türkmenbaşy
Krasnoyarsk Russian Federation 96 D4
Krasnyy Luch Ukraine 91 H3
Kremenchuk Ukraine 91 F2
Kremenchuts'ke Vodoskhovyshche Reservoir Ukraine 91 E2
Krems an der Donau Austria 77 E6
Kretinga Lithuania Ger. Krottingen 88 B3
Krichev see Krychaw

Krishna *river* India 114 C1

Kristiansand Norway 67 A6

Kristianstad Sweden 67 B7

Kríti *island* Greece *Eng.* Crete 87 C7

Kritikó Pélagos *see* Crete, Sea of

Krivoy Rog *see* Kryvyy Rih

Krk *island* Croatia 82 A3

Kroonstad South Africa 60 D4

Krottingen *see* Kretinga

Krung Thep *see* Bangkok

Kruševac Serb. & Mon. (Yugo.) 83 E4

Krušné Hory *see* Erzgebirge

Krychaw Belarus *Rus.* Krichev 89 E6

Kryms'kyy Pivostriv *peninsula* Ukraine *var.* Crimea 90 F4

Kryvyy Rih Ukraine *Rus.* Krivoy Rog 91 E3

Kuala Lumpur *capital of* Malaysia 120 B3

Kuala Terengganu Malaysia 120 B3

Kuang-tung *see* Guangdong

Kuantan Malaysia 120 C3

Kuba *see* Quba

Kuching Malaysia 120 C3

Kuçovë Albania *prev.* Qyteti Stalin 83 D6

Kudus Indonesia *prev.* Koedoes 120 D5

Kuei-chou *see* China Guizhou

Kugluktuk Canada *prev.* Coppermine 19 E3

Kuito Angola 60 C2

Kuldīga Latvia *Ger.* Goldingen 88 B3

Kullorsuaq Greenland 64 C2

Kůlob Tajikistan *Rus.* Kulyab 105 E3

Kulyab *see* Kůlob

Kum *see* Qom

Kuma *river* Russian Federation 93 B7

Kumamoto Japan 113 B6

Kumanovo Macedonia 83 E5

Kumasi Ghana 57 E5

Kumayri *see* Gyumri 99 F2

Kumo Nigeria 57 G4

Kumon Range *mountain range* Myanmar 118 B1

Kunashir *island* Japan/Russian Federation (disputed) 112 E1

Kunduz Afghanistan *var.* Kondūz, Qondūz, Kondoz 105 E3

Kunja-Urgenç *see* Köneürgench

Kunlun Mountains *see* Kunlun Shan

Kunlun Shan *mountain range* China *Eng.* Kunlun Mountains 106 B3

Kunming China 111 B6

Kununurra Australia 128 D3

Kupang Indonesia 120 E5

Kür *see* Kura

Kura *river* Azerbaijan/Georgia *Az.* Kür 99 G2

Kurashiki Japan 113 B5

Kurdistan *region* Turkey 99 F4

Küre Dağları *mountains* Turkey 98 C2

Kuressaare Estonia *prev.* Kingissepp, *Ger.* Arensburg 88 C2

Kurgan–Tyube *see* Qŭrghonteppa

Kurile Islands *islands* Pacific Ocean 112 E1

Kurile Trench *undersea feature* Pacific Ocean 134 C2

Kurnool India 114 D2

Kushiro Japan 112 E2

Kushka *see* Gushgy

Kustanay *see* Kostanay

Kütahya Turkey *prev.* Kutaiah 98 B3

Kutaiah *see* Kütahya

K'ut'aisi Georgia 99 F2

Kutch, Rann of *see* Kachch, Rann of

Kuujjuaq Canada 21 E2

Kuujjuarapik Canada 20 D2

Kuusamo Finland 66 E3

Kuwait *country* SW Asia 102 C4

Kuwait City *capital of* Kuwait 102 C4

Kuytun China 108 C2

Kvitøya Island Svalbard 65 G1

Kwangju South Korea 111 E4

Kwango *river* Dem. Rep. Congo 59 C7

Kwangtung *see* Guangdong

Kweichow *see* Guizhou

Kyklades *island group* Greece *prev.* Kikládhes, *Eng.* Cyclades 87 D6

Kyrenia *see* Girne

Kyrgyzstan *country* C Asia *var.* Kirghizia 105

Kýthira *island* Greece 87 B6

Kyushu-Palau Ridge *undersea feature* Pacific Ocean 124 B1

Kyyiv *see* Kiev

Kyyivs'ke Vodoskhovyshche *Reservoir* Ukraine 91 E1

Kyōto Japan 113 C5

Kyūshū *island* Japan 113 B6

Kyzylorda Kazakhstan 96 B5

— **L** —

Laâyoune Western Sahara 52 B3

Labé Guinea 56 C4

Laborca *see* Laborec

Laborec *river* Slovakia *Hung.* Laborca 81 E5

Labrador *region* Canada 21 F2

Labrador Sea Atlantic Ocean 64 B5

Laccadive Islands *see* Lakshadweep

La Ceiba Honduras 34 D2

Lachlan River *river* Australia 131 C6

La Coruña *see* A Coruña

La Crosse Wisconsin, USA 22 A2

Ladoga, Lake *see* Ladozhskoye Ozero

Ladozhskoye Ozero *lake* Russian Federation *Eng.* Lake Ladoga 92 B3

Ladysmith Wisconsin, USA 22 A2

Lae Papua New Guinea 126 B3

La Esperanza Honduras 34 C2

Lafayette Louisiana, USA 30 B3

Laghouat Algeria 52 D2

Lagos Nigeria 57 F5

Lagos Portugal 74 C4

Lagouira Western Sahara 52 A4

La Grande Oregon, USA 26 C3

La Habana *see* Havana

Lahore Pakistan 116 C2

Laï Chad 58 C4

Laila *see* Laylá

Lajes Brazil 44 D3

Lake Charles Louisiana, USA 30 B3

Lake District *region* England, UK 71 C5

Lakewood Colorado, USA 24 D4

Lakshadweep *island group* India *Eng.* Laccadive Islands 114 B2

La Ligua Chile 46 B4

La Louvière Belgium 69 B6

Lambaré Paraguay 44 B3

Lambaréné Gabon 59 B6

Lamía Greece 86 B4

Lancaster England, UK 71 D5

Lancaster California, USA 27 C7

Lancaster Sound *sea feature* Canada 19 F2

Landsberg *see* Gorzów Wielkopolski

Land's End *coastal feature* England, UK 71 C7

Landshut Germany 77 D6

Lang Son Vietnam 118 D3

Länkäran Azerbaijan *Rus.* Lenkoran'. 99 H3

Lansing Michigan, USA 22 C3

Lanzarote *island* Spain 52 B3

Lanzhou China 110 B4

Laon France 72 D3

La Oroya Peru 42 B3

Laos *country* SE Asia 118

La Palma *island* Spain 52 A3

La Paz *capital of* Bolivia 42 C4

La Paz Mexico 32 B3

La Pérouse Strait *sea feature* Japan 112 D1

Lapland *region* N Europe 66 C3

La Plata Argentina 46 D4

Lappeenranta Finland 67 E5

Laptev Sea *see* Laptevykh, More

Laptevykh, More Arctic Ocean *Eng.* Laptev Sea 97 F2

L'Aquila Italy 78 C4

Laramie Wyoming, USA 24 C4

Laredo Texas, USA 29 F5

La Rioja Argentina 46 C3

Lárisa Greece 86 B4

Lārkāna Pakistan 116 B3

Larnaca Cyprus *var.* Larnaka, Larnax 98 C5

Larnaka *see* Larnaca

Larnax *see* Larnaca

La Rochelle France 72 B4

La Roche-sur-Yon France 72 B4

La Romana Dominican Republic 36 E3

Las Cruces New Mexico, USA 28 D3

Las Piedras Uruguay 44 C5

La Serena Chile 46 B3

La Spezia Italy 78 B3

Las Tablas Panama 35 F5

Las Vegas Nevada, USA 27 D7

Latakia *see* Al Lādhiqīyah

Latvia *country* NE Europe 88

Launceston Tasmania 131 C8

Laurentian Basin *see* Canada Basin

Laurentian Mountains *upland* Canada 16 D4

Lausanne Switzerland 77 A7

Laut, Pulau *prev.* Laoet. *Island* Indonesia 120 D4

Laval France 72 B4

Lawton Oklahoma, USA 29 F2

Laylá Saudi Arabia 103 C5

Lazarev Sea *sea* Antarctica 136 B2

Lebanon *country* SW Asia 100-101

Lebu Chile 47 B5

Lecce Italy 79 E5

Leduc Canada 19 E5

Leeds England, UK 71 D5

Leeuwarden Netherlands 68 D1

Leeward Islands *see* Sotavento, Ilhas de

Lefkáda *island* Greece *prev.* Levkás 87 A5

Lefkoşa *see* Nicosia

Lefkosia *see* Nicosia

Legaspi Philippines 120 E2

Legnica Poland *Ger.* Liegnitz 80 B4

Le Havre France 72 B3

Leicester England, UK 71 D6

Leiden Netherlands 68 C3

Leipzig Germany 76 D4

Lek *river* Netherlands 68 C4

Le Léman *see* Geneva, Lake

Lelystad Netherlands 68 D3

Léman, Lac *see* Geneva, Lake

Le Mans France 72 B4

Lemesos *see* Limassol

Lemnos *see* Límnos

Lena *river* Russian Federation 97 F3

Leninabad *see* Khŭjand

Leninakan *see* Gyumri

Leningrad *see* St Petersburg

Leninsk *see* Türkmenabat

Lenkoran' *see* Länkäran

León Mexico 33 E4

León Nicaragua 34 C3

León Spain 74 D1

Léopoldville *see* Kinshasa

Lepel' *see* Lyepyel'

Le Puy France 73 C5

Lérida *see* Lleida

Lerwick Scotland, UK 70 D1

Lesbos *see* Lésvos

Leshan China 111 B5

Leskovac Serb. & Mon. (Yugo.) 82 E4

Lesotho *country* southern Africa 60

Lesser Antarctica *region* Antarctica 134 B3

Lesser Antilles *island group* West Indies 37 G4

Lésvos *island* Greece *Eng.* Lesbos 86 D4

Lethbridge Canada 19 E5

Leti, Kepulauan *island group* Indonesia 121 F5

Leuven Belgium 69 C6

Leverkusen Germany 76 A4

Levin New Zealand 132 D4

Levkás *see* Lefkáda

Lewis *island* Scotland, UK 70 B2

Lewiston Idaho, USA 26 C2

Lewiston Maine, USA 23 G2

Lexington Kentucky, USA 22 C5

Lezhë Albania 83 D5

Lhasa China 108 C5

Lhazê China 108 C4

L'Hospitalet de Llobregat *var.* Hospitalet. Spain 75 G2

Liao *see* Liaoning

Liaoning *province* China *var.* Liao, Shengking; *hist.* Fengtien, Shenking. Admin. region 110 D3

Libau *see* Liepāja

Liberec Czech Republic *Ger.* Reichenberg 80 B4

Liberia *country* W Africa 56

Liberia Costa Rica 34 D4

Libreville *capital* of Gabon 59 A5

Libya *country* N Africa 53

Libyan Desert *desert* N Africa 50 C3

Lichuan China 111 B5

Liechtenstein *country* C Europe 77 B7

Liège Belgium 69 D6

Liegnitz *see* Legnica

Lienz Austria 77 D7

Linz Austria 77 D7

Liepāja Latvia *Ger.* Libau 88 B3

Liffey *river* Ireland 71 B5

Ligurian Sea Mediterranean Sea 78 A3

Likasi Dem. Rep. Congo 59 E8

Lille France 72 D2

Lillehammer Norway 67 B5

Lilongwe *capital* of Malawi 61 E2

Lima *capital* of Peru 42 B4

Limassol Cyprus *var.* Lemesos 98 C5

Limerick Ireland 71 A6

Límnos *island* Greece *var.* Lemnos 86 D4

Limoges France 72 C5

Limón Costa Rica 35 E4

Limpopo *river* southern Africa 60 D3

Linares Chile 46 B4

Linares Spain 75 E4

Linchuan China 111 D6

Lincoln England, UK 71 D5

Lincoln Nebraska, USA 25 F4

Lincoln Sea Arctic Ocean 64 E1

Linden Guyana 41 G2

Lindi Tanzania 55 C8

Line Islands *island group* Kiribati 127 G2

Linköping Sweden 67 C6

Linz Austria 77 D6

Lion, Golfe du *sea feature* Mediterranean Sea 73 D6

Lipari, Isola *island* Italy 79 D6

Lipari Islands *see* Isole Eolie

Lira Uganda 55 B6

Lisbon *capital* of Portugal *Port.* Lisboa 74 B3

Litani *river* SW Asia 91 B4

Lithuania *country* E Europe 88-89

Little Andaman *island* India 115 G2

Little Minch *sea feature* Scotland, UK 70 B3

Little Rock Arkansas, USA 30 B2

Liuzhou China 111 C6

Liverpool England, UK 71 D5

Livingstone Zambia 60 D3

Livno Bosnia & Herzegovina 82 B4

Livorno Italy 78 B3

Ljubljana *capital* of Slovenia 77 D7

Ljusnan *river* Sweden 67 B5

Llanos *region* Colombia/Venezuela 41 E2

Lleida Spain *Cast.* Lérida 75 F2

Lobatse Botswana 60 D4

Lobito Angola 60 B2

Locarno Switzerland 77 B7

Lodja Dem. Rep. Congo 59 D6

Łódź Poland *Rus.* Lodz 80 D4

Lofoten *island group* Norway 66 B3

Logroño Spain 75 E2

Loire *river* France 72 B4

Loja Ecuador 40 A5

Lokitaung Kenya 55 C5

Loksa Estonia *Ger.* Loxa 88 D2

Lombok, Pulau *island* Indonesia 120 D5

Lomé *capital* of Togo 57 E5

Lomond, Loch *lake* Scotland, UK 70 C4

London Canada 20 C5

London *capital* of UK 71 E6

Londonderry Northern Ireland, UK 70 B4

Londonderry, Cape *coastal feature* Australia 128 D2

Londrina Brazil 44 D2

Long Beach California, USA 27 C8

Long Island *island* Bahamas 34 D2

Long Island *island* NE USA 23 G3

Longreach Australia 130 C4

Long Strait *Strait* Russian Federation 95 H2

Longview Texas, USA 29 G3

Longview Washington, USA 26 B2

Longyearbyen Svalbard 65 F2

Lop Nur *lake* China 108 C3

Lorca Spain 75 E4

Lord Howe Island *island* Australia 124 C4

Lord Howe Rise *undersea feature* Pacific Ocean 124 D4

Lorient France 72 A4

Los Alamos New Mexico, USA 28 D1

Los Angeles California, USA 27 C7

Loslau *see* Wodzisław Śląski

Los Mochis Mexico 32 C3

Losonc *see* Lučenec

Losontz *see* Lučenec

Lot *river* France 73 B5

Louangphrabang Laos 118 C3

Loubomo Congo 59 B6

Louisiana *state* USA 30 B3

Louisville Kentucky, USA 22 C5

Louisville Ridge *undersea feature* Pacific Ocean 125 E4

Lovech Bulgaria 86 C2

Lower California *see* Baja California

Lower Hutt New Zealand

Loxa *see* Loksa

Loyauté, Îles *island group* New Caledonia 126 D5

Loznica Serb. & Mon. (Yugo.) 82 C3

Lu *see* Shandong

Luanda *capital of* Angola 60 B1

Luanshya Zambia 60 D2

Lubango Angola 60 B2

Lubbock Texas, USA 29 E2

Lübeck Germany 76 C3

Lublin Poland *Rus.* Lyublin 80 E4

Lubny Ukraine 91 F2

Lubumbashi Dem. Rep. Congo 59 E8

Lucapa Angola 60 C1

Lucena Philippines 120 E2

Lučenec Slovakia *Hung.* Losonc, *Ger.* Losontz 81 D6

Lucerne *see* Luzern

Lucknow India 117 E3

Lüderitz Namibia 60 C4

Ludhiāna India 116 D2

Lugano Switzerland 77 B7

Lugo Spain 74 C1

Luhans'k Ukraine 91 H3

Luleå Sweden 66 D4

Lumsden New Zealand 133 A7

Lüneburg Germany 76 C3

Luninyets Belarus 89 C6

Luoyang *var.* Honan, Lo-yang. China 110 C4

Lusaka *capital of* Zambia 60 D2

Lushnjë Albania 83 D6

Lūt, Baḥrat *see* Dead Sea

Luts'k Ukraine 90 C1

Luxembourg *country* W Europe 69 D8

Luxembourg *capital of* Luxembourg 69 D8

Luxor Egypt 54 B2

Luzern Switzerland *Fr.* Lucerne 77 B7

Luzon *island* Philippines 121 E1

Luzon Strait *sea feature* Philippines/Taiwan 107 E3

L'viv Ukraine *Rus.* L'vov 90 C2

L'vov *see* L'viv

Lyepyel' Belarus *Rus.* Lepel' 89 D5

Lyon France 73 D5

Lyublin *see* Lublin

— **M** —

Ma'ān Jordan 101 B6

Maas *see* Meuse

Maastricht Netherlands 69 D6

Macao *external territory* Portugal, E Asia *var.* Macau 111 C7

Macapá Brazil 43 F1

Macau *see* Macao

Macdonnell Ranges *mountains* Australia 130 A4

Macedonia *country* SE Europe officially Former Yugoslav Republic of Macedonia, *abbrev.* FYR Macedonia 83

Maceió Brazil 43 H3

Machala Ecuador 40 A5

Mackay Australia 130 D4

Mackay, Lake *lake* Australia 128 D4

Mackenzie *river* Canada 19 E4

Mackenzie Bay *sea feature* Atlantic Ocean 136 D3

Macleod, Lake *lake* Australia 128 A4

Mâcon France 72 D5

Macon Georgia, USA 31 E2

Madagascar *country* Indian Ocean 61

Madagascar Basin *undersea feature* Indian Ocean 123 B5

Madagascar Plateau *undersea feature* Indian Ocean 123 A6

Madang Papua New Guinea 126 B3

Madeira *river* Bolivia/Brazil 42 D2

Madeira *island group* Portugal 52 A2

Madhya Pradesh *state* India 117 E4

Madison Wisconsin, USA 22 B3

Madiun *prev.* Madioen. Indonesia 120 D5

Madona Latvia *Ger.* Modohn 88 D3

Madras *see* Chennai

Madre de Dios *river* Bolivia/Peru 42 C3

Madrid *capital of* Spain 75 E3

Madurai India 114 D3

Magadan Russian Federation 97 G3

Magallanes *see* Punta Arenas

Magallanes, Estrecho de *see* Magellan, Strait of

Magdalena *river* Colombia 40 B2

Magdeburg Germany 76 C4

Magelang Indonesia 120 C5

Magellan, Strait of *sea feature* S South America *Sp.* Estrecho de Magallanes 47 B8

Maggiore, Lake *lake* Italy/Switzerland 78 B2

Mahajanga Madagascar 61 G3

Mahalapye Botswana 60 D4

Mahanādi *river* India 117 F5

Mahārāshtra *state* India
116 D5
Mahé *island* Seychelles 61 H1
Mahilyow Belarus *Rus.* Mogilëv
89 E6
Mährisch-Ostrau *see* Ostrava
Maicao Colombia 40 C1
Maiduguri Nigeria 57 H4
Maimana *see* Meymaneh
Maine *state* USA 23 G1
Maine, Gulf of *gulf* USA 23 G2
Mainz Germany 77 B5
Maio *Island* Cape Verde
56 A3
Maíz, Islas del *islands*
Nicaragua 35 E3
Majorca *see* Mallorca
Majuro *island* Marshall Islands
126 D1
Makarska Croatia 82 B4
Makarov Basin *undersea*
feature Arctic Ocean 137 G3
Makassar Strait *strait* Indonesia
120 D4
Makeyevka *see* Makiyivka
Makhachkala Russian
Federation 93 B7 96 A4
Makiyivka Ukraine *Rus.*
Makeyevka 91 G3
Makkah Saudi Arabia *Eng.*
Mecca 103 A5
Makkovik Canada 21 F2
Malabo *capital of* Equatorial
Guinea 59 A5
Malacca, Strait of *sea feature*
Indonesia/ Malaysia 106 C4
119 C8 120 B3
Maladzyechna Belarus *Rus.*
Molodechno, *Pol.*
Molodeczno 89 C5
Málaga Spain 74 D5
Malakal Sudan 55 B5
Malang Indonesia 120 D5
Malanje Angola 60 C2
Malatya Turkey 99 E3
Malawi *country* southern
Africa 61
Malay Peninsula *peninsula*
Malaysia/Thailand 119 D8
Malaysia *country* Asia 120

Malden Island *atoll* Kiribati
125 F2
Maldives *country* Indian Ocean
114 C4
Male' *capital of* Maldives
114 C4
Malekula *island* Vanuatu 124 D3
Mali *country* W Africa 57
Malindi Kenya 55 C7
Mallorca *island* Spain *Eng.*
Majorca 75 H3
Malmö Sweden 67 B7
Malta *country* Mediterranean
Sea 79 C8
Malta Montana, USA 24 C1
Malta Channel *sea feature*
Mediterranean Sea 79 C7
Maluku *island group* Indonesia
var. Moluccas 107 E4 121 F4
Maluku, Laut Pacific Ocean
Eng. Molucca Sea 121 F4
Mamberamo *river* Indonesia
121 H4
Mamoudzou *capital of*
Mayotte 61 G2
Man, Isle of *island* UK 71 C5
Manado Indonesia 121 F3
Managua *capital of* Nicaragua
34 D3
Manama *capital of* Bahrain *Ar.*
Al Manāmah 103 C5
Mananjary Madagascar 61 G3
Manaus Brazil 42 D2
Manchester England, UK 71 D5
Manchester New Hampshire,
USA 23 G2
Manchurian Plain *plain* E Asia
107 E1
Mandalay Myanmar 118 B3
Mangalia Romania 90 D5
Mangalore India 114 C2
Manicouagan, Réservoir
Reservoir Canada 21 E3
Manihiki *atoll* Cook Islands
125 F3
Maniitsoq Greenland 64 C3
Manila *capital of* Philippines
121 E1
Manisa Turkey *prev.* Saruhan
98 A3

Manitoba *province* Canada
19 G4
Manizales Colombia 40 B3
Manjimup Australia 129 B7
Mannar Sri Lanka 115 E3
Mannar, Gulf of *sea feature*
Indian Ocean 114 D3
Mannheim Germany 77 B5
Manono Dem. Rep. Congo
59 E7
Mansel Island *island* Canada
20 C1
Mansfield Ohio, USA 22 D4
Manta Ecuador 40 A4
Mantes-la-Jolie France 72 C3
Mantova Italy *Eng.* Mantua
78 B2
Mantua *see* Mantova
Manurewa New Zealand 132 D3
Manzhouli China 109 F1
Mao Chad 58 B3
Maoke, Pegunungan
mountains Indonesia
121 H4
Maputo *capital of*
Mozambique 61 E4
Mar, Serra do *mountains* Brazil
38 D4
Maracaibo Venezuela 40 C1
Maracaibo, Lago de *inlet*
Venezuela 40 C1
Maracay Venezuela 40 D1
Maradi Niger 57 F3
Marāgheh Iran 102 C3
Marajó, Ilha de *island* Brazil
43 F2
Marañón *river* Peru 42 B2
Maraş *see* Kahramanmaraş
Marash *see* Kahramanmaraş
Marbella Spain 74 D5
Marble Bar Australia 128 B4
Mar Chiquita, Laguna *salt lake*
Argentina 46 C3
Mardān Pakistan 116 C1
Mar del Plata Argentina 47 D5
Mardin Turkey 99 E4
Margarita, Isla de *island*
Venezuela 41 E1

Mārgow, Dasht-e- *desert* Afghanistan 104 C5

Mariana Trench *undersea feature* Pacific Ocean 124 B1 126 B1

Marías, Islas *islands* Mexico 32 C4

Maribor Slovenia 77 E7

Marie Byrd Land *region* Antarctica 136 B4

Mariehamn Finland 67 D6

Marijampolė Lithuania *prev.* Kapsukas 88 B4

Marília Brazil 44 D2

Maringá Brazil 44 D2

Marion, Lake *lake* South Carolina, USA 31 F2

Mariscal Estigarribia Paraguay 44 B2

Maritsa *river* SE Europe 86 D3

Mariupol' Ukraine *prev.* Shdanov 91 G3

Marka Somalia 55 D6

Marmara, Sea of *see* Marmara Denizi

Marmara Denizi Turkey *Eng.* Sea of Marmara 98 B2

Marne *river* France 72 D3

Marotiri *island group* French Polynesia 125 F4

Maroua Cameroon 58 B3

Marowijne *river* French Guiana/Suriname 41 H3

Marquesas Fracture Zone *tectonic feature* Pacific Ocean 125 G3

Marquesas Islands *island group* French Polynesia *Fr.* Îles Marquises 125 G3

Marquette Michigan, USA 22 B1

Marquises, Îles *see* Marquesas Islands

Marrakech Morocco *Eng.* Marrakesh 52 C2

Marrawah Australia 131 C8

Marree Australia 131 B5

Marsala Italy 79 C6

Marseille France 73 D6

Marshall Islands *country* Pacific Ocean 126-127

Martin Slovakia *prev.* Turčiansky Svätý Martin, *Ger.* Sankt Martin, *Hung.* Turócszentmárton 81 C5

Martinique *external territory* France, West Indies 37

Mary Turkmenistan *prev.* Merv 104 C3

Maryborough Australia 131 E5

Maryland *state* USA 23 F4

Masai Steppe *grassland* Tanzania 55 C7

Mascarene Basin *undersea feature* Indian Ocean 123 B5

Mascarene Islands *island group* Indian Ocean 61 H4

Mascarene Plain *undersea feature* Indian Ocean 123 B5

Mascarene Plateau *undersea feature* Indian Ocean 123 B5

Maseru *capital of* Lesotho 60 D4

Mas-ha Bank 101 D6

Mashhad Iran *var.* Meshed 100 E3

Masindi Uganda 55 B6

Maşīrah, Jazīrat *Island* Oman 103 E6

Maşīrah, Khalīj *bay* Oman 103 E6

Mason City Iowa, USA 25 F3

Masqaṭ *see* Muscat

Massachusetts *state* USA 23 G3

Massawa Eritrea 54 C4

Massif Central *upland* France 73 C5

Massoukou Gabon 59 B6

Masterton New Zealand 133 D5

Matadi Dem. Rep. Congo 59 B7

Matagalpa Nicaragua 34 D3

Matamoros Mexico 33 E2

Matanzas Cuba 36 B2

Matara Sri Lanka 115 E4

Mataram Indonesia 120 D5

Mataró Spain 75 G2

Mato Grosso *upland* Brazil 43 E3

Matosinhos Portugal 74 C2

Matsue Japan 113 B5

Matsuyama Japan 113 B5

Matterhorn *peak* Italy/Switzerland 77 B7

Maturín Venezuela 41 E1

Maun Botswana 60 D3

Mauritania *country* W Africa 56

Mauritius *country* Indian Ocean 61 H4 123 B5

Mayaguana *island* Bahamas 36 D2

Mayfield New Zealand 133 C6

Mayotte *external territory* France, Indian Ocean 61 G2

Mayyit, Al Baḥr al *see* Dead Sea

Mazār-e Sharīf Afghanistan 104 D3

Mazatlán Mexico 32 C3

Mažeikiai Lithuania 88 B3

Mazury *region* Poland 80 D3

Mazyr Belarus *Rus.* Mozyr' 89 D7

Mbabane *capital of* Swaziland 61 E4

Mbaké Senegal 56 B3

Mbala Zambia 61 E1

Mbale Uganda 55 C6

Mbandaka Dem. Rep. Congo 59 C5

Mbeya Tanzania 55 B8

Mbuji-Mayi Dem. Rep. Congo 59 D7

McKinley, Mount *peak* Alaska, USA *var.* Denali 18 C3

Mead, Lake *lake* SW USA 28 A1

Mecca *see* Makkah

Mechelen Belgium 69 C5

Mecklenburger Bucht *bay* Germany 76 C2

Medan Indonesia 120 B3

Medellín Colombia 40 B2

Médenine Tunisia 53 F2

Medford Oregon, USA 26 A4

Medina *see* Al Madīnah

Mediterranean Sea Atlantic Ocean 84-85

Mörön Mongolia 108 D2

Morondava Madagascar 61 F3

Moroni *capital of* Comoros
61 F2

Morotai, Pulau *island*
Indonesia 121 F3

Morova Poland 80 C6

Morris Jesup, Kap *headland*
Greenland 65 E1

Moscow *capital of* Russian
Federation *Rus.* Moskva 92
B4 96 B2

Mosel *river* W Europe *Fr.*
Moselle 77 A5

Moselle *river* W Europe *Ger.*
Mosel 72 E4

Mosgiel New Zealand 133 B7

Moshi Tanzania 55 C7

Moskva *see* Moscow

Mosquito Coast *coastal region*
Nicaragua 35 E3

Moss Norway 67 B6

Mossendjo Congo 59 B6

Mossoró Brazil 43 H2

Most Czech Republic *Ger.* Brüx
80 A4

Mostaganem Algeria 52 D1

Mostar Bosnia & Herzegovina
82 C4

Mosul *see* Al Mawşil

Motril Spain 75 E5

Motueka New Zealand 133 C5

Moulins France 72 C4

Moulmein Myanmar 118 B4

Moundou Chad 58 C4

Mount Gambier Australia
131 B7

Mount Isa Australia 130 B4

Mount Magnet Australia 129 B5

Mount Vernon Illinois, USA
22 B5

Mouscron Belgium 69 A6

Moyobamba Peru 42 B2

Moyu China 108 B2

Mozambique *country*
SE Africa 61

Mozambique Channel *sea*
feature Indian Ocean 61 F3

Mozyr' *see* Mazyr

Mpika Zambia 61 E2

Mtwara Tanzania 55 C8

Muang Không Laos 119 D5

Muang Xaignabouri *see*
Xaignabouri

Mudanjiang China 110 E3

Mufulira Zambia 60 D2

Mugla Turkey 98 A4

Mulhouse France 72 E4

Mull *island* Scotland, UK 70 B3

Muller, Pegunungan *mountains*
Indonesia 120 C3

Multãn Pakistan 116 C2

Mumbai India *var.* Bombay
117 C5

München Germany *Eng.*
Munich 77 C6

Muncie Indiana, USA 22 C4

Munich *see* München

Münster Germany 76 B4

Muqdisho *see* Mogadishu

Mur *river* C Europe 77 E7

Murchison River *river* Australia
129 B5

Murcia Spain 75 F4

Mures *river* Hungary/Romania
81 D7

Murfreesboro Tennessee, USA
30 D1

Murgab Tajikistan 105 F3

Murgap *river* Turkmenistan
var. Murghab 104 C3

Murghab *see* Murgap

Müritz *lake* Germany 76 D3

Murmansk Russian Federation
92 C2 96 C3

Murray *river* Australia 131 B6

Murray Fracture Zone *tectonic*
feature Pacific Ocean 135 E2

Murray Ridge *Undersea feature*
Arabian Sea 122 B3

Murwillumbah Australia 131 E5

Murzuq Libya 53 F3

Muş Turkey 99 F3

Muscat *capital of* Oman *Ar.*
Masqaţ 103 E5

Musgrave Ranges *mountain*
range Australia 129 D5

Musters, Lago *lake* Argentina
46 C6

Mu Us Shamo *Desert* China
109 E3

Mvonioälv *river*
Finland/Sweden 66 D3

Mwanza Tanzania 55 B6

Mwene-Ditu Dem. Rep. Congo
59 D7

Mweru, Lake *lake* Dem. Rep.
Congo/Zambia 59 D7

Myanmar *country* SE Asia *var.*
Myanmar 118-119

Mykolayiv Ukraine *Rus.*
Nikolayev 91 E4

Mykonos *island* Greece 87 D5

Mysore India 114 D2

Mzuzu Malawi 61 E2

N

Naberezhnyye Chelny Russian
Federation *prev.* Brezhnev
93 C5

Nablus West Bank *var.* Nãbulus,
Heb. Shekhem 101 D6

Nãbulus *see* Nablus

Nacala Mozambique 61 F2

Naga Philippines 120 E2

Nagano Japan 112 C4

Nagasaki Japan 113 A6

Nãgercoil India 114 D3

Nagorno-Karabakh *region*
Azerbaijan 99 G2

Nagoya Japan 113 C5

Nãgpur India 116 D4

Nagqu China 108 C5

Nagykanizsa Hungary *Ger.*
Grosskanizsa 81 C7

Nagyszombat *see* Trnava

Naha Japan 113 A8

Nain Canada 21 F2

Nairobi *capital of* Kenya 55 C6

Najaf *see* An Najaf

Najrãn Saudi Arabia 103 B6

Nakamura Japan 113 B6

Nakhichevan' *see* Naxçivan

Nakhon Ratchasima Thailand
119 C5

Northern Mariana Islands *external territory* USA, Pacific Ocean 124 C1

Northern Sporades *see* Voreioi Sporades

Northern Territory *territory* Australia 130 A3

North European Plain *region* N Europe 62 E3

North Frisian Islands *islands* Denmark/Germany 76 B2

North Island *island* New Zealand 132 G2

North Korea *country* E Asia 110

North Little Rock Arkansas, USA 30 B1

North Platte Nebraska, USA 25 E4

North Platte *river* C USA 24 D3

North Pole *ice feature* Arctic Ocean 137 G3

North Sea Atlantic Ocean 70 E2

North Siberian Lowland *lowlands* Russian Federation 94-95

North Taranaki Bight *gulf* New Zealand 132 D3

North Uist *island* Scotland, UK 70 B3

Northwest Territories *territory* Canada 19 E3

Norway *country* N Europe 66-67

Norwegian Sea Arctic Ocean 137 G5

Norwich England, UK 71 E6

Noteć *river* Poland *Ger.* Netze 80 C3

Nottingham England, UK 71 D6

Nottingham Island *island* Hudson Strait 20 D1

Nouâdhibou Mauritania 56 B2

Nouakchott *capital of* Mauritania 56 B2

Nouméa *capital of* New Caledonia 126 D5

Nova Gradiška Croatia 82 C3

Nova Iguaçu Brazil 43 F5 45 F2

Novara Italy 78 B2

Nova Scotia *province* Canada 21 F4

Novaya Zemlya *islands* Russian Federation 137 H4

Novaya Zemlya Trench *see* East Novaya Zemlya Trench

Novgorod Russian Federation 92 B4 96 B2

Novi Sad Serb. & Mon. (Yugo.) 82 D3

Novokuznetsk Russian Federation *prev.* Stalinsk 96 D4

Novopolotsk *see* Navapolatsk

Novosibirsk Russian Federation 96 D4

Novosibirskiye Ostrova *islands* Russian Federation *Eng.* New Siberian Islands 95 F1

Novo Urgench *see* Urgench

Novyy Margilan *see* Farg'ona

Nsanje Malawi 61 E3

Nsawam Ghana 57 E5

Nubian Desert *desert* Sudan 54 B3

Nu'eima West Bank 101 D7

Nuevo Laredo Mexico 33 E2

Nuku'alofa *capital of* Tonga 127 F5

Nukus Uzbekistan 104 C2

Nullarbor Plain *region* Australia 129 D6

Nunap Isua Island *coastal region* Greenland *var.* Uummannaruaq *Dan.* Kap Farvel 64 C5

Nunavut *Territory* Canada 19 F3

Nunivak Island *island* Alaska, USA 18 B2

Nuoro Italy 79 A5

Nuremberg *see* Nürnberg

Nürnberg Germany *Eng.* Nuremberg 77 C5

Nusa Tenggara *islands* East Timor / Indonesia 120 E5

Nuuk Greenland *var.* Godthåb 64 C4

Nyainqêntanglha Shan *mountain range* China 108 D5

Nyala Sudan 54 A4

Nyasa, Lake *lake* E Africa 51 D5

Nyeri Kenya 55 C6

Nyima China 108 C4

Nyíregyháza Hungary 81 E6

Nyitra *see* Nitra

Nykøbing Denmark 67 B8

Nyköping Sweden 67 C6

Nyngan Australia 131 D6

Nyoman *see* Neman

O

Oakland California, USA 27 B6

Oakley Kansas, USA 25 E4

Oamaru New Zealand 133 B7

Oaxaca Mexico 33 F5

Ob' *river* Russian Federation 96 D4

Oban Scotland, UK 70 C4

Obihiro Japan 112 D2

Obo Central African Republic 58 D4

Oceania 124-125

Ocean Island *see* Banaba

Oceanside California, USA 27 C8

Ochamchira *see* Och'amch'ire

Och'amch'ire Georgia *Rus.* Ochamchira 99 E1

Ödenburg *see* Sopron

Odense Denmark 67 B7

Oder *river* C Europe 80 C4

Odesa Ukraine *Rus.* Odessa 91 E4

Odessa *see* Odesa

Odessa Texas, USA 29 E3

Odienné Côte d'Ivoire 56 D4

Oesel *see* Saaremaa

Ofanto *river* Italy 79 D5

Offenbach Germany 77 B5

Ogaden *plateau* Ethiopia 55 D5

Ogallala Nebraska, USA 24 D4

Ogbomosho Nigeria 57 F4

Ogden Utah, USA 24 B3

Ogdensburg New York, USA 23 F2

Oger *see* Ogre

Ogre Latvia *Ger.* Oger 88 C3

Ogulin Croatia 82 B3

Ohio *state* USA 22 D4

Ohio *river* N USA 22 B5

Ohrid Macedonia 83 D6

Ohrid, Lake *lake* Albania/Macedonia 83 D6

Ohře *river* Czech Republic/ Germany *Ger.* Eger 81 A5

Ôita Japan 113 B6

Okavango *river var.* Cubango southern Africa 60 C3

Okavango Delta *wetland* Botswana 60 C3

Okayama Japan 113 B5

Okazaki Japan 113 C5

Okeechobee, Lake *lake* Florida, USA 31 F4

Okhotsk Russian Federation 97 G3

Okhotsk, Sea of Pacific Ocean 134 C1

Okinawa *island* Japan 113 A8

Oki-shotō *island group* Japan 113 B5

Oklahoma *state* USA 29 F1

Oklahoma City Oklahoma, USA 29 F2

Okushiri-tō *island* Japan 112 C2

Okāra Pakistan 116 C2

Öland *island* Sweden 67 C7

Olavarría Argentina 46 D4

Olbia Italy 79 A5

Oldenburg Germany 76 B3

Oleksandriya Ukraine *Rus.* Aleksandriya 91 E3

Olenëk Russian Federation 97 E3

Ölgiy Mongolia 108 C2

Olhão Portugal 74 C4

Olita *see* Alytus

Olmaliq *see* Almalyk

Olmütz *see* Olomouc

Olomouc Czech Republic *Ger.* Olmütz 81 C5

Olsztyn Poland *Ger.* Allenstein 80 D2

Olt *river* Romania 90 B5

Olympia Washington, USA 26 B2

Omaha Nebraska, USA 25 F4

Oman *country* SW Asia 103 D6

Oman, Gulf of *sea feature* Indian Ocean 103 E5 122 B3

Omdurman Sudan 54 B4

Omsk Russian Federation 96 C4

Onega *river* Russian Federation 92 C4

Onega, Lake *see* Onezhskoye Ozero

Onezhskoye Ozero *lake* Russian Federation *Eng.* Lake Onega 92 B3

Ongole India 115 E2

Onitsha Nigeria 57 F5

Onslow Australia 128 A4

Ontario *province* Canada 18 B3

Ontario, Lake *lake* Canada/USA 17 D5

Oostende Belgium *Eng.* Ostend 69 A5

Opole Poland *Ger.* Oppeln 80 C4

Oporto *see* Porto

Oppeln *see* Opole

Oradea Romania 90 B3

Oran Algeria 52 D1

Orange River *river* southern Africa 60 C4

Oranjestad Netherlands Antilles 37 E5

Orantes River Asia 100 B3

Ordu Turkey 98 D2

Ordzhonikidze *see* Vladikavkaz

Örebro Sweden 67 C6

Oregon *state* USA 26

Orël Russian Federation 93 A5

Orem Utah, USA 24 B4

Orenburg Russian Federation 93 C6 96 B4

Orense *see* Ourense

Oreor *capital of* Palau *var.* Korov 126 A1

Orestiáda Greece 86 D3

Orinoco *river* Colombia/Venezuela 41 E3

Oristano Italy 79 A5

Orkney *islands* Scotland, UK 70 C2

Orlando Florida, USA 31 E4

Orléans France 72 C4

Örnsköldsvik Sweden 67 C5

Orantes *river* SW Asia 100 B3

Orosirá Rodópis *see* Rhodope Mountains

Orsha Belarus 89 E5

Orsk Russian Federation 93 D6 96 B4

Oruro Bolivia 42 C4

Ōsaka Japan 113 C5

Osborn Plateau *undersea feature* Indian Ocean 123 C5

Ösel *see* Saaremaa

Osh Kyrgyzstan 105 F2

Oshawa Canada 20 D5

Oshkosh Wisconsin, USA 22 B2

Osijek Croatia 82 C3

Oslo *capital of* Norway 67 B6

Osmaniye Turkey 98 D4

Osnabrück Germany 76 B3

Osorno Chile 47 B5

Oss Netherlands 68 D4

Ossora Russian Federation 97 H2

Ostend *see* Oostende

Östersund Sweden 67 C5

Ostrava Czech Republic *Ger.* Mährisch-Ostrau, *prev.* Moravská Ostrava 81 C5

Ostrołęka Poland 80 D3

Ostrowiec Świętokrzyski Poland 80 D4

Ōsumi-shotō *island group* Japan 113 A7

Otago Peninsula *peninsula* New Zealand 133 B7

Otaru Japan 112 D2

Oti *river* Africa 57 E4

Otranto, Strait of *sea feature* Albania/Italy 79 E5

Ottawa *capital of* Canada 20 D4

Ottawa *river* Canada 20 D4

Ou *river* Laos 118 C3

Ouachita *river* SE USA 30 B2

Ouagadougou *capital of* Burkina 57 E3

Ouarâne *desert* Mauritania 56 D2

Ouargla Algeria 53 E2

Ouessant, Île d' *island* France 72 A3

Ouésso Congo 59 C5

Oujda Morocco 52 D2

Oulu Finland 66 D4

Oulu *river* Finland 66 D4

Oulujärvi *lake* Finland 66 E4

Ounasjoki *river* Finland 66 D3

Our *river* W Europe 69 E7

Ourense Spain *Cast.* Orense 74 C2

Ourinhos Brazil 44 D2

Ourthe *river* Belgium 69 D6

Outer Hebrides *island group* UK *var.* Western Isles 70 B3

Outer Islands *island group* Seychelles 61 H2

Ouyen Australia 131 C6

Oviedo Spain 74 D1

Owando Congo 59 C6

Owen Fracture Zone *tectonic feature* Arabian Sea 122 B3

Owensboro Kentucky, USA 22 B5

Oxford England, UK 71 D6

Oxnard California, USA 29 C7

Oyem Gabon 59 B5

Oyo Nigeria 57 F4

Ozark Plateau *plain* Arkansas/Missouri, USA 25 G5

Ózd Hungary 81 D6

P

Paamiut Greenland 64 B4

Pachuca Mexico 33 E4

Pacific-Antarctic Ridge *undersea feature* Pacific Ocean 136 B5

Pacific Ocean 134-135

Padang Indonesia 120 B4

Paderborn Germany 76 B4

Padova Italy *Eng.* Padua 78 C2

Padre Island *island* Texas, USA 29 G5

Padua *see* Padova

Paducah Kentucky, USA 22 B5

Paeroa Waikato, New Zealand 132 D3

Pafos *see* Paphos

Pag *island* Croatia 82 A3

Pago Pago *capital of* American Samoa 127 F4

Paide Estonia *Ger.* Weissenstein 88 D2

Paihia New Zealand 132 D2

Painted Desert *desert* SW USA 28 C1

País Valenciano *cultural region* Spain 75 F3

Pakistan *country* S Asia 116

Pakokku Myanmar 118 A3

Palagruža *island* Croatia 83 B5

Palau *country* Pacific Ocean *var.* Belau 124 B2 126

Palawan *island* Philippines 121 E2

Palawan Passage *passage* Philippines 121 E2

Paldiski Estonia *prev.* Baltiski, *Eng.* Baltic Port, *Ger.* Baltischport 88 C2

Palembang Indonesia 120 C4

Palencia Spain 74 D2

Palermo Italy 79 C6

Palikir *capital of* Micronesia 126 C2

Palioúri, Akrotírio *coastal feature* Greece *var.* Akra Kanestron 86 C4

Palk Strait *sea feature* India/Sri Lanka 115 E3

Palliser, Cape *headland* New Zealand 133 D5

Palm Springs California, USA 27 D8

Palma Spain 75 G3

Palmer Land *physical region* Antarctica 136 A3

Palmerston North New Zealand 132 D4

Palmyra *see* Tudmur

Palmyra Atoll *external territory* USA, Pacific Ocean 125 F2

Palu Indonesia 121 E4

Pamir *river* Afghanistan/Tajikistan 105 F3

Pamirs *mountains* Tajikistan 105 F3

Pampa Texas, USA 29 E2

Pampas *region* South America 46 C4

Pamplona Spain *var.* Iruña 75 F1

Pānāji India 114 C2

Panama *country* Central America 35

Panamá, Golfo de *sea feature* Panama 35 F5

Panama Canal *canal* Panama 35 F4

Panama City *capital of* Panama 35 F5

Panama City Florida, USA 30 D3

Pančevo Serb. & Mon. (Yugo.) 82 D3

Panevėžys Lithuania 88 C4

Pantanal *region* Brazil 38 C4

Pantelleria *island* Italy 79 B7

Papeete *capital of* French Polynesia 127 H4

Paphos Cyprus *var.* Pafos 98 C5

Papua *province* Indonesia *prev.* Irian Jaya 121 H4

Papua New Guinea *country* Pacific Ocean 126

Paracel Islands *disputed territory* Asia 120 D1

Paragua *river* Venezuela 41 E3

Paraguay *country* South America 44

Paraguay *river* C South America 38 C4 44 B2

Parakou Benin 57 F4

Paramaribo *capital of* Suriname 41 G2

Paraná Argentina 46 D4

Paraná *river* C South America 46 D3

Paranaíba Brazil 43 G2

Paraparaumu New Zealand 132 D4

Qaṭṭâra, Monkhafad el *desert basin* Egypt *Eng.* Qattara Depression 54 A1
Qena Egypt 54 B2
Qeqertarsuaq Greenland 64 B3
Qeqertarsuaq *island* Greenland 64 B3
Qian see Guizhou
Qilian Shan *mountain range* China 108 A4
Qimusseriarsuaq *bay* Greenland 64 C2
Qingdao China 110 D4
Qinghai *province* China *var.* Chinghai, Koko Nor, Qing, Tsinghai 108 D4
Qinghai Hu *lake* China *var.* Koko Nor 108 D4
Qingzang Gaoyuan *plateau* China *Eng.* Plateau of Tibet 110 A4
Qiong see Hainan
Qiqihar China 110 D3
Qira China 108 B4
Qitai China 108 C3
Qom Iran *var.* Kum 102 C3
Qondūz *river* Afghanistan 105 E4
Qondūz see Kunduz
Qo'qon Uzbekistan *prev.* Kokand, *var.* Khokand, 105 E2
Quba Azerbaijan *Rus.* Kuba 99 H2
Québec Canada 21 E4
Quebec *province* Canada 20 D3
Queen Charlotte Islands *islands* Canada 18 D4
Queen Charlotte Sound *sea feature* Canada 18 D5
Queen Elizabeth Islands *islands* Canada 19 F1
Queensland *state* Australia 130 C4
Queenstown New Zealand 133 B6
Quelimane Mozambique 61 E3
Querétaro Mexico 33 E4
Quetta Pakistan 116 B2
Quezaltenango Guatemala 34 B2

Quibdó Colombia 40 B2
Quimper France 72 A3
Qui Nhon Vietnam 119 E5
Qing see Qinghai
Quito *capital of* Ecuador 40 A4
Qürghonteppa Tajikistan *Rus.* Kurgan–Tynbe 105 E3
Qyteti Stalin see Kuçovë

R

Raab see Győr
Raab see Rába
Rába *river* Austria/Hungary *Ger.* Raab 81 C7
Rabat *capital of* Morocco 52 C2
Race, Cape *coastal feature* Canada 21 H4
Rach Gia Vietnam 119 D6
Radom Poland 80 D4
Radviliškis Lithuania 88 C4
Ragusa Italy 79 D7
Rahīmyār Khān Pakistan 116 C3
Raipur India 117 E5
Rājahmundry India 115 E1
Rājasthān *state* India 116 C3
Rājkot India 116 C4
Rājshāhi Bangladesh 117 G4
Rakaia *river* New Zealand 133 C6
Rakvere Estonia *Ger.* Wesenberg 88 D2
Raleigh North Carolina, USA 31 F1
Ralik Chain *islands* Marshall Islands 126 D1
Râmnicu Vâlcea Romania *prev.* Rîmnicu Vîlcea 90 B4
Ramallah West Bank 101 D7
Ramree Island *island* Myanmar 118 A3
Rancagua Chile 46 B4
Rānchi India 117 F4
Randers Denmark 67 A7
Rangiora New Zealand 133 C6

Rangitikei *river* New Zealand 132 D4
Rangoon *capital of* Myanmar *Bur.* Yangon 118 B4
Rankin Inlet Canada 19 G3
Rapid City South Dakota, USA 24 D3
Rarotonga *island* Cook Islands 127 G5
Rasht Iran 102 C3
Ratak Chain *islands* Marshall Islands 126 D1
Ratchaburi Thailand 119 C5
Rat Islands *island group* Alaska, USA 18 A2
Raukumara Range *mountain range* New Zealand 132 E3
Rauma Finland 67 D5
Ravenna Italy 78 C3
Rāwalpindi Pakistan 116 C1
Rawson Argentina 47 C6
Razgrad Bulgaria 86 D1
Reading England, UK 71 D6
Rebecca, Lake *lake* Australia 129 C6
Rebun-tō *island* Japan 112 D1
Rechytsa Belarus 89 D7
Recife Brazil 43 H3
Recklinghausen Germany 76 G4
Red Deer Canada 19 E5
Redding California, USA 27 B5
Red River *river* S USA 30 B3
Red River *river* China/ Vietnam 118
Red Sea Indian Ocean 122 A3
Reefton New Zealand 133 C5
Regensburg Germany 77 C5
Reggane Algeria 52 D3
Reggio di Calabria Italy 79 D6
Reggio nell' Emilia Italy 78 B3
Regina Canada 19 F5
Rehoboth Namibia 60 C4
Reichenberg see Liberec
Reid Australia 129 D6
Reims France *Eng.* Rheims 72 D3
Reindeer Lake *lake* Canada 17 C4
Reni Ukraine 90 D4

Rennes France 72 B3
Reno Nevada, USA 27 B5
Resistencia Argentina 46 D3
Reşiţa Romania 90 B4
Resolute Canada 19 F2
Réunion *external territory* France, Indian Ocean 123 B5
Reus Spain 75 G2
Reutlingen Germany 77 B6
Reval *see* Tallinn
Revel *see* Tallinn
Revillagigedo, Islas *island* Mexico 32 B4
Rey, Isla del *island* Panama 35 F5
Reykjavík *capital of* Iceland 65 E5
Reynosa Mexico 33 E2
Rēzekne Latvia *Ger.* Rositten, *Rus.* Rezhitsa 88 D4
Rezhitsa *see* Rēzekne
Rheims *see* Reims
Rhine *river* W Europe 62 D3
Rhode Island *state* USA 23 G3
Rhodes *see* Ródos
Rhodope Mountains *mountain range* Bulgaria/Greece *Gk.* Orosirá Rodópis, *Bul.* Despoto Planina 86 C3
Rhône *river* France/Switzerland 62 C4
Ribeirão Preto Brazil 45 E1
Riberalta Bolivia 42 C3
Rîbniţa Moldova 90 D3
Richfield Utah, USA 24 B4
Richland Washington, USA 24 C2
Richmond Kentucky, USA 22 C5
Richmond New Zealand 133 C5
Richmond Virginia, USA 23 E5
Richmond Range *mountain range* New Zealand 133 C5
Ricobayo, Embalse de *reservoir* Spain 74 D2
Riga *capital of* Latvia *Latv.* Rīga 88 C3
Riga, Gulf of *sea feature* Baltic Sea 88 C3
Riihimäki Finland 67 D5

Rijeka Croatia *It.* Fiume 82 A3
Rimah, Wādī ar *dry watercourse* Saudi Arabia 103 B5
Rimini Italy 78 C3
Rîmnicu Vîlcea *see* Râmnicu Vâlcea
Riobamba Ecuador 40 A4
Rio Branco Brazil 42 C3
Río Cuarto Argentina 46 C4
Rio de Janeiro Brazil 45 F2
Río Gallegos Argentina 47 C7
Rio Grande Brazil 44 D4
Rio Grande *river* N America 16 B6
Rio Grande Rise *undersea feature* Atlantic Ocean 49 C6
Río Verde Mexico 33 E3
Rishiri-tō *island* Japan 112 D1
Rivas Nicaragua 34 D3
Rivera Uruguay 44 C4
Riverside California, USA 27 C8
Riverton New Zealand 133 A7
Rivne Ukraine *Rus.* Rovno 90 C2
Riyadh *capital of* Saudi Arabia *Ar.* Ar Riyāḍ 103 C5
Rize Turkey 99 E2
Rkiz Mauritania 56 C3
Road Town *capital of* British Virgin Islands 37 F3
Roanne France 73 D5
Roanoke Virginia, USA 23 E5
Roanoke *river* SE USA 31 G1
Robinson Range *mountain range* Australia 129 B5
Rochester Minnesota, USA 25 F3
Rochester New York, USA 23 E3
Rockford Illinois, USA 22 B3
Rockhampton Australia 130 D4
Rock Island Illinois, USA 22 B3
Rock Springs Wyoming, USA 24 C3
Rockstone Guyana 41 G2
Rocky Mountains *mountain range* Canada/USA 18-19 D4
Rodez France 73 C6
Ródhos *see* Ródos

Ródos *island* Greece *var.* Ródhos, *Eng.* Rhodes 87 E6
Ródos Greece *Eng.* Rhodes 87 E6
Rodosto *see* Tekirdağ
Roeselare Belgium 69 A5
Roma Australia 131 D5
Roma *see* Rome
Romania *country* SE Europe 90
Rome *capital of* Italy *It.* Roma 78 C4
Rome Georgia, USA 30 D2
Rønne Denmark 67 B8
Ronne Ice Shelf *ice feature* Antarctica 136 B3
Roosendaal Netherlands 68 C4
Rosario Argentina 46 D4
Roseau *capital of* Dominica 37 G4
Rosenau *see* Rožňava
Rositten *see* Rēzekne
Ross Ice Shelf *ice feature* Antarctica 136 B4
Ross Sea Antarctica 136 B4
Rostak *see* Ar Rustāq
Rostock Germany 76 C2
Rostov-na-Donu Russian Federation 96 A3
Roswell New Mexico, USA 28 D2
Rotorua New Zealand 132 D3
Rotorua, Lake *lake* New Zealand 132 D3
Rotterdam Netherlands 68 C4
Rouen France 72 C3
Rovaniemi Finland 66 D3
Rovno *see* Rivne
Rovuma *river* Mozambique/ Tanzania 61 E2
Roxas City Philippines 121 E2
Rožňava Slovakia *Ger.* Rosenau, *Hung.* Rozsnyó 81 D6
Rozsnyó *see* Rožňava
Ruatoria New Zealand 132 E3
Ruawai New Zealand 132 D2
Rudnyy Kazakhstan 96 C4
Rudolf, Lake *see* Lake Turkana

Salso *river* Italy 79 C7
Salt *see* As Salṭ
Salta Argentina 46 C2
Saltillo Mexico 33 E2
Salt Lake City Utah, USA 24 B4
Salto Uruguay 44 B4
Salton Sea *lake* California, USA 27 D8
Salvador Brazil 43 G4
Salween *river* SE Asia 111 A6
Salzburg Austria 77 D6
Salzgitter Germany 76 C4
Samara Russian Federation 93 C6 96 B3
Samarinda Indonesia 121 E4
Samarkand Uzbekistan 104 D2
Sambre *river* Belgium 69 B7
Samoa *country* Pacific Ocean 127 F4
Samobor Croatia 82 B3
Sámos *island* Greece 87 D5
Samothrace *see* Samothráki
Samothráki *island* Greece *Eng.* Samothrace 86 D3
Samsun Turkey 98 D2
Samui, Ko *island group* Thailand 119 C6
San *river* Poland 81 E5
Saña Peru 42 A3
Sana *capital of* Yemen *var.* Ṣanʿā’ 103 B7
Sanandaj Sinneh. Iran 102 C3
San Andrés, Isla de *island* Colombia 35 E3
San Angelo Texas, USA 29 F3
San Antonio Chile 46 B4
San Antonio Texas, USA 29 F4
San Antonio *river* S USA 29 G4
San Antonio Oeste Argentina 47 C5
Sanāw Yemen 103 C6
San Bernardino California, USA 27 C7
San Carlos Uruguay 44 C5
San Carlos de Bariloche Argentina 47 B5
San Clemente Island *island* W USA 27 C8
San Cristóbal Venezuela 40 C2

San Diego California, USA 27 C8
Sandwich Island *see* Efate
San Fernando Trinidad & Tobago 37 G5
San Fernando Venezuela 40 D2
San Fernando de Noronha *island* Brazil 43 H2
San Francisco California, USA 27 B6
Sangir, Kepulauan *island group* Indonesia 121 F3
San Ignacio Belize 34 C1
San Joaquin Valley *valley* W USA 27 B6
San José *capital of* Costa Rica 34 D4
San Jose California, USA 27 B6
San José del Guaviare Colombia 40 C3
San Juan Argentina 46 B3
San Juan *river* Costa Rica/Nicaragua 34 D4
San Juan *capital of* Puerto Rico 37 F3
San Juan Bautista Paraguay 44 B3
San Juan de los Morros Venezuela 40 D1
Sankt Martin *see* Martin
Sankt-Peterburg *see* St Petersburg
Sankt Pölten Austria 77 E6
Şanlıurfa Turkey *prev.* Urfa 98 E4
San Lorenzo Honduras 34 C3
San Luis Potosí Mexico 33 E3
San Marino *country* S Europe 78 C3
San Matías, Golfo *sea feature* Argentina 39 C6
San Miguel El Salvador 34 C3
San Miguel de Tucumán Argentina 46 C3
San Nicolas Island *island* W USA 27 B8
San Pedro Sula Honduras 34 C2
San Remo Italy 78 A3
San Salvador *capital of* El Salvador 34 C3

San Salvador de Jujuy Argentina 46 C2
San Sebastián Spain *Bas.* Donostia 75 E1
Santa Ana El Salvador 34 B2
Santa Ana California, USA 27 C8
Santa Barbara California, USA 27 B7
Santa Catalina Island *island* W USA 27 C8
Santa Clara Cuba 36 B2
Santa Cruz Bolivia 42 D4
Santa Cruz California, USA 27 B6
Santa Cruz Islands *island group* Solomon Islands 126 C4
Santa Fe Argentina 46 D3
Santa Fe New Mexico, USA 28 D2
Santa Maria Brazil 44 C4
Santa Marta Colombia 40 C1
Santander Spain 75 E1
Santanilla, Islas *islands* Honduras 35 E1
Santarém Brazil 43 E2
Santarém Portugal 74 C3
Santaren Channel *Channel* Bahamas 36 C2
Santa Rosa Argentina 47 C4
Santa Rosa California, USA 27 A6
Santa Rosa de Copán Honduras 34 C2
Santa Rosa Island *island* W USA 27 B8
Santiago *island* Cape Verde 56 A3
Santiago *capital of* Chile 46 B4
Santiago Dominican Republic 37 E3
Santiago Panama 35 F5
Santiago de Compostela Spain 74 C1
Santiago de Cuba Cuba 36 C3
Santiago del Estero Argentina 46 C3
Santo Antão *island* Cape Verde 56 A2
Santo Domingo *capital of* Dominican Republic 37 E3

Sinnamary French Guiana 41 H2

Sinop Turkey 98 D2

Sint-Niklaas Belgium 69 B5

Sintra Portugal 74 B3

Sion Switzerland 77 B7

Sioux City Iowa, USA 25 F3

Sioux Falls South Dakota, USA 25 E3

Siracusa Italy *Eng.* Syracuse 79 D7

Siret *river* Romania/Ukraine 90 C4

Sirikit Reservoir *Reservoir* Thailand 118 C4

Sirte, Gulf of *see* Surt, Khalīj

Sisak Croatia 82 B3

Sisimiut Greenland 64 C3

Sittang *river* Myanmar 118 B4

Sittwe Myanmar *prev.* Akyab 118 A3

Sivas Turkey 98 D3

Sjælland *island* Denmark 67 B7

Skagerrak *sea feature* Denmark/Norway 67 A6

Skellefteå Sweden 66 D4

Skopje *capital of* Macedonia 83 E5

Skövde Sweden 67 B6

Skovorodino Russian Federation 97 F4

Skye *island* Scotland, UK 70 B3

Slavonski Brod Croatia 82 C3

Sligo Ireland 71 B5

Sliven Bulgaria 86 D2

Slonim Belarus 89 C6

Slovakia *country* C Europe 81

Slovenia *country* SE Europe 77

Slov'yans'k Ukraine 91 G3

Słupsk Poland *Ger.* Stolp 78 C2

Slutsk Belarus 89 C6

Smallwood Reservoir *reservoir* Canada 21 E3

Smara Western Sahara *var.* Semara 52 B3

Smederevo Serb. & Mon. (Yugo.) 82 D3

Smolensk Russian Federation 92 A4

Smyrna *see* İzmir

Snake *river* NW USA 26 D4

Snowdonia *mountains* Wales, UK 71 C5

Sobradinho, Represa de *Reservoir* Brazil 43 G3

Sochi Russian Federation 93 A7 96 A3

Société, Îles de la *islands* French Polynesia *Eng.* Society Islands 127 H4

Society Islands *see* Société, Îles de la

Socotra *see* Suquţrá

Sodankylä Finland 66 D3

Sofia *capital of* Bulgaria *var.* Sofija, *Bul.* Sofiya 86 C2

Sofija *see* Sofia

Sofiya *see* Sofia

Sognefjorden *inlet* Norway 67 A5

Sohâg Egypt 54 B2

Sokhumi Georgia *Rus.* Sukhumi 99 E1

Sokodé Togo 57 E4

Sokoto Nigeria 57 F3

Sokoto *river* Nigeria 57 F3

Solāpur India 116 D5 114 D1

Sol, Costa del *coastal region* Spain 75 E5

Soligorsk *see* Salihorsk

Solomon Islands *country* Pacific Ocean 126

Solomon Islands *island group* PNG/Solomon Islands 124 C3

Solomon Sea Pacific Ocean 126 B3

Somalia *country* E Africa 54-55

Somali Basin *undersea feature* Indian Ocean 122 A4

Sombor Serb. & Mon. (Yugo.) 82 C3

Somerset Island *island* Canada 19 F2

Somme *river* France 72 C3

Somoto Nicaragua 34 D3

Songea Tanzania 55 C8

Songkhla Thailand 119 C7

Sonoran Desert *see* Altar, Desierto de

Sopron Hungary *Ger.* Ödenburg 81 B6

Soria Spain 75 E2

Sorocaba Brazil 43 F5 45 E2

Sorong Indonesia 124 G4

Sotavento, Ilhas de *island group* Cape Verde *var.* Leeward Islands 56 A3

Soûr Lebanon *anc.* Tyre 100 A4

Sousse Tunisia 53 F1

South Africa *country* southern Africa 60-61

South America 38-39

Southampton England, UK 71 D7

Southampton Island *island* Canada 17 G3

South Andaman *island* India 115 G2

South Australia *state* Australia 131 A5

South Australian Basin *undersea feature* Southern Ocean 124 B5

South Bend Indiana, USA 22 C3

South Carolina *state* USA 31 F2

South Carpathians *see* Carpaţii Meridionali

South China Sea Pacific Ocean 119 E7

South Dakota *state* USA 24-25 E3

South East Point *coastal feature* Australia 131 C7

Southeast Indian Ridge *undersea feature* Indian Ocean 123 E6

Southeast Pacific Basin *undersea feature* Pacific Ocean 135 E5

Southend-on-Sea England, UK 71 E6

Southern Alps *mountain range* New Zealand 133 B6

Southern Cook Islands *islands* Cook Islands 127 G5

Southern Cross Australia 129 B6

Talamanca, Cordillera de *mountains* Costa Rica 35 E4

Talas Kyrgyzstan 105 F2

Talaud, Kepulauan *island group* Indonesia 121 F3

Talca Chile 46 B4

Talcahuano Chile 46 B4

Taldykorgan Kazakhstan 96 C5

Tallahassee Florida, USA 30 D3

Tallinn *capital of* Estonia *prev.* Revel, *Ger.* Reval, *Rus.* Tallin 88 D2

Talsen *see* Talsi

Talsi Latvia *Ger.* Talsen 88 B3

Tamale Ghana 57 E4

Tamanrasset Algeria 53 E4

Tambo Australia 130 C4

Tambov Russian Federation 93 B5

Tamil Nādu *state* India 114 D2

Tampa Florida, USA 31 E4

Tampere Finland 67 D5

Tampico Mexico 33 F3

Tamworth Australia 131 D6

Tana *river* Finland/Norway 66 D2

Tananarive *see* Antananarivo

Tanega-shima *island* Japan 113 B7

Tanga Tanzania 55 C7

Tanganyika, Lake *lake* E Africa 51 D5

Tanger Morocco *var.* Tangiers 52 C1

Tangiers *see* Tanger

Tangra Yumco *lake* China 108 B5

Tangshan China 110 D4

Tanimbar Islands *see* Tanimbar, Kepulauan

Tanimbar, Kepulauan *island group* Indonesia *Eng.* Tanimbar Islands 121 F5

Tanjungkarang *see* Bandarlampung

Tan-Tan Morocco 52 B3

Tanzania *country* E Africa 55

Taoudenni Mali 57 E2

Tapa Estonia *Ger.* Taps 88 D2

Tapachula Mexico 33 G5

Tapajós *river* Brazil 43 E2

Taps *see* Tapa

Ţarābulus *see* Tripoli, Lebanon

Ţarābulus al-Gharb *see* Tripoli, Libya

Taranto Italy 79 E5

Taranto, Golfo di *sea feature* Mediterranean Sea 79 E5

Tarapoto Peru 42 B2

Tarawa *island* Kiribati 127 E2

Taraz Kazakhstan *prev.* Dzhambul, Zhambyl 96 C5

Tarbes France 73 B6

Tarcoola Australia 131 A5

Târgovişte Romania *prev.* Tîrgovişte 90 C4

Târgu Mureş Romania *prev.* Tîrgu Mureş 90 C4

Tarija Bolivia 42 C5

Tarim Basin *basin* China 108 B3

Tarim He *river* China 108 B3

Tarn *river* France 73 C6

Tarnów Poland 81 D5

Tarragona Spain 75 G2

Tarsus Turkey 98 D4

Tartu Estonia *prev.* Yur'yev, *var.* Yurev, *Ger.* Dorpat 88 D3

Ţarţūs Syria 100 B3

Tashauz *see* Daşoguz

Tashkent *capital of* Uzbekistan *var.* Taškent, *Uzb.* Toshkent 105 E2

Taškent *see* Tashkent

Tasman Bay *inlet* New Zealand 132 C4

Tasmania *state* Australia 131 C8

Tasman Basin *undersea feature* Tasman Sea 124 D5

Tasman Plateau *undersea feature* Pacific Ocean 124 C5

Tasman Sea Pacific Ocean 134 C4

Tassili-n-Ajjer *desert plateau* Algeria 53 E4

Tatabánya Hungary 81 C6

Tatar Pazardzhik *see* Pazardzhik

Taubaté Brazil 43 F5 45 E2

Taumarunui New Zealand 132 D3

Taunggyi Myanmar 118 B3

Taunton England, UK 71 D7

Taupo New Zealand 132 D3

Taupo, Lake *lake* New Zealand 132 D3

Tauragė Lithuania 88 B4

Tauranga New Zealand 132 D3

Taurus Mountains *mountain range* Turkey *see* Toros Dağları 94 D4

Tavoy Myanmar 119 B5

Tawau Malaysia 120 D3

Taymyr, Ozero *lake* Russian Federation 97 E2

Taymyr, Poluostrov *peninsula* Russian Federation *Eng.* Taymyr Peninsula 97 E2

Taymyr Peninsula *see* Taymyr, Poluostrov

Tbilisi *capital of* Georgia *Geor.* T'bilisi, *prev.* Tiflis 99 F2

Te Anau New Zealand 133 A7

Te Anau, Lake *lake* New Zealand 133 A7

Tedzhen Turkmenistan *Turkm.* Tejen 104 C3

Tegal Indonesia 120 C5

Tegucigalpa *capital of* Honduras 34 C3

Teheran *see* Tehrān

Tehrān *capital of* Iran *prev.* Teheran 102 C3

Tehuacán Mexico 33 F4

Tehuantepec, Golfo de *sea feature* Mexico 33 G5

Tejen *see* Tedzhen

Tejo *see* Tagus

Te Kao New Zealand 131 C1

Tekirdağ Turkey *It.* Rodosto 98 A2

Te Kuiti Waikato, New Zealand 132 D3

Tel Aviv-Yafo Israel 101 A5

Teles Pires *river* Brazil 43 E3

Tell Atlas *plateau* Africa 84 C3

Telschen *see* Telšiai

Telšiai Lithuania *Ger.* Telschen 88 B4

Temuco Chile 47 B5

Ténéré *physical region* Niger 57 G2

Tenerife *island* Spain 52 A3

Tennant Creek Australia 130 A3

Tennessee *state* USA 30 D1

Tennessee *river* SE USA 31 C1

Tepelenë Albania 83 D6

Tepic Mexico 32 D4

Teplice Czech Republic *Ger.* Teplitz, *prev.* Teplice-Šanov, *Ger.* Teplitz-Schönau 80 A4

Teplice-Šanov *see* Teplice

Teplitz *see* Teplice

Teplitz-Schönau *see* Teplice

Teraina Kiribati 127 G2

Teresina Brazil 43 G2

Termez Uzbekistan 105 E3

Terneuzen Netherlands 69 B5

Terni Italy 78 C4

Ternopil' Ukraine *Rus.* Ternopol' 90 C2

Ternopol' *see* Ternopil'

Terrassa Spain 75 G2

Terre Haute Indiana, USA 22 B4

Terres Australes et Antarctiques Françaises *see* French Southern and Antarctic Territories

Terschelling *island* Netherlands 68 C1

Teruel Spain 75 F3

Teseney Eritrea 54 C4

Tessalit Mali 57 E2

Tete Mozambique 61 E3

Tétouan Morocco 52 C1

Tetovo Macedonia 83 D5

Tetschen *see* Děčín

Tevere *river* Italy 78 C4

Texas *state* USA 28–29 F3

Texarkana Arkansas, USA 30 A2

Texas City Texas, USA 29 G4

Texel *island* Netherlands 68 C2

Thailand *country* SE Asia 118–119

Thailand, Gulf of *sea feature* South China Sea 119 C6

Thames *river* England, UK 71 D6

Thar Desert *desert* India/Pakistan 116 C3

Tharthār, Buḥayrat ath *lake* Iraq 102 B3

Thásos *island* Greece 86 C3

Thaton Myanmar 118 B4

Theiss *see* Tisza

Thermaic Gulf *see* Thermaïkós Kólpos

Thermaïkós Kólpos *sea feature* Greece *Eng.* Thermaic Gulf 86 B4

Thessaloniki Greece *var.* Salonica 86 B3

The Valley *dependent territory capital* Anguilla 37 G5

Thimphu *capital of* Bhutan 117 G3

Thionville France 72 E3

Thira *island* Greece 87 D6

Thompson Canada 19 F4

Thorn *see* Toruń

Thorshavn *see* Tórshavn

Thracian Sea Greece *Gk.* Thrakikó Pélagos 86 D3

Thrakikó Pélagos *see* Thracian Sea

Three Kings Islands *island group* New Zealand 132 C1

Thule *see* Qaanaaq

Thunder Bay Canada 20 B4

Thuner See *lake* Switzerland 77 B7

Thurso Scotland, UK 70 C2

Tianjin China *var.* Tientsin 110 D4

Tiberias, Lake *lake* Israel *var.* Sea of Galilee, *Heb.* Yam Kinneret, *Ar.* Bahrat Tabariya 101 B5

Tibesti *mountains* Chad/Libya 50 C3

Tibet *autonomous region* China *Chin.* Xizang 108 C5

Tibet, Plateau of *see* Qingzang Gaoyuan

Tienen Belgium 69 C6

Tien Shan *mountain range* C Asia 105 G2

Tientsin *see* Tianjin

Tierra del Fuego *island* Argentina/Chile 47 C8

Tiflis *see* Tbilisi

Tighina Moldova *prev.* Bendery 90 D4

Tigris *river* SW Asia 94 B4

Tijuana Mexico 32 A1

Tiki Basin *undersea feature* Pacific Ocean 135 E3

Tiksi Russian Federation 97 F2

Tilburg Netherlands 68 C4

Timaru New Zealand 133 B6

Timişoara Romania 90 A4

Timmins Canada 20 C4

Timor *island* Indonesia 121 F5

Timor Sea Indian Ocean 121 F5

Tindouf Algeria 52 B3

Tinos *island* Greece 87 D5

Tirana *capital of* Albania 83 D6

Tiraspol Moldova 90 D4

Tîrgovişte *see* Târgovişte

Tîrgu Mureş *see* Târgu Mureş

Tirol *region* Austria *var.* Tyrol 77 C7

Tiruchchirāppalli India 114 D3

Tisa *see* Tisza

Tisza *river* E Europe *Ger.* Theiss, *Cz./Rom./SCr.* Tisa 81 D6

Titicaca, Lake *lake* Bolivia/Peru 42 C4

Tlemcen Algeria 52 D2

Toamasina Madagascar 61 G3

Toba, Danau *lake* Indonesia 120 B3

Tobago *island* Trinidad and Tobago 37 G5

Toba Kākar Range *mountains* Pakistan 116 B2

Tobruk *see* Ţubruq

Tocantins *river* Brazil 43 F3

Tocopilla Chile 46 B2

Togo *country* W Africa 57 E4

Tokat Turkey 98 D3

Tokelau *external territory* New Zealand, Pacific Ocean 127 F3

Tokmak Kyrgyzstan 105 F2

Tokuno-shima *island* Japan 113 A8

Tokushima Japan 113 B5

Tokyo *capital of* Japan 113 D5

Toledo Spain 75 E3

Toledo Ohio, USA 22 C3

Toledo Bend Reservoir *Reservoir* S USA 29 H3

Toliara Madagascar 61 E3

Tol'yatti *prev.* Stavropol' Russian Federation 93 C5

Tomakomai Japan 112 D2

Tombouctou Mali 57 E3

Tombua Angola 60 B2

Tomini, Gul of *sea feature* Indonesia 121 E4

Tomsk Russian Federation 96 D4

Tonga *country* Pacific Ocean 127

Tongatapu *island* Tonga 125 E3

Tongking, Gulf of *sea feature* South China Sea *var.* Gulf of Tonkin 111 B7

Tongliao China 109 G2

Tongtian He *river* China 108 C4

Tonkin, Gulf of *see* Tongking, Gulf of

Tônle Kông *river* Cambodia/Vietnam 118 E5

Tônlé Sap *lake* Cambodia 119 D5

Tonopah Nevada, USA 27 C6

Toowoomba Australia 131 D5

Topeka Kansas, USA 25 F4

Top Springs Australia 130 A3

Torino Italy *Eng.* Turin 78 A2

Tornio Finland 66 D4

Tornionjoki *river* Finland/Sweden 66 D3

Toronto Canada 20 D5

Toros Dağları *mountain range* Turkey *Eng.* Taurus Mountains 98 C4

Torre del Greco Italy 79 D5

Torrens, Lake *lake* Australia 131 B5

Torreón Mexico 32 D2

Torres Strait *sea feature* Arafura Sea/Coral Sea 126 B4

Torrington Wyoming, USA 24 D3

Tórshavn *capital of* Faeroe Islands *Dan.* Thorshavn 65 F5

To'rtko'l Uzbekistan *prev.* Petroaleksandrovsk, *prev.* Turtkul', *Uzb.* Türtkül 104 C2

Tortoise Islands *see* Galapagos Islands

Tortosa Spain 75 F2

Toruń Poland *Ger.* Thorn 80 C3

Toscana *region* Italy *Eng.* Tuscany 78 B3

Toscano, Archipelago *island group* Italy 78 B4

Toshkent *see* Tashkent

Tottori Japan 113 B5

Touggourt Algeria 53 E2

Toulon France 73 D6

Toulouse France 73 B6

Toungoo Myanmar 118 B4

Tournai Belgium 69 B6

Tours France 72 C4

Townsville Australia 130 D3

Toyama Japan 112 C4

Tozeur Tunisia 53 E2

Trâblous *see* Tripoli, Lebanon

Trabzon Turkey *Eng.* Trebizond 99 E2

Tralee Ireland 71 A6

Trang Thailand 119 C7

Transantarctic Mountains *mountain range* Antarctica 136 B3

Transylvania *region* Romania 90 B3

Transylvanian Alps *see* Carpaţii Meridionali

Trapani Italy 79 C6

Traralgon Australia 131 C7

Trasimeno, Lago *Lake* Italy 78 C4

Traverse City Michigan, USA 22 C2

Travis, Lake *lake* Texas, USA 29 F4

Trebinje Bosnia & Herzegovina 83 C5

Trebizond *see* Trabzon

Trelew Argentina 47 C6

Trenčín Slovakia *Ger.* Trentschin *Hung.* Trencsén 81 C6

Trencsén *see* Trenčín

Trento Italy *Ger.* Trient 78 C2

Trenton New Jersey, USA 23 F4

Trentschin *see* Trenčín

Tres Arroyos Argentina 47 D5

Treviso Italy 78 C2

Trient *see* Trento

Trieste Italy 78 D2

Trikala Greece 86 B4

Trincomalee Sri Lanka 115 E3

Trindade *external territory* Brazil, Atlantic Ocean 49 C6

Trinidad Bolivia 42 C4

Trinidad Uruguay 44 B5

Trinidad *island* Trinidad & Tobago 38 C2

Trinidad & Tobago *country* West Indies 37 G5

Trípoli Greece 87 B5

Tripoli Lebanon *var.* Trâblous, Ţarābulus 100 B4

Tripoli *capital of* Libya *Ar.* Ţarābulus al-Gharb 53 F2

Tristan da Cunha *external territory* UK, Atlantic Ocean 49 D6

Trivandrum India 114 D3

Trnava Slovakia *Ger.* Tyrnau, *Hung.* Nagyszombat 81 C6

Trois-Rivières Canada 21 E4

Trollhättan Sweden 67 B6

Tromsø Norway 66 C2

Trondheim Norway 66 B4

Trondheimsfjorden *inlet* Norway 66 B4

Troyes France 72 D4

Trujillo Honduras 34 D2

Trujillo Peru 42 A3

Tsarigrad *see* İstanbul

Tschenstochau *see* Częstochowa

Tselinograd *see* Astana

Tsetserleg Mongolia 108 D2

Tshikapa Dem. Rep. Congo 59 C7

Tsinghai *see* Qinghai

Tsumeb Namibia 60 C3

Tsushima *island* Japan 113 A5

Tuamotu Fracture Zone *tectonic feature* Pacific Ocean 125 H3

Tuamotu Islands *island group* French Polynesia 125 G3

Tubmanburg Liberia 56 C4

Ţubruq Libya *Eng.* Tobruk 53 H2

Tucson Arizona, USA 28 B3

Tucupita Venezuela 41 F1

Tucurui, Represa de *Reservoir* Brazil 43 F2

Tudmur Syria *var.* Tadmur, *Eng.* Palmyra 100 C3

Tuguegarao Philippines 121 E1

Tuktoyaktuk Canada 137 E2

Tula Russian Federation 93 B5 96 A3

Tulancingo Mexico 33 E4

Tulcán Ecuador 40 B4

Tulcea Romania 90 D4

Ţūlkarm West Bank 101 D7

Tully Australia 130 D3

Tulsa Oklahoma, USA 29 G1

Tundzha *river* Bulgaria 86 D2

Tungaru *island group* Kiribati *prev.* Gilbert Islands 127 E2

Tunis *capital of* Tunisia 53 F1

Tunisia *country* N Africa 53 F2

Tunja Colombia 40 C2

Tupiza Bolivia 42 C5

Turan Lowland *lowland* Turkmenistan/Uzbekistan *var.* Turan Plain, *Rus.* Turanskaya Nizmennost' 104 C2

Turan Plain *see* Turan Lowland

Turanskaya Nizmennost' *see* Turan Lowland

Turčiansky Svätý Martin *see* Martin

Turin *see* Torino

Turkana, Lake *lake* Ethiopia/Kenya *var.* Lake Rudolf 50 D4 55 C5

Turkey *country* SW Asia 98-99

Türkmenabat Turkmenistan *prev.* Chardzhev, *prev.* Chardzhou, *prev.* Leninsk, *Turkm.* Chärjew 104 D3

Türkmenbaşy Turkmenistan *prev.* Krasnovodsk 104 A2

Turkmenistan *country* C Asia 104

Turks & Caicos Islands *external territory* UK, West Indies 37

Turku Finland 67 D5

Turnagain, Cape *headland* New Zealand 132 E4

Turnhout Belgium 69 C5

Turnu Severin *see* Drobeta-Turnu Severin

Turócszentmárton *see* Martin

Turpan China 108 C3

Turtkul' *see* To'rtko'l

Türtkül *see* To'rtko'l

Tuscany *see* Toscana

Tuvalu *country* Pacific Ocean 127

Tuxtla Mexico 33 G5

Tuz Gölü *lake* Turkey 98 C3

Tuzla Bosnia & Herzegovina 82 C3

Tver' Russian Federation 92 B4

Twin Falls Idaho, USA 26 D4

Tyler Texas, USA 29 G3

Tyre *see* Soûr

Tyrnau *see* Trnava

Tyrol *see* Tirol

Tyrrhenian Sea Mediterranean Sea 78 C6

Tyup Kyrgyzstan 105 G2

U

Ubangi *river* C Africa 59 C5

Uberaba Brazil 43 F5 45 E1

Uberlândia Brazil 43 F5 45 E1

Ubon Ratchathani Thailand 119 D5

Ucayali *river* Peru 42 B3

Uchkuduk Uzbekistan *Uzb.* Uchquduq 104 D2

Uchquduq *see* Uchkuduk

Udine Italy 78 C2

Udon Thani Thailand 118 C4

Uele *river* Dem. Rep. Congo 58 D5

Ufa Russian Federation 96 B3

Uganda *country* E Africa 55

Uíge Angola 60 B1

Ujungpandang Indonesia 121 E4

Ukhta Russian Federation 92 D4

Ukiah California, USA 27 A5

Ukmergė Lithuania 88 C4

Ukraine *country* E Europe 90-91

Ulaanbaatar *see* Ulan Bator

Ulaangom Mongolia 108 C2

Ulan Bator *capital of* Mongolia *var.* Ulaanbaatar 109 E3

Ulan-Ude Russian Federation 97 E4

Ullapool Scotland, UK 70 C3

Ulm Germany 77 C6

Ulster *region* Ireland/UK 71 B5

Ulungur Hu *lake* China 108 C2

Uluru *peak* Australia *var.* Ayers Rock 129 E5

Ul'yanovsk Russian Federation 93 C5

Umeå Sweden 66 D4

Umnak Island *island* Alaska, USA 18 B3

Una *river* Bosnia & Herzegovina/Croatia 82 B3

Unalaska Island *island* Alaska, USA 18 B3

Ungava, Péninsule d' *peninsula* Canada 20 D1

Ungava Bay *sea feature* Canada 21 E1

United Arab Emirates *country* SW Asia 103 D5

United Kingdom *country* NW Europe 70-71

United States of America *country* North America 16-17

Uppsala Sweden 67 C6

Ural *river* Kazakhstan/Russian Federation 96 B4

Ural Mountains *mountain range* Russian Federation *var.* Ural'skiy Khrebet, Ural'skiye Gory 92-93

Ural'sk Kazakhstan 96 B3

Ural'skiy Khrebet *see* Ural Mountains

Ural'skiye Gory *see* Ural Mountains

Urfa *see* Şanlıurfa

Urganch *see* Urgench

Urgench Uzbekistan *prev.* Novo Urgench, *Uzb.* Urganch 104 C2

<hr>

V

W